I0796105

# CHINA'S MAHAN

# CHINA'S MAHAN

## ADMIRAL LIU HUAQING AND THE RISE OF THE MODERN CHINESE NAVY

XIAOBING LI

NAVAL INSTITUTE PRESS
Annapolis, Maryland

Naval Institute Press
291 Wood Road
Annapolis, MD 21402



ISBN: 978-1-68247-960-5 (hardcover)
ISBN: 978-1-68247-967-4 (ebook)

**Library of Congress Cataloging-in-Publication Data is available.**

♾ Print editions meet the requirements of ANSI/NISO z39.48–1992 (Permanence of Paper).
Printed in the United States of America.

34 33 32 31 30 29 28 27 26 9 8 7 6 5 4 3 2 1
First printing

*All maps created by Brad Watkins.*

For Tran, Kevin, Sharon, and Christina

# CONTENTS

# MAPS

# PHOTOS

## ABBREVIATIONS

| | |
|---|---|
| AAA | anti-aircraft artillery |
| ADIZ | air defense identification zone |
| AIP | air-independent propulsion |
| AMS | Academy of Military Science |
| ARVN | Army of Vietnam (South Vietnam) |
| ASBM | anti-ship ballistic missile |
| A2/AD | anti-access/area denial |
| BRI | Belt and Road Initiative |
| CAS | China Academy of Sciences |
| CCFA | Central China Field Army |
| CCG | China Coast Guard |
| CCP | Chinese Communist Party |
| CCYL | Chinese Communist Youth League |
| CG | cruiser, guided missile |
| CMC | Central Military Commission (CCP) |
| CPPCC | Chinese People's Political Consultative Conference |
| CPVF | Chinese People's Volunteers Force (the Korean War) |
| CSTIND | Commission of Science, Technology, and Industry for National Defense |
| CVBG | carrier battle group |
| CVFAV | Chinese Volunteer Forces to Assist Vietnam |
| CWIHP | Cold War International History Project (Wilson Center) |
| DDG | destroyer, guided missile |
| DGA | Department of General Armament |
| DGL | Department of General Logistics |

| | |
|---|---|
| DGPT | Department of General Political Tasks |
| DGS | Department of General Staff |
| ECFA | East China Field Army |
| ECMR | East China Military Region |
| ECMRN | East China Military Region Navy |
| EEZ | exclusive economic zone |
| ESF | East Sea Fleet |
| HQ | headquarters |
| IOC | Intergovernmental Oceanographic Commission (UNESCO) |
| KMT | Kuomintang (Chinese Nationalist Party) |
| LNB | Lüshun Naval Base |
| NDU | National Defense University |
| NKPA | North Korean People's Army |
| NLF | National Liberation Front (Viet Cong) |
| NPC | National People's Congress |
| NSF | North Sea Fleet |
| NVA | North Vietnamese Army |
| NVAN | North Vietnamese Army's Navy |
| OLS | optical landing system |
| PC | patrol craft |
| PLA | People's Liberation Army |
| PLAAF | PLA Air Force |
| PLAN | PLA Navy |
| PLANAF | PLA Navy Air Force |
| Politburo | Political Bureau (CCP Central Committee) |
| POW | prisoner of war |
| PRC | People's Republic of China |
| PT | patrol torpedo boat |
| QNBC | Qingdao Naval Base Command |

| | |
|---|---|
| QSD | Quadrilateral Security Dialogue |
| RAD | rear admiral |
| R&D | research and development |
| RMB | renminbi (Chinese currency) |
| ROC | Republic of China |
| ROK | Republic of Korea |
| RVN | Republic of Vietnam (South Vietnam) |
| SAF | Second Artillery Force (strategic force) |
| SAM | surface-to-air missile |
| SLOC | sea lines of communication |
| SMAG | Soviet Military Advisory Group (China) |
| SNIE | *Special National Intelligence Estimate* (U.S.) |
| SRV | Socialist Republic of Vietnam |
| SSBN | nuclear ballistic missile submarine |
| SSF | South Sea Fleet |
| SSN | nuclear attack submarine |
| TCAF | theater command air force |
| UAV | unmanned aerial vehicle |
| UN | United Nations |
| UNCLOS | UN Convention on the Law of the Sea |
| UNF | UN Force (the Korean War) |
| UNSC | UN Security Council |
| U.S. | United States |
| USAF | U.S. Air Force |
| USMC | U.S. Marine Corps |
| USN | U.S. Navy |
| VNN | Vietnamese Navy (South Vietnam) |
| VWP | Vietnam Workers' Party (Communists) |
| WWI | World War I |
| WWII | World War II |

# ACKNOWLEDGMENTS

Many people at the University of Central Oklahoma (UCO) have contributed to this book and deserve recognition. First, I would like to thank Elizabeth Maire, dean of the College of Liberal Arts (CLA); Theresa A. Vaughan, associate dean of the CLA; and Katrina Lacher and Marc Goulding, chairpersons of the Department of History and Geography, respectively. They have been very supportive of the project over the past years. As the Don Betz Endowed Chair in International Studies since 2020, I received funding from the UCO Foundation for my research and conference trips. The UCO Research, Creative, and Scholarly Activities grants sponsored by the Office of High-Impact Practice made student research assistants available for the project during the past four years.

I wish to thank my Chinese colleagues and collaborators at the PLA Academy of Military Science, China Academy of Social Sciences, Military Archives of the PLA, National Defense University, Peking University, East China Normal University, Ji'nan University, China Society for Strategy and Management, China Foundation for International and Strategic Studies, Logistics College of the PLA, Nanjing Political Academy of the PLA, and provisional academies of social sciences and history museums in Heilongjiang, Jilin, and Liaoning. They made the many arrangements neccssary for interviewing PLAN officers and retired admirals in 2017–2019 and 2023–2024. I am grateful to Rear Admiral Xu Changyou, Major General Chen Zhiya, Major General Wang Baocun, Senior Colonel Ke Chunqiao, Senior Colonel Wang Zhongchun, Colonel Yang Shaojun, Li Danhui, Liu Zhiqing, Niu Jun, Shen Zhihua, Shao Xiao, Yang Dongyu, Yang Kuisong, Zhang Baijia, and Zhang Pengfei for their help and advice for my research in China.

I also thank the Sun Yat-sen Foundation, China Reunification Alliance, and Mainland Affairs Council, Republic of China (ROC). They provided financial assistance for my research trips to Taiwan in 2017 and 2022–2023 and arranged many interviews with the military and political leaders like ROC president Ma Ying-jeou. I am grateful to the staff of Academia Sinica at Taipei, National Palace Museum, National Military Archives, and Taiwan National University for their assistance and advice on my research in Taiwan.

Special thanks to Chen Jian, Bruce A. Elleman, Sherman X. Lai, Steven I. Levine, Peter Lorge, Robert J. McMahon, Matt Muehlbauer, Hai Nguyen, John Prados, David Shambaugh, Harold M. Tanner, David Ulbrich, James Willbanks, Peter Worthing, Yafeng Xia, Qiang Zhai, Shuguang Zhang, and Xiaoming Zhang, who made important comments on earlier versions of some chapters as conference papers. Brad Watkins drew the maps. Travis Chambers and Hamilton Bloodworth copyedited the chapters. Gabrielle S. Bottger provided secretarial assistance. Several graduate and undergraduate students at UCO traveled with me to meet the veterans, transcribed the interviews, and read parts of the manuscript.

I also wish to thank the two readers for the Naval Institute Press who offered many valuable suggestions and criticism on the manuscript. At the press, Padraic (Pat) Carlin, senior acquisitions editor, guided the review process of this project over the past two years. Any remaining errors of facts, language usage, and interpretation are my own.

During the research and writing period over the past years, my wife, Tran; our son, Kevin, and daughter-in-law, Sharon; and our daughter, Christina, shared with me the burden of overseas traveling through China, Hong Kong, Taiwan, and Vietnam. Their understanding and love made the completion of this history project possible. I dedicate this book to them.

# NOTE ON TRANSLITERATION

The Hanyu Pinyin romanization system is applied to Chinese names of persons, places, and terms. The transliteration is also used for the titles of Chinese publications. A person's name is written in the Chinese way, the surname first, such as with Liu Huaqing. Some popular names—such as Mao Zedong (Mao Tse-tung)—have traditional Wade-Giles spellings appearing in parentheses after the first use of the Hanyu Pinyin, as do popular names of places like the Yangzi (Yangtze) River and Guangzhou (Canton). Exceptions are made for a few figures, whose names are widely known; in these cases the Hanyu Pinyin spellings appear in parentheses after the first use, as with Chiang Kai-shek (Jiang Jieshi) and Sun Yat-sen (Sun Zhongshan). A few places and terms such as Tibet and Kuomintang (KMT) are not transliterated.

# INTRODUCTION

## *"Red Mahan" or China's Gorshkov?*

Admiral Liu Huaqing, commander of the PLA (People's Liberation Army, China's armed forces) Navy from 1982 to 1988, stated publicly, "I am not the Chinese Mahan!" In 1996, Lieutenant Commander Jeffery B. Goldman (U.S. Navy) published an article titled "China's Mahan" and cited commentators' comparing "Admiral Liu's impact on the PLA Navy to that of Alfred Thayer Mahan on the U.S. Navy (USN) and Sergei Gorshkov on the Soviet Navy."[1] When his staff passed on the U.S. Naval Institute's magazine *Proceedings* to Liu, the Chinese admiral laughed and said, "It counts for nothing what Americans said whether [I am] Mahan or not." Liu Huaqing died in 2011. Hu Jintao, chairman of the CCP (Chinese Communist Party) from 2002 to 2012, all top Chinese leaders, PLA chiefs, and naval officers attended his funeral in Beijing. Admiral Wu Shengli, PLA Navy (PLAN) commander from 2008 to 2017, and Admiral Liu Xiaojiang, PLAN political commissar from 2008 to 2014, coauthored a memorial article stating that Liu Huaqing "established our own maritime consciousness and new strategy to defend China's oceanic sovereignty. His doctrine guides our naval development in the new century."[2]

In 2013, an official biographer, Commodore Shi Changxue, attributed China's new naval strategy—submarine capability of second nuclear strike, the pursuit of aircraft carriers, and penetration of the first island chain in the Pacific[3]—to Liu Huaqing as the "father of the modern Chinese navy."[4] In 2016, Xi Jinping, CCP chairman, spoke at a commemoration symposium for Liu Huaqing's one hundredth birthday in Beijing. The PLA commander in chief spoke highly of Liu's contribution to China's naval reforms and development. Xi called for more efforts to promote the "red tradition" and learn more from Liu Huaqing.[5] Meanwhile, the Chinese official blog and social media described Liu Huaqing as China's Mahan and

Gorshkov.[6] Was Liu Huaqing a "Red Mahan" or "China's Sergey Gorshkov"? How did he become China's legendary naval leader? What did the Chinese learn from Mahan and Gorshkov? How much do Liu Huaqing's theories, doctrines, and strategy impact the PLA Navy today?

As a biography of the admiral, this book covers Liu Huaqing's naval career, military leadership, and political struggle from 1952 to 1998. As the first book of its kind, *China's Mahan: Admiral Liu Huaqing and the Rise of the Modern Chinese Navy* focuses on Liu's forty-six years of service in the Chinese navy and the PLA high command. Based on Liu's papers, PLA documents, and naval materials, this research examines the relatively neglected subject of Liu's revolutionary experience and professional development beyond the battle of the South China Sea and the Tiananmen Square incident. *China's Mahan* situates the admiral in the context of the Chinese Civil War, global Cold War, CCP power struggles, military reforms, and a changing society. It provides a Communist tale from "the other side of the ocean" to describe China's maritime evolution, interests, and the PLAN's cognitive process in the pursuit of sea power. Liu Huaqing's story provides fresh insight from the Chinese naval command by identifying its motivations, operations, and perceptions. The historical narrative in the book humanizes and contextualizes China's naval modernization, while revealing aspects of China's naval growth, problems, and limitations previously unknown to Western readers. Admiral Liu Huaqing transformed the Chinese navy, and his legacy defined the PLAN's characteristics in the twenty-first century.

## MAHAN IN CHINA (1900–1953)

Alfred T. Mahan (1840–1914) was a USN captain, rear admiral, globally known military theorist, historian, president of the U.S. Naval War College, and "the most important American strategist of the nineteenth century."[7] Among his strategic works were *The Influence of Sea Power upon History, 1660–1783* (1890), his best-known book, if not his masterpiece.[8] Mahan believed in sea power, national greatness determined by its command of sea, national maritime interests, and oversea trade.[9] Mahan explained in his works the interdependence of military and commercial control of sea-lanes, decisive naval battles, effective blockades, overseas trade, and a nation's economic interests. He also emphasized the importance of the individual in shaping history with an emphasis on loyalty, courage, and service to the country. Mahan's ideas influenced all navies in the late nineteenth and early twentieth centuries, but the American, German, British, and Japanese navies aligned themselves most closely with his strategic vision.[10] During the first half of the twentieth century, Mahan's theory even had some influence on the Qing dynasty (1644–1911) and Republic of China (ROC) from 1912 to 1949.

Mahan's writings were introduced to China between 1900 and 1910 from Japanese translations. The first translation into Chinese of Mahan's *The Influence of Sea Power upon History* was made by a Japanese writer in March 1900. Titled "On Fundamentals for Sea Power," translations from Japanese to Chinese were published in installments in a monthly magazine, *Eastern Asian Times*, in Shanghai.[11] Although the Shanghai magazine only published Mahan's translations in two issues, it was the first time Chinese readers could learn about Mahan and his book. In 1910, another translation started in Tokyo by a Chinese naval student Qi Xi (Ch'i Hsu). With a different title, Qi published his installments in a quarterly journal, *Naval Forces*, by Qing-sent naval cadets in Japan.[12] The overseas Chinese naval students were inspired and excited about Mahan's theory and policy, which they considered the solutions for the Qing dynasty's frequent defeats at seas against European powers as well as the Japanese Empire. The journal published Qi's translations from Japanese to Chinese in four issues.[13] After the early translations, various newspapers and periodicals in China began citing Mahan's theory, discussing naval construction, calling for maritime sovereignty, and reporting disputes over fisheries, sea boundaries, and islands. The sea power awareness effectively promoted the spread of maritime interest concept and became "China's first astonishing discovery about sea power theory in the twentieth century."[14]

The fundamental elements in these late Qing translations included the core of Mahan's sea power strategy that any country that fully controlled the high seas could control the world's wealth and thus the entire world. Therefore, if China wanted to become one of the world powers, it had to have a well-equipped and well-trained naval force. Most translations also highlighted the six conditions for a maritime power: geographic location, land shape, territorial scope, population, national character, and government policies. It seemed to many Qing scholars and officials that since

China had at least four out of six conditions in its favor, all they needed were a country willing to engage in maritime business guided by government policy. In general, sea power itself was a national act.[15]

Mahan's theory rebounded to the scholarly and official policy discussions and heightened the reshaping of Chinese worldview.[16] One of the late Qing reform leaders, Liang Qichao (1873–1929), published his article "On Sea Power in the Pacific and the Future of China" in the Chinese journal *New People's Voices* in 1903 in Japan. He argued, "To become one of the world powers, [China] must fight for its sea power as the priority."[17] In 1905, the Qing government purchased three cruisers from Germany, named them as *Hai Yung* (2,950 tons displacement with 19.5 knots speed), *Hai Chou*, and *Hai Chen*. The Qing delegation also purchased two larger cruisers from Britain: *Hai Qi* (4,515 tons and 24.15 knots) and *Hai Tian*.[18] (The cruiser *Hai Qi* would remain the largest warship China ever had until the late Cold War.) In November 1906, the Advanced Academy of Anhui launched a campus-wide fundraising to support naval purchases. The donations came in not only from students, faculty, and staff, but also from local communities, city residents, and many businesses, organizations, and schools across Anhui Province.

Late Qing translations also focused on Mahan's writings about China and East Asia's maritime tradition, status, problems, and future. Chinese scholars understood that China had traditionally been a land power despite its long coastline and the massive oceanic territory. Chinese people experienced—as Mahan detailed in his writings—China's weakness, chaos, and uncertainty after their defeat in the First Sino-Japanese War of 1894, when China lost its power position in East Asia. Qing officials worried about domestic chaos and foreign powers' attempts to carve up China. The Qing government paid more attention to its maritime sovereignty and naval development. On August 30, 1906, an official report to the Qing court emphasized the importance of sea power: "The current international affairs became more critical, and the sea power became more important. To strengthen self-defense, [Qing] must revitalize the naval force."[19] After Beijing was informed of Japanese ships reaching the Dongsha Islands, the Qing court sent warships to the South China Sea to protect the islands. In 1909, the court ordered the Guangdong Provincial Government to conduct a maritime survey around the Dongsha and Paracel Islands. As the governor suggested in his report, Qing established the Paracel Affairs Office in the provincial capital.[20]

Nevertheless, China's naval development became intertwined with its military history and revolutionary movement. Mahan's strategy could not save the empire because the Manchu rulers refused to carry on the military reform into institution and organization apart from buying Western weapons and hiring European instructors. Li Hongzhang (1823–1901), the Qing court's grand secretary, said once publicly that "Chinese civil and military systems are much superior in every aspect to these of the Westerners; only our firearms are far inferior to theirs."[21] Manchu grandees' refusal of further reform and brutal suppression against the reformers also alienated the regular seamen and undermined their loyalty to the emperor.[22] Moreover, the naval officers were soon disillusioned by the government's corruption, mismanagement, and, the worst of all, its failure against European, American, and Japanese forces during the 1900 Boxer Rebellion.[23] By the end of the first decade, the Qing dynasty's political order and economic system crumbled under Western invasions and increasing dissatisfaction, rapidly eroding Manchu authority in Beijing.

Sun Yat-sen (Sun Zhongshan, 1866–1925) led the 1911 Revolution to end the Qing dynasty and found the Republic of China (ROC). Mahan's theory had established the Chinese perception of sea power and connection between naval power and national development among the Republican revolutionaries. On January 1, 1912, Sun Yat-sen founded the ROC Navy right after his inauguration. He recognized the importance of maritime development in China's modernization. In his *Industrial Plans*, Sun emphasized construction of naval bases and commercial ports, which would link to railways and highways as international trade network to promote China's trade.[24] Sun and the other Nationalist (Kuomintang, KMT; or Guomindang, GMD) leaders, however, failed to establish a republican state and never had control of any armed force. Soon Marshal Yuan Shikai replaced Sun in 1912 as the ROC president. After Yuan's death, the country entered the Warlord Era (1916–1927), when some warlords established their own naval forces as they fought against each other to seize control of the whole country.

In 1927, Chiang Kai-shek (Jiang Jieshi, 1887–1975) and his Nationalist Army achieved the victory of their Northern Expeditionary War by defeating several major warlords. In April, Chiang reestablished the ROC government under KMT control in Nanjing. The national reunification and establishment of the Department of Navy in the Chiang administration brought new hope for China's sea power. In 1927, the *Journal of Naval Force* published Tang Baogao's first Chinese translation of Mahan's *Sea Power upon History* from English.[25]

From 1928 to 1948, Chen Shaokuan (1889–1969) became the first Chinese naval commander who called for China's sea power and intended to build a strong KMT Navy according to Mahan's theory. Captain Chen Shaokuan studied naval theory and technology in England from 1916 to 1918. During World War I, Chen participated in three British submarine battles against the Germans and received British navy's Distinguished Service Order in 1918. After the war, he was ranked commander and served as military attaché in Chinese embassies in London, Paris, and Rome. After his return to China, Chen was promoted to rear admiral in 1923, vice admiral in 1928, and full admiral in 1932. He served as commander of the navy's Second Fleet in 1929 and secretary of the ROC Navy Department in 1932. Chen Shaokuan dreamed of a strong Chinese navy. In 1928, Chen Shaokuan submitted his naval development plan to build one aircraft carrier, three cruisers, four destroyers, and two submarines within two years. His long-term plan would build 600,000 tons of warships in fifteen years.[26] Although Admiral Chen never had a chance to build a strong navy as Mahan described, he founded China's first naval university in July 1934 at Mawei, where Mahan's books became required texts for all KMT naval officers. Naval commander Chen Shaokuan was ranked fleet admiral in 1935.[27]

On Christmas Day of 1934, Chiang Kai-shek invited Admiral Chen to spend the new year with him and his family at Chiang's hometown Xikou, Fenghua. One morning, when China's president asked his naval commander what books he had read recently, Chen told Chiang, "I read U.S. Rear Admiral Mahan's book on naval strategy." He explained to Chiang Kai-shek that Mahan's book was the first systematic theoretical work of the naval power.[28] At that time, Chen believed that "the whole country must clearly recognize the importance of the power at sea. . . . If [our] sea power can develop, our industry and commerce will win. It totally depends on the Navy."[29] Chen's navy dream, however, did not become the ROC's reality because of KMT power struggles and foreign invasion.

When Japan invaded China in 1937, the ROC Navy was weak. Its warships totaled merely 59,000 tons and were no match against the invading Japanese navy. At that time, the Imperial Japanese Navy totaled 1.15 million tons of warships, including four aircraft carriers, nine battleships, twelve heavy cruisers, thirteen light cruisers, seventy destroyers, and forty-four submarines. The Chinese warships totaled just over 5 percent of Japanese total tonnage.[30] Without naval and air defense, Chiang Kai-shek suffered humiliating defeats and lost almost all of the eastern and southern coastal port cities that had once been his power base.[31] By March 1938, almost all of north China had fallen into Japanese hands. From July 1937 to November 1938, Chiang lost 1 million KMT troops, and he had to move the seat of his government from Nanjing to Chongqing, Sichuan, in 1939. In the wake of the Allied forces' campaign against fascism and militarism across the globe, China's War of Resistance against Japan under the CCP-KMT united front launched partial counteroffensives and won some victories against Japanese invading army in 1942–1944.

Celebrating the victory of the war, in August 1945, Admiral Chen made another naval development plan for Chiang Kai-shek. His postwar ROC fleet would include three aircraft carriers, four battleships, four heavy cruisers, sixteen light cruisers, twenty-four destroyers, twenty-four submarines, twelve submarine chasers, and forty torpedo speed boats.[32] However, during the Chinese Civil War from 1946 to 1949, Chiang focused his military efforts on the ground warfare against the Chinese Communist army in the country. Any major naval buildup became impossible until Chiang Kai-shek removed the seat of his ROC government from the mainland to Taiwan in 1949. However, his naval commander did not follow him but instead stayed on the mainland at the end of the civil war. After the CCP took over the country, Chen Shaokuan was appointed by Beijing as vice chairman of a military and political committee to help the PLA build a new navy from 1950 to 1954 and then as lieutenant governor of Fujian Province from 1955 to 1968.[33]

During the Chinese Civil War, the PLA did not have a naval force capable of engaging the KMT Navy. On April 23, 1949, the PLA's Third Field Army established the East China Military Region's Navy (ECMRN) to receive former KMT seamen and vessels. April 23 is celebrated as the birthday of the PLA Navy. In December, the CCP Central Military Commission (CMC) reorganized the PLA's 12th Army Group Headquarters into the PLA Navy Department.[34] On January 12, 1950, Mao Zedong (Mao Tse-tung, 1893–1976), CCP chairman, appointed the army group commander Xiao Jinguang (Hsiao Ch'in-guang, 1903–1989) as the first commander of the new "Chinese People's Navy." On February 3, the Third Field Army transferred its 35th Army to the ECMRN HQ under Zhang Aiping's command.[35] Then the PLA transferred additional 30,000 soldiers and 1,500 officers to the navy—Liu Huaqing was one of them. In 1952, PLAN commander Xiao Jinguang appointed Liu as vice superintendent and deputy political commissar of PLA Dalian Naval Academy.

The newly established PLA Navy had no experience in naval warfare and no knowledge about naval technology and training, including Commander Xiao Jinguang himself, an army commander for twenty-eight years. In 1950, there were no PLAN officers or sailors capable of moving a ship, and many had never seen the ocean before.[36] As such, former enemy seamen, or defected and realigned KMT sailors, operated PLAN ships and gunboats in the rivers and at sea. The PLAN had to rely on ex-KMT naval officers, who had received their training from British, American, and Japanese navies through both world wars. After the CMC decided to establish the naval academy, college, and training schools in 1949, the PLAN had to hire four thousand former KMT naval officers as the instructors and administrators to run PLA naval schools and train PLA officers. Liu Huaqing learned about Mahan and his sea power theory for the first time from the instructors at the Dalian Naval Academy in 1952–1953.[37]

## GORSHKOV AND RUSSIAN INFLUENCE: MAO'S COLD WAR NAVY (1954–1992)

Throughout the 1950s, the new PLA Navy depended entirely on Russian naval doctrine, technology, curriculum, and training. The PLAN purchased Soviet warships, submarines, maritime planes, naval equipment, and coastal artillery and radars. Beijing hired Russian advisors, instructors, and experts for its coastal defense, offshore landing campaigns, shipbuilding, and naval education and training. By 1959, more than six hundred

Chinese naval officers had studied naval engineering, maritime science, and aviation technology in Soviet naval colleges and institutes. From 1954 to 1958, Liu Huaqing studied at the Voroshilov Naval Command Academy (currently Kuznetsov Naval Academy) in St. Petersburg. Mahanian maritime policy and naval power strategy had a historical impact in Russian military curriculum and their naval classroom. Although Liu Huaqing learned more about Mahan's sea power theory in the Soviet Union, the Cold War world had entered the "post-Mahan era."[38] China's need to build a new naval force, offshore islands crises, and its increasing security risks did not have much to do with Mahanian theory. Moreover, Liu Huaqing and other naval officers criticized Mahan's sea power theory, arguing that its marine activities aimed at competing for sea power fully reflected the imperialist ambitions of aggression.[39]

Meanwhile, Liu Huaqing studied Russian fleet admiral Sergey Gorshkov's naval strategy and sea power theory in several courses he took at the Soviet naval academy. Sergey Gorshkov (1910–1988) was commander in chief of Soviet Navy from 1956 to 1985. He became a Russian naval war hero in World War II after several successful landing campaigns and his command of 150 ships in a breakout to the Black Sea to save Soviet troops. Soviet leader Joseph Stalin (1878–1953) appointed Gorshkov commander of the Black Sea Fleet in 1951 and promoted him to admiral in 1953. After Stalin's death, Nikita Khrushchev appointed Gorshkov as commander in chief of the Soviet Navy in January 1956. Gorshkov was promoted to fleet admiral in 1962 and also served as deputy defense minister of the Soviet Union. After the Cuban Missile Crisis of 1962, Fleet Admiral Gorshkov transformed the Soviet Navy from a "fortress fleet" for near-shore defense to an "ocean-going missile nuclear navy" for far sea offense. Meanwhile, the Soviet Union also completed a strategic transformation from a traditional Euro-Asian land power to global sea power. With support of four Soviet leaders, Khrushchev (in power from 1954 to 1964), Leonid Brezhnev (1964–1982), Yuri Andropov (1982–1984), and Konstantin Chernenko (1984–1985), Gorshkov created a "balanced naval force" capable of challenging Western naval power by the 1970s.[40] His massive naval building included aircraft carriers, nuclear submarines, nuclear weapons, ballistic missiles, and shipboard helicopters. As a global maritime power, his fleets operated in the Atlantic, Pacific, and Indian Oceans and in the Mediterranean Sea. Fleet

Admiral Gorshkov is described in Russia as the "Father of the Modern Soviet Navy."[41]

From the 1960s through the 1970s, Fleet Admiral Sergey Gorshkov published a series of works such as *The Navy in War and Peace* and *The Power of the Nation at Sea*. Gorshkov argued in his works that sea power was a systematic power system that included maritime scientific research and development, oceanic transportation, and naval power. These contents supported and promoted each other, and the naval power was the core of a country's sea power. Therefore, he believed in large naval force, decisive naval battles, and control of high seas. The fleet admiral explained his ideas of "active offense," which became a doctrine on the Soviet military theory and a core value in naval academy curriculum. Gorshkov's sea power theory guided the development and practice of the Soviet Union's maritime strategy during the Cold War. As a result, Gorshkov's doctrines and Soviet naval theories and tactics strongly influenced Chinese naval development through its technological aid and advisory assistance during the PLAN's formative years.[42]

Russian research on Gorshkov's theory is divided into two groups. First, the naval academic scholars centered their research on the core of the Soviet sea power development. They argued that the primary determinant of the sea power was the size and capability of the Soviet Navy, and that its foundation was the national economic strength. Second, Russian naval historians focused their research on Soviet military history and provided a naval development in the context of the Soviet overall military modernization. While they pointed out the "Great Patriotic War" (World War II) as a historical defining movement in Soviet naval history, they argued that the 1962 Cuban Missile Crisis was the turning point in Soviet naval modernization. The historical perspective was applicable for Chinese learning and thinking how to build a strong naval force as part of the PLA's modernization, while Liu Huaqing always emphasized the distinguished nature of naval force and special needs of naval construction.

Liu Huaqing was familiar with Gorshkov's concept of the Communist military since he had served in the Red Army and PLA for almost twenty years. The Soviet fleet admiral was following Vladimir Lenin's (1870–1924) principle of the Russian armed forces serving the political goals of the party. To build a combat-effective peasant army in China, Mao Zedong employed the CCP to control the officer corps and politicize the Red Army institution. The party and the army established an interdependent relationship before World War II to create a center in rural areas for revolutionary authorities. The party mobilized the peasants, trained the officers, and received instructions and aid from the Soviet Union. The army protected the Communist base against a stronger enemy force.[43] Mao emphasized the party leadership by stating that the party must control the gun, and the gun must never control the party.[44] Liu Huaqing understood both war of politics and politics of war. He believed that they would eventually build strong armed forces if they maintained the party-army institution.

Meanwhile, Liu Huaqing's understanding of Gorshkov's military theory and naval building came from not only their similar political ideology, but also their geostrategic roots. The Soviet Union, like the People's Republic of China (PRC), was traditionally a land power and landlocked on three sides. During the Cold War, however, Gorshkov began a historical transition of the Soviet Union from a Eurasian continental power to a global sea power. Although it was a long historical process, Gorshkov's theory and strategy clearly indicated such a strategic transformation was possible and necessary for Soviet survival in the Cold War. During its formative years, the Chinese navy had close ties with the Soviet Navy. Chinese naval officers like Liu Huaqing wanted to learn from the experience and lessons of the Soviet Navy's development. Liu's military experience in China and naval learning in Russia intersected well during his years in the Soviet Union. His higher education in the Soviet Navy completed his transition from an army officer to a naval commander and made him more "China's Gorshkov" than "Red Mahan." Liu was made a rear admiral in 1955.[45]

During the second half of the 1960s, however, Mao Zedong shifted his defense focus and national security concerns from the United States to the Soviet Union. The PLA high command was convinced that the United States had lost its power and control in the Asian-Pacific region because of its failure in the Vietnam War and serious problems in other parts of the world. As the United States tried to withdraw from Asia, Moscow filled the power vacuum, replacing the United States as the "imperialist" aggressor in the region and a new threat to China. The Vietnam War transformed the Cold War from a bipolar standoff to a multifront confrontation, forcing both superpowers to use the "China card" and play a different game in the early 1970s. Washington's strategic needs eventually led to President Richard Nixon's visit to Beijing in 1972 and the PRC and Japan's establishment of diplomatic relations in 1973. Soon the East China Sea, South China Sea, and the Pacific Ocean opened for China's trade and overseas exchanges. China needed more naval power to serve its new maritime interests and oceanic territorial claims. The early 1970s became the turning point in Chinese naval development and modernization. Liu Huaqing saw the great opportunity and maximized his political capital in his advantage. In 1975, he wrote directly to Deng Xiaoping, the chief of the PLA General Staff.

Liu Huaqing served in the PLA Navy under three generations of CCP leadership—Mao Zedong's from 1952 to 1976, Deng Xiaoping's from 1975 to 1990, and Jiang Zemin's from 1990 to 2002. A seldom direct superior-subordinate relationship developed in the Eighth Route Army between Liu Huaqing and Deng Xiaoping from 1938 during the War of Resistance against Japan until 1952 after the Chinese Civil War. Deng Xiaoping knew Liu Huaqing well, and Liu's political loyalty to Deng earned him Deng's trust and promotions in the army. The personal connection played a more important role in Liu's high-ranking appointments in the navy from 1982 to 1988 and the PLA high command from 1988 to 1998. Although Deng's rise and fall had some impacts on Liu's military career, Liu Huaqing survived the political movements and personality struggles. Liu was in and out of the navy three times, each return at the right moment and under better political conditions during the PLAN's definitive historical moments. Liu Huaqing joked about it later: "While other people lost their jobs in the Cultural Revolution, I got promoted in the middle of it."[46]

In 1975, Rear Admiral Liu Huaqing, head of the Shipbuilding Office in the PLAN headquarters, called for a strong Chinese navy in his ten-thousand-character plan, which was directly sent to Deng Xiaoping. Liu's naval plan included manufacturing a 40,000-ton aircraft carrier and numerous 4,000-ton destroyers and 2,000-ton frigates.[47] From his observations, Liu argued that the world's successful navies operated increasingly farther from their coasts and that international trade was progressively more important to China's economy. Liu predicted that it was only a matter of time before the Chinese navy would have to engage in operations to protect China's sea lines of communications (SLOCs). It became a historical moment when Deng Xiaoping, PLA chief of general staff, read the middle-ranking officer's proposal and accepted Liu's strong navy's idea. On the next day, impressed and excited, Deng Xiaoping forwarded Liu's plan to the navy's leaders with his instruction to "take this report into consideration. Some points deserve our attention."[48]

In 1978, when Deng Xiaoping became the country's commander in chief, he commenced economic reform. Rapid economic growth and overseas trade made the coastal regions, sea-lanes, and maritime development more important to national security interests and the country's economic activities. The Party Center supported Liu's naval strategy and shifted the focus of its military reform to the navy's modernization. Liu Huaqing was promoted to deputy chief of the PLA General Staff in January 1981.

## LIU AND THE PLAN: LITERATURE REVIEW

When Liu Huaqing became PLAN commander in 1982, the Chinese navy was a sizable regional naval power with nearly all types of warships. Then, Liu highlighted three major transformative phases from the 1980s to the 2010s. First, the PLAN transformed from a Russian-built coastal brown-water navy from the 1950s to 1970s to an offshore defensive force in the 1980s; then, to a near sea blue-water navy along the first island chain in the 1990s–2010s; and then, to a far sea navy with offensive capability and nuclear deterrence in the 2010s–2020s. These defining historical changes aid in comprehending Chinese naval strategy and characteristics. After his promotion to CMC deputy secretary general and then vice chairman, Liu continued his efforts to build a strong navy.

From 1992 to 1998, Admiral Liu served as a member of the CCP Politburo's Standing Committee and became one of China's seven top leaders. He administrated the PLA's daily operations, managed China's defense budget, and continued promoting naval development as the CMC first vice chairman next to Deng's successor Jiang Zemin. Jiang Zemin supported Liu Huaqing's endeavor to build a modern, blue-water naval force. In 1992, under Jiang's leadership, the National People's Congress (NPC) passed China's First Maritime Law that codified Liu's conception of "sea as territory," including the country's "sovereignty" over 3 million square kilometers of ocean and seas. From that point, China considered the oceans and seas as new frontiers. Although Admiral Liu Huaqing retired in 1998, his strategy envisioned the Chinese navy with capabilities in the Pacific and Indian Oceans by the end of the twentieth century. His near sea defense and far sea protection became PLAN strategy in the twenty-first century. His sea power theory laid foundation for China's oceanic sovereignty, maritime policy, and international diplomacy in the Indo-Pacific region.

After Jiang Zemin left office, new Chinese leader Hu Jintao (in office 2002–2012) launched a nationwide campaign to promote China's maritime interest and fully support naval development. With a rapid increasing of naval power, at the CCP Sixteenth National Congress in 2002, the Party Center for the first time called for "implementing maritime development" and "developing the maritime economy" as one of the party's new tasks in the twenty-first century. In August 2004, Hu Jintao chaired a Politburo meeting to mobilize national resources and promote naval modernization. Hu emphasized the escalation of naval transformation and special attention to its combat readiness. During the Hu administration, the navy improved its equipment and weapon systems, and received numbers of new warships, including aircraft carrier. Liu Huaqing's persistent efforts in aircraft carrier research and development eventually led to the completion of China's first aircraft carrier in 2011. His continuing efforts in nuclear submarine manufacturing and improvement resulted in the commission of the PLAN's third generation of nuclear submarines, giving it a second nuclear strike capability. By 2010, the PLAN had a total force of 300,000 personnel and more than 600 warships. The Chinese navy has an air arm of 430 warplanes and 35,000 personnel, and commands China's 12,000-strong Marine Corps. The Chinese navy evolved and became one of the world naval powers by 2012.

The PLAN's ongoing development and its inevitable implications for Indo-Pacific security have attracted great academic attention in the West, especially in the United States. Combined scholarly efforts provide solid groundwork for a new study of the PLAN's leadership. Nevertheless, there is no comprehensive history of Admiral Liu Huaqing available in English yet. Research by Western military historians is constrained, as they have focused on the 1980s–2010s when the Chinese navy enjoyed a tremendous development. Many research monographs examined Liu's naval strategy from 1982 when he became the PLAN commander. However, the Chinese navy did not become a global naval power overnight in the 1990s. There are few historical explanations in the West about the rise of Liu Huaqing from the 1950s to the 1990s.

In the United States, the study of the PLAN's history is relatively new. Since the 1990s, American naval scholars and military historians have focused on Chinese naval history in response to the PLA's reform and modernization in the 1980s. As Chinese naval scholarship advanced, they emphasized the importance of Chinese naval history and provided fresh interpretations, new concepts, and research frameworks to better understand the PLAN in terms of party control, national defense, state-building, economic growth, and international relations. Rear Admiral Michael A. McDevitt provides a well-researched volume on the PLAN, *China as a Twenty-First Century Naval Power: Theory, Practice, and Implications.* In this pathbreaking volume, his book addresses important questions like "why China seeks to become a maritime power" and why Chinese leader Xi Jinping needs a "world-class" navy by mid-century.[49] While redefining "world-class navy," his analysis focuses on Chinese maritime security theory, strategic practice and implications, and civil-military relations between the party-state and the navy. McDevitt puts the PLAN into a broader context of China's national goal to become a global economic power. His discussions about Liu Huaqing include Liu's argument in 1986 that China needed carrier-based airpower for the country's maritime interests; Liu and the 1988 Sino-Vietnamese naval battle over the disputed Spratly Islands in the South China Sea; and Liu's use of a Japanese case in World War II to justify the need of China's own carrier.[50] However, Rear Admiral McDevitt's book is present-oriented analyses, not histories. It "is not a history of PLA Navy; that book has already been well written, twice, by Dr. Bernard Cole."[51]

As the leading historian in the field, Bernard D. Cole offers a comprehensive and insightful assessment of the PLAN in a second edition of his essential book *The Great Wall at Sea: China's Navy in the Twenty-First Century.* He traces the trajectory of the Chinese navy from the 1950s to the twenty-first century. His historical research examines Chinese naval reforms with an emphasis on the continuity and changes in PLAN doctrine, organization, force composition, strategy, technology, readiness, and utility as vital instruments of national power. His book links Chinese naval efforts to "the nation's economic development" and to "dependence on overseas trade," which have been principally overlooked by other works in the field.[52] He pays special attention to the roles played by ideology, economy, international trade, energy resources, Russian relations, and geographic setting. Cole points out that "Beijing's inflexibilities" over its territorial claims are determined by its "increasing dependence on offshore energy resources."[53] He has a section titled "Liu Huaqing's Vision" that offers general coverage of Liu's strategy and plans from 1982 to 2010. Cole also provides several brief introductions and general descriptions of Liu's policy throughout the book. A historical portrait of Liu's strategic thinking will prove helpful in better understanding the PLAN's leadership.

James C. Bussert and Bruce A. Elleman surveyed PLAN technological advantages and shortcomings in its "increasingly modern combat system." The coauthored book *People's Liberation Army Navy: Combat Systems Technology, 1949–2010* provides "a warp of plainly technical threads of equipment characteristics and capabilities and ship construction programs."[54] With a technical focus, the coauthors explain how the PLAN is rapidly advancing in technology diffusion and why China is preparing to fight "informationized warfare." As a contemporary Chinese naval study, it contains only one chapter (out of twelve) as a historical background on "China's Naval Technology Growth." The book mentions Liu Huaqing once when he directed a 1997 purchase of a high-tech naval platform that included Su-27 and Su-30 aircraft.[55]

The leading Asia-Pacific security scholars Toshi Yoshihara and James R. Holmes offer an overview of Chinese maritime strategy in the second edition of their coauthored book *Red Star over the Pacific*. They discuss how China's rise challenges the security order and U.S. maritime strategy in the Asia-Pacific region and increases conflict and confrontation that has already been seen in maritime territorial disputes and other regional security issues. The book surely fills some major gaps in strategy research and indicates the destabilizing factors in the region largely deriving from China's rise. The coauthors examine Liu Huaqing's naval strategic development in the 1980s, combat experience, influence, and conceptions of near seas and offshore active defense on sixteen pages. They provided a historical direction in the recent past, rarely venturing further back than the Deng Xiaoping era (1979–1992), and a broader context for the understanding of the PLAN's strategy.

Yoshihara and Holmes warn readers about Mahan's "comeback," this time, to China, as "the Chinese are the Mahanians now" in a "modern, neo-Mahanian" Asia.[56] They delve into questions of Mahan's sea power theory and naval strategy and their influence on China during the late twentieth and early twenty-first centuries. The coauthors also offered Chinese maritime interests, naval strategy, and their historical background. "But to understand how Mahanian and Maoist strategic traditions may intersect with Chinese maritime strategy, we must first appreciate why China is taking to the sea."[57] Although they pointed out three major reasons for China to take to the seas, including security, economy, and Taiwan, the book does not look further back into earlier military experience of Chinese revolution.

Nevertheless, Toshi Yoshihara does offer a historical account of the PLA's navy, *Mao's Army Goes to Sea*. Through his research on the PLAN since the late 1990s, he "became convinced that an understanding of China's prospects at sea in the twenty-first century requires an acquaintance with its maritime past."[58] Andrew S. Erickson points out Yoshihara's "portraying one of the most valuable perspective of all: how China's navy views its own past, present, and potential future."[59] Yoshihara criticizes the "conventional wisdom held that China's maritime thought was largely a Soviet derivative and that the founding naval officers—army officers selected for their loyalty to the Chinese Communist Party—contributed little to the nautical enterprise."[60] Yoshihara pointed out the Western argument on "the emergence of a coherent and modern naval strategy to Liu Huaqing's intellectual contributions in the 1980s . . . is also incomplete. It understates the role that earlier combat experiences and associated doctrinal debates played in the formulation of Chinese naval strategy in the post-Mao era." Although the author offers the little-known story of Mao Zedong's founding of the PLAN, the book only covers a short period (about eighteen months) of the PLAN's history from 1949 to 1950.

This work complements these books by providing a historical perspective of Liu Huaqing's military career since 1935. His strategic thinking, naval doctrines, and reform policies resulted from a half century of sea battles, contested island landings, oceanic operations, shipbuilding, naval education, and technology improvements. Many early experiences from his inception in the Cold War are relevant to contemporary Chinese naval leaders as they consider specific strategic and even operational challenges like those in the Taiwan Strait and South China Sea. Current Chinese naval organization, operation, weapon systems, and training originated during, and draw on the experience and maritime policies, of the Cold War, including "nuclear deterrence," "active defense," "defensive offense," and "local warfare." The book's historical perspective provides an answer to the ongoing questions among academia and the public: Why does China want a naval war against the USN? What did Chinese learn from Mahan? What made Liu Huaqing Mahanian?

## NAVAL HISTORY: A NOTE ON THE SOURCES

This book examines Liu Huaqing's military career by discussing how China's strategic goal shifted from a land defense in the 1950s to sea defense in the 2020s. Through his biography, the book establishes naval development as a fundamental factor for changes in national strategy and maritime interests. Successful naval operations were a driving force behind China's requests for oceanic sovereignty and sea power. Admiral Liu played a historical role in making the crucial connections between the navy, state, and the party. As a man of both action and letters, the admiral composed a large body of naval literature, including strategic theory, naval war doctrine, operational principles, and technological development for the new century. His doctrine demonstrates an acute awareness of complex and intermingling philosophies including modern, Western naval influences like Mahan and Gorshkov. His writings continue to influence the navy and the PLA in the twenty-first century. The conclusions in this volume are supported by both primary and secondary Chinese sources made available in recent years.

The party and the government documents are housed in the First National Historical Archives of China (Zhongguo diyi lishi dang'anguan) in Beijing. Although the First Archives opened 4.7 million historical files to the public by 2022, there are only a few thousand that address the CCP's military history and the PLA's developments. Since 2016, the PLA's naval documents are housed in both the PLA Archives (Jiefangjun dang'anguan) under the Security and Archives Bureau (SAB) of the CCP's Central

Military Commission and the PLAN Archives (Haijun danganguan) under the naval headquarters. Although most PLAN archival materials remain closed to scholars, some of Liu Huaqing's strategic thoughts, war plans, and naval reports are selected and published in two volumes, *Liu Huaqing junshi wenxuan* (*Selected Military Writings of Liu Huaqing*), by the PLA Press in 2008.[61] The first volume includes Liu's military papers from September 1939 to January 1988, and the second volume selects his papers from February 1988 to September 1997, before his retirement in 1998. He also left behind many published recollections, memorial articles, op-eds, book chapters, and journal articles.[62]

Other primary sources include Liu Huaqing's letters, inscriptions, speeches, and images that were collected and published after he died in 2011.[63] His photo album was published in 2016 by Long March Press. Some local archives also host Liu's conference remarks, telegrams, and speeches when he served as commander, deputy commander, and political commissar at the Lüshun Naval Base and North Sea Fleet (NSF) at Qingdao. His early military career can be traced in the archives at the War Museum of the Eighth Route Army at Changzhi, Shanxi; Hong'an County Archives, Hubei; Nanzhao Archives; and Wuhan Metropolitan Archives. Local archival materials are also vital for military historians who study Chinese naval warfare, not simply for filling in factual gaps but also to serve as the main source for discovering new topics in the field.

It is important to note that during most of the PLAN's history, the CCP Political Bureau and the CMC, the top decision-making body of the party, micromanaged naval strategic and even tactical decisions. This book explores official Chinese documents, strategic writings, military instructions, PLAN speeches, and high command communications by top leaders like Mao Zedong, Deng Xiaoping, Jiang Zemin, Zhu De, Liu Shaoqi, Zhou Enlai, Hu Jintao, and Xi Jinping.[64] Their manuscripts and military works were collected and published by the CCP Central Archival and Manuscripts Press. The General Office of the PRC Ministry of Foreign Affairs also published large numbers of government documents in recent years.[65] After the Cold War ended, some former Soviet documents were declassified at the Archives of the President, Party Central Committee, and General Staff of the Soviet Armed Forces, which revealed new perspectives on Russo-Chinese military relations and

Soviet aid and advisory to the PLAN.[66] Some translated Russian documents were printed in the *Bulletin* of the Cold War International History Project (CWIHP) at the Wilson Center.[67] Many China-related Soviet archives were translated into Chinese and published by the Archives and Manuscripts of Social Sciences Press in Beijing in thirty-four volumes.[68] Some sensitive Russian archives on the Korean War are published by the Institute of Modern History, Academia Sinica, Taipei, in three volumes.[69]

The PLA collected and published military papers from top marshals and generals like Peng Dehuai, Lin Biao, Liu Bocheng, Nie Rongzhen, Xu Xiangqian, Chen Yi, He Long, and Ye Jianying.[70] Their writings on strategy, campaign plans, reform projects, conference records, and telegrams are crucial for comprehending the PLAN's development and modernization during the Cold War. Certainly, the writings and memoirs of the naval leaders like Xiao Jinguang, Su Zhenhua, Ye Fei, and the others are essential for this research.[71] The exploration of their strategic thoughts, operational systems, and internal weaknesses shapes the PLAN's characteristics in the twenty-first century and differentiate the PLAN from other naval forces in the world. Liu Huaqing's autobiography, *Liu Huaqing huiyilu* [*Memoir of Liu Huaqing*], published by the PLA Press in 2007, is another helpful source for this work.

In recent years, my research trips to China focused on the recollections and interviews of PLAN sailors and officers. I collected their memoirs and interviewed retired PLAN admirals and officers like General Ye Fei, PLAN political commissar (1979–1982); Rear Admiral Xu Changyou, former political commissar of the East Sea Fleet's (ESF's) Air Force; and Major General Chai Chengwen, Senior Colonel Guan Zhichao, Major Huo Zhenlu, Captain Wang Xuedong, and others in Beijing, Shanghai, Guangzhou, Nanjing, Wuhan, Hangzhou, and Hainan.[72] The rich details from their experience remarkably contributed to this study by adding alternate perspectives. From 2017 to 2019, and again in 2023, I also researched ROC government documents and interviewed Taiwanese leaders, KMT generals, naval officers, and POWs of the PLA in Taiwan. No matter how politically indoctrinated they may be, the veterans are culturally bound to cherish the memory of the past. During my 2017 trip, I had an opportunity to meet Ma Ying-jeou, president of the ROC from 2008 to 2016, and discussed the naval conflict and disputed islands in the East and South

China Seas. The Taiwanese president gave me some of his own research papers and one of his three books on the legal status of the disputed islands from an international maritime legal perspective.[73]

After Liu Huaqing died in 2011, many personal interviews, memorial articles, and research papers exploring the life and experience of the admiral became available as interest in China's naval strategy and maritime power increased. Xi Jinping attended five commemorative symposiums for the most influential Chinese in history, including Confucius, Sun Yat-sen, Mao Zedong, Deng Xiaoping, and Liu Huaqing. Commodore Shi Changxue published Liu's official biography in 2013. There are several biographies of Liu Huaqing by other authors.[74] The August First Film Studio produced and aired on CCTV (China Central Television) a nine-episode documentary *Liu Huaqing*, offering important historical archives, detailed naval sources, and many personal interviews with retired admirals, PLAN officers, naval war veterans, naval pilots, and marines. Some doctoral dissertations and master's theses also focused on Liu's naval career and maritime strategy.[75]

The chapters follow Liu Huaqing's military career in the context of a development of China's recognition of its maritime interests and naval power. Chapter 1 begins with Liu's military career in the army from 1934 to 1951 and his transfer from the army to the navy in 1952. It also traces his naval education in the Soviet Union from 1954 to 1958, which broadened his worldview and shaped his belief in a strong naval force for China. Chapter 2 examines Liu's early naval career as a base commander from 1958 to 1961 and president of national research institute for naval development from 1961 to 1965. It also explained why Liu Huaqing left the navy in 1965 and became vice minister of China's Sixth Machinery Ministry from 1965 to 1966, then vice chairman of the Commission of Science, Technology, and Industry for National Defense (CSTIND) from 1966 to 1969. Chapter 3 examines his return to the navy as the "shipbuilding chief" in 1969, his perception and facilitation of a "strong navy with combat capability," and his plan for the PLAN's future development from 1975 to 1985. It explains why Liu Huaqing left the navy again in 1975 and later resumed his position as CSTIND vice chairman in 1977. Chapter 4 focuses on Liu's new naval strategy of "near sea defense" when he served as the PLAN commander from 1982 to 1988. It also covers Liu's role as the commander in chief of the PLA's Capital Martial Law Forces that cracked down on student demonstrations at Tiananmen Square on June 4, 1989. Chapter 5 explains how Liu became one of the top seven national leaders and served as the PLA high commander next to Jiang Zemin from 1990 to 1998, where Liu continued naval buildup and completed a Chinese model of naval power development. Liu's maritime strategy became China's new national policy under Hu Jintao's and Xi Jinping's leaderships from 2002 to 2020. The conclusion investigates Xi's new efforts to materialize Liu's vision and make the PLAN a "world-class navy" by 2049.

CHAPTER 1

# FROM A POLITICAL COMMISSAR TO A REAR ADMIRAL

When Liu Huaqing reported to the PLAN's headquarters in Beijing in 1952, navy commander Xiao Jinguang (Hsiao Chin-guang) appointed him as party secretary and vice political commissar of the Dalian Naval Academy. A surprised Liu said he had been fighting in the mountains and had never seen the ocean before.[1] Xiao related to Liu's reservations; the naval commander himself had transferred from the army as well.[2] This chapter begins with Liu Huaqing's early revolutionary career when he joined the CCP movement at thirteen in 1929 and became a Red Army officer in 1935. It examines his military experience during the CCP's Agrarian Revolutionary War (1927–1937), China's Resistance War against Japan (1937–1945), and the Chinese Civil War (1946–1949). It also explains how Xi Jinping identified the "red tradition" (or red DNA) of the CCP armed forces, or the "miliary soul" of the PLA, in Liu's service in the army.[3]

Three important factors in Liu Huaqing's army career from 1932 to 1952 prepared him for his future naval career. First, the CCP adopted a meritocratic system for PLA appointments and promotions. Liu's lengthy service in the Red Army and early revolutionary career provided him with a solid seniority standing for the PLAN's leadership. Second, Liu Huaqing worked directly under Deng Xiaoping during the Resistance War against Japan. Deng trained him as one of his staff members in his political tasks department and then appointed Liu as a political commissar in the Chinese Civil War. Liu's personal relations, working experience, and earned trust from Deng Xiaoping played an important role in his naval career when Deng became the leader of the CCP and PRC in 1978. Third, Liu served as a political commissar at regimental, brigade, division, and army commands in the PLA army from 1943 to 1949. By the end of the civil war, Liu was vice political commissar of the 11th Army in the PLA's Second Field Army commanded by Deng Xiaoping and Marshal Liu Bocheng.[4] Liu Huaqing's army career as a political commissar for ten years helped him build a strong political loyalty to Mao Zedong and Deng Xiaoping and provided him rich administrative experience in military institutions. Liu Huaqing was familiar with what Russian fleet admiral Sergey Gorshkov said about the Red Army as the Communist Party's "instrument or tool" to reach political goals.[5] Liu became a believer of Mao's adage that "the Party controls the gun" and a strong supporter of the party-army system, which propelled him to command Beijing's Martial Law Force during the 1989 Tiananmen Square incident. From 1992 to 1998, Liu Huaqing was the top military leader in China next to Jiang Zemin.

The chapter focuses on Liu's career change from an army officer to a naval college administrator of the PLA's First Naval Academy in Dalian in 1952. His study of Soviet naval theory and technology at Voroshilov Naval Command Academy in St. Petersburg from 1954 to 1958 broadened his worldview, completed his transition from an army political commissar to a naval officer, and made him a student of Admiral Sergey Gorshkov's naval theory. Liu Huaqing became a rear admiral in 1955 as one of the first Russian-educated Chinese naval officers.

## A MOUNTAIN GUERRILLA AND A RED ARMY OFFICER

On August 1, 1927, when CCP members within the KMT 20th Army revolted against the ROC government at Nanchang, Jiangxi, the CCP began its independent military revolution. The Nanchang Uprising marked the beginning of the CCP's Second Civil War (also known as the Revolutionary War for Land, or the Agrarian Revolutionary War, from 1927 to 1937) against Chiang Kai-shek's regime. Mao Zedong believed "political power grows out of the barrel of a gun."[6] August 1 is celebrated as the birth of China's armed forces. After Chiang Kai-shek launched counterattacks against insurgent troops, the CCP-led armed rebellions in cities like Nanchang, Guangzhou, and Changsha failed. Mao recognized the party's need to mobilize peasants, then the majority Chinese population, into its newly established Red Army. However, the peasants held no interest in such a large-scale rebellion unless the party was willing to center the movement in their areas where a victory would benefit the peasants.[7] Soon the CCP shifted its strategic focus from cities to the countryside. To avoid further losses and save the Red Army from Chiang's suppression campaigns, the CCP created six Red Army military bases in southern and southeastern China from 1927 to 1930.[8] For survival's sake, all Red Army bases were located in areas where the KMT's control was weakest—along provincial borders, in remote mountains, and among the country's poorest areas. One of them was the E-Yu-Wan Base in the Dabei (Ta-pieh) Mountains, within which nestled Liu Huaqing's hometown.

Liu Huaqing was born Liu Jinfa (meaning "golden boomer") in 1916 into a peasant family of Dawu County, situated in the Dabie Mountains along the borders of Hubei, Henan, and Anhui Provinces. According to his upbringing, Jinfa should not have been part of the peasants protesting the KMT government. At age seven, his parents were able to send Jinfa, one of their six children, to a traditional private school in the village. From 1923 to 1926, he learned how to read and write by studying *Three Character Classic* (三字经), *Analects of Confucius* (论语), *Mencius* (孟子), and the *Great Learning* (大学).[9] In 1926, Liu left the old village school and enrolled in a new school with a modern curriculum, studying geography, mathematics, and literature. The teacher also taught the students about Sun Yat-sen, nationalism, and republican revolution. He thought Jinfa's name too old fashioned and referred to him as "Huaqing" (meaning "Chinese blue") starting in 1927.[10] Later in the Resistance War against Japan, Liu Huaqing added a water element to the last characters of his new name, changing the meaning to "pure" or "unsullied."

In 1928, the remnants of the Red Army's 31st Division, merely 120 men, withdrew into the Dabie Mountains and established a small military base. The Dabie Mountains are an important mountain range in central China, about 250 miles from east to west and 110 miles north-south, with their highest point at 5,830 feet. It is a major mid-country watershed separating the Huai River's system in the north and the Yangzi River in the south. The mountain range covers about twenty counties and marks the boundary between Hubei (its abbreviation in Chinese as E) and its neighboring provinces of Henan (abb. Yu) and Anhui (abb. Wan). There, the Red Army developed a weak army's guerrilla strategy against superior enemy forces.[11]

The Red Army was able to improve their weapons and training and win small-scale battles by surprise hit-and-run attacks and active defense. In 1929, the 31st Division created a Communist authority, E-Yu-Wan District Soviet government, including Dawu County.[12] The Soviet government mobilized the peasants and their families to support the Red Army. In 1930, the 31st Division grew to 1,200 men and created the 32nd Division. The E-Yu-Wan Base expanded and became the Red Army's second largest military base by the early 1930s. The Red Army also organized village youths into CCP Children's Leagues (Er Tong Tuan). At the age of fifteen, Liu Huaqing joined the Children's Leagues and started working for the county Soviet government in 1930. Since he was one of the few who knew how to read and write, Liu was tasked with oral message and instruction delivery, paper distribution, and being poster maker and holder at political rallies.[13]

In the E-Yu-Wan base region, the Red Army launched the land reform movement, including land redistribution and rent reduction, which appealed to the landless peasants living in one of the country's poorest regions. After taking over a village, CCP officers helped organize a peasant association, a village committee, self-defense team, and provided weapons and basic training for a village militia. The peasant militia protected their newly acquired land and sent new recruits to the Red Army. With local supplies and manpower, the 31st Division grew into a new army. In 1932, the E-Yu-Wan troops were reorganized into the Fourth Army with Marshal Xu Xiangqian as its commander.[14] After a few victories over KMT forces, the E-Yu-Wan Soviet reached its peak by wresting control of forty thousand square kilometers including more than two dozen counties.[15] However, later that year, Chiang Kai-shek organized a large-scale military expedition against the Fourth Army in the Dabie Mountains. The Fourth Army withdrew from the Dabie Mountains in October.

After the Red Army's main forces moved out, the E-Yu-Wan Soviet reorganized all the local guerrillas into the 25th Army, about seven thousand men, in November 1932. They vacated the Soviet capital, used the mountains to engage the KMT in guerrilla warfare, maintained base areas as much as possible, and protected wounded and sick soldiers abandoned by the Fourth Army. At this time Liu Huaqing, age sixteen, left home and joined the 25th Army.[16]

With his communication experience, Liu Huaqing became a staff member working in the army's headquarters, which provided opportunities to read documents and instructions, learn civil-military relations, and work with field communications. He witnessed the 25th Army's brutal battles and heavy losses, dropping from seven thousand men in November 1932, to five thousand men in June 1933, and to three thousand in October.[17] In November, the army command decided on a long northward march, leaving central China, and traveling two thousand miles to northwestern China. From November 1934 to September 1935, Liu Huaqing left the Dabie Mountains and served in the army's department of political tasks during the Long March from Hubei to Shaanxi.[18] In October 1935, Mao Zedong and the Central Red Army also arrived at northern Shaanxi, completing the eight-thousand-mile Long March from southern to northwestern China.

Xi Jinping identified the first "red tradition" or "red DNA" in Liu Huaqing's early military career as "sacrificing his life to the revolutionary cause." Xi stated in 2016 that Liu Huaqing "began his revolutionary career at the age of 13 and gave 82 years of his life" to the party, people, and the army. Before the Long March, Liu wrote down his oath of "throwing away everything I have, carrying on the revolution to the end."[19] Indeed, few of his fellow villagers wanted to leave their hometown for the Red Army's Long March. It was not only the Confucian tradition of "not traveling far, while your parents were around," but also the Red Army's escape seemingly having no future at all. Moreover, Xi Jinping pointed out that "after Liu was badly wounded in the Battle of Dushuzhen, he refused to stay behind with a local peasant family" as most wounded Red Army soldiers did. "He definitely wanted to stay in the Red Army, . . . saying, 'I must be with my troops, even though I would die.' Suffering through terrible pain, Liu continued the Long March in the Red Army by holding on to a horse's tail."[20] Xi Jinping considered the soul of a PLA officer is willingness to sacrifice everything for the Chinese revolution.

After the Long March, the Red Army reorganized all troops into four army corps. Each army corps had two or three group armies; and each group army had two or three armies. The 25th, 26th, and 27th Armies were reorganized into the 15th Army Group. The 15th and First Army Groups were under the command of the First Army Corps commanded by Marshal Peng Dehuai and Mao Zedong as political commissar. Liu Huaqing began working at the 15th Army Group headquarters as the propaganda office director in the department of political tasks. At the age of nineteen, Liu Huaqing rejoined the CCP in October 1935, even though he completed the membership process several years prior.[21] He met Mao Zedong for the first time when the new army corps political commissar talked to the 15th Army Group's staff in November. Mao soon set up a Chinese Soviet government in Yan'an, a small town in northern Shaanxi, as CCP capital from 1936 to 1948. In 1936, Liu Huaqing was transferred from the 15th Army Group to the 31st Army and served as the chief of the army's operational office.[22]

On July 7, 1937, the Japanese Army attacked KMT troops at the Marco Polo Bridge (Lugouqiao), southwest of Beijing, marking the beginning of the Second Sino-Japanese War or China's Resistance War against Japan. On August 13, Japanese forces seized Shanghai and threatened Nanjing, Chiang's capital. The KMT government came to an agreement with the CCP on joint resistance through a united front.[23] According to the agreement, the main force of the Red Army in northern Shaanxi, about 46,000 troops, became the Eighth Route Army (Balujun) of the KMT government in August 1937. Zhu De served as commander in chief of the Eighth Route Army, Peng Dehuai as deputy commander, and Ye Jianying as chief of staff.[24] The Eighth Route army had three divisions, the 115th, 120th, and 129th, commanded by Lin Biao, Nie Rongzhen, and Liu Bocheng, respectively. Liu Huaqing's 31st Army was reorganized into the 129th Division under the command of Liu Bocheng. His division was the smallest division, totaling 13,000 men, while the 115th Division had 15,000 troops and 120th Division 14,000 strong. The 129th Division was also poorly equipped with merely 4,136 rifles, 93 light machine guns, 29 heavy machine guns, and 6 mortars. Each rifle had fewer than ten bullets.[25] In the south, 10,300 CCP guerrilla troops reorganized into the New Fourth Army (Xinsijun) with Ye Ting as commander, including four field columns (divisions).

However, the 129th Division grew from the Eighth Route Army's smallest division to its largest division from 1937 to 1945. Liu Huaqing experienced how the weakest division swelled in rank through the Resistance War against Japan. In September 1937, at the age of twenty-one, Liu Huaqing began working at the 129th Division headquarters as chief of secretariats for Marshal Liu Bocheng. After the division moved out of Shaanxi with 9,300 troops to the front line in the Taihang Mountains, Liu Huaqing prepared the marshal's daily briefing, collected and analyzed field reports and intelligence, issued division instructions and orders, drafted telegrams and reports to the Eighth Route Army's headquarters, arranged division commanders' meetings, trips, and visits, provided their secretary details, and filed documents in divisional archives. Liu Huaqing had to understand Marshal Liu Bocheng's strategic thinking, operational intention, battlefield analysis, and problems the commander faced.[26]

Working directly under Liu Bocheng, Liu Huaqing benefited greatly during those years from learning about Chinese classics, Russian military theories, and warfighting skills at the division headquarters. Chinese generals described Liu Bocheng as one of the PLA's "war gods." He was well received as one of China's top military experts, both in theory and in practice, with few equals at home or abroad. Liu Bocheng participated in the Nanchang Uprising that created the Chinese Red Army. He considered Sunzi's *Art of War* not only a Chinese military classic, but also the universal law for conducting war.[27] He compared it with Western military classics, which he learned in the Soviet Union. In 1927, he was sent by the CCP to study Soviet military and technology in Moscow and was transferred to the prestigious Frunze Military Academy to study strategy and tactics from 1928 to 1930. He became a master of the Russian language and the first translator of Russian military theoretic works. After his return from the Soviet Union, Liu Bocheng became president and political commissar of Red Army University in 1932. He significantly shaped and developed Mao Zedong's thinking on military matters, and became one of the PLA's ten marshals in 1955.

From 1937 to 1938, Liu Huaqing learned a pragmatic and adaptative view of war from the marshal. Liu Bocheng's realistic thinking resulted from necessity and awareness of the 129th Division's geographic location as a remote, mountainous, northern provincial border, and its demographic characteristics with a small population and backward economy. His troops' weakness, including their lack of funds, ammunition, and new recruits, led him to a cautious way of war, primarily mountainous guerrilla warfare. His flexibility and commonsense approach came from his military experience and warfighting tactics. Marshal Liu Bocheng employed both guerrilla and mobile war strategies that saw the 129th Division engage in many small-scale battles across a vast conjunction of three provinces in the Taihang Mountains. His artistic battle planning focused on the weakest link of the Japanese line and used guerrilla tactics, deception, surprise attacks, and close combat to produce victories. After several battle victories, the division tripled its size, growing from 9,300 to 30,000 men in mid-1938. With more troops, Liu Bocheng was able to divide his division into three battle groups to expand the "liberated areas" into the Taiyue Mountains and southern Hebei Province.

Liu Huaqing learned the most from Liu Bocheng's strategic thinking by drafting the marshal's speeches and writing battle evaluation reports for him. Marshal Liu Bocheng said, "Our division has established an assessment system to provide a military and political report after each battle in the war."[28] To prepare the division's report, Liu Huaqing had to collect the post-battle reports from all the brigades, analyze the Japanese field communication from captured documents, and edit the 129th Division's battle planning, troops mobilization and preparation, execution, and outcomes. Liu Huaqing learned even more from the marshal's feedback on his drafted reports, including Liu Bocheng's corrections, revisions, and comments. The marshal told his secretaries that the division should learn from its experience and develop its own approaches to winning war and its different methods to conduct military operations against the Japanese army. The division doubled its troops from thirty thousand men in 1938 to sixty thousand in 1939.

Liu Huaqing also learned the importance of strategic theory and concepts. According to his "Study Notes on Liu Bocheng's Strategic and Tactic Thinking," he understood why "Liu Bocheng paid special attention to strategic theory" and where his strategic thinking came from.[29] The marshal's strategic concept of realism and flexibility became the essence of his military thought, which guided the division's operations. In 1939, Chiang Kai-shek moved the seat of his government from Nanjing to Chongqing (Chongking), Sichuan. The situation in north China worsened by 1940. The Japanese and Wang Jingwei's collaborationist forces conducted a systematic pacification of their occupied regions as part of a "caging" strategy aimed at limiting Peng Dehuai's mobile warfare and the CCP's military expansion.[30] The strategy was designed to use major rail lines to separate the Eighth Route Army's troops and stop their movements from one area to another in the northern plain. The Japanese established road connections between their strongpoints with the capability of rapid reinforcement from each other. Liu Bocheng described that "to use the rail lines as bars, roads as chains, and strongpoints as locks."[31] Marshals Zhu De and Peng Dehuai knew decisive action was necessary to stop the Japanese "cage" strategy and slow Japanese occupation of north China.

The 129th Division participated in what became known as the "Hundred Regiments Campaign," when the Eighth Route Army utilized 105 regiments, about 400,000 men, from August to December 1940 to launch the Communists' largest raids in the war. The campaign targeted Japanese-held railways, small cities, towns, and supply depots in northern and eastern China. The 129th Division engaged in the campaign with nearly 40 regiments and a total of 110,000 troops. In 1940, the division established three military district commands in its theater, including the Taihang, Taiyue, and Ji-nan (South Hebei, abb. Ji) Military Districts. In November 1941, just before Japan's surprise attack on Pearl Harbor, the CMC issued another order, "Instructions on Military Buildup in the Base Areas," urging all Communist troops to mobilize the masses and enlist more new recruits.[32] In the wake of the Allied forces' campaign against fascism and militarism across the globe, the "liberated areas" under Marshal Liu Bocheng's control launched partial counteroffensives and won important victories against Japan from 1942 to 1944.

By the summer of 1944, Liu Bocheng's forces established four large, liberated regions, including 110 counties with a population of 30 million. His force totaled 300,000 troops by the summer of 1945, known as "Liu–Deng's Big Army," and became one of the PLA's main forces. Deng Xiaoping praised Liu Bocheng, stating that, as "a great strategist" in the PLA, Liu "knew a great deal about the art of war. He drew on the best military theories, both ancient and modern, Chinese and foreign, and applied them in the Chinese revolutionary war."[33] By the fall, the CCP's regular army grew to 1,270,000 men, supported by militias numbering another 2.68 million.[34] The Eighth Route Army increased from three divisions and 46,000 men in August 1937 to more than forty divisions in August 1945. The New Fourth Army increased from four divisions in 1937 to seven divisions, totaling 268,000 men, in 1945.[35]

During the Resistance War against Japan, Liu Huaqing also became close to Deng Xiaoping after Deng became the 129th Division's political commissar in January 1938. At the age of twenty-two, Liu Huaqing met Deng Xiaoping for the first time when he carried out Liu Bocheng's order, led a security platoon, and escorted Deng Xiaoping from the Eighth Route Army's headquarters to the 129th Division Command for his new position. They spent three days together and arrived at the 129th Division safely. Commodore Shi Changxue states, "Thereafter, Liu Huaqing had never left Deng Xiaoping's sight for fourteen years." Their wartime relations "created a special trust and connection" between Deng Xiaoping and Liu Huaqing.[36]

Later that year, Deng Xiaoping appointed Liu Huaqing as the head of the propaganda office, working directly under Deng daily. Deng Xiaoping carried out political tasks in mass mobilization, party organization, civil-military relations, troop morale, propaganda, political education, psychological warfare, and discipline. When his political officers executed a soldier who raped a young woman, Deng called for a mass meeting and made a public speech to criticize any disciplinary violations and criminal behavior in his division. As a political officer, Liu Huaqing drafted political instructions and divisional documents, reviewed reports on morale, disciplines, and recommendations, discussed appointments, promotions, awards, and punishments, collected local information, and traveled with Deng to the front line during the War of Resistance against Japan. Later Deng appointed Liu Huaqing as the director of the department of political tasks of the 129th Division's Logistics Department. Gu Yue comments that "Deng Xiaoping knew more about politics than other military leaders; and knew more about military than many political leaders."[37] At the CCP Seventh National Congress in 1945, Deng was elected one of the forty-four members of the Central Committee.

## FROM POLITICAL TASKS DEPARTMENT TO ARMY COLLEGE ADMINISTRATION

After Deng Xiaoping became the Secretary of the CCP Northern Bureau in charge of the Eighth Route Army headquarters in 1943, he summoned Liu Huaqing in June 1944 and appointed him as the head of the organization office in the Department of Political Tasks of the newly established Ji-Lu (Shandong's abb.)-Yu Military Region. Then, in January 1945, Liu Huaqing was promoted to the political commissar of the Sixth Military District of the Ji-Lu-Yu Military Region Command, which commanded four regiments. In late 1945, Liu became a brigade political commissar.

During his service in the Red Army from 1932 to 1945, Liu understood party-army relations and supported the CCP's absolute leadership over the army. From 1927 to 1929, the CCP designed a party-army system during the Red Army's formative years by appointing a political instructor to each company and a political commissar to each battalion, regiment, brigade, division, army, and army group. The Red Army detailed tasks for political officers to mobilize and train peasant soldiers and its political indoctrination permitted the CCP to form an army different from previous warlord and KMT armies. Their political works included mobilization, recruitment, civil-military relations, retention, political education, literature studies, performance evaluations, recommendations for promotion and awards, discipline, and punishments. Officers considered political tasks as the lifeline for the Red Army's survival and success.

Xi Jinping emphasized the party's control of the PLA in 2021 at the CCP's one hundredth anniversary celebration. As another part of the PLA's DNA, according to Xi, the party's leadership is "the soul and the lifeline of our armed forces. Never change! Never lose it!"[38] Xi said, "We commemorate Comrade Liu Huaqing by carrying on his party spirit. As our role model, he was always listening to the party, wholeheartedly following the party, and fighting where the party pointed."[39] Xi Jinping tried to prove it through Liu Huaqing's early military career and example as a PLA tradition for its soldiers to be loyal to the party, defend the party, and fight for the party.

During the formative period, Mao Zedong also laid groundwork for the Red Army and created a new military system for the CCP. He established three major tasks for his Fourth Army: fighting battles, raising money for the revolutionary cause (later changed to production), and social work of the masses. As the political commissar of the Fourth Army, Mao formulated the "Three Main Rules of Discipline" and the "Eight Points for Attention" for the Red Army.[40] By establishing a new merit and punishment system, Mao added moral and social values to the CCP military institution. In Chinese tradition, military culture considered man as a social and political being, highlighting his duty within an agrarian society. This was in sharp contrast to the emphasis that Indian and Mediterranean civilizations place on the holy war and the man as God's soldier. At northern Shaanxi, Liu Huaqing accomplished a historical composition in the PLA history by making the Red Army's Three Main Rules of Discipline and the Eight Points for Attention into a popular army song still used today.

During the Chinese Civil War, Liu Huaqing continued to serve as political commissar in the PLA's Second Field Army under the command of Liu Bocheng and Deng Xiaoping. In November 1946, he was appointed as political commissar of the Sixth Brigade. Liu Huaqing spent a lot of time working on defected former KMT soldiers and officers, including the brigade commander, by introducing communist ideology, CCP policy, and PLA regulations. With his commander, Liu Huaqing commanded the brigade in several battles against the KMT troops in southern Hebei. The Sixth Brigade had excellent battle performance in the offensive campaigns, growing from 4,100 to 6,700 men, and received commendation from the army command in 1947. From June 1946 to March 1947, the Liu–Deng Army defeated Chiang Kai-shek's offensive campaigns in Shangdang, Handan, and Long-Hai. When Chiang's attacks slowed, Liu Bocheng and Deng Xiaoping led 120,000 troops from their base areas in the north and crossed the Yellow River in June 1947. They broke through Chiang's line and marched more than 350 miles south into the Dabie Mountains near the Yangzi River. Their strategic southward advance ended the KMT offensive against CCP-occupied regions in central China and brought the civil war into Chiang's occupied southern regions.[41] Mao Zedong commented on Liu and Deng's southward advance as "a historical turning point" in the revolutionary wars against Chiang Kai-shek in the past twenty years. The PLA eventually ended their defense and began a strategic offensive thereafter.[42] In October 1947, the PLA issued a manifesto that called on the people to "overthrow Chiang Kai-shek and liberate all China."[43] In 1948, Deng Xiaoping became the party secretary of the CCP Central China Bureau.

In November 1948, the CMC reorganized its troops into field armies and army groups as the "Chinese People's Liberation Army" (PLA). In

January 1949, the CMC established four field armies in four different regions. The PLA's First Field Army, under the command of Peng Dehuai in northwestern China, had two army groups, including six armies. The Second Field Army, under Deng Xiaoping and Liu Bocheng's command in central China, had three army groups, including nine armies. The Third Field Army, commanded by Chen Yi and Su Yu in eastern China, had four army groups, totaling fifteen armies. The Fourth Field Army, under Lin Biao and Luo Ronghuan's command in the northeast (Manchuria), had four army groups, twelve armies. In addition, the CMC directly commanded nine armies in three army groups. In the spring of 1949, the PLA had a total of sixteen army groups—fifty-eight infantry armies, numbering 4 million men.[44] The Second Field Army under Liu Bocheng and Deng Xiaoping had three army groups—nine infantry armies totaling 300,000 troops. Its Third Army Group commanded the 10th, 11th, and 12th Armies. Liu Huaqing served as the director of the Department of Political Tasks of the 11th and 10th Armies and vice political commissar of the 10th Army in the Chinese Civil War (see photo 1). The Third Army Group entered the Korean War in early 1951.[45]

From November 6, 1948, to January 10, 1949, the PLA launched its largest offensive campaign against Chiang Kai-shek's army, the Huai-Hai Campaign. The PLA high command concentrated 600,000 troops, from both the Central China Field Army (CCFA) under the command of Deng Xiaoping and Liu Bocheng and the East China Field Army (ECFA) under the command of Chen Yi and Su Yu. On November 25, Liu–Deng's CCFA deployed seven armies, about 200,000 men, to encircle the KMT 12th Army Group under the command of General Huang Wei at Shuangduiji, in southern Su County, about thirty miles southeast of Xuzhou. When KMT General Huang Wei ordered his 85th Army to break through the PLA's encirclement on the 27th, the 110th Division of the 85th Army defected to the PLA on the front. Liu Huaqing's brigade joined the blocking defense to stop Huang Wei's escape.

Meanwhile, Su Yu's ECFA joined CCFA's encirclement with five armies arriving at Shuangduiji. The KMT 12th Army Group was totally isolated without supply and depended on airdrops. The KMT Air Force was unable to provide food and ammunition for 120,000 men. Chiang Kai-shek ordered Du Yuming to lead three army groups from Xuzhou

**PHOTO 1.** Political commissar Liu Huaqing posts on September 6, 1945, after his 19th Regiment seized Xiajin County, Shandong, from the KMT army two days before. 光明日报 [*Guangming Daily*]

on November 30 to relieve the 12th. The rescue forces were stopped by Su Yu's ECFA armies on December 4. Su attacked and destroyed the KMT 16th Army Group first on December 6. The CCFA armies then turned to Huang Wei's 12th Army Group on December 12. Three days later, the PLA annihilated the 120,000 men of the 12th and captured General Huang Wei at Shungduiji. After destroying three out of six KMT army groups, the PLA launched the final attack on January 6, 1949. Three days later, the KMT Second and 13th Army Groups were annihilated. Deputy commander General Du Yuming was captured and General Qiu Qingquan, commander of the Second Army Group, was killed. The Huai-Hai Campaign ended on January 10. The PLA's offensive campaign proved catastrophic for Chiang Kai-shek and the KMT army. According to PLA statistics, the KMT army lost 555,099 men, including 171,151 killed and wounded, 320,355 captured, 35,093 defected (who fled), and 28,500 revolted (who joined the PLA).

In early 1949, Liu Huaqing was promoted to the director of the Department of Political Tasks of the 11th Army, Third Army Group, PLA Second Field Army. On April 20, the PLA's central group, including the Seventh and Ninth Army Groups with seven armies and 300,000 men, crossed the Yangzi River. The PLA troops broke through the KMT's defense and marched east toward Nanjing and Shanghai. On April 21, Liu Huaqing's 11th Army crossed the Yangzi and seized KMT-defended Anqing. On April 22, the KMT government fled Nanjing, the capital of the ROC, and removed the seat of the government to Guangzhou. In May, the 11th Army chased the KMT troops southward into Zhejiang. During the Chinese Civil War, the PLA's Second Field Army destroyed more than 2 million enemy troops, including 1.6 million defected and captured KMT officers and soldiers. The Second Field Army lost 37,000 men, including 200 officers at and above the regimental level.[46]

In late May 1949, Liu Bocheng summoned Liu Huaqing to Nanjing and appointed the latter as the Party Secretary of the Military and Political University of the PLA Second Field Army in Nanjing. Liu Huaqing hesitated to accept the new appointment in higher education since he never completed his elementary education. Liu Bocheng, however, accounted for his administrative experience in military training and education. In 1938, Liu Huaqing served as the party secretary at the Eighth Route Army's party school where Zhu De was its president. In 1944, Liu served as deputy superintendent of a cadre training school of the Ji-Lu-Yu Military District. Although these positions were temporary, they provided some experience in PLA education. The marshal also told Liu Huaqing that his longtime superior Liu Bocheng would serve as the university's president and political commissar himself.

Since Liu Bocheng, as the commander of the Second Field Army, was preoccupied by the military operations of the ongoing civil war, Liu Huaqing ran the campus administration with Xu Lixing, provost of the university. Xu served in the Eighth Route Army in the Resistance War against Japan and the Second Field Army in the civil war. He was made a major general in 1964. After the university started its classes on June 23, 1949, with more than 13,000 students, Liu Bocheng and Deng Xiaoping came to Nanjing and spoke to the faculty, students, and staff. Meanwhile, Mao Zedong appointed Liu Bocheng as mayor of Nanjing. On October 1, 1949, Mao declared the birth of the People's Republic of China (PRC) in Beijing after the PLA controlled the mainland except Tibet, Taiwan, and some offshore islands (see map 1).

In March 1950, the Second Field Army's Military University moved from Nanjing to Chongqing, Sichuan, as the PLA Southwestern Military and Political University in April with Liu Bocheng as its president and political commissar.[47] The university took on a new task to reeducate more than 900,000 former KMT officers and soldiers who defected or surrendered to the PLA, or were captured by the PLA during the last phase of the Chinese Civil War. After the Second Field Army defeated the KMT defense and seized Chongqing in November 1949, many KMT generals and local leaders in southwestern China, including Sichuan, Guizhou, Yunnan, and Xikang Provinces, defected or surrendered to the PLA. Refusal to follow Chiang Kai-shek to Taiwan expanded beyond political factors and often involved personal reasons. Many KMT officers and soldiers had families, savings, and owned property on the mainland, but nothing on Taiwan. If they decided to remain on the mainland, KMT defectors did so out of political consideration as well.

After the PLA's Second Field Army marched into the southwest in early November, many KMT generals and governors declared their defections to the CCP. On December 9, KMT governor and general Lu Han

MAP 1. The People's Republic of China

announced the defection of his troops and province of Yunnan from the KMT. On the same day, Liu Wenhui, Governor of Xikang and commander of the KMT 24th Army, also declared defection. Then, generals Deng Xihou and Pan Wenhua publicly announced their defections. Deng Xihuo commanded the 95th Army and Pan the 235th Division. The KMT 19th and 22nd Army Groups also defected and undermined the KMT's defense of southwestern China. The 19th Army Group commanded the 49th and 89th Armies with General He Shaozhou as its commander. After He fled Hong Kong with his family, his 49th Army defected first, followed by the 89th. When the PLA seized Chengdu by December 30, the Second Field Army received more than 910,000 KMT troops, including 95,640 defected, 401,000 surrendered, and 196,100 captured, plus 230,000 local KMT troops surrendered.

On January 17, 1950, Deng Xiaoping chaired a commander conference at Chongqing where it was decided to turn as many former KMT officers and soldiers as possible into the PLA through reeducation. In February, the KMT 7th, 15th, 16th, and 20th Army Groups, totaling 113,764 troops, joined the PLA's northwestern and eastern forces, and continued their reeducation and reorganization. Meanwhile, 124,533 KMT officers and soldiers were incorporated into the PLA's southwestern forces. More than 11,000 KMT officers and soldiers from the 7th Army Group were transferred to the PLA's 19th Army Group.

To carry on the new mission, the Second Field Army's Military and Political University at Chongqing designed a special curriculum for ex-KMT officers and soldiers to realign with the PLA. To serve the large number of KMT troops, the university opened eight branch campuses over southwestern China to realign the former KMT personnel with the PLA's political doctrines, military tradition, and troop regulations. Liu Huaqing established the CCP system in the former KMT armies and appointed political commissars and instructors to the divisions, regiments, battalion, and companies. The political commissars and political instructors organized the ex-KMT officers and soldiers to study communism, CCP theories, and PLA history. They also recruited some politically active ex-KMTs to join the Chinese Communist Youth League (CCYL) and CCP. The newly established PRC government also offered executive positions for the KMT generals. For example, Liu Wenhui and Deng Xihou served as lieutenant governors.

In June 1950, the Korean War broke out and Beijing intervened in the fall. By October, the first echelon of the Chinese People's Volunteer Force (CPVF) entered the Korean War, consisting of 260,000 troops from the 13th Army Group of the Fourth Field Army. In November, the Third Field Army sent its Ninth Army Group with 150,000 troops to join the first wave.[48] By January 1951, the first wave included two PLA army groups and totaled 450,000 troops in Korea. The strongest forces in the second wave were the Third Army Group for the Second Field Army, which had three armies, totaling 120,000 men, and entered the war in March. Meanwhile, the 19th Army Group also crossed the Yalu River. With the arrival of two more army groups in the second wave, the CPVF doubled in strength to 950,000 men in mid-April.[49] By the fall of 1951, total Chinese forces in Korea had increased to 1.15 million men (see map 2).

Starting in 1952 during the stalemate stage of the war, the PLA implemented troop rotations into Korea to gain modern warfighting experience. Not only could PLA troops gain experience fighting American forces, but

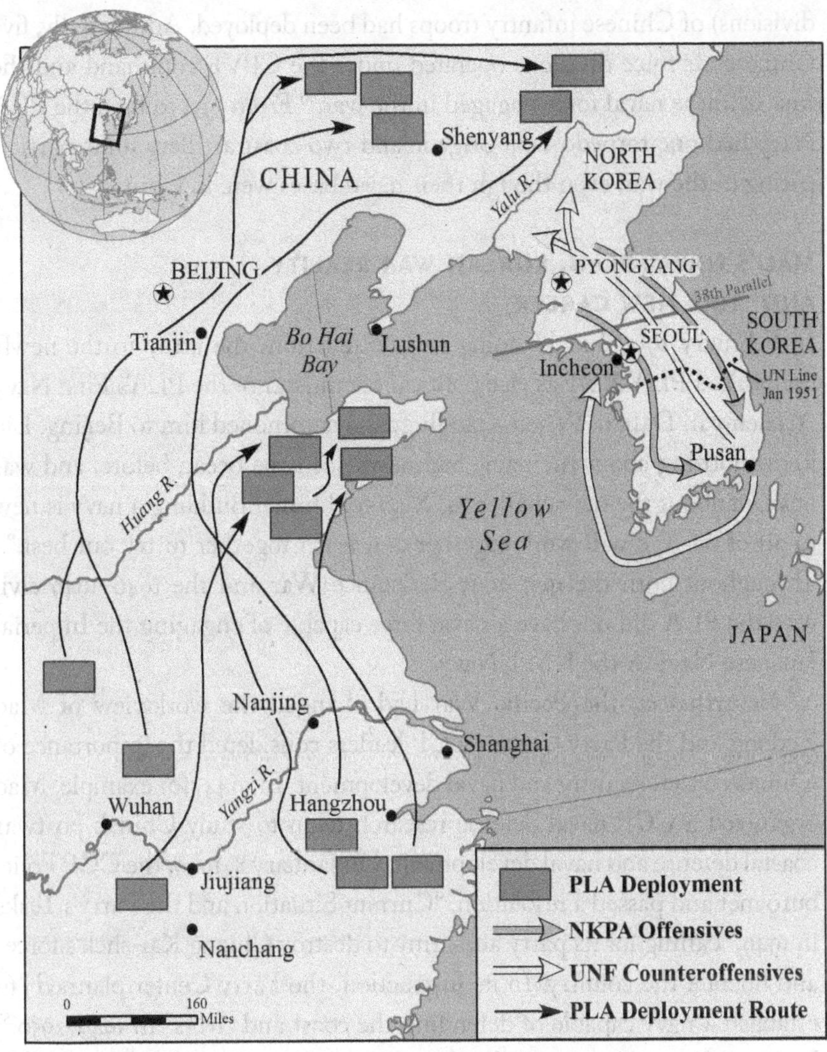


**MAP 2.** The Korean War and PLA Deployment, June–October 1950

exhausted CPVF troops already in Korea could be relieved for needed recuperation through rotation. The Chinese army had previously fought in wars against the Japanese army and Chinese Nationalist Army, but it knew little about the American, British, Canadian, and other technologically equipped Western forces. Korea became a combat laboratory that offered Chinese officers and soldiers essential combat training. By the end of the war, about 73 percent (25 out of 34 armies, or 79 of 109 infantry divisions) of Chinese infantry troops had been deployed. Additionally, five Chinese air force divisions operated under the CPVF command and the first Chinese naval force engaged in the war.[50] From 1951 to 1953, the PLA Navy had one torpedo-boat brigade and two coast artillery units participating in the war, even though their naval bases were in China.

## MAO'S NAVAL PLAN, KOREAN WAR REALITY, AND LIU'S NEW CAREER

In February 1952, Liu Huaqing transferred from the army to the newly established PLA Navy as vice political commissar of the PLA's First Navy Academy in Dalian. When Xiao Jinguang summoned him to Beijing, Liu knew nothing about the navy, had never seen the ocean before, and was hesitant about the new challenge. Xiao told him, "Building a navy is new to all of us. We will work together and learn together to try our best."[51] Throughout both the 1937–1945 Resistance War and the 1946–1949 civil war, the PLA did not have a naval force capable of engaging the Imperial Japanese Navy or the KMT Navy.

Nevertheless, the Pacific War had changed the worldview of Mao Zedong and the Party Center. CCP leaders considered the importance of China's coastal security and naval development. In 1944, for example, Mao organized a CCP naval defense research team to study China's postwar coastal defense and naval development. On January 8, 1949, the CCP Politburo met and passed a resolution, "Current Situation and the Party's Tasks in 1949," calling for its party and army to destroy Chiang Kai-shek's forces and liberate the country. In its instruction, the Party Center planned "to establish a navy capable of defending the coast and rivers" in 1949–1950.[52] Its immediate intention to develop a naval force derived primarily from the CCP's plan to eliminate all enemy forces on the mainland and offshore islands. From February to December, there were 14 KMT naval defections, including 98 warships and gunboats and 3,800 KMT naval officers and sailors. On April 20, the PLA's Third Field Army exchanged artillery fire with four British warships on the Yangzi River, also known as the Yangtze Incident. HMS *Amethyst* was damaged and grounded. As a result, Mao drafted a statement for the PLA high command on April 30, demanding all foreign governments "quickly withdraw their armed forces—their warships, military aircraft and marines . . . from China's territorial inland waters, seas, land and air."[53]

On April 23, 1949, the PLA's Third Field Army established the East China Military Region's Navy (ECMRN) to receive defecting KMT seamen and vessels. April 23 is celebrated as the PLA Navy's birthday. Marshal Chen Yi (Ch'en Yi), Third Field Army commander, appointed General Zhang Aiping, deputy commander of the Central China Military Region, as the ECMRN commander and political commissar.[54] When the report reached the CMC, Mao Zedong and Zhu De cheered and said, "We now have our own warships and our own navy!"[55] On January 12, 1950, Mao appointed the PLA's 12th Army Group commander General Xiao Jinguang as the inaugural commander of the new "Chinese People's Navy."

From his initiation, Commander Xiao Jinguang faced three major problems in building a new navy. First, he had a deplorable personnel situation since the PLA had no officers or soldiers with previous naval background or experience. From 1949 to 1951, the army had to transfer more than 30,000 officers and soldiers to establish the navy. Building an army-based navy, Xiao Jinguang shaped PLA naval doctrine by adopting army doctrine and tradition and modifying in a naval environment. On April 14, 1950, Xiao's army group command commenced operating as the PLA naval headquarters in Beijing.[56] The PLAN was established through "an arduous birth from the flame of war," as PLA Naval Command College's Gao Xiaoxing describes.[57] Second, Xiao Jinguang had only 200 medium and small warships and support vessels, left by the KMT Navy, totaling 43,000 tons. It was a random collection of ex-American and ex-Japanese ships; all were World War II vintage or older. After the defected cruiser *Chongking* sank, the major units remaining were nine ex-Japanese frigates, fifty landing craft, and a few minesweepers. The newly established PLAN seemed no match for the ROC Navy that boasted 428 warships and naval vessels in the Taiwan Strait.[58] Third, what Xiao Jinguang worried most was that all PLAN ships were controlled by ex-KMT officers and sailors, who were former enemies in the civil war. No Communist officers or sailors could move a ship. Xiao desperately needed to transform the defected KMT seamen into a PLA navy.

The PLA then established a naval school to provide political reeducation, with communist ideology and PLA tradition, for the defected KMT naval officers and sailors. In May 1949, the PLAN opened the Andong (or Dandong) Naval School in Liaoning. More than 550 former KMT naval officers and sailors who defected from the KMT Navy cruiser *Chongking* were the first class to arrive. Seventy-four more ex–KMT Navy officers and sailors from KMT warship *Lingfu* joined them in the summer. The Andong Naval School's first superintendent was *Chongking*'s Captain Deng Zhaoxiang, an honored graduate of British Greenwich Royal Naval College. After the *Chongking*'s defecting, Captain Deng was appointed superintendent of the PLAN's Andong Naval Academy in March 1949 and Torpedo Training School at Qingdao in August 1950. He was ranked PLAN rear admiral in 1955 and joined the CCP in 1965. Vice superintendent of the Andong Naval School and later Rear Admiral Zhang Xuesi was the brother of KMT marshal Zhang Xueliang (Chang Hsueh-liang). The PLA high command soon ordered Zhang Xuesi to plan a new naval academy to train PLA naval officers. Mao needed his own red navy.

After founding the PRC in October 1949, Mao Zedong still confronted more than 1 million KMT soldiers on Taiwan and in southwestern China.[59] At Taipei, the ROC's new capital, Chiang Kai-shek deployed 200,000 troops to defend Taiwan and other offshore islands, including 100,000 men on Hainan Island, 120,000 on Zhoushan Island, and 60,000 on Jinmen Island.[60] Chiang's navy had 428 warships and naval vessels, totaling 100,000 tons. Chiang Kai-shek used Taiwan as a base and relied on the coastal islands for counterattacks, air bombings, and naval blockades against the PLA-occupied mainland. Bruce Elleman argues, "Chiang shifted from a land-based offensive to a naval one, supporting a blockade strategy against the PRC."[61] After the disastrous failure of the PLA's landing at Jinmen in October and loss of nearly 10,000 men, Mao realized that the PLA faced an entirely new task of amphibious landing campaigns. In mid-December, Mao developed an amphibious landing strategy for the PLA to include naval and air support.[62] To successfully execute any significant amphibious operations, the PLA required combined air and naval operations.

The CCP Party Center recognized the discrepancies between the ROC and PRC navies and realized that a successful landing campaign against Taiwan necessitated a strong naval force. Chinese leaders considered Soviet naval assistance as a quick solution to their problem.[63] The CCP Party Center sent a delegation led by CCP vice chairman Liu Shaoqi to visit Moscow for Russian naval assistance and military aid in June–July 1949. Soviet leader Joseph Stalin proposed to Chinese leaders, that "China should have its own navy, and we are ready to help you build naval fleets." Stalin's detailed suggestions included coastal defense, naval cooperation in the offshore areas, shipbuilding and repair, and warship weapons and ammunition.[64] To follow up Stalin's proposal for a new Chinese naval force, the PLA high command sent a naval delegation to the Soviet Union in August–September 1949. The Chinese delegation visited several Russian naval academies and negotiated three Soviet assistance agreements for Chinese naval academies.[65] On September 13, ECMRN commander Zhang Aiping led another naval delegation to Moscow. They spent forty-three days in the Soviet Union and negotiated more agreements on Russian naval aid, advisory, and naval educational assistance.

During Mao's first visit to Moscow, from December 1949 to February 1950, he requested Russian aid in building a Chinese navy. Stalin agreed and further advised that "you send sailors, and we provide ships. After completing their training, these Chinese naval officers can sail these warships back to China."[66] After extensive negotiation, Beijing and Moscow established a military alliance by signing the "Sino-Soviet Friendship and Mutual Assistance Treaty" on February 14. Mao used the loan from the treaty to purchase ships, aircraft, and equipment for the new Chinese naval force. Two days later, Stalin signed the $150 million naval purchase agreement, about half of the total loan. Upon Mao's request, Stalin also agreed to send a couple hundred Soviet naval officers to serve in the Soviet Naval Advisory Group for the Chinese navy.[67] Mao was satisfied with the outcome of his visit and told Soviet ambassador Pavel Yudin after his return to Beijing that "you can help us build a navy. You can be our advisors. . . . You can train Chinese [officers] to fight against imperialism while you work as advisors."[68] By the summer of 1950, the Chinese navy had received 7 gunboats, 19 airplanes, and 431 artillery guns from the Russians.[69]

On August 10, 1950, Mao Zedong and Zhou Enlai, CMC vice chairman and China's premier, chaired a PLA high command meeting about the new naval and air force developments. To carry out the CMC decisions, Commander Xiao Jinguang held the first PLAN high command conference in Beijing from August 11 to 30. Chinese naval leaders discussed naval development strategy and made a three-year plan (1950–1953) for the Chinese navy. With limited time and resources, naval leaders viewed large warships as unrealistic and unnecessary. Instead, they endeavored to build a small, agile navy with practical and effective applications like airplanes, submarines, and torpedo boats for immediate and capable operations.[70]

The Chinese leaders placed total trust in the Soviet Union's technology, advisement, and experience in building their new navy. After approving the PLAN's "Three-Year Plan," Mao Zedong cabled Stalin on October 8, 1950, asking for more Soviet naval aid and advisors. His lengthy shopping list focused on China's three priorities, including 7 destroyers and frigates, 36 torpedo bombers, 124 pursuit airplanes, 10 coast transit airplanes, 500 vehicles, 194 heavy coastal guns, and 6,550 naval mines and depth charges. The Chinese also requested an additional 408 naval advisors.[71] Mao cabled Stalin again on October 28 and informed him that Beijing would send a naval delegation to Moscow to finalize the arms purchase. The Chinese delegation included Xiao Jinguang, Luo Shunchu, and Soviet chief advisors in the PLAN. Xiao Jinguang's six years of higher education and military training in the Soviet Union established his close contacts and affiliation with Russian admirals, made him successful in Sino-Soviet naval negotiations and agreement for Soviet aid.[72] The Chinese delegation made a formal proposal to the Soviet government on December 18 that included the purchase of naval aircraft and submarines, advisory assistance, and naval education.[73]

Nevertheless, throughout the Korean War, the Chinese army and air force were prioritized over the navy as they desperately needed more financial resources and Russian aid. Mao Zedong visited the PLAN headquarters on December 12, 1952, to convince his admirals to reduce, if not cancel, their naval purchases from the Soviet Union. Mao told Xiao Jinguang, Liu Daosheng, and Wang Hongkun that "currently [the War of] Resisting the U.S. and Aiding Korea demanded airplanes. We have to concentrate our foreign currency on helping the Air Force. . . . Our foreign currency is not enough [for both air and naval forces]. How are about purchasing airplanes first for the Air Force? Is it OK to postpone your planned purchase of warships to a later time?" Naval leaders agreed to accept Mao's request to reduce their budget and cancel their orders from the Soviet Union.[74] Many senior naval officers attributed the PLAN's slow start, a decade-long budget restraint, and poor performance in the 1950s to the PLA's intervention in the Korean War.

Perhaps most detrimental to the PLAN's inception was that all PLA naval officers, including Generals Xiao Jinguang and Zhang Aiping, came from an infantry background without any basic naval knowledge or training. Xiao Jinguang became a CCP member in 1922 during his study of military science in the Soviet Union from 1921 to 1924. Fluent in Russian, he was sent to Russia by the Party Center in 1927 and received a degree from the Leningrad Military and Political Academy in 1930.[75] After returning, Xiao became a chief of staff, political commissar, and army commander in the Red Army. He then served as political commissar and superintendent of the CCP Central School for Military and Politics until 1937. During China's Resistance War against Japan, Xiao was the Eighth Route Army's garrison force commander. After the civil war broke out in 1946, Xiao Jinguang served as deputy commander and chief of staff for the Shandong Regional Command. In 1948, the PLA Fourth Field Army appointed him commander of its 12th Army Group. Thereafter, Xiao served as the PLAN Commander for twenty-six years from 1949 to 1966 and again from 1971 to 1980. He became vice defense minister in 1954 and a fleet admiral in 1955. (The PLA did not have ranks until 1955.)[76] In 1950, Xiao Jinguang strongly suggested "opening naval schools before building a navy."[77]

The newly established PLA Navy lacked experience in offshore operations and sea warfare and had no knowledge about naval technology and training. In 1949–1950, there were no PLA commanders or soldiers capable of moving a ship. As such, former enemy seamen, mostly KMT sailors, operated PLA ships and gunboats in the rivers and at sea. After his delegation returned from Moscow in October 1949, Vice Admiral Zhang Xuesi proposed opening a PLA naval academy at Dalian, Liaoning. Again, the former KMT naval officers administrated the naval academy and developed its training curriculum.

After the founding of the PRC, the Soviet Union supported China's building a new navy. The Chinese naval force received more Russian advisory assistance and technology than other services. According to the Sino-Soviet agreement, on October 25, 1949, the first group of eighty-four Soviet naval advisors arrived in Dalian to establish the Chinese naval academy. On November 22, the PLA's first naval academy was established in Dalian with Xiao Jinguang as its president and political commissar and Zhang Xuesi as vice president and vice political commissar. Dalian was and still is a coastal resort city. The PLAN could not find a site large and suitable for its new naval campus in Dalian. On November 24, Rear Admiral Kuzmin and his high-ranking Russian naval advisory group arrived in Beijing. After negotiations, Kuzmin removed a Russian coastal artillery regiment from the city and made the oceanfront land available for the new naval academy. Later, Stalin appointed RAD Kuzmin as the Soviet Navy's chief advisor to the PLAN.[78] On February 1, 1950, naval classes began. The Dalian Naval Academy trained and transformed the PLA infantry officers into sailors by preparing them for naval warfare, marine navigation, and surface warship technology.[79]

When Xiao Jinguang summoned Liu Huaqing in Beijing, the naval commander told Liu, "We must develop good naval schools before we can build a strong navy."[80] The PLA Navy desperately needed its own naval higher education leadership and administrators, who commanded the Red Army and participated in the CCP's wars. Liu Huaqing shared Xiao's belief in military education since he had worked at the army universities for three years. However, after arriving at Dalian in May 1952, he faced many new issues at the naval academy.

Both Russian advisors and former KMT naval officers served as the instructors and administrators at the Dalian Naval Academy. Liu Huaqing had never worked with Russians before. The Russian navy strongly influenced the Chinese navy's development through advisory assistance in the early 1950s. At the Dalian Naval Academy, the Soviet naval advisors, totaling ninety-two in 1951, decided on the campus layout, designed shipyards, planned training programs, implemented entire curricula and instructions for seafaring technicians and helmsmen, and provided hundreds of naval texts and tens of thousands of Russian books.[81] General Vasilievich Zahalov, deputy chief of the Soviet General Staff and head of the Soviet Military Advisory Group (SMAG) in China, assigned 711 Soviet advisors to the PLAN HQs and naval bases in 1950–1951.[82] The Russian military advisors were under the Soviet Red Army high command. Major General Kecherjin wrote in his report to the Soviet General Staff on June 16, 1951, that "the Chinese comrades are very friendly to our military advisors. They always listen carefully to all of our advice, suggestions, and considerations."[83] After General Zahalov left China, General Mikhail Kalasovski became SMAG chief in 1951–1953.[84] In December 1950, the second group of 621 Soviet naval advisors arrived. The PLAN faced a serious shortage of Russian translators. In January 1951, the Soviet Navy sent twenty-four Russian translators to the PLAN for one year. Soon the Russians extended the translators' contracts for one more year until 1953.

As a vice political commissar, Liu Huaqing worked closely with the Russian advisors. However, disagreements between Russian advisors and Chinese naval officers fomented at all levels. In his report to Moscow, Major General Kecherjin complained on June 16, 1951, "Whenever they felt like [we forced something on them], they would immediately say that 'our opinion is different from your opinion on these issues.'" He also complained about the Russian advisors: "Our advisors did not express their supposed determination and persistence when they helped Chinese comrades to overcome the wrong ideas and practices on their troop deployments and operation tactics. Whenever the Chinese declined their advice (by saying please wait for the next time or no hurry), [our advisors] often stepped back and gave up."[85]

Liu Huaqing dealt with the disagreements by identifying the major issues between Chinese faculty and Russian advisors. He realized that the Russian advisors were very friendly and tried their best to help the Chinese any way they could. But disagreements and arguments persisted as the Russian advisors wanted to enforce Russian standards, regulations, and systems on the Chinese, and were not interested in developing a new Chinese naval institution. Their recommendations were inflexible and sometimes unrealistic for the PLAN.[86] Some Chinese officers opposed Russian attempts to copy their naval system at Dalian. Although the Russian advisors intended to make the PLAN as good as the Soviet Navy, they often ignored the geographic settings, demographical characters, cultural tradition, and military experience unique to the Chinese. Russian advisors did not conduct research on Chinese coasts, offshore islands, and near sea areas. Many had only brought their handbooks and training manuals to

China. Some of their ideas, plans, and decisions did not apply to China's situation. Then, Liu Huaqing instructed the Chinese faculty that, first, they must patiently learn from the Soviet Navy. Second, they should learn selectively according to China's conditions and PLAN needs. The Dalian Naval Academy successfully trained the first generation of Chinese naval officers by the early 1950s. By 1953, the academy opened two branch campuses for rapidly increased enrollment at Dalian.

Liu Huaqing also worked closely with Vice President Zhang Xuesi and former KMT naval officers who served on the faculty and administration at the naval academy. Zhang Xuesi participated in the establishment of the first naval academy in Dalian by following the Andong Naval School's model. After the Dalian Naval Academy opened, the majority of former KMT naval personnel transferred from Andong, a city at the Chinese-Korean border, to Dalian due to the Korean War. Liu Huaqing used his successful experience in reeducation, transformation, and unity from the PLA's Southwestern Military and Political University in Chongqing and provided political studies and training for the former KMT seamen on communist ideology and PLA tradition. Liu's Department of Political Tasks at Dalian carried out a series of reeducation programs with an emphasis on "consultation, inclusion, education, and thought reform."[87] The political instructors in the administration, departments, and labs organized the ex-naval officers to study communism, CCP theories, and PLA tradition. They also recruited politically active ex-seamen to join the CCYL (Chinese Communist Youth League) and CCP. The PLAN command points out that most ex-KMT naval officers and seamen at naval academies and schools successfully realigned with the PLAN and "made their important contribution" to the construction of the new Chinese navy.[88]

Liu Huaqing learned about Mahan and his sea power theory from ex-KMT administrators and instructors like Zhang Xuesi. They collected Mahan's books for the naval library and introduced his theory to the PLAN students. Liu learned still more about Mahan and his career from KMT naval experts returning from Great Britain and America. Liu supported Professor Zhou Yiqing, who returned from America, and his lectures on USN development, including Mahan's naval strategy and tactics.[89] Xiao Jinguang, satisfied with Liu's administration at Dalian, said,

"Liu Huaqing has great skills in political tasks."[90] However, by the mid-1950s, the PLAN gradually retired former KMT officers from administrative posts as more PLA officers completed their naval education and training programs. During the Chinese Cultural Revolution (1966–1967), many former KMT naval seamen were purged from the Chinese navy.

Although he was a vice political commissar, Liu Huaqing emphasized naval education as the academy's primary task by concentrating resources and administrative efforts on teaching, training, curriculum development, and naval internships. He instructed the political department to support and serve the technical departments, testing labs, and logistical staff. In March 1953, after Zhang Xuesi was promoted to the deputy chief of staff of the PLAN, Liu Huaqing became the vice president of the Dalian Naval Academy in charge of daily administration, including political tasks, academic affairs, administrative managements, and campus construction. He developed two educational tracks in a four-year degree program for two different needs. A comprehensive academic program made up the first track to include general education, science, theory, methodology, and liberal arts, for future naval research, professional, and academia needs. The second track focused on a special field in naval operations, shipbuilding, and maintenance for future warship officers, shipyard managers, and coastal service leadership. Many transferred army officers, with only an elementary education background, enrolled in the second track program and successfully completed their academic requirements.[91]

In the summer of 1953, Liu Huaqing's first naval exercise was also his first trip to the ocean (the Yellow Sea). During his administration, Liu organized sailing exercises twelve weeks every year. First-year sailing exercises included daily routines of sailors, technicians, gunners, and logistical staff. The second-year students served as interns to sergeants, second mates, second stewards, and other officers. During their third-year exercise, students gained experience as boatswains, first mates, chief stewards, sergeant majors, and as other ship officers. In 1953, Liu Huaqing and other officers sailed with their students for ten weeks aboard the tank landing ship *Siming Shan*. Bad weather, rough seas, and constant technical problems from the retired landing vessel made the excursion difficult, forcing them to cut it short and return to Qingdao naval base for safety. Liu Huaqing remembered the poor conditions from his first time sailing. After he became PLAN commander, he ordered the 5,000-ton *Zhenghe* far sea exercise warship and a 10,000-ton *Shichang* multipurpose training ship to be built in the 1980s.[92]

In 1953, Marshals Zhu De and Liu Bocheng visited the Dalian Naval Academy aboard landing ships, and they were impressed by Liu's leadership and the academy's achievements. By 1954, the Dalian Naval Academy had constructed 120,000 square meters of campus buildings, including forty-eight naval labs and twenty-one displacement rooms. The naval academy became the "cradle of Chinese naval officers" and graduated nearly one thousand naval officers by 1954.[93] During the celebration of its forty-fifth birthday, the naval academy established a monument with Fleet Admiral Liu Huaqing's handwritten inscription, "The Cradle of Naval Officers." By 1994, the Dalian Naval Academy had produced more than 10,000 naval officers, including 180 PLAN admirals. In April 1954, the two branch campuses reorganized into the Naval Command College and Naval Engineering College. At the same time, Liu Huaqing was summoned to Beijing to prepare his study of naval warfare in the Soviet Union from 1954 to 1958.

## RUSSIAN HIGHER EDUCATION WITH A CHINESE VISION

During the 1950s, the CCP carried out a Soviet-style social and economic reform. Soviet financial, technological, and educational support aided China's reconstruction and economic growth, marking the "closest collaboration" between China and the Soviet Union.[94] In 1953, Mao called for a national movement to learn from the Soviet Union. The chairman remarked that "we are facing tremendous difficulties because we are building a great country. We do not have enough experience. Thus, we must carefully learn from the Soviet success."[95] Mao asked the PLA to do the same. The chairman said that the Chinese military "must learn all of the Soviet experience and really master all of their advanced technology in order to change our army's backward condition. We must re-construct our army as the second finest modern army in the world."[96]

Throughout the 1950s, the PLA sent a large group of young and promising officers to the Soviet Union to study military science and technology, operational tactics, and logistics. Many of them later became the second (1970s–1990s) and third (1990s–2010s) generations of Chinese military leaders. For example, China's defense minister from 2003 to 2008, General Cao Gangchun was one of the students "studying in the Soviet Union" (*liusu*). Born in 1937 in Wugang, Henan, Cao joined the PLA and CCP in 1956. He enrolled in the PLA's Dalian Russian Language Special School. In September 1957, he attended the Leningrad Advanced Artillery Military Engineering School for further studies. After six years in Russia, Cao graduated from the Soviet Army Artillery Academy and returned to China in 1963. Speaking fluent Russian, he became an instructor at the First Artillery Ordnance Technical School. Cao Gangchuan was promoted to staff officer of the Comprehensive Planning Section, Equipment Department of the Department of General Staff (DGS) in April 1975.[97] Cao's study in the Soviet Union built a solid groundwork of military technology and personal connections that helped his military career. In September 1988, when the PLA restored the military ranking system, he was given the rank of major general. In 1993, Can was promoted to lieutenant general, and in 1998 to general.

By 1959, more than six hundred Chinese naval officers had studied military technology, aviation, and maritime science in Soviet naval colleges and institutes, including high-ranking officers like Liu Daosheng, PLAN vice political commissar and Political Tasks Department's director; Fang Qiang, commander and political commissar of the SCMRN from 1950 to 1953; and Zhang Xuesi, vice superintendent and vice political commissar of the Dalian Naval Academy from 1950 to 1955. Fang Qiang, Zhang Xuesi, and Liu Huaqing were classmates and all three studied at the Voroshilov Naval Command Academy (currently Kuznetsov Naval Academy) in St. Petersburg. During his study in Russia, Fang Qiang was ranked a vice admiral in 1955. After his graduation, Fang served as PLAN deputy political commissar from 1959 to 1965 and vice commander from 1979 to 1982.[98] Zhang Xuesi was ranked a rear admiral in 1955 and became PLAN chief of staff from 1960 to 1966.[99]

The Soviet Naval Command Academy established an international training division after 1945 to offer a four-year program for foreign naval officers. At the Soviet Naval Academy, Liu Huaqing learned more about Alfred Mahan's sea power theory and naval strategy. Although the Cold War world had entered the "post-Mahan era," Mahanian maritime policy and naval power strategy had a historical impact in Russian military curriculum and its naval classroom. In the 1950s, a major technological change took place in the Soviet Navy, which applied nuclear power to submarine propulsion and developed the cruise missile.

Meanwhile, Admiral Sergey Gorshkov, known as the Russian Mahan, believed that the Soviet Navy should be a global sea power to guarantee the Soviet Union's great power status during the Cold War. As the Soviet naval theorist, Gorshkov agreed with Mahan's perception of a strong navy as core for a nation to control seas and then the world. That naval force had to be large enough to defeat an enemy in the far sea. There were similarities and overlapping between Mahan's sea power theory and Gorshkov's large fleet justification. With new technology and nuclear power available, Gorshkov emphasized submarine propulsion and development of the cruise missiles. Soviet naval theory, doctrine, and tactics strongly influenced Chinese naval development through its technological aid and advisory assistance during PLAN formative years. Liu Huaqing appreciated new naval technology and admired the battleships and big guns of the Soviet Navy. He became an articulate advocate of China's sea power during his study in Russia.[100]

Moreover, Gorshkov emphasized Communist ideology and the party's political control as necessary for a strong Russian navy. He argued that the party-navy would make the Soviet Union as a great world power. Gorshkov followed Vladimir Lenin's party-state-building theory on the principle of the military serving the political agenda of the Communist Party.[101] It resonated well with Liu Huaqing's military experience as the CCP won the civil wars and took over China. Liu Huaqing understood Gorshkov's work since he was quite familiar with the PLA's role as a party-army in which he served as a political commissar for more than twelve years. Thereby, Liu was more influenced by, or had more in common with, Sergey Gorshkov's theory than Alfred Mahan's theory. His learning from Gorshkov's perspective and strategic thinkings in the 1950s prepared him to be the architect of today's Chinese navy—the world's second largest navy only after the U.S. Navy. This is important to understand Liu Huaqing's political ambition and naval career for the next forty years.

When Liu Huaqing and his group of ten Chinese officers arrived in August 1954, they met many Communist naval officers from Romania, Bulgaria, East Germany, Poland, and North Korea. Liu served as the class leader of the Chinese officers during the four years. Their first semester in the fall of 1954 provided preparatory classes like Russian, Bolshevik history, international war history, and history of the Soviet Red Army. The first-year curriculum in 1955 required classes on naval operation and weapon systems, including warship maneuvers and grouping, surface battle tactics, torpedo attack, mine laying and sweeping, submarine combat, naval aviation, and coastal support. The second year (1956) offered naval command classes covering joint operations, landing campaigns, sea communication, naval intelligence, history of Soviet naval warfare, and historiography of the Soviet Navy. The third-year classes in 1957 included naval staff work at the general headquarters like naval strategy, maritime laws, international conventions, maritime geography, global naval warfare, and World War II at sea.

Liu Huaqing's formal naval education in the Soviet Navy not only completed his transition from an army political commissar to a naval officer but also prepared him to change the Chinese navy forever. Liu Huaqing systematically learned about Russian naval theory, Soviet naval warfare, and international naval conflicts, and developed a broader worldview and a belief in sea power. He accepted a Russian perception of a "great country with a strong navy," established and shared by many Soviet naval leaders including Admiral Sergey Gorshkov. Gorshkov was six years older than Liu Huaqing. When Liu studied at the Voroshilov Naval Command Academy, Sergey Gorshkov was already serving as the Soviet Navy's commander. Liu Huaqing told his biographer many years later that he "had full respect of professional naval officer for the Russian naval marshal." Liu believed that Gorshkov was "fully worth of the name of the father of Soviet modern blue-water navy."[102]

As Soviet instructors explained Gorshkov's concept of the military to the Chinese officers in the classroom, Liu Huaqing was familiar with the Red Army's role as the Communist Party's instrument to reach the political goals since he served as a political commissar in both the PLA army and navy for twelve years. The Chinese understanding of maritime theory and naval building was derived from the similar intellectual and institutional roots as Communist ideology and Eurasian geopolitics. Liu Huaqing had more in common with Gorshkov's thinking and began his navy dream during his study in Russia.[103] In fact, the Russian naval marshal negotiated the Sino-Soviet agreement with his Chinese counterpart Xiao Jinguang in 1957, promising new naval technology and equipment for a modern Chinese navy.[104]

Liu's naval education in Russia convinced him that China should build a strong, large navy and prepared him to challenge the PLAN's naval strategy of a "light, small navy for coastal defense and landing assistance" in the 1970s. After the establishment of the Chinese navy in 1949, the PLA high command and the PLAN developed a plan in 1950 for China's coastal defense to focus on light and small vessels because of limited resources, the army's needs for landing campaigns, and the breakout of the Korean War. The naval commanders all agreed that the navy's immediate tasks were assisting the army's landing campaigns to eliminate KMT remnants, fighting against KMT naval blockades and harassment, and defending the coast to guarantee China's security. To reach these objectives with limited time and resources, the naval leaders believed it unrealistic and unnecessary to have large warships. Instead, they endeavored to build a light, small navy with practical and effective means like airplanes, submarines, and torpedo boats for immediate and capable operations. This light navy would develop its "air, sub, and speed" (空 *kong*, 潜 *qian*, 快 *kui*) capacities for coastal defense, landing assistance, and surprise and ambush attacks. The three priorities included the establishment of naval aviation, submarine force, and torpedo fleets from 1950 to 1953.[105] Xiao Jinguang's "Three-Year Plan" seemingly lacked a long-term vision for a modern Chinese navy. Nevertheless, Liu Huaqing pointed out that the conference prioritized naval education and training for China's naval development.[106]

During the Korean War, Mao Zedong realized China's military limits. He modified its civil war strategy in 1954. Moreover, the CCP adopted a moderate foreign policy to relax international tensions in East Asia after Stalin's death in 1953. Mao cooperated with the new post-Stalin Soviet leaders who strived for détente with the United States. Following recent settlements that ended two conflicts close to Chinese borders, namely, the Korean armistice in 1953 and the Indochina settlement in 1954, Chinese leaders did not want any major international crisis, or a war with the United States, especially in the Taiwan Strait. After Mao's foreign policy shift, the PLA high command postponed its naval development again. To avoid any confusion and high expectation from naval officers, Mao told the navy at an enlarged CCP Politburo meeting on December 4, 1953, "We should make a plan to gradually develop a strong navy step by step in a relatively long period time according to [our] industrial growth and financial availability."[107]

Thereby, the PLAN's short-term plan, or the "Three-Year Plan," focused merely on "air (空 *kong*, naval aviation), sub (潜 *qian*, submarines), and speed (快 *kuai*, speed boats)," became a long-term plan from the 1950s through the 1970s. This meant that the Chinese navy remained a light navy with no large ships. In 1955, the navy established its East Sea Fleet (ESF), South Sea Fleet (SSF), and North Sea Fleet (NSF), but naval development remained slow and limited through the 1960s as the navy's modernization was secondary to that of the army and air force. Because of Mao's decision, as Major General Xu Yan of PLA National Defense University argues, the Chinese navy did not become an independent armed service during the 1950s–1960s. "In fact, the Navy merely served the Army as its auxiliary force. . . . In retrospect, the PLA did not have an independent naval strategy during that period."[108]

Sherman Xiaogang Lai adds another reason for the weak navy, "The decline of the PLAN's combat efficiency in the late 1950s was closely linked to Mao's catastrophic Great Leap Forward Movement campaign in 1958 and the resulting famine that coast over 30 million lives."[109] Commodore Wu Dianqing of the PLAN's Political Tasks Department believes the "short-term plan" "became the foundation of the PLAN's development for the next three decades" from 1950 to 1980, rather than three years from 1950 to 1953.[110] Thereby, the short-term, quick-fix plan handicapped the PLAN's future development for more than twenty years. Eventually, Liu Huaqing's visionary plans ended the outdated naval strategy in 1975.

Liu's Russian naval education, especially field trips and naval internships in the Soviet Navy, provided him with the direction, methods, and practical approaches to build a strong Chinese navy. The Soviet Naval Command Academy emphasized the importance of internship and field experience and organized a monthlong naval study tour every year for international naval officers. During their first-year trip in 1955, Liu Huaqing and his Chinese class traveled to the Gulf of Finland, working with the equipment, weapons, and command system on the battleship *October*

*Revolution*, built by the Russian czar and with a displacement of 40,000 tons. They also visited coastal defense works with 130mm, 180mm, and 203mm heavy artillery guns. They traveled to Estonian and Latvian naval and naval aviation bases along the Baltic Sea during their second study tour in 1956 (see photo 2). The Chinese officers spent their time on Russian destroyers, submarines, torpedo boats, and reconnaissance planes, working

**PHOTO 2.** Liu Huaqing is ranked PLAN rear admiral in October 1955. 中国国史网 [History of the PRC Net]

with the captains and sailors and participating in their naval exercises. Through his study and internships in Russia, Liu was convinced and passionately believed that China needed a strong navy with big warships and effective weapon systems. In 1985, then–PLAN commander admiral Liu Huaqing proposed a large naval building plan for a strong, oceangoing navy.

Liu Huaqing endeavored to modify the Soviet system to better fit China's situation. He spent his third-year internship at Lüshun (formerly Port Arthur) Naval Base, Liaoning, in 1957, for his graduation thesis, and analyzed the advantage and disadvantage of the Soviet Navy's influence during the naval base transfer from Russia to China. In May 1955, the Port Arthur Naval Base was returned to the PLA Navy, after sixty years of foreign military occupations (by Imperial Russia from 1895 to 1904, Imperial Japan from 1905 to 1945, and the Soviet Union from 1945 to 1955), when 12,000 Soviet ground, air, and naval troops withdrew.[111] The PLAN received surplus Russian aircraft, vessels, vehicles, and equipment, including 64 torpedo bombers, 14 training airplanes, 39 torpedo boats, 12 frigates, 18 support ships, 412 torpedoes and naval mines, 122 anti-aircraft artillery (AAA) guns, 66 heavy coast artillery pieces (180mm and 130mm), 3,250,000 artillery shells, 2,642 tons of explosives and bombs, 35 radar sets, 1,684 vehicles, and 22,000 tons of gasoline. The Soviet Navy also returned shipyards, coastal defense works, training facilities, hospitals, warehouses, research labs, and additional naval equipment in Dalian to the Chinese navy.[112] The PLA ground force received 357 Russian tanks and 1,113 heavy artillery pieces. The air force also received 328 Russian airplanes and assumed nine airfields in Liaoning Province. The PLA renamed Port Arthur Lüshun Naval Base.

Liu Huaqing used the Lüshun Naval Base as a case study and focused his thesis on the staff duties and responsibilities in the newly established Chinese base command. He criticized Soviet missions, regulations, and base administration to serve Moscow's interests and ignore China's needs and conditions. He suggested learning Soviet naval experience and base management critically and electively. Liu Huaqing graduated from the Russian Naval Command Academy with outstanding academic achievements in the spring of 1958. (Much later, in 1990, when Admiral Liu Huaqing led a Chinese military delegation to Moscow, the Russian navy arranged for him to revisit the Russian Naval Command Academy during his trip.)

Liu Huaqing's early experience in naval education, both domestic and foreign, from 1952 to 1958 manifested in lack of maritime experience, centralized coordination, modern warships, and seamen training. The PLAN, building on the army's historical legacy, carried on army organizational systems, including the party's control, and ground combat tactics. When Russian naval assistance became available, the PLAN slowly evolved through Chinese interactions with and observations of Russians, and naturally outgrew the formative years. Liu's official biographer, Shi Changxue, concluded that Liu's naval study in the Soviet Union from 1954 to 1958 "was a very valuable, life-time opportunity for him to generate a worldwide strategic thinking, theocratize his military command experience and skills, and explore his problem-solving methods and abilities in the future."[113] After his graduation from Russia, Liu served as the PLAN's commander of the Lüshun Naval Base and deputy commander of North Sea Fleet (NSF) from 1958 to 1961. Acquisition and assimilation of Russian naval technology and naval experience sparked debate among Chinese naval officers for the rest of the century. The lessons learned in the 1950s informed the PLAN's reform, reconstruction, and technological improvements. In retrospect, the Chinese navy's adaptation to a new naval war environment resulted from the assimilation of Russian experience and technology.

CHAPTER 2

# REFORMER OF THE RUSSIAN MODEL

Rear Admiral Liu Huaqing began his naval career in 1958 after his graduation from the Russian Naval Command Academy. From 1958 to 1960, the one-star admiral served as deputy commander and chief of staff of the PLAN Lüshun Naval Base (the base command equivalent to the PLA's army command). He carefully adopted Russian naval systems and maintained a stable base management through Mao's political shift from "following the Soviet model" from 1954 to 1959 to ridding the PLA of Russian influence in 1960.[1] Liu Huaqing was promoted to base commander and deputy commander of the PLAN North Sea Fleet (NSF) in 1960. After the Sino-Soviet split in 1960, Liu successfully moved away from the Russian operational systems and established the core responding force of Lüshun Naval Base (LNB) with Chinese characteristics. His strategic planning reflected his potential to build a weak fleet into a strong naval force by identifying immediate security needs, concentrating resources, focusing on combat capability, and emphasizing speed, firepower, and effectiveness.

This chapter also discusses Liu Huaqing's transfer out of the navy to ship research and development as the inaugural president of the Defense Ministry's Seventh Institute (Naval Ship Research Institute) in 1961.[2] Liu initially declined the offer because, in his mind, he was not a naval scientist or an academic scholar qualified for a research leadership position, but Fleet Admiral Xiao Jinguang persuaded him to accept the new position. Thanks to Xiao Jinguang, Liu was not only promoted to a two-star admiral position (equivalent to PLA army group command level), but also left the navy and survived the PLAN's political purge after Marshal Peng Dehuai's fall in 1959. In 1965, Liu became vice minister of the Sixth Machinery Ministry (China's Shipbuilding Ministry) in addition to his presidency at the institute. The new deputy cabinet position in 1965–1966 helped him integrate naval research with commercial ship development and identify the PLAN's problems and needs for its modernization. Although the Chinese navy claimed three offshore victories over the Taiwanese navy in 1965, Liu realized that the PLAN would need larger warships and more firepower in future naval wars. He required more surface naval power over certain distances against Taiwan's naval power.

In 1966, Liu Huaqing was promoted to vice chairman of the Commission of Science, Technology, and Industry for National Defense (CSTIND), at a three-star admiral level, working directly under Marshal Nie Rongzhen, CMC vice chairman, vice premier, and CSTIND chairman, as the top national leader of China's defense industry. CSTIND characterized the administration of China's defense industry as a highly centralized system with new emphasis on naval development when Rear Admiral Liu began to serve as branch chief for warship research and development, nuclear submarines, weapon systems, and aviation technology.[3] In CSTIND, he started the journey of transforming the PLAN to a naval power.

From 1961 to 1969, Liu Huaqing founded and led a national naval research center, designed ship development agenda and methods, and executed his research programs to meet the PLAN's operational needs in the Taiwan Strait. He began to emerge as a Chinese Sergey Gorshkov, who appreciated new technology and advocated naval research and development. His initiatives and continuing efforts eventually started a historical transformation of the PLA from a ground force to a multiservice army. Since the founding of the PRC in 1949, China had been a land power with 6 million troops in 1969. The Party Center's strategic shift in 1970 opened the Pacific for China's development. Liu's decade-long efforts in shipbuilding and research showed a new direction of PLA balanced naval capability.

Liu Huaqing's story also offers a perspective on new civil-military relations that shaped innovation and technological development, revealing the complicated interactions between the state and military. In his centralized and militarized research and development system, the military mobilized civilian professionals and utilized national resources for its strategic weapon programs by centralizing the nation's science and technology development. China's naval and nuclear programs throughout the 1960s were characterized by centralization and bureaucratic power, which guaranteed the program's success.[4] The chapter explains how the new appointment did not only save him from possible purge, criticism, and even accusations as many of his colleagues experienced during the first two years of the Cultural Revolution from 1966 to 1968, but also promoted him from two-star admiral to a three-star position (equivalent to PLA regional command level) during one of the darkest periods in PRC history. It was during these years from 1966 to 1969 when Liu began to design, produce, and equip a modern naval force with strategic power and new technology that he also became a strategic naval thinker, who appreciated new technology and set up a new direction for the PLAN's modernization.

## LNB REFORMER: ADOPTION AND EVOLUTION

The Soviet Union played an active role in Chinese military modernization in the 1950s. The Soviet naval aid and advisory assistance did not only develop communist military cooperation but also created a new PLA Navy capable of fighting against the technologically advanced KMT naval force in the Taiwan Strait. From 1954 to 1959, Defense Minister Peng Dehuai continued Chinese military modernization begun during the Korean War. Following the Soviet model, Marshal Peng improved military technologies, reorganized defense industries, and spent about $2 billion on arms purchases from Russia.[5] In April–June 1958, fleet admiral and PLAN commander Xiao Jinguang proposed to Peng Dehuai more Russian assistance to update naval technologies and adaption of Russian naval systems.

RAD Liu Huaqing was familiar with Russian systems after his graduation from the Russian Naval Command Academy.[6] He planned to apply Russian naval technology and experience to the Chinese navy. In March 1958, he was appointed deputy commander and chief of staff of the PLAN's Lüshun Naval Base, in charge of operations, base administration, and training. Liu began his command with what he had learned from Russia. He spoke at a base officer conference that "Soviet naval weaponry, equipment, and technology are absolutely much superior to ours; we must learn from the Soviet Navy. Their military has a lot of experiences, and their experiences are universal and suitable to our military."[7] Lüshun Naval Base was at the front line and China's closest naval base to the Korean Peninsula (see map 3). Liu implemented Russian coastal defense strategy by focusing his efforts on coastal artillery work, offshore patrol, and

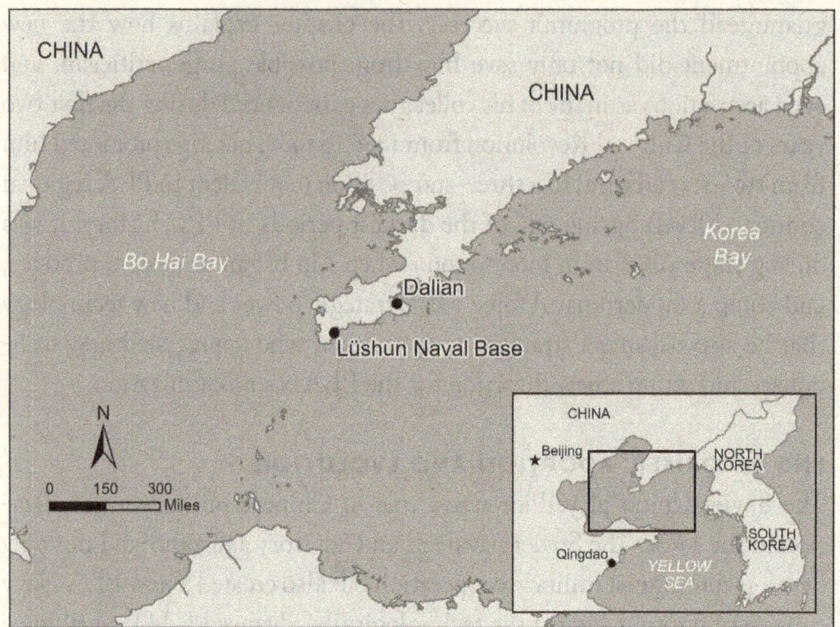


MAP 3. PLAN Lüshun Naval Base

anti-landing exercises to improve base defense, fleet combat effectiveness, and joint operational capability. To reach his objectives to improve base management and operation, Liu Huaqing followed the Russian system closely, including base regulations, operational handbooks, naval technical manuals, and training procedures, all of which were passed on by Russian commanders to the PLAN after they returned the base to China. Familiar and comfortable with the existing system, Liu administrated the base by Russian naval books.[8]

In 1958, Fleet Admiral Xiao Jinguang and PLAN Command submitted the "PLAN Ten-Year Development Agenda" to Marshal Peng, CMC, and Mao recommending the PLAN's transformation to a medium navy with large surface warships and missile submarines for near-shore defense.[9] The proposal required more Russian technology and naval assistance. Defense Minister Peng Dehuai agreed and supported Xiao's agenda, which argued the importance of continuing Soviet naval aid, advisory, and technology assistance. The last huge naval purchase before the Sino-Soviet split, the so-called 2–4 Agreement, was finalized on

February 4, 1959, and provided the PLAN with ballistic submarine-to-surface missiles and ship-to-ship missiles, submarines armed with missiles, and missile launching ships. The agreement was then considered a "high-tech" deal for the PLAN.[10]

To maintain base facilities and adopt newly imported Russian missile technology, Liu and base command hired back more than 140 Russians as advisors to train Chinese naval officers at Lüshun Naval Base in 1958–1959.[11] As they imparted rudimentary naval knowledge to the base officers, Russian advisors developed unique ways in working with their Chinese counterparts at the base. In most cases, Liu Huaqing and Chinese officers listened to Russian recommendations, accepted their comments and suggestions, and implemented Russian advice in the orders and instructions. In 1958, there were a total of 3,390 Russian naval advisors in the PLAN.[12] At that time, Soviet aid and advisory remained available and as a result, the PLAN maintained its slow, steady development by following the Soviet model with new, but limited capacities.

Toward the end of the 1950s, the PLAN boasted twenty-three naval brigades with 860 vessels, including four destroyers, twenty-eight frigates, sixteen submarines, two hundred small warships and gunboats, and more than two hundred torpedo boats. There were six air force divisions and two independent regiments under the PLAN Air Force command. The PLANAF had more than five hundred fighters, bombers, reconnaissance, and cargo planes.[13] The PLAN also commanded nineteen artillery regiments and eight anti-aircraft artillery (AAA) regiments along the coast areas. These artillery regiments had nearly seven hundred heavy (130mm) coastal cannons and AAA guns with Russian-made fire-control radar.[14] The PLAN totaled 188,000 men, including 114,000 transferred infantry soldiers (80.6 percent of the total), 6,000 transferred air force personnel (3.2 percent), 30,000 new recruits of high school graduates (16 percent), and 4,000 former ROC sailors (2.1 percent). With an exceptionally low annual operational budget, about 100 million renminbi (about $40 million at that time) throughout the 1950s, the Chinese navy managed to integrate Russian naval technology with its own experience and lessons learned from naval battles. Mao Zedong spoke at the PRC Central Government's 33rd Plenary that "Taiwan will be unified when our naval and air forces get stronger."[15]

Due to ideological and political disagreements, complicated domestic and international factors, and differences over nuclear doctrines, Soviet and Chinese leaders split at the close of the 1950s. In November 1957, Mao attended celebrations for the Russian Revolution's fortieth anniversary, while international Communists met in Moscow. In his speech, Mao emphasized that, although meaning a large sacrifice of lives, worldwide communism should not fear nuclear war initiated by the imperialists as it would bring imperialism to its grave.[16] Chen Jian points out that Mao's statement was "a deliberate challenge to Khrushchev's emphasis on the necessity and possibility of 'peaceful coexistence' with Western imperialist countries," and "it inevitably worried Moscow's leaders."[17]

During international communism's great polemic from 1958 to 1960, the Sino-Soviet alliance's ideological foundation collapsed. One major contributing factor was China's newly acquired position as the dominant center of international communism in East Asia.[18] Mao Zedong criticized Nikita Khrushchev as a "new revisionist," who "betrayed international communist movements" with "socialist imperialist" aggressive policy.[19] Khrushchev labeled Mao as "an ultra-leftist, an ultra-dogmatist and a left revisionist." On a broader scale, the new confrontation between Beijing and Moscow changed the dynamics of the global Cold War.[20] The Sino-Soviet split undermined the characteristics of the Cold War as a confrontation between the contentious ideologies of communism and capitalism.[21] What once existed as the cornerstone of international communism in the 1950s was dealt a final blow by strategic differences on naval developments within the Sino-Soviet military alliance.

The dramatic Sino-Soviet split buried previously shared perceptions, among Communists internationally, that communism solved problems created by worldwide, capitalistic modernization. Soon, political conflicts between the two Communist parties extended to their diplomatic relations, defense coordination, and military operations. From July 31 to August 3, 1958, when Khrushchev visited Beijing, the Soviet leader proposed to Mao Zedong a Russo-Chinese joint fleet, a permanent naval force including both the PLA and Soviet Navies, and a long-wave radio system between the two countries. Mao declined the Soviet offer by denouncing it as an attempt to control the Chinese navy. In June 1959, the Soviet Union met in Geneva with the United States and Britain on partially banning the use of nuclear weapons. On June 20, the Central Committee of the Soviet Communist Party informed the CCP Central Committee that in order to achieve an agreement to partially ban nuclear tests, the Soviet Union had to terminate the Sino-Soviet agreement on cooperation of nuclear development. On July 16, the Soviet government informed the Chinese government that it would withdraw all of its nuclear scientists and experts. By August 13, 1960, all 12,000 Soviet experts left China with their blueprints and designs. Among them were more than 200 working on the nuclear research and development programs. The Soviets also stopped shipments of the equipment and materials that the Chinese nuclear program desperately needed.[22]

The Sino-Soviet split and Mao's failed Great Leap Forward divided Chinese leaders between the so-called rightists, or the pragmatic group, and the leftists, or the radical group in accordance to their loyalty toward Mao. The gap between the military and the party caused a series of political problems, and eventually led to Defense Minister Peng Dehuai's fall and the termination of the Russian-modeled programs. The marshal was purged at the party's Lushan Conference in the summer of 1959.[23] On July 14, Peng wrote a long letter to Mao expounding on his grievances regarding the Great Leap Forward's failure. Peng Dehuai asserted that they were not only economic, but also "political."[24] Worried about Peng's disloyalty and military power, Mao launched a major assault on Peng, whose criticism would have potentially been tolerated had another military leader raised it. Mao addressed the Lushan Conference on July 23, rebuking Peng's letter. Peng's military career ended when Mao accused him of forming a "rightist-opportunist clique" and conducting "unprincipled factional activity" in the party and army, charges that often-reflected pro-Soviet political positions, and removed him from his post as minister of defense. Peng Dehuai was under house arrest for many years until he died during the Cultural Revolution.

In 1959–1960, Liu Huaqing risked his military career by maintaining the Russian system at Lüshun Naval Base and convincing the NSF Command that the navy differed from the army since it had its own situation and needs at seas. Lüshun could not abolish the Russian system immediately without establishing a new, workable system.[25] Naval leaders continued using Russian regulations, manuals, and codes for

PHOTO 3. Lüshun Base commander Liu Huaqing accompanies Marshal Zhu De, PLA commander in chief, on a visit to Lüshun Naval Base on June 10, 1959. 人民网 [People's Net]

a while because they agreed with Liu. In August 1960, the PLAN established the North Sea Fleet (NSF) at Qingdao and Liu became deputy commander of NSF and commander of Lüshun Naval Base (see photo 3).

In late 1959, Marshal Lin Biao assumed the administration of the CMC and Defense Ministry. New defense minister Lin Biao terminated most reform programs initiated by Peng Dehuai. Policy shifts and political pressure forced Liu Huaqing to end the Russian system and develop Chinese ways of naval operations at Lüshun Naval Base. Although it proved difficult for the Russian-educated rear admiral to abandon what he had learned, Liu knew where and how to transform the Russian model into China's own naval system. Comparing the Russian model with Chinese naval needs were an important part of his learning experience since Liu began his study at the Soviet Naval Command Academy. He always questioned if Russian regulations, technology, or experience were useful, adaptable, or manageable for the Chinese navy. From the beginning of

1960, Liu determined to change the Soviet system to better fit the Chinese coastal defense situation.[26]

First, RAD Liu Huaqing designed his new naval defense strategy by creating a small elite response squadron as a "fist" of Lüshun Naval Base (LNB) in 1960. As the "pocket of excellence," the quick and effective naval force was designed to fight against a surprise attack, enemy landing, and local foreign intervention. Lüshun Naval Command defended a long coastline, including the capital city Beijing, and 8 million square kilometers of the northern Yellow Sea, surrounded by Japan in the east and the Korean Peninsula in the west. Liu realized that, although Russian advisors intended to make Lüshun as good as a Russian naval base, they ignored the geographic settings of China's northeastern coast, combat experience of the PLAN, and inadequate naval defense with small warships and weak firepower. Russian defense plans simply divided all coastal areas and sovereign waters among Lüshun ships and troops. Moreover, the Russian advisors wanted to enforce their standard and procedure but ignored defensive capability of Lüshun. LNB was one of China's smaller bases, ranked fifth in 1960 after Qingdao (NSF headquarters), Shanghai (East Sea Fleet headquarters), Ningbo (ESF), and Zhanjiang (South Sea Fleet headquarters). All four destroyers (newly purchased from Russia) anchored at Qingdao Naval Base.

Liu Huaqing replaced the Russian operational system with a new Lüshun defense plan. After Russian advisors were recalled, in February 1960, Liu organized the concentration of available sources and built the core coastal defense fleet at LNB. His quick responding force included one frigate squadron, one torpedo boat squadron, three submarines, one patrol boat squadron, three coast artillery companies, three AAA companies, one combat engineering company, and one infantry battalion.[27] From 1960, the base command provided its best support to the core combat force and guaranteed its mobility, firepower, and logistics. This core naval fleet was combat ready for a surprise attack, enemy landing, or a foreign intervention at any location around the north Yellow Sea, or all water territory, defended by LNB. The core combat fleet was also prepared for and trained as a striking force capable of launching defensive attacks on enemy warships or hostile fishing boats which conducted illegal activities over Chinese sovereign waters, including China's fishing areas. Liu designed training programs for the core combat force, and organized their offshore exercises, landing practices, and joint operations.[28] The establishment of LNB naval core combat force reflected Liu's strategic thinking on how to defend territorial waters and make a strong, effective defense out of a weak force.

Second, Rear Admiral Liu offered effective protection for the Chinese fishing fleet in the Yellow Sea. During the fishing seasons, hundreds and thousands of fishermen from Hebei, Shandong, Liaoning, and other coastal provinces flocked to the Yellow Sea for commercial fishing. They often faced harassment by large numbers of Japanese and Korean fishermen in the same area. A conceptual gap on civil-military relations also existed between the Russians and Chinese. The Russians separated the populace from naval operations, but the PLAN considered naval protection of civilian life and maritime commerce an important task for Chinese naval forces. Liu made detailed plans to guarantee Chinese fishermen's safety at sea. He first coordinated with local governments and established communication between the fishing fleet and LNB patrol ships at sea. He then organized naval exercises around Chinese fishing areas as a show of naval power. If a situation occurred, his frigates or patrol boats could reach the area immediately. Additionally, Liu sent LNB officers to local villages and trained fishermen militias on firearms, self-defense, communication, foreign languages, and close combat at sea. Before the fishing groups sailed out, LNB issued small arms, ammunition, hand grenades, and other weapons to the militias for their self-protection. Upon returning to shore, the naval officers recollected the weapons and ammunition.[29]

In 1961, Liu Huaqing was appointed as the inaugural president of the Defense Ministry's Seventh Research Institute (Naval Ship R&D Institute), and he left the navy. Liu Huaqing's transfer saved him from a political purge in the PLAN in 1962–1963. After Marshal Peng Dehuai's fall in 1959, a top-down purge permeated the army in 1960–1961. In less than a year, 1,848 generals, high-ranking commanders, and middle-ranking officers were dismissed or jailed for their support or sympathies toward Peng.[30] Ellis Joffe describes it as "the most serious leadership struggle since the establishment of the Communist regime."[31] After Peng's dismissal, the new defense minister, Marshal Lin Biao, emphasized "leftist" politics for the PLA and promoted Mao's personality cult. In 1962, Lin appointed Lieutenant General Li Zuopeng, his longtime lieutenant, as the navy's first deputy commander in an attempt to wrest naval leadership from Fleet Admiral Xiao Jinguang. (Li Zuopeng was ranked a vice admiral in 1963.)

In March 1962, Lin sent an investigation team led by Li Zuopeng to the navy to investigate a naval aviation pilot's defection to Taiwan along with his MiG-15 jet fighter. In April, Li Zuopeng and his team completed the investigation and submitted their report to Lin Biao and the CMC, accusing the navy's leadership of failing "to raise high the flag of Mao Zedong's Thought."[32] The report describes the "rampant existence of phenomenon of discord" through the navy's party hierarchy. Li knew that the internal factional struggles inhibited the CCP's networks from working effectively. Among the consequences of the party's loss of control was erosion of discipline. Warship captains held drinking parties on board while on duty. Some prominent officers pursued "corruptive ways of life." A reflection of the problems in the navy's leadership was a series of scandals ranging from sailors' suicides and revenge homicides to murders of civilian officials and attempts by officers to organize mass defections to Taiwan.[33]

After receiving Li Zuopeng's report, Lin Biao appointed Vice Admiral Li as standing deputy commander of the navy in April 1962, and then the navy's political commissar from June 1967 to 1972. Li was appointed the PLA deputy chief of the General Staff in October 1968 as one of the top military leaders.[34] After taking the naval command, Li launched a political campaign in the navy, "helping" Xiao Jinguang to deal with the problems as Xiao's health declined.[35] With Defense Minister Lin Biao's support, Li chaired a series of high-ranking naval commander conferences to identify the major issues, target responsible parties, and undermine Xiao's leadership while establishing his own authority in the PLAN. Mao Zedong approved the navy's new leadership. Sherman Xiaogang Lai points out, "Xiao was not happy with this arrangement and wrote to Mao, but Mao ignored him. From this moment until his official retirement in 1980, Xiao was the PLAN's commander in name only."[36] Starting in 1963, 158 senior naval officers, above division level, were dismissed or jailed. The extended political struggle and large-scale purge caused fear among the navy's rank and file about their career, positions, and even their own life.

## SHIP R&D ARCHITECT: MISSION, STRATEGY, AND METHODS

On June 7, 1961, the CMC issued the order to establish China's first ship research and development institute, officially the Seventh Research Institute of the Defense Ministry, with Liu Huaqing as its inaugural president. With the Party Center's support, Liu started new ship research and developed naval force at a national level. As in other countries, there was always a debate between the military and industry over who should lead the country's research and development of strategic weapons. However, China differed from the Western countries in that Chinese leaders reached an agreement that the party, or the CCP Central Committee, would lead the research and development of military technology and strategic weapons, including nuclear bombs, strategic submarines, and ballistic missiles. Chen Jian argues that "the Chinese leadership resolved not to abandon the nuclear project . . . on July 16, 1961, the CCP leadership decided to mobilize the whole country's resources to enhance the development of China's nuclear industry."[37]

Departure from Soviet technological and material aid almost scuttled China's four-year-old nuclear and missile programs. Disappointed by the Soviet's unilateral termination of their agreements, the CCP Central Committee met at Beidaihe, Hebei, on July 18, 1959, over how to handle the termination of Soviet aid. Having lost Soviet nuclear protection, Mao Zedong expedited the PLA's efforts to develop a strategic force in the early 1960s. The Communist Cold War not only triggered the development of nuclear and missile programs, but also determined their eventual targets. Mao felt that the Chinese should undertake the task of advanced technology themselves, and that it was a good thing that Khrushchev refused to give China advanced technology.[38] At the meeting, the party's Central Committee agreed that China should continue its nuclear research and development without any interruption, regardless of the Soviet withdrawal. The new proposal deemed "Project 596," symbolized June 1959, when the Soviets withdrew all technology and personnel. "Project 596" endeavored to develop China's own nuclear bomb and submarines within eight years.[39]

On November 17, 1962, the CCP Central Committee organized a "Central Special Commission" in charge of strategic weapons research and nuclear development to ensure cooperation between research, manufacturing, military, and civilian officials and to strengthen the leadership of China's nuclear and missile programs. The Party Center established a highly centralized system for strategic weapons, based upon close cooperation between civil government and the military, a concentration of national resources, and a series of social and political incentives for professionals. The Central Special Commission consisted of fifteen top leaders, including seven vice premiers, five vice chairmen of the CMC, and some ministers; Zhou Enlai served as the chairman.[40] On November 29, the Central Special Commission met a second time to centralize structures, coordinate defense and civilian industries, and concentrate materials and manpower. By December, the commission transferred 126 senior experts and scientists plus 6,000 college graduates to the program.

Marshal Nie Rongzhen became the czar of China's strategic weapon development. Since Premier Zhou was preoccupied by foreign affairs, CMC vice chairman and vice premier Nie Rongzhen was the next top leader in the Central Special Commission responsible for the entire research and development process. Nie was one of Mao's closest working colleagues and trusted marshals.

Nie Rongzhen was sent to the Soviet Union in the fall of 1924 and attended the Oriental University in Moscow. In February 1925, he was transferred to the special "class for Chinese officers" in the Soviet Academy of the Red Army. While in Red Army uniform, Nie studied and drilled with Red Army officers, learning the Soviet military system from inside.[41] On his return to China in the late 1920s, Nie Rongzhen worked as secretary and instructor at Huangpu Military Academy. He served as the secretary of the CCP's Northern Bureau in the 1930s and commanded the PLA's Northern Military Region in the mid-1940s. In 1948–1949 he worked with Mao daily after CCP leadership moved from Yan'an to North China. Nie successfully protected the CCP HQs and PLA high command by defeating KMT attacks and personally saved Mao's life once during an air raid.[42] When Mao founded the PRC, Nie was appointed mayor of Beijing, Beijing-Tianjin garrison commander, and deputy chief of the PLA General Staff. He practically ran the PLA's General Staff because Zhou Enlai, as its chief, was preoccupied with the premiership and foreign ministry. Moreover, the entire General Staff were Nie's former Northern Military Region staff, people who worked under him and Mao during the civil war and moved to Beijing with him.[43]

After the founding of the PRC, Nie Rongzhen became acting chief of the General Staff in 1950, vice chairman of the CMC in 1951. After 1954, he was one of the party's top eleven national leaders and a member of the Politburo's Standing Committee. In 1955, he became one of the ten marshals of China.[44] By that spring, Nie was one of the top three leaders in charge of nuclear research and development. In 1956, Vice Premier Nie "assumed overall supervision of the entire strategic weapons program."[45] He organized the Aviation Industry Committee for aerospace technology that same year. In October 1958, the CMC founded the Commission of Science, Technology, and Industry for National Defense (CSTIND) and Mao appointed Marshal Nie as its chairman. CSTIND was a highly centralized top military authority in charge of the defense industry and military technological development.

In 1962, Marshal Nie coordinated CSTIND with the Central Special Commission, worked through the bureaucratic system, and created new government offices, research institutes, and testing facilities for defense projects. The number of science and technology research institutes and facilities increased from 380 in 1956 to 1,300 in 1962.[46] The Central Special Commission and CSTIND established three new PLA research institutes for military technological improvement and defense modernization, including aviation and missile development, electronics and computers, and naval technology. On June 7, 1961, the CMC issued a proclamation establishing the Defense Ministry's Seventh Research Institute. In the fall, Fleet Admiral Xiao Jinguang summoned Liu Huaqing and appointed him as the first president of the Seventh Research Institute.[47]

In 1961, Liu Huaqing positioned himself to establish a top naval research institute and lead ship research and development at the national level. He perfectly understood the party-navy system and fully utilized the Party Center's decision, which he described as the "Sword of State" with highest authoritarian power.[48] From 1961 to 1966, Liu established the PLA's naval research complex by centralizing, militarizing, and institutionalizing China's ship research institutes, academies, schools, labs, testing sites, experiment facilities, and training centers. He created the "dragon head of the nation's ship research" and set the national stage for naval modernization.

He firmly believed that naval development depended on the country's maritime research and scientific ability in nautical studies. It needed all available talents, experts, and nationwide coordination of all elements to make it happen.

First, Liu Huaqing used the Party Center's order to centralize the country's ship R&D and made the Seventh Research Institute the head of the nation's naval research. He collected and reorganized three ship research institutes from the First Industrial Ministry, three institutes from the Third Industrial Ministry, five institutes from the navy, and the Research Division of the PLAN HQs.[49] These institutes were in six provinces and eleven different cities, including their research facilities, labs, testing sites, office buildings, and naval vessels. There were different opinions against Liu's centralization of China's ship R&D. Opponents argued that the Soviet Union had two separate ship research systems, one was under the military, the other belonging to the state industry. Liu justified the necessity of concentrating human and material resources in naval research in his report to the Defense Ministry on August 23, 1962. "The Soviet Union has sufficient human and financial resources, and they can establish two separate [research] systems. Our country with limited research resources and weak industrial foundation cannot afford two ship research systems."[50] It was approved that his concentration and centralization of the nation's naval research resources would guarantee the design and manufacturing of China's new warship in the 1960s.

Second, Liu Huaqing militarized the Seventh Research Institute by reorganizing academic, civilian, and industrial research institutes into defense facilities. Some local officials opposed Liu's militarizing their ship research under the PLA (Defense Ministry). Liu believed in a division of labor between the shipbuilding industry and ship research and development as the "two hands" of a modern navy. The ship R&D should be under the military, while shipbuilding belonged to the state industry. Both worked together, but he insisted that "the brain [of the two hands] must be military. The hands cannot replace the brain."[51]

Third, Liu Huaqing conscripted civilian scientists, experts, engineers, technicians, and lab assistants into military service. In the mid-1950s, the PRC passed its first Military Service Law and created a compulsory system by which both conscripts and volunteers were combined in the Chinese military. Liu Huaqing's militarization did not stop at the institutionalization and organizational levels, but also extended to personal level by drafting his civilian researchers and other professionals into the navy as active PLAN officers if they met age, physical, and other requirements.[52] The Seventh Research Institute's naval programs and national defense projects offered a few benefits to professionals and intellectuals like political protection, economic security, social privileges, and future career, which were not provided by any industrial, academic, and civilian research institute.[53]

Political security was a major concern for Chinese intellectuals in the 1960s. By 1961, Mao Zedong had launched several nationwide political campaigns targeting intellectuals and academics in China. Society radicalized throughout the late 1950s. The first serious campaign against the intellectuals and academics occurred in 1957 when Mao launched the Anti-Rightist Movement (Fanyou yundong) across the country. In the field of science and technology, the movement targeted nonparty members and those who were not interested in Communist politics. In schools, academies, and mass media, party committees and branches mobilized the masses and identified the "rightists" among faculty members, researchers, and educated employees. Many scientists, engineers, and technicians were criticized as "rightists," dismissed from their jobs, and exiled to the frontier or remote border land, thousands of miles away from their families, as manual laborers and for their "reeducation." Some were jailed, tortured, and even executed. It was called "taking out white flags" (*babaiqi*). The fear factor worked as Mao's harsh and endless political campaigns against intellectuals in society pushed scientists and researchers into the military.[54]

The Seventh Research Institute worked on national defense projects and provided security and protection for its staff and employees. Liu Huaqing tried to reduce political pressures on his own personnel throughout the movements. Most naval scientists and experts faced less criticism and avoided certain investigations and political purges in the 1960s. This was particularly important for these returning students from the United States and the West. When their American training and work experience brought suspicion, they had no choice but to stay in the military and work for the strategic weapon programs for their own political safety and family security. Liu also carried out a rehabilitation program of "hat off and ranking up," removing some researchers' bad labels like the "rightists" from the previous political movement and then offering them military ranks for political protection.[55]

From 1959 to 1961, the defense research institutes became the nation's priority and continued receiving adequate finances and logistics. In these three years, China experienced a serious economic depression that claimed more than 30 million lives due to severe food shortages. This resulted from the massive failure of Mao Zedong's Great Leap Forward movement, an industrialization effort through labor power and collectivization instead of technology and private enterprises. The total grain production decreased from 200 million tons in 1958 to 144 million tons in 1960. The government, however, blamed it on bad weather and called it a "natural disaster."[56] Moreover, the main culprit became the Soviet Union when its ideological split with China became public in 1961. The Party Center, however, decided in July 1961 to continue its strategic weapons research and development. Mao said, "We have to make up our mind to focus on the most sophisticated technology. Khrushchev refused to give us advanced branches of science. It is great! We would not be able to pay him back if he had given them to us."[57] Marshal Chen Yi supported the idea but commented that they would have to "sell their pants" to continue the programs.[58] The Seventh Research Institute continued offering its researchers and staff daily needs and family support through these difficult years.

For scientists and technicians, defense facilities and nuclear programs offered better career opportunities than the academic institutes and civilian enterprises could. By the early 1960s, many academic scientists, college researchers, industrial engineers, and shipbuilding technicians were willing to join the navy and acquire professional development for their careers. The military academies and facilities were usually not implicated to the same degree of personal connection, corruption, "red tape," or bureaucratic issues as their civil counterparts.[59] Under Liu's leadership, the Seventh Research Institute also made changes to the "security clearance system" allowing more civilian researchers to work on defense technology and open up for promotions. Thousands of scientists and researchers became active servicemen through the militarization of the research institute. By 1965, the Seventh Research Institute had 15 research institutes, 11 testing sites, 12 manufacturing factories, and 187 major departments and labs, totaling 16,000 researchers.[60]

After the founding of the Seventh Research Institute, Liu Huaqing and his researchers initiated domestic ship development by imitating Russian naval technology. In 1953, China purchased from the Soviet Navy all the blueprints, technical data, and some shipbuilding materials for five ships, including a torpedo speedboat, frigate, submarine chaser, submarine, and minesweeper. According to the Sino-Soviet "2–4 Agreement" in 1959, when the Russian navy shipped the PLAN ballistic missiles and missile launching ships and submarines, they also provided designs, blueprints, equipment, sample missiles, and ship parts.[61] Liu started by imitating three Russian surface ships and two submarines, including a large missile speedboat, small missile speedboat, torpedo boat, missile submarine, and medium-size torpedo submarine. Nevertheless, some naval scientists and experts were not interested in imitating existing Russian ships and believed that imitations belonged to shipyards. Under the fever of the Great Leap Forward, they wanted to research new cutting-edge ships, high-tech weapons, and computerized equipment to surpass Soviet, or even American and British, naval technology. At the institute's executive conference on June 22, 1962, Liu clarified that "research policy is very important [for the institute]. Our current policy is that the imitation is our priority."[62]

He concentrated 65 percent of his research personnel on imitating "two boats and a missile" and "two boats and a torpedo." The "two boats and a missile" were Russian-designed missile submarines, missile speed boats, and ship-to-ship missiles. The "two boats and a torpedo" were Russian-made torpedo boats, torpedo submarines, and torpedoes. In late 1961, the Seventh Research Institute imitated the Russian T-123 (or P-4, and then P-6) torpedo boat with 22 tons of displacement, two 12.7mm dual-barreled antiaircraft machine guns, 2 torpedo tubes, and a speed of 52 knots. The small surface combatant was an effective weapon against large Taiwanese warships because of its speed, agility, and torpedoes. However, torpedo boats (PTs) had only two 450mm torpedoes (imitated Russian Type 53–39), and they were inshore craft with a limited fuel load for short distance.[63] Soon they were manufactured at the Guangzhou and Wuhu Shipyards as Chinese Type 026 torpedo boats. By March 1964, the Seventh Research Institute had completed the imitation of five Russian-modeled boats. They also successfully imitated and began manufacturing the Russian Type

53–39 torpedo in 1965. Their imitations produced new combat ships and naval weapons for the PLAN's ongoing naval warfare against the Taiwanese navy in the Taiwan Strait throughout the 1960s.

Although Liu learned, digested, imitated, and selected Russian naval technology, he considered adaptations in design and development to better fit Chinese needs. Before the 1960s, Chinese shipbuilding was based on existing Russian designs and reverse-engineered Soviet components and equipment. From 1962, the Seventh Research Institute began designing China's own naval combat ships. Liu understood that the PLAN's immediate tasks were to assist the army's landing campaigns, fight back Taiwanese naval raids and blockades, and defend the coastal areas and near-shore islands.

To meet the urgent need for a light naval force with limited time and resources, he knew that it was unrealistic and unnecessary to design large warships. From 1962, Liu instead focused on designing and developing effective combat ships for immediate and capable operations like torpedo boats and small frigates (or patrol craft, PC). It was the first time for the Chinese admiral to integrate national strength and resources, coordinate research and development, shipbuilding, and logistics, and create an effective and capable naval force. After knowing how to build a new navy from scratch, Liu knew now how to take it from weak to strong. Under his leadership, the Seventh Research Institute maintained a balance between high-tech, cutting-edge research and design and development of conventional naval vessels like torpedo boats and patrol ships.[64]

The first-generation Chinese-designed and manufactured frigates were the backbone of the PLAN's combat power in the early days. They performed brilliantly in offensive operations on near-shore islands and safeguarding coastal and territorial waters (12 nautical miles off the shore) in the 1960s. In 1962, the Seventh Research Institute designed its first frigate as Type 062. The Chinese designed the frigate as a patrol craft with a displacement of 125 tons. The design emphasized speed and firepower equipped with both 75mm and 37mm cannons, two 25mm double-barrel guns, and a capable top speed of 27 knots. The frigates were tested in 1962, manufactured in 1963, and began their service in the PLAN by 1964. China produced more than 300 Type 062 frigates in the 1960s.[65] In the mid-1960s, frigate development and manufacturing shifted from small to medium-sized ships. In September 1966, the Type 065 frigates were delivered to the navy with a standard displacement of 1,263 tons and cruising speed of 16 knots. By the end of the 1960s, the PLAN had established a capable torpedo boat fleet, developed frigate combat tactics, and transformed the Chinese navy from an inshore defensive fleet to a light naval force capable of offshore attacks.[66] With more new ships commissioned, the total tonnage of the PLAN surface ships increased from 60,000 tons in 1961 to 100,000 tons in 1971.

During China's nationwide famine, Chiang Kai-shek called for a "return to the mainland" in 1962 and launched new, small-scale attacks along China's coast during the Sino-Soviet split. By 1964, the Taiwanese navy had launched twenty-four raids against China's commercial shipping, offshore fishing, and island defenses, and captured 370 Chinese fishing boats. In early 1964, Mao Zedong instructed Commander Xiao Jinguang and the navy to fight back against "Chiang Kai-shek's harassments and sabotages along the southeastern coast."[67] In 1965, the Chinese navy engaged in two major naval battles, and newly made Chinese gunboats claimed all victories over the Taiwanese navy.

During the Battle of August Sixth, a newly commissioned patrol craft (PC) sank two larger Taiwanese warships. On August 5, two Taiwanese submarine hunters, *Jianmen* (PCE 45) and *Zhangjiang* (PC 118), landed special forces units on a Chinese-held offshore island. *Jianmen* was a large U.S. submarine hunter (MSF 387) transferred to the Taiwanese navy in April 1965. With a Taiwanese ship hull number of 045, it had a standard displacement of 595 tons, 18 nautical miles speed, one 76.2mm cannon, four 40mm guns, and four 20mm guns. *Zhangjiang*, a smaller U.S. submarine chaser (PC-1232), transferred to Taiwan in 1954 as Taiwanese naval ship 118, displaced 298 tons, one 76.2mm cannon, one 40mm gun, and five 20mm guns. The Chinese navy sent five frigates and twelve torpedo boats to attack the two large Taiwanese warships. As the first generation of Chinese speedy frigates, the newly designed and improved *Shanghai*-class (Types 0109 and 0110) PC had a displacement of 105 to 120 tons with more firepower. China manufactured more than 200 *Shanghai*-class frigates in the 1960s.

In the early morning of August 6, 1965, the Chinese PCs ambushed Taiwanese warships around the offshore island. From 2:41 to 3:20 a.m., four PLAN PCs concentrated their fire on Taiwanese *Zhangjiang* from 500 to 100 meters. The guns fitted on the PCs were of small caliber, but their firing rate was very high. Although the Chinese frigate PC 611 was badly damaged after sustaining seventeen hits and losing three out of four of its engines, it continued to fire on *Zhangjiang*.[68] Eventually, the Taiwanese sub-hunter's magazine exploded and caught fire after the PCs' repeated attacks. After a one-and-a-half-hour fight, Taiwanese *Zhangjiang* sank at 3:33 a.m., 25 nautical miles southeast of Dongshan Island. Its captain and most of the crew were lost at sea.[69] While the Chinese PCs turned to the Taiwanese *Jianmen* about 5:19 a.m., PLAN PT 119 also ordered the five torpedo boats to fire. Three of the ten Chinese torpedoes hit their target. Three minutes later, *Jianmen* sank at 38 nautical miles southeast of Dongshan. In the battle, Taiwanese Rear Admiral Hu Jiaheng was killed with 170 sailors and soldiers. *Jianmen* captain Wang Yunshan and 33 sailors were captured. The August 6 naval battle was a PLAN victory by sinking two Taiwanese warships with only four PLAN officers and sailors killed, twenty-eight wounded, and two PCs and two PT boats damaged.[70] Chinese battle tactics employed small PC boats to provide covering gunfire to silence the enemy guns while the high-speed PTs charged and torpedoed the Taiwanese ships (see map 4).

The PLAN assessed its battle performance on August 6. Three days later, the navy relayed the battle report to PLA high command. The report considered the Battle of August Sixth "the largest victory of naval engagements in the recent years. . . . This battle victory has proved not only small boats can attack large warships, but also they can sink enemy warships."[71] On August 15, Mao Zedong read and approved their report. The navy deemed the PC 611 the "Heroic Ship at Sea" and TP 119 the "Heroic Speedboat." The Seventh Research Institute continued meeting naval needs and battle situations in their ship research and development.

The Taiwanese naval leaders blamed their defeats on their underestimation of the effectiveness and firepower of small Chinese ships. Disappointed by the lost naval battle, Chiang Kai-shek removed Admiral Liu Guangkai from his post as commander of the Taiwanese navy on August 11. Although the American naval advisors tried to convince Chiang to give Liu's a second chance, Chiang Kai-shek stayed with his decision.[72]

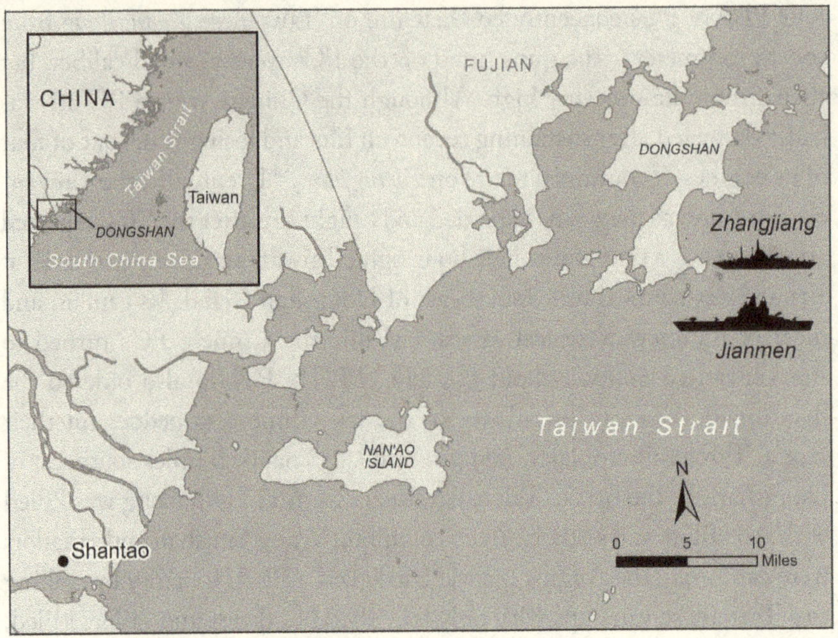


MAP 4. The Battle of August Sixth, 1965

The Chinese admirals realized the newly designed and manufactured *Shanghai*-class PC boats had made a big difference in combat because they had better speed and stronger firepower than the imitated Russian model *Guangzhou*-class PC craft. These Chinese-made boats enabled the PLAN to maintain its initiative in the Taiwan Strait, develop its naval combat tactics at sea, and take advantage of offshore areas for battle opportunities. The PLAN depended on the new PCs and PTs and continued to employ their successful tactics of using small boats to attack large enemy warships. The ships and tactics worked again in the next naval engagement, the Battle of East Chongwu (also known as the "Battle of Wuqiu," or Wuchiu, in Taiwan), in November 1965 (see map 5).

On November 13, *Yongtai* and *Yongchang*, two Taiwanese submarine hunters with displacements of 600 tons each and strong firepower, departed Magong Island for the Chinese coast at 1:20 p.m.[73] The PLAN ordered six PCs and six PTs to attack the enemy warships. At 11:33 p.m., when the PLAN's PCs met *Yongchang* about five cable lengths from its right, the Chinese opened fire. Four PCs concentrated their guns on *Yongchang*'s

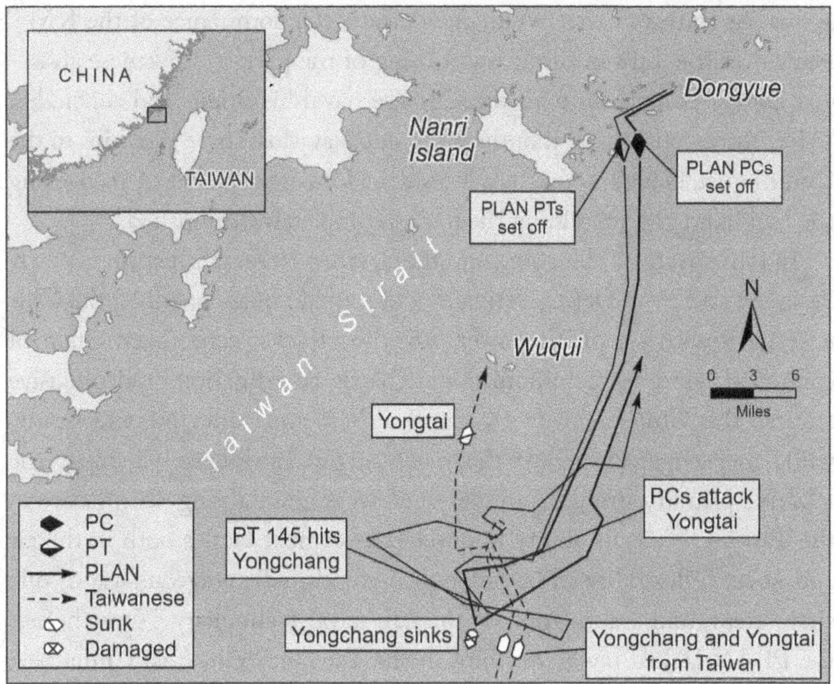


MAP 5. The Battle of East Chongwu, 1965

deck and rapidly fired 2,000 shells within several minutes.[74] Around 12:30 a.m., one of the PTs reached *Yongchang* within four cable lengths and fired two torpedoes within three hundred meters. One of them hit *Yongchang* and it began to sink. At 1:06 a.m., *Yongchang* (PG 61) sank about fifteen nautical miles south of Wuqiu. Soon after the battle, two U.S. destroyers from the Seventh Fleet (or Task Force 72), USS *O'Brien* (DD 725) and USS *Leonard F. Mason* (DD 852), arrived and rescued the captain and fifteen officers and sailors from the water.[75]

From 1962 to 1966, the PLA Navy sank thirty-five Taiwanese boats and ships and captured twenty-six to stop Taiwan's harassment and sabotage.[76] The domestically designed and produced new PCs and PTs maintained the PLAN's initiative in the Taiwan Strait, developed its combat tactics both in the air and at sea, and allowed it to take advantage of offshore areas for battle opportunities. Naval Command College's Gao Xiaoxing and other PLAN historians argue, "Further, the three naval defeats came as severe blows to the KMT Navy in Taiwan, altering the military balance across the Taiwan Strait. With the defeats, the dominance of the KMT Navy over the Taiwan Strait was a thing of the past."[77] Taiwanese strategist Zhong Jian agrees with the Chinese naval historians and concludes, "After three consecutive months when our Navy lost three warships to the Communist Navy's ambushes, President Chiang's dream of recovering the mainland and rebuilding the nation completely diminished."[78]

In retrospect, Liu Huaqing and the Seventh Research Institute's newly designed and manufactured frigates and torpedo boats provided the Chinese navy with speed, firepower, surprise attacks, centralized chain of command, land-sea communications, battle coordination, and offensive tactics. The Chinese-made PCs and TPs seemed effective and deadly while they engaged against the much larger Taiwanese warships. The PLAN's primary strengths in 1961–1966 were maintaining its initiative in the Taiwan Strait, its ability to develop its combat tactics both in the air and at seas, flexibility in obstruction methods, advantageous use of offshore areas, and assimilation of Russian naval technology. Nevertheless, the PLAN lacked major warships in the Taiwan Strait, East China Sea, and South China Sea, and was not capable of far sea operation as a strategic naval force yet in the late 1960s.

## STRATEGIC SHIFT: DESTROYER, SUBMARINE, AND SUBCHASER

In January 1965, the Seventh Research Institute came under China's Sixth Machinery Ministry (responsible for shipbuilding). Liu Huaqing was appointed as vice minister of the Sixth Machinery Ministry while continuing to run the Seventh Research Institute. Initially, Liu Huaqing strongly opposed the merge of his research institute into China's shipping industry.[79] However, he soon realized that he was able to lead not only China's warship research, but also the country's shipbuilding industry as a deputy cabinet member in the State Council. He understood that naval development reflected China's industrial capabilities and demonstrated the country's progress in terms of modernization. Naval modernization required solid economic foundation and strong leadership to mobilize nationwide efforts. He believed both CCP mechanism and PRC administration could be instrumental in leading the pathway to a modern navy.

In August 1966, Liu Huaqing was promoted to vice chairman of CSTIND at a three-star admiral level. He became one of the top defense industrial leaders. He worked directly under Marshal Nie Rongzhen, who as CSTIND chief was responsible for China's strategic weapons programs, including atomic bombs, missiles, satellites, and nuclear submarines.[80] John W. Lewis and Xue Litai point out that after Nie became the overall head of China's nuclear research and development, he played a vital role in supervising the entire strategic weapons program. When almost everything failed in China from the late 1950s to the late 1960s, he managed to save the country's nuclear, missile, and space programs, which "stand as a major accomplishment, a marked contrast to China's general fate in that decade."[81] Working closely with Marshal Nie Rongzhen, Liu Huaqing pushed several major naval projects through research and development from 1965 to 1971, including conventional submarines, nuclear submarines, destroyers, missile destroyers, submarine chasers, and ship-to-ship missiles. Gao Xiaoxing of the PLA Naval Command University claims Liu Huaqing made three important achievements in Chinese warship design and manufacturing in the late 1960s.

First, Liu's vision and leadership moved design and development away from small surface ships like patrol gunboats and torpedo speedboats to building medium-sized warships like destroyers and submarine hunters. He was not satisfied with the PLAN's small ships and weak firepower and argued such a backward naval force could not defend the country's oceanic sovereignty and would fail to protect China's maritime interests.[82] In April 1967, as vice chairman of CSTIND and vice minister of the Sixth Machinery Ministry, Liu Huaqing commenced the research, development, and manufacturing of four new warships, including destroyers, during the peak of the Cultural Revolution. He recalled that moment: "As a Chinese naval officer, I always dreamed of commanding our own new warships, patrolling our country's oceanic frontier, and sailing to the oceans all over the world. We are like 'addicted' to developing naval ships and equipment."[83] He chaired joint conferences that included research institutes, industrial ministries, and the navy to discuss the destroyers' development and manufacturing. From 1967, China constructed eight Type 051 *Lüda* destroyer keels, a copy of the Soviet *Kotlin*. Bussert and Elleman point out, "Most significant was the replacement of the torpedo tubes with two twin CSS-N-1 Styx SSM missile launchers, including an FC radar." Throughout the 1980s, the

PLAN received seventeen *Lüda*-class destroyers as "primary open-ocean surface combatants."[84]

In the late 1960s, the navy also received Type 037 and 037I submarine chasers, Type 027 large torpedo boats, Type 520T missile boats, and Type 082 minesweeping ships.[85] Under Liu's leadership, the Seventh Research Institute began designing China's own medium-sized submarine chasers. After imitating and reproducing several Russian sub-hunters (Model 6641, or 201M) as Type 0111 and 0112, the institute designed China's Type 037 submarine chasers in 1962. The first subchaser was launched at Guangzhou Huangpu Shipyard and tested in 1963.[86] After modifications and changes, the improved Type 037 was tested in 1964. A year later, the new subchaser was finalized, and Type 037 batch production began at both Huangpu and Shanghai Qiuxin Shipyards. The Chinese-made subchaser had a standard displacement of 375 tons, maximum speed of 30 knots, a double-barrel 57mm cannon, and two double-barrel 37mm guns. They were delivered to the navy in 1966.[87] The Chinese-made subchasers participated in the Battle of the Paracels (*Xisha* in Chinese and *Quan Dao Hoang Sa* in Vietnamese) in the South China Sea in 1974 and sank one frigate of the South Vietnamese Navy (VNN). In 1978, the Type 037 subchaser was further improved with new radar, depth charges, communication, and electronic systems.[88]

Second, in the 1960s, the Seventh Research Institute researched and developed China's own medium-sized, conventionally powered submarines. Before the Sino-Soviet split, the Soviet Union agreed to a compensated transfer to China of the license to build the new *Romeo*-class, SSK design, conventional torpedo submarine (Type 033) and *Golf*-class conventionally powered ballistic missile submarine (Type 035). In the early 1960s, the Type 033 submarine was manufactured at the Jiangnan Shipyard in Shanghai by using Russian technology accompanying production kit provided by the Soviet Union. Its submerged displacement is 1,881 tons, submerged maximum 300 meters within 600 hours, and submerged speed is 13 knots. Its main weapons are torpedoes.[89] In the early 1960s, the PLAN had ten submarines with a total of 20,000 tons. After the Sino-Soviet split in 1960, the Seventh Research Institute put together what the Soviet experts and advisors left behind and continued their own submarine design and manufacturing.

Third, Liu Huaqing emphasized firepower and replaced guns with missiles as the main weapon system for surface warships.[90] He studied missile technology and pushed the Seventh Institute to develop anti-ship, anti-air, and ship-to-shore missiles. Some of them became available and were delivered to the navy by 1966.[91] At CSTIND executive conference on December 20, 1967, the vice chairman told the nation's top defense scientists, experts, executives, and administrators that missile technology was their top priority.[92] Having learned from American missile technology during the Vietnam War, Liu worked with rocket scientists and experts to design small-sized naval missiles with advanced guidance systems and more firepower. In 1968, the *Shangyou-01* ship-to-ship missile was tested and finalized for production. It had a self-guided system, an effective fire range between eight and thirty-five miles, and a hit rate of 70 percent. That year, Chinese speedboats, frigates, and destroyers were equipped with the *Shangyou-01*.[93] In 1970, an improved *Haiying-01* anti-ship missile replaced the *Shangyou-01*. The new missile had a self-control, radar-guided system and a fire range between fifteen and fifty miles. Soon a *Haiying-02* missile became available with a new fire range of twenty to ninety-five miles.[94]

However, the PLA was not immune to the nationwide political struggle and massive purges during the "Great Proletarian Cultural Revolution" from 1966 to 1976. To fight his political rivals, Mao Zedong launched the Cultural Revolution on May 16, 1966, by issuing a Party Center's circular to purge the "bourgeois representatives who wormed their way into the party, government, and armed force."[95] Targeted at China's president, Liu Shaoqi, and Party Secretary General Deng Xiaoping, Mao used student organizations like the "Red Guards" to "bomb the bourgeois headquarters." In June, all K-12 schools, universities, and colleges dismissed classes and encouraged tens of millions of students to join the Red Guards and participate in the new revolution. In the summer, the Red Guards occupied schools, patrolled neighborhood streets, and controlled local businesses, public transportation, and mass media by attacking officials, administrators, and local party leaders. Their radical actions quickly devolved into a spree of home searches, kidnappings, detainment of residents, property confiscation, tortures, and even murder (see photo 4).

PHOTO 4. Liu Huaqing with his family in 1967 during the Cultural Revolution. 中国海军 [*China's Navy*], January 2, 2021

Marshal Lin Biao was elected the CCP vice chairman at a plenary session of the party's Eighth National Congress on August 12, 1966, second only to Mao. Later that month, Lin Biao called the PLA to participate in the Cultural Revolution through "three months of turmoil." In October, the PLA high command dismissed all classes in the military academies, naval colleges, and aviation institutes to allow cadets to join the Red Guards in the revolution. Soon the Red Guards seized school administrations, attacked PLA headquarters and departments in Beijing, and kidnapped generals, admirals, and their families. By 1967, it was reported that there were 80,000 generals and officers detained and tortured. About 1,169 of them died of physical abuse, starvation, or by execution. PLAN political commissar Li Zuopeng, one of Lin Biao's loyalists, called for revolution in the navy, criticizing Fleet Admiral Xiao Jinguang and labeling Xiao's leadership as the "Rightists' Headquarters." Li orchestrated a "struggle between the two headquarters" in the navy, the "Leftist Headquarters" and "Rightist Headquarters." In 1966–1967, 258 senior naval officers above divisional command levels were dismissed, purged, or jailed. Twenty-three of them died by torture and two died in jail. Eleven committed suicide, including Vice Admiral Tao Yong, deputy commander of the PLAN and commander of the East Sea Fleet, and Rear Admiral Zhang Xuesi, chief of the staff of the PLAN.[96]

In early 1967, the situation worsened across the country as the Cultural Revolution entered the phase of a "total takeover" of the authorities. The Red Guards controlled government offices at all the levels, jailed officials, and administered provincial and local affairs. But various factions within the Red Guards had contradictory political orientations and different goals, often leading to violent internal conflicts resembling a civil war. To stop the national turmoil, Mao ordered the PLA to control the situation by "three supports and two militarizations" (support Leftist masses, manufacturing production, and agricultural production; and martial laws with military administration and training of civilians, "*Sanzhi liangjun*"). Mao employed the PLA to restore social and political order and to prevent a possible civil war in the country. On January 23, 1967, the Central Committee, CMC, State Council, and Central Cultural Revolution Leading Team, issued a joint directive about the PLA's new task. On March 19, the CMC ordered all PLA units fully engaged in the "three supports and two militaries" to stop armed conflicts and stabilize the social order across the country. Thereafter, tasking headquarters were established at regional and provincial commands, and tasking offices were opened at the army and divisional levels.

Moving to center stage and under Lin's command, the Chinese military replaced civilian governments at the provincial, district, county, and city levels through its military administration, or the "Military Administrative Committee," from 1967 to 1972. The PLA used its officers as administrators for schools, factories, companies, villages, and farms.[97] More than 2.8 million officers and soldiers participated in the tasks. By February 1967, military administration assumed control of nearly 7,000 enterprises including mass media, defense industry, law enforcement, foreign affairs, transportation, finance, and other pivotal activities. By 1967, the PLA administered all universities, colleges, high schools, and elementary schools across the country. The military teams also organized professors, teachers, administrators, and students for military training and daily drills. The PLA takeover promoted military-civilian integration and contributed to more favorable conditions for defense industry militarization in China.[98]

**STRATEGIC THINKER: NUCLEAR SUBMARINES**

The PLAN's intervention in the Vietnam War shocked Chinese admirals not only because Liu Huaqing quickly realized the disparity between Russian-made ships and weapons and American naval technology, but also because he knew the technological gap between Chinese and U.S. naval technology had widened from five years in the Korean War to twenty years in the Vietnam War. The technology gap caused Chinese naval casualties in the air and coastal defense in North Vietnam.[99]

From 1965 to 1969, Liu focused his effort on the designs and development of strategic ships and weapons like nuclear submarines and missile technology. According to Liu, "I have spent the best years of my entire life on our own nuclear submarines' design, development, experiment, manufacture, testing, commission, and combat-readiness."[100] He had a long-term plan for China's nuclear submarine research and development since "it took eight years for the U.S., ten years for the Soviet Union, and planned for thirteen years for France developing their nuclear submarines." China needed to start its "nuclear submarine R&D as soon as possible," as Liu suggested in 1963.[101] As the president of the Seventh Research Institute, Liu Huaqing establish the 15th Research Institute for nuclear submarine's R&D, including nuclear power system, submarine design and testing, and missile technology. On March 13, 1965, the Second and Sixth Machinery Ministries proposed establishing the Joint Institute of Nuclear Submarine to design and manufacture nuclear submarines. The Party Center approved the nuclear submarine proposal later that month.

China's first nuclear bomb test on October 16, 1964, promoted its nuclear-powered submarine research and development. Beijing's limited nuclear deterrence strategy aimed at attacking vulnerable enemy targets, with fewer bombs, when making reprisals. The basic strategic thinking limited the use of nuclear weapons to achieve an asymmetrical balance with formidable enemies that had many nuclear warheads. Thereby, China's few nuclear bombs would deter enemies from attacking China with nuclear weapons. To pursue such a limited nuclear deterrence strategy, China required second-strike capabilities and the ideal reliable means employed nuclear-powered, missile-bearing submarines to provide a concealed nuclear retaliation under water. After China's first successful nuclear test in 1964, Liu Huaqing and his institute also worked on research and development of China's nuclear-powered submarines. In 1974, China launched a Type 091 *Han*-class nuclear submarine, the first nuclear-powered SSN in Asia.

While leading nuclear submarine research at the Seventh Research Institute and the Sixth Machinery Ministry, Liu Huaqing drafted a proposal for nuclear submarine development and submitted it to the Central Special Committee on March 13, 1965.[102] As the chairman of the CCP Central Special Commission, Premier Zhou Enlai held a civil-military hearing in Beijing on March 20–21 that included the research institutes, universities, PLAN, and the three machinery ministries (the First, Second, and Sixth Machinery Ministries) under the State Council.[103] The testimony convinced the Central Special Commission that China was ready for its own nuclear submarines development. After the hearing, Zhou Enlai chaired twenty-two nuclear submarine working conferences from 1965 to 1970, evaluating progress, discussing issues, coordinating collective efforts, and solving administrative and material problems. Cole points out, "Beijing invested heavily in developing nuclear-armed missiles and the nuclear-powered submarines," and considered them as the "national projects."[104] As vice chairman of CSTIND, Liu continued leading the nuclear submarine's manufacturing, tests, and improvement from beginning to end.

On July 10, 1965, the Sixth Machinery Ministry and the Seventh Research Institute reported a detailed plan about organization, management, resources, and technology for nuclear submarine development. The project included two submarine types. The first type was a torpedo nuclear submarine, to be launched in 1972. The second was a missile nuclear submarine. In August 1965, the Central Special Commission approved the nuclear submarine plan. In 1966, the CMC issued the "Third Five-Year Plan for National Defense Industry," which included development and manufacture of nuclear submarines. From then on, Liu Huaqing remained in his leadership position throughout the entire research, tests, production, and assessment process.

In November 1966, the Joint Institute of Nuclear Submarine finished its first design.[105] From December 7 to 10, Marshal Nie Rongzhen chaired an assessment conference, including the navy, all industrial ministries and research institutes to evaluate the design, provide improvement suggestions, and discuss how to cope with the chaotic first year of the Cultural Revolution. Vice premier and CMC vice chairman Nie Rongzhen militarized the nuclear research institutes to save the researchers and protect the programs. The most serious campaign against the intellectuals and academics since Mao founded the PRC in 1949 occurred in 1966. In 1967, Marshal Nie sent PLA troops to all research institutes and nuclear testing facilities and transferred most civilian employees into military service.

Thereby, nuclear submarine development and production continued throughout the Cultural Revolution. The first step of nuclear submarine research focused on a nuclear power system, which was decided by Premier Zhou and the Central Special Commission's conferences. The Sixth Machinery Ministry was charged with design and manufacturing of the nuclear power system for submarines. As the vice minister in charge of research and development, Liu Huaqing organized and chaired several research conferences and signed numerous documents facilitating and coordinating the nuclear power system's development with hundreds of research institutes, experimental labs, and testing facilities from 1966 to 1969.[106] On November 23, 1968, construction of the torpedo nuclear submarine began at Bohai Shipyard in Huludao, Hebei. As the first *Han*-class Type 91 attack submarine, it was completed in April 1969. From July 23 to August 28, 1970, its nuclear reactor was tested and reached designed levels. On December 26, 1970, China's first nuclear-powered submarine launched with its hull number as 401. After a few delays, its trial voyage lasted from 1972 to 1974.

During the torpedo nuclear submarine's manufacturing, Liu Huaqing also commenced research and design of missile nuclear submarines from 1967 to 1972. He chaired the first meeting on March 18, 1967, to plan the missile development details, divide the assignments, and concentrate the resources. Liu planned to finish the design, manufacturing, and land tests in 1970. Underwater tests would then take place in 1971.

In retrospect, from 1961 to 1969, Liu Huaqing's naval research, innovation, and development took advantage of the PLA's party-army, or "party in uniform," status and greatly expanded its utilization of civil-military integration. His naval research institute and national defense industry commission mobilized civilian professionals and utilized national resources for their strategic weapon programs by centralizing the nation's science and technology development. China's nuclear programs from 1964 to 1969 were characterized by centralization and bureaucratic power, which guaranteed the program's success. The country was willing and able to focus on its defense-oriented innovation and nuclear weapon development. In the meantime, however, our findings also explore the reasons and factors for the PLA's constraints and limits on military technology improvement. Although the chapter captures the essence of successive generations of the PLA while illuminating the patterns of its modernization, it shows such a military transformation demanded an industrialized economy and supportive society. The major features of the principal existing social characteristics of the PLA as it was confronted by the superpowers in the Cold War failed in adapting significantly to the modern military system during this period.

CHAPTER 3

# NAVY BUILDER
## *From the Weak to the Strong*

The PLA experienced its most dangerous and turbulent decade as Chinese armed forces fought simultaneous wars against the United States and the Soviet Union from the second half of the 1960s to the early 1970s. Starting in 1965, the PLA sent 430,000 troops to Vietnam and Laos to fight a "limited war" against U.S. armed forces until 1973. From 1969 to 1972, the PLA fought Soviet forces along the Sino-Russian border in northwestern Xinjiang and northeastern Heilongjiang. The Soviet Union deployed up to 48 divisions along the border, constituting nearly 1 million troops. Reportedly, Moscow considered using a "preemptive nuclear strike" against Beijing.[1] China was on the brink of a nuclear showdown with the Soviet Union.

The decade from 1968 to 1978 was the most crucial for the CCP and PRC as the Party Center experienced at least four major political earthquakes. Each political crisis tremendously impacted Communist rule in China. The first political conflict emerged between Mao Zedong and Lin Biao in 1970, after the former was officially named Mao's successor at the CCP Ninth National Congress in 1969. The power struggle peaked after Lin's son attempted to assassinate Mao. On September 13, 1971, Defense Minister Lin and his family fled the country. Their plane apparently crashed in Mongolia, conveniently killing everyone on board. The second political crisis occurred between Deng Xiaoping and Maoist leaders in Beijing. Mao Zedong returned Deng to the Party Center as the PLA's chief of general staff and vice premier in 1973. Deng's pragmatic policy upset radical leaders, including Mao's wife, Jiang Qing. Mao supported his wife, dismissed Deng for the second time, and launched the "Criticizing Deng and Fighting Back the Rightist Reversal Attempt" movement. The third political earthquake occurred after Mao died in September 1976. Mao's successor, Hua Guofeng, and Marshal Ye Jianying arrested the Maoist

"Gang of Four," including Jiang Qing and Mao's cousin Mao Yuanxin, in an October military coup. The fourth political earthquake occurred in 1978 when Deng Xiaoping made his third return as China's new leader. Deng initiated economic reform and opening relations with the outside world. In addition, the worst literal earthquake in the PRC's history occurred on July 28, 1976, in Tangshan, Hebei, and killed more than 242,000 people.

Nevertheless, the decade would see a shift in Chinese naval modernization. In 1968–1969, Mao Zedong changed his security concerns from the United States to the Soviet Union as China's major threat. Mao's strategic shift led to President Richard Nixon's visit to China in 1972 and the normalization of Sino-Japanese relations by 1973. The Sino-American rapprochement also resulted in the United Nations' acceptance of the PRC's membership as well, replacing Taiwan as one of five of its permanent members of the UN Security Council (UNSC). Though the Pacific was opening for China's new diplomacy, trade, and exchanges, the navy's lack of capability to face new challenges and missions concerned Mao. In 1973, Mao resurrected Deng Xiaoping's political career to help Premier Zhou Enlai with four modernizations (industry, agriculture, science and technology, and national defense). Deng Xiaoping prepared a military reform in the mid-1970s with an emphasis on naval research and development, including larger warships, nuclear submarines, and new weapon systems. In 1974, the Chinese navy was tested when it fought its first foreign naval war in the South China Sea against much larger, U.S.-made warships.

The chapter explains how Liu Huaqing comprehended the high command's historical shift, facilitated Mao and Deng's ideas for a large navy, and commenced building a strong navy from 1969 to 1981. After returning to the navy in 1969, Liu was tremendously pressured and politically challenged after eight years of absence. As PLAN shipbuilding chief from 1969 to 1975, Liu centralized naval research and development, concentrated national resources in manufacturing and testing, and utilized military power to guarantee the shipbuilding programs' success. Frustrated by bureaucratic red tape and politics and dissatisfied with naval capability, he criticized naval command's ten-year plan (1975–1985) and demanded reform for a modern navy. In 1975, Liu took a huge career risk and wrote directly to Deng Xiaoping in his famous 10,000-character "policy statement" of the Chinese navy's modernization. Liu proposed a major development plan that included designing and manufacturing 40,000-ton aircraft carriers, 4,000-ton destroyers, and 2,000-ton frigates.[2]

As a reformer and a modern navy builder, Liu's vision—led by naval research and development for the PLAN's future—impressed Deng Xiaoping. After he left the navy again in 1975, Liu was able to put Deng's reform ideas into a science-technology-led reform when he served as a member of the core leadership team at the China Academy of Sciences (CAS) from 1975 to 1977, the vice chairman of CSTIND from 1977 to 1981, and eventually assistant to Deng Xiaoping, when Deng made his third return to power and served as the PLA's chief of the general staff, CMC vice chairman, and vice premier in 1978.

## STRATEGIC SHIFT AND NEW NAVAL DEVELOPMENT

After China's ship research, design, and manufacture planning were transferred from CSTIND to the navy, Liu Huaqing returned to the navy in 1969. Although Chinese naval leadership was traumatized during the Cultural Revolution, Liu took the opportunity and made significant progress in naval research and development to continue PLAN modernization from 1969 to 1975. New opportunity came when Mao Zedong changed his security concerns from the United States to the Soviet Union. In October 1968, Marshal Lin Biao, China's defense minister, warned the army and the country that Soviet forces would invade China soon. At the CCP's Ninth National Congress in 1969, Lin Biao made the keynote speech and called for "preparing a war, fighting it early; fighting it in large-scale; and fighting a nuclear war against the Soviet Union and the United States."[3] Major General Xu Yan of the PLA National Defense University argues that Moscow's intention to overthrow Mao Zedong and change Beijing's leadership was one of the reasons for Mao launched a nationwide anti-Soviet movement in the 1960s.[4]

In late 1968, Marshal Chen Yi argued in his strategy report that the United States and Soviet Union had different intentions, and that the Soviet Union was China's main enemy.[5] In February 1969, Mao chaired a high command meeting to discuss China's new strategy. Premier Zhou Enlai and Marshals Lin Biao, Chen Yi, Xu Xiangqian, Nie Rongzhen, and Ye Jianying agreed that American power had declined because of its failures in Vietnam and in other parts of the world. As the United States withdrew from Vietnam, the Soviet Union filled in the power vacuum and replaced the United States as a new "imperialist" aggressor. Therefore, China, like other Asian countries, became a target and victim of the new, aggressive, "Soviet socialist imperialist" policy.[6] Nicholas Khoo argues, "The threat represented by the Soviet Union was the central and overriding concern of Chinese foreign policymakers."[7]

To avoid two wars against both superpowers, Beijing intended to undermine the rising power of the Soviets in Asia by playing the "American card" and opening a new relationship with the United States.[8] Chen Jian argues that "it was Zhou [Enlai] who made the decision" to resume the Sino-American ambassadorial talks in Warsaw after the new Nixon administration made the proposal in early 1969.[9] Both Nixon and his national security advisor Henry Kissinger saw an improvement in relationship with China as beneficial to the United States as it would, in the short run, help get America out of the Vietnam War, and, in the long term, dramatically enhance the strategic position of the United States in a global confrontation vis-à-vis the Soviet Union.[10] It paved the way for Nixon's visit of Beijing in February 1972. In September, only months after Nixon's visit, China and Japan established formal diplomatic relations. Thereafter, the two countries went further and signed a treaty of friendship and mutual cooperation, including trade, foreign investment, technology, and cultural exchanges.

From then on, Beijing perceived the Pacific less with hostility, containment, and threat and more as an open, cooperative, and beneficial opportunity. New questions emerged: Was China was ready for oceangoing exploration and adventures? Was the PLAN able to support and protect China's new foreign policy and international trade? Mao's strategic shift provided a new opportunity for naval development and modernization. On June 13, 1969, the navy established the Office of Ship Development and Manufacturing (also known as the "Ship Office," a divisional level office in the Naval Commanding Headquarters) with Liu Huaqing as its inaugural chief until 1975.[11] Liu continued research-led ship development and manufacturing, balanced high-tech with conventional equipment, and concentrated national resources on new, larger warship manufacturing.

After becoming the navy's shipbuilding chief, Liu Huaqing chaired a national naval ship development conference in October–November 1969 to reorganize the country's ship research and manufacturing. There were

284 research institutes, naval labs, factories, shipyards, testing sites, PLA regional commands, and provincial and local governments in attendance for thirty-eight days. At the naval ship development conference, Liu continued emphasizing the civil-military integration, branch coordination, one-stop research, streamlined development, and centralized manufacturing. Centralization helped the design, development, and manufacturing of China's new warships in the 1970s. The military mobilized civilian professionals and utilized national resources for its strategic weapons programs by centralizing the nation's science and technology development during the Cultural Revolution (1966–1976). The conference began a new era of Chinese naval modernization. In December 1970, Liu Huaqing was appointed as deputy chief of the PLAN in charge of naval ship development and manufacturing.

The change of Mao Zedong's mindset toward the Pacific Ocean determined China's new direction for a powerful navy beginning in 1969. The Cultural Revolution had created Mao Zedong's personality cult and established a totalitarian government. In the highly centralized Maoist system, other Chinese leaders showed their loyalty by carrying out Mao's ideas. In early 1970, Defense Minister Lin Biao followed Mao's strategic shift and ordered the navy to start aircraft carrier research and development. When the Soviet Union refused to help China develop the nuclear-powered submarine after the Sino-Soviet split, Mao Zedong famously said, "Even if it takes us 10,000 years, we must manufacture our own nuclear-powered submarines!"[12] The chairman saw a strong navy as a vital of China's great power status in the Pacific. Premier Zhou Enlai chaired twenty-two national meetings from 1969 to 1972 to organize, supervise, and evaluate China's nuclear submarine design, manufacturing, and testing.

At the navy's Ship Office from 1969 to 1975, Liu Huaqing focused on research and development of new missile destroyers, nuclear submarines, and aircraft carrier. He chaired several planning meetings in 1967, to discuss the missile research and development. The meetings divided assignments among three research institutes and aimed to finish design, trial production, and land tests by 1970. After his plan was approved, the Seventh Institute also researched and developed anti-ship and shore-to-ship missiles. Beginning in 1968, China built its first guided missile destroyer at Dalian Shipyard. In 1970, an improved Haiying-01 ship-to-ship missile replaced Shangyou-01. The new missile used a self-controlled radar-guided system and could effectively fire between fifteen and fifty miles. Soon the "Haiying-02" missile became available with a new firing range of twenty to ninety-five miles.[13]

In May 1970, Liu Huaqing organized an executive meeting to coordinate the Type 051 missile destroyers' tests, finalization, and sea trial. The Chinese-designed missile destroyer *Lüda* Type 051 had a standard displacement of 3,500 tons, maximum speed of 36 knots, six SSM missile launchers, twenty guns from 130mm to 25mm, and maximum cruise distance of 4,000 nautical miles.[14] Several dozen research institutes, four machinery ministries, and thirteen naval units attended. The first Type 051 missile destroyer was launched in July 1970 with its hull number as 105. This type of the missile destroyer became the PLAN's star warship equipped with new missile technology and electronics system.[15] On December 31, 1971, Liu Huaqing commissioned the PLAN Ship 105 at the Lüshun Naval Base. In February 1972, Marshal Xu Xiangqian boarded the destroyer 105 with Cambodian prince Sihanouk and PLAN commander fleet admiral Xiao Jinguang. They sailed from Lüshun Naval Base to Dalian and observed a naval exercise. The new kind of Chinese-made missile destroyer amazed the Cambodian guests. In September 1973, Marshal Ye Jianying visited the missile destroyer and watched the missile firing exercise. In August 1974, Marshal Zhu De visited the destroyer 105 with Xiao Jinguang and the destroyer sailed for three hours to observe a naval exercise.[16] Eventually, the CMC and State Council approved the Type 051's production finalization on February 3, 1975. By the end of the 1970s, the PLAN received seventeen *Lüda*-class missile destroyers as "primary open-ocean surface combatants" before 1993.[17] In the 1970s, the navy also manufactured improved Type 051G missile destroyers.

As naval shipbuilding chief, Liu Huaqing firmly believed that both nuclear submarines and aircraft carriers reflected the magnitude of China's industrial and technological development. Under Premier Zhou Enlai and Marshal Nie Rongzhen's leadership, Liu continued work on conventional submarine improvements, nuclear submarine manufacturing, and nuclear missile submarine development. In the 1960s, the Type 033 torpedo submarine was manufactured at the Jiangnan Shipyard in Shanghai using Russian technology. The first Type 033 was delivered to the PLAN in 1965.

Its submerged displacement was 1,881 tons and submerged speed 13 knots. In April 1974, the first Chinese-made Type 035 *Ming*-class diesel submarine launched in Wuhan. Its submerged displacement was 2,325 tons and submerged speed 18 knots. In August, it was commissioned into the PLAN's battle array. By 1975, the second Type 035 was delivered to the navy. This marked a new era of China's own, self-designed and manufactured, conventionally powered *Romeo*-class submarines.[18] From 1972 to 1982, the PLAN's submarine force increased from 35 to 100 conventional submarines.

The PLAN worked for nearly thirty years toward sailing on the open ocean, as this had been the dream of the Chinese leaders. On the last day of 1976, a Chinese submarine with hull number 252 surfaced in the Pacific Ocean. From the 1950s to 1970s, due to technological limitations, patrols could only be conducted near shorelines and within the first island chain. By the late 1970s, the Chinese navy could move from the yellow waters of the near shore to the blue waters of the far sea. Captain Xu Zhiming and his submarine 252 cruised the Pacific underwater for 30 days over 3,200 nautical miles. On January 24, 1977, the sub 252 returned to its base in Qingdao. By opening new routes for the Chinese navy, the 252's voyage was a landmark for the PLAN's sailing history. It indicated China's new capabilities in shipbuilding, navigation technology, and long-distance communication and logistics. These oceangoing voyages convinced Liu Huaqing that the Chinese navy was no longer a "small navy," constrained to traversing only the near sea; it had become a modern navy, capable of reaching the oceans' deep waters. In April 1980, the submarine 256 expanded its range and sailed into the Pacific. Afterward, more submarines sailed the Pacific and reached the second island chain.[19]

During the conventional torpedo submarine's manufacturing, Liu Huaqing continued research and design on China's missile submarines, nuclear submarines, and nuclear missile submarines. Construction of the first *Han*-class Type 91 nuclear-powered attack submarine began in 1968. It was completed in April 1969 at Bohai Shipyard in Huludao. From July 23 to August 28, 1970, the nuclear reactor was tested and reached designed levels. On December 26, China's first nuclear-powered submarine launched with hull number 401. In May 1971, the nuclear submarine began its maiden voyage, and underwater tests took place in 1972.[20] It underwent more than twenty trial voyages, 6,000 nautical miles in total. In August 1974, it was commissioned into the PLAN's battle array as the *Long March 1*. After completing all testing, the first nuclear missile submarine launched in late 1976.[21] The second *Han*-class nuclear submarine began its construction in 1975 and became operational in 1980 with hull number 402.

In the late 1960s, Mao Zedong's strategic shift led to a détente with Washington and Tokyo as Beijing prepared for new international trade and exchanges across the Pacific. China needed naval support and far seas protection for its oceangoing development. By early 1970, Marshal Lin Biao followed Mao's strategic shift, ordering the navy to start aircraft carrier research and development. In April, naval leader Li Zuopeng chaired the PLAN's party committee meeting and explained the significance and urgency of building China's own aircraft carrier. He told naval commanders that "the chief [Lin Biao] is very happy to see the strategic change and new international situations."[22] Then, Vice Admiral Li Zuopeng proposed the aircraft carrier's research and construction. The meeting instructed the PLAN Shipbuilding Office to work on a feasibility study and report it to the high command as soon as possible.

On May 5, 1970, as the chief of the Shipbuilding Office, Liu Huaqing called for an aircraft carrier design and development conference, including CSTIND, Third Research Institute (missile research), Sixth Research Institute (aviation research), Seventh Research Institute, First and Sixth Machinery Ministries, navy, and air force. On May 16, Liu drafted the plan and submitted it to the Navy Command. The "Preliminary Proposal of Building an Aircraft Carrier" became the first official plan detailing China's aircraft carrier construction. Liu Huaqing first, provided an overview of American and Russian aircraft carriers' capabilities, technologies, manufacturing cost, and service problems. Second, he recommended China initially build an escort aircraft carrier with a displacement of 30,000 tons, speed of 35 knots, carrying 50 jet fighters and antisubmarine helicopters for both air and water control. The fighters would take off and land vertically to save in size, cost, and time of the carrier's manufacturing. The carrier would be armed with mid-range anti-ship missiles, antiaircraft missiles, and different cannons. Third, Liu examined the issues of carrier fighters, electronic equipment, power systems, and weaponry. He planned to finish the overall design in 1971, begin construction in 1972, and start sea trials in 1973.[23]

On May 27, 1970, Liu Huaqing chaired a carrier development conference to discuss his plan, designating it "Project 707." Liu assigned carrier design to the Seventh Research Institute, two carrier airplanes' designs to the Sixth Research Institute, and ship-based missiles development to the Third Research Institute. Rear Admiral Zheng Ming recalled the conference as a "historical moment in China's carrier history" from a "carrier dream" to a "carrier reality."[24] From July 20 to August 5, the navy's Shipbuilding Office organized a national high-tech shipbuilding conference, including 729 admirals, generals, governors, mayors, company CEOs, scientists, and experts from 333 military and civilian enterprises, to discuss the issues and schedule of nuclear submarines and aircraft carrier manufacture.[25] On September 28, the Shipbuilding Office chaired another executive meeting to reschedule the completion of carrier design by the end of 1972, the beginning of construction in 1973, and the launch of the carrier toward the end of the Fourth Five-Year Plan (1971–1975).[26] Before the end of 1970, Liu Huaqing submitted "The Fourth Five-Year Plan for China's Naval Ships Research, Development, and Manufacturing," in which the aircraft carrier was prioritized second only to nuclear submarines in China's high-tech naval development from 1971 to 1975.[27] Nevertheless, the September 13 Lin Biao incident ended Liu's plan for aircraft carrier development.

In 1970, a new political conflict emerged between Mao Zedong and Lin Biao in Beijing due to their different worldviews, defense strategies, and personalities. Their contradictions erupted at the Ninth Party Central Committee's Second Plenum in August 1970. Fang Zhu argues, "By disagreeing with Mao during the plenum, for whatever reason, Lin had provided Mao with hard evidence of his political ambition. The relationship between the two men had deteriorated to the point of open confrontation."[28] Threatened by Lin's ambitions and control of the military, Mao decided to remove Lin from leadership. Lin and his family felt Mao directed his political spearhead against them. The power struggle intensified after Lin's son attempted to assassinate Mao. On September 13, 1971, the Lin family plane fell from the sky and crashed in Mongolia, killing all aboard.[29]

After Marshal Lin Biao's death, there was another top-down purge through the PLA. On September 24, the Central Committee dismissed all key members of Lin's group from their positions. On October 3, Mao dissolved the CMC Executive Office, formerly controlled by Lin, and created a new CMC office under Marshal Ye Jianying. On the next day, Mao chaired the new office's first meeting, stating that Lin had controlled the armed forces for more than ten years and created many problems for the military. "The PLA must unify and prepare for war."[30] On October 6, the Central Committee issued a report regarding the "criminal activities of the Lin Biao clique." Lin was accused of forming an "anti-revolutionary clique," conducting a military coup, planning the assassination of Mao, and betraying his country. In mid-October, the document circulated to all local CCP branch secretaries. On the 24th, the Central Committee sent it to all party members throughout the land.[31] Thereafter, Marshal Ye Jianying, with consultation from Premier Zhou Enlai, took charge of the PLA's daily affairs. This Zhou-Ye system replaced the Lin system of 1960–1971.[32]

One of those purged was Vice Admiral Li Zuopeng, one of Lin's lieutenants who had controlled the PLAN for ten years (1962–1971).[33] Li Zuopeng's naval programs, including Project 707, were terminated, but China's carrier dream did not die with Lin Biao. The ideas and urgent need for an aircraft carrier enjoyed continued endorsement by Chinese leaders. For example, on October 25, 1973, Zhou Enlai imparted to his foreign guests: "Without [our] aircraft carrier, South Vietnam occupied our Nansha (Spratly) and Xisha (Paracel) Islands. We cannot send our naval force to fight with bayonet[s] again. I worked on [China's] military and politics for my entire life, I haven't seen a Chinese aircraft carrier. I am not reconciled without seeing a carrier!"[34] Zhou Enlai died in January 1976.

In March 1972, Admiral Su Zhenhua, former PLAN political commissar, was released from custody by Mao's order and returned to the navy's leadership from 1973 to 1979. Su Zhenhua had been dismissed from all his positions in June 1967 and sent to a labor camp in the mountains of Hunan as a farm field hand for nearly five years.[35] After replacing Li Zuopeng and reassuming his position as PLAN political commissar in 1973, the CMC appointed Su Zhenhua as the navy's first deputy commander on May 22, 1974. On September 21, Admiral Su conducted a large-scale naval review for China's defense minister Marshal Ye Jianying that included Chinese-made conventionally powered submarines, nuclear submarines, guided missile destroyers, missile frigates, and naval fighter-bombers.

By the late 1970s, the navy had improved Type 053K and Type 053H frigates, and new Type-H2 missile frigates. In December 1975, Chinese-made

Type 053H missile frigates went into service with a standard displacement of 1,469 tons, 100mm cannons, 37mm guns, ship-to-ship missiles, and depth charge launchers. The navy also received Type 037 and Type 037I submarine chasers, Type 027 large torpedo boats, Type 520T missile boats, and Type 082 minesweeping ships.[36] The submarine chasers and minesweepers played an important role in the 1972–1973 minesweeping operations in North Vietnam and the 1974 Battle of the Paracel Islands against the South Vietnamese Navy in the South China Sea. The navy also developed and manufactured survey vessels, including salvage-and-rescue ships, rescue tugboats, comprehensive depot ships, mine layers, and other service ships for engineering, reconnoitering, transport, maintenance, medical care, and other tasks. The ocean survey vessels displaced more than 11,000 tons. The PLAN also developed new weapons and equipment for the Marine Corps and Navy Coastal Defense units. Thereby, the navy was equipped with a modern framework to carry out maritime combat operations, base defense operations, sea-based self-defense nuclear counterattack with near-shore combat as a focus and operational and tactical maneuvers as a complement. Guo Xiaoxing states, by that time, "the overall technological level of the PLAN's equipment and vessels rose to international levels."[37]

## THE VIETNAM WAR AND THE SOUTH CHINA SEA

From 1965 to 1973, the PLAN's participation in the Vietnam War allowed new opportunities to learn from the most advanced navy in the world, the U.S. Navy. The Chinese navy engaged in the Vietnam War in five operations: First, the navy sent its AAA troops to North Vietnam in air defense against U.S. warplanes in Operation Rolling Thunder. Second, the PLAN transported NVA (North Vietnam Army) troops to South Vietnam and delivered military supplies to the NLF (National Liberation Front, or Viet Cong) via a water route. Third, the Chinese navy transported PLA troops, weapons, ammunition, and logistics from China to North Vietnam. Fourth, the PLAN opened the "Ho Chi Minh Trail at Sea" to transport supplies from China to Cambodia and to South Vietnam via a sea route and the Sihanoukville Seaport. Fifth, the Chinese navy launched minesweeping operations at the major seaports of North Vietnam (see map 6).[38]

MAP 6. The Vietnam War, 1965–1973

During the naval operations in Vietnam, the PLAN collected information on U.S. naval and aviation technology. Field agents in South Vietnam and those near U.S. Navy bases in Thailand relayed information back to Hanoi where PLAN intelligence worked at the embassy.[39] Major U.S. naval bases were targeted by more than thirty NVA-assisted PLAN agents gathering information on U.S. and ARVN (Army of Vietnam, South Vietnam) naval technology from May 9 to November 28, 1968.[40] Chinese naval officers traveled to ARVN naval wreck sites and airplane crash sites to examine U.S. technology and problems. They also traveled to a few major seaports such as Da Nang and Hue in South Vietnam, reporting details of American naval technology and ARVN naval operations.[41] Among the naval research officers were five mine experts from the Seventh Research Institute. They were briefed by NVA counterparts and provided three types of American water mines captured by the Vietnamese, including MK-42, MK-50, and MK-52.[42] The Chinese tested mines and familiarized themselves with NVA mine-clearing equipment and techniques. After returning on June 26, 1969, the PLAN's shipbuilding office and research institute cohosted a conference on naval mine warfare, a new category in Chinese naval history.

Although Chinese naval leadership remained traumatized through the Cultural Revolution, the PLAN significantly developed and expanded its operations in Vietnam, including a minesweeping operation along the coast of North Vietnam from 1971 to 1973. In August 1971, Liu Huaqing organized a naval "Symposium on Anti-Water-Mine Equipment and Technology," including the First and Sixth Machinery Ministries and Seventh Research Institute. The symposium updated the PLAN's minesweeping capability, coordinated technological improvements among different units, and established a central factory for minesweeping equipment manufacturing and assembly. In addition to aquatic mine research and development, the naval conference developed China's Type 311 and later Type 312 mine dredgers, which would later prove useful during the minesweeping operations from 1972 to 1973.[43]

On May 8, 1972, President Richard Nixon announced the United States would mine the major harbors along North Vietnam's coast. Hours later, U.S. warships and planes began mine-laying operations. "Navy A-6 and A-7 bombers dropped 2,000-pound mines at the entrance to Hai Phong Harbor, beginning the isolation of the DRV from seaborne resupply."[44] All major seaports, including Haiphong, were totally blocked by mines, and the sea routes in and out of North Vietnam were paralyzed in less than ten days. During their emergency meeting in Beijing on May 9, the Vietnamese ambassador made an urgent request to Premier Zhou Enlai for China's immediate help in minesweeping. Zhou and Marshal Ye Jianying summoned Liu Huaqing and other naval officers to discuss a PLAN minesweeping plan that evening. On May 10, the Central Committee's Politburo met and approved the navy's plan to help the Vietnamese clear mines.[45] Mao Zedong approved the plan on May 20.

After the Zhou–Ye meeting on May 9, Liu Huaqing briefed Fleet Admiral Xiao Jinguang on his minesweeping research and plan. PLAN commander Xiao ordered the North and East Sea Fleets to form a minesweeping research team.[46] The PLAN's research team entered Vietnam on May 27 with three Type 312 and one Type 311 mine dredgers escorted by two warships and four supply vessels under the command of Zhang Shouying.[47] On May 30, Liu Huaqing and Zhang Ruiji, deputy chief of PLAN Logistics, met and discussed how to help North Vietnam sweep U.S. mines deployed in Haiphong Harbor. The meeting focused on operational coordination, offshore communication, minesweeping vessels, equipment, technological assistance, logistical support, and personnel. On June 4, Commodore Zhang Shouying reported to the Chinese embassy in Hanoi the research and operational plan.[48] Zhang and his team then departed for Beijing on June 6 to brief the PLAN Command on June 8.[49]

In July, the PLAN minesweeping fleet arrived in North Vietnam with twelve Type 312 minesweepers, four technology-support vessels, seven logistics vessels, and three escort frigates, with 1,380 sailors and soldiers.[50] The task force command's minesweeping operation used depth charges to clear mines and then guide commercial ships out of Haiphong Harbor. From late July, Fleet Commodore Zhang recalled, the Chinese minesweeping fleet worked closely with the North Vietnamese Navy.[51] Though they welcomed the large Chinese minesweeping force's arrival, NVA Navy Command disagreed with them after Chinese naval officers reported their plan to the Vietnamese.[52]

The North Vietnamese proposed prioritizing targets and made a joint plan with the Chinese on where and how to clear the mines. On August 2, the Vietnamese Navy Command held a joint operation conference and decided that the Chinese minesweeping fleet start its operation according to Vietnamese shipping priorities. Around 7 p.m. on August 12, the Chinese minesweeping operation began with the Chinese minesweeper's number MS 05 (Type 312) sailing to the Haiphong minefield. Next evening,

Vietnamese ship HQ 412 sailed to the same minefield for sweeping operations. HQ 412 minesweeper was one of the Chinese-made landing vessels transferred to the NVA Navy and remodeled into a minesweeping boat. After it successfully detonated one MK-52, HQ 412 hit another mine and sank with all its crew.[53] The Chinese and Vietnamese learned from the HQ 412's failure. On August 14, Chinese minesweepers MS-02, MS-04, and MS-05 successfully cleared and detonated five MK-52 mines.[54] Meanwhile, Fleet Commodore Zhang Zhouying transferred three Type 311 dredgers to the North Vietnamese Navy, and trained Vietnamese naval officers and sailors to operate them. The joint minesweeping improved the operation by doubling the number of mines discovered and destroyed.[55] It took another month for the port of Haiphong to reopen in October 1972. To accelerate the minesweeping, Liu Huaqing sent more minesweeping ships to North Vietnam on December 23.

After American troops pulled out of Vietnam in March 1973, the PLA high command took the opportunity for its South Sea Fleet (SSF) to seize disputed islands in the South China Sea from South Vietnam. Beijing's propaganda campaign started on January 11, 1974, when the PRC's Foreign Ministry issued an official statement claiming China's sovereignty over the Spratly (Nansha, or South Sandbar), Paracel (Xisha, West Sandbar), Macclesfield Bank (Zhongsha, Central Sandbar), and Pratas (Dongsha, East Sandbar) Islands with all their accompanying natural resources (see map 7).[56] On January 15, the ARVN navy (VNN, Vietnamese navy) sent one of their destroyers to the Paracel's Yongle Island. On the 16th, the Vietnamese destroyer HQ 16 (also known as *Li Changjie* in Chinese) shelled Ganquan Island, driving Chinese fishing boats out of the area. On the next day, ARVN transported soldiers to occupy Ganquan and Jinyin Islands and to remove the Chinese national flag, which had been erected two days earlier.

The PLA high command ordered the navy to engage the South Vietnamese navy at the Paracel Islands. SSF had only seven frigates capable of sailing to the disputed islands. However, five of them were assigned to the Vietnam War and unavailable for the island campaign. The other frigates were either overhauled or out of order. The remaining escort and patrol ships were small, about 300 tons each, with limited voyage capability and could not be used for naval operations in off-lying sea.[57] South

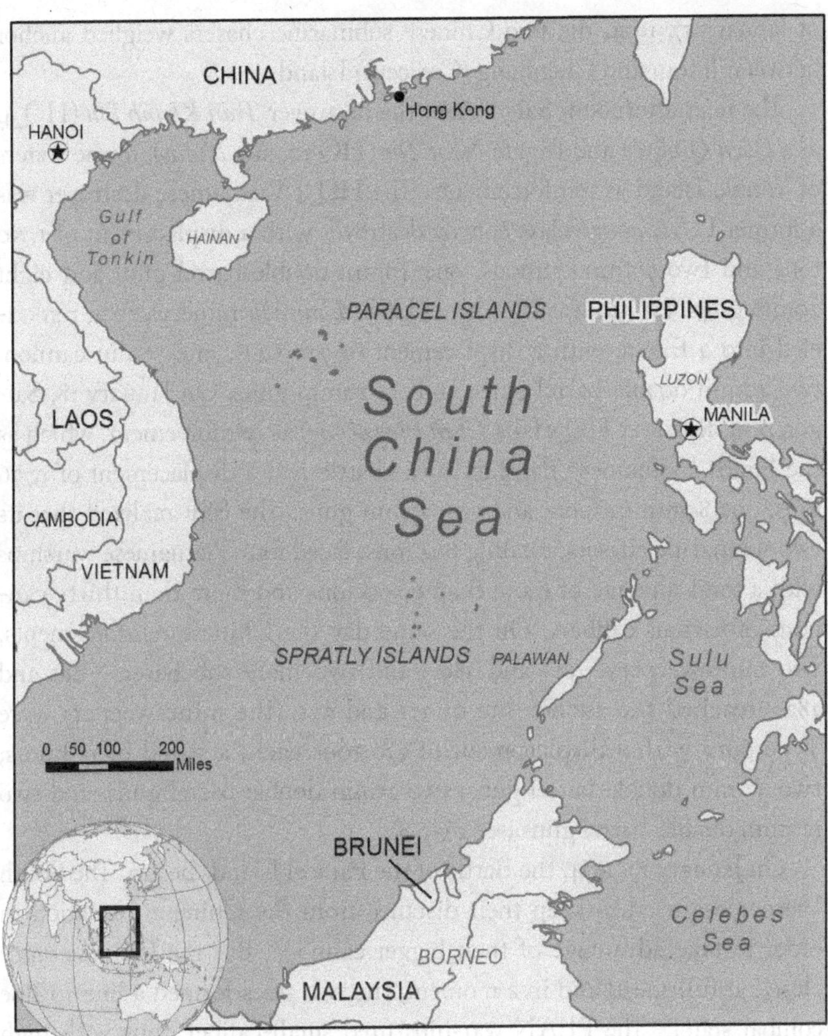


MAP 7. The South China Sea

Vietnamese destroyer HQ 16 had a displacement of 2,040 tons with a 127-mm cannon and 40mm double-barrel guns. The remaining SSF surface ships consisted of six Type 6604 (or 037) submarine chasers, which had just returned from Vietnam. SSF considered two submarine chasers, *Jinzhou* with ship hull number 271 and *Luzhou*, 274. The Chinese submarine hunters were 332 tons each with maximum speeds of 18 knots, in the best condition and fitted with the best equipment and weapons. On the morning of January 17, 1974, the two Chinese submarine chasers weighed anchor between Jinqin and Chenhang (Crescent) Islands.

The next afternoon, Saigon sent the destroyer *Tran Khanh Du* (HQ 4, aka *Chen Qingyu*) and frigate *Nhat Tao* (HQ 10, aka *Nutao*), to the waters of Yongle Island as reinforcements. The HQ 4 Vietnamese destroyer was a former U.S. *Savage*-class convoy destroyer with a displacement of 1,750 tons and two 76mm cannons, one 40mm double-barrel gun, and eight 20mm guns. HQ 10 was the former USS *Admirable* minesweeper, remodeled into a frigate with a displacement of 720 tons, one 76mm cannon, two 40mm double-barrel guns, and six 20mm guns. On January 18, Saigon sent destroyer HQ 5 (aka *Chen Pingzhong*) as reinforcement, which as the South Vietnamese flagship in the battle had a displacement of 1,776 tons, one 85mm cannon, and two 37mm guns. The SSF realized that its two submarine chasers, totaling 664 tons, faced four Vietnamese warships with a total tonnage of more than 6,300 tons and more than thirty cannons of various calibers. On the same day the Chinese reinforcements, two minesweepers—396 and 389—and two more subchasers—281 and 282—reached the anchor site of 271 and 274. The minesweepers were Type 6610 with a displacement of 570 tons each, a speed of 15 knots, two 37-mm double-barrel guns, two 25mm double-barrel guns, and two 12.5mm double-barrel guns (see map 8).

On January 19, 1974, the Battle of the Paracel Islands began. The South Vietnamese tried to keep their distance from the Chinese formation in order to take advantage of their bigger cannons. But the Chinese ships closed at full speed and in a moment, the two sides formed a line-to-line combat state.[58] The PLAN warships fired small-caliber guns with high firing rates at the Vietnamese.[59] The Chinese ship 271 found HQ 4 *Tran Khanh Du*'s dead zone and concentrated its fire on the bridge, cutting off its communications. Irreparably damaged by the Chinese submarine chasers, the Vietnamese HQ 4 fled to the open seas trailed by smoke.[60] Then, the Chinese ships concentrated their fire on *Nhat Tao* (HQ 10). The Chinese 281 and 282 moved to *Nhat Tao*'s starboard side and sprayed it with bullets and shells. Soon, the Vietnamese frigate caught fire. The Chinese 281 pursued the damaged *Nhat Tao*, which attempted to move to Antelope Reef, but failed. As their ship closed to within a dozen yards, the 281's crew peppered the South Vietnamese sailors with machine guns and grenades.

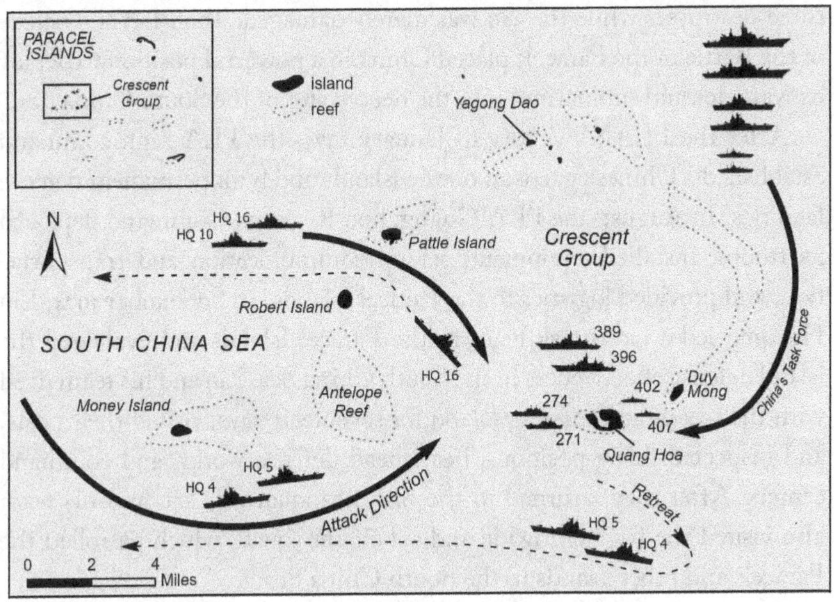


MAP 8. The Battle of the Paracel Islands, 1974

The Vietnamese frigate exploded and sank at 2:52 p.m. south of Antelope Reef. After a one-and-a-half-hour fight, the rest of the Vietnamese warships fled the Paracel Islands.[61]

After the VVN vessels left, on January 20, the Chinese began landing operations against the South Vietnamese troops defending the islands. Under gunfire from both warships and landing troops, ARVN soldiers on Robert Island surrendered. Those on Pattle and Money Islands continued a stubborn defense from several positions. Later that day, after Chinese troops took the beachhead, most of the South Vietnamese soldiers surrendered and laid down their weapons. During the Battle of the Paracels, more than one hundred ARVN officers and soldiers were killed or wounded, and forty-nine captured, including one American; sixty-seven Chinese sailors were wounded and eighteen killed.[62] The battle was the first time the Chinese navy conducted operations in the far sea. It was also the first time the PLAN fought a foreign navy since its establishment in 1949. PLAN officers and sailors mastered the Chinese-made small ships, maximized their firepower, and fought successfully by using shrewd naval tactics. The Chinese navy sank one South Vietnamese frigate and damaged three destroyers while the 389 was merely damaged. The PLAN's victory of the Battle of the Paracels placed China in a powerful position to deploy its warships and submarines into the deep water of the South China Sea.

After the PLAN's victory in January 1974, the PLA high command established a Chinese garrison on the islands and built permanent defense facilities. In August, the PLA Guangzhou Regional Command deployed its troops, installed equipment, set up communication and transportation, and provided logistics to the Paracel Islands. In September 1974, Liu Huaqing led a naval task team to the Paracel Islands and evaluated the island defense effectiveness in the South China Sea. Liu and his team lived with the troops at Yongxing Island for seventeen days, visited their posts, and inspected firing positions, beachhead defense works, and command centers. After they returned to the SSF headquarters, Liu and his team also visited the frigate brigade and subchaser squad, which patrolled the Paracels and other islands in the South China Sea.

After their return to Beijing, Liu Huaqing briefed the naval command about the Paracel defense on November 14, 1974. He strongly suggested that, to maintain an effective and permanent garrison, the defense should be under the command of the navy rather than the army regional command in Guangzhou on the mainland. Naval command opened sea routes for the Paracels' supply, built harbors and airstrips, established radio communication with warships, and received immediate air support from naval aviation. It proved more practical and effective for the navy to provide all support and defense at sea than the army from the mainland. The navy supported Liu's proposal and forwarded it to the PLA high command. Deng Xiaoping and the CMC approved the naval proposal. In 1982, when Liu Huaqing became navy commander, the Paracel Harbor was completed.

## LIU'S VISION FOR A MODERN NAVY

The Sino-Soviet Border War from 1969 to 1971 pushed China to finalize its strategic priority shift from the United States to the Soviet Union. Tension between Beijing and Moscow mounted in the late 1960s. After the Soviet Red Army invaded Czechoslovakia in 1968, its troops broke into the Chinese embassy and "savagely" beat Chinese diplomats.[63] By the end of 1968, the Soviet Union had increased its troops along the disputed Russo-Chinese border from seventeen divisions to twenty-seven divisions.[64] In October, Marshal Lin Biao warned the army that Soviet forces would invade China soon. In April 1969, China's defense minister called the country for "preparing a war, fighting . . . against the Soviet Union."[65] Thereafter, active war preparation became the party's and country's priority.

Beginning in March 1969, small-scale border skirmishes erupted at the Zhenbao (Damansky) and Bacha Islands in Heilongjiang and at Taskti and Tieliekti in Xinjiang.[66] By the early 1970s, the Soviet Union deployed up to forty-eight divisions, nearly 1 million troops, along the Russian-Chinese border. China prepared for total war, including possible Russian nuclear attacks. Although the border conflict did not escalate into a total war between the two Communist countries, it ushered Sino-Soviet relations into a two-decade ebb during which both saw each other as the archenemy. Mao turned his attention from the north to the south, looking for new resources of international trade, technology, and foreign investment by normalizing relations with the United States and Japan in the Pacific. Premier Zhou Enlai supported the improvement of Sino-U.S. relations and expected to open the Pacific with a naval support.[67]

However, Mao Zedong realized Chinese naval force was ill-prepared for new challenges presented by the strategic shift. On July 29, 1970, Mao mentioned the naval problems with General O Jin-u, chief of the general staff of the North Korean People's Army (NKPA), in Beijing. Mao said: "Our naval force does not look like [a navy]. . . . Comparing with Japan, [we] have the same kind of shipyard but could not manufacture that many ships. What is the reason for that? Have to find the reasons."[68] On September 25, Mao Zedong met Vice Admiral Muzaffar Hassan, Pakistan's navy commander, in Beijing. He told his guest that "talking about the navy, ours is not good enough. . . . At the present, some big countries bully us . . . and dominate the Indian Ocean and Pacific Ocean. Therefore, we should develop our navy."[69]

At that time, Mao considered naval power as an indispensable attribute of China's international status. After Lin Biao was killed in September 1971, Marshal Ye Jianying took charge of the PLA's daily affairs as defense minister and CMC vice chairman under Premier Zhou Enlai's consultation. This Zhou-Ye system replaced Lin's leadership of the PLA from 1959 to 1971. Defense Minister Ye Jianying was one of the four marshals who submitted the policy report suggesting the strategic shift.

In 1973, Mao Zedong rehabilitated Deng Xiaoping, appointed him vice premier, and renewed his membership on the Central Committee. During the Cultural Revolution, Deng was purged along with Liu Shaoqi as the head of the "Bourgeoisie Headquarters within the Party" and ousted from the CCP and PLA hierarchy in 1966. Deng and his wife were placed under house arrest in Beijing for two years before being sent to Jiangxi to work at a tractor-repair factory in 1969.[70] "Rehabilitated" by Mao, Deng was then appointed as the chief of PLA General Staff, vice chairman of the CMC, vice chairman of the Central Committee, and a member of the Politburo Standing Committee in 1975.[71]

As a survivor of the Cultural Revolution, Deng Xiaoping announced economic and military reforms and tried to "repair the damage" done to the PLA during the Cultural Revolution.[72] Contrasted with previous reforms, Deng did not aim at an external, American or a Soviet threat, but addressed serious, internal problems within the PLA. At a General Staff meeting in January 1975, Deng Xiaoping criticized the PLA for losing many of its "fine traditions," being a "seriously bloated" organization, and that "an over-expanded and inefficient army is not combat worthy."[73] At an enlarged meeting of CMC in July, he criticized the PLA's problems with five words: "bloating, laxity, conceit, extravagance, and inertia." While blaming these faults on "sabotage by Lin Biao and his followers," Deng called for an immediate military reforms to solve the PLA's problems through consolidation, including the problems of the PLA Navy. Deng Xiaoping's return and Mao Zedong's leaving offered a great opportunity for resetting the direction of the Chinese navy in 1975. Liu Huaqing saw the historical moment and took his chance to demonstrate the necessity of a strong surface sea power as part of the military reform agenda later that year.

Mao's strategic shift and Deng's reform provided a new opportunity for naval development and modernization. On May 2–3, 1975, Mao Zedong chaired his last Politburo meeting in Beijing. He held Admiral Su Zhenhua's hands at the end of the meeting and asked him "to build a good navy, which should make the enemy afraid of."[74] Unsatisfied and disappointed, Mao stretched out his little finger and said to Su, "Our naval force has a such size." After the meeting, Su organized a planning committee, coordinated with the State Council, and rushed to draft the "Ten-Year Plan (1975–1985) for Naval Development." Mao approved it immediately on May 23, "Agree. Work hard to reach the goal in ten years!"

Liu Huaqing, however, was disappointed by the "Ten-Year Plan." Since Su Zhenhua did not include Liu Huaqing in his planning committee, Liu did not see the Ten-Year Plan until much later. Surprised and frustrated, Liu could not believe that Su's plan laden with old coastal defense, "small navy" development, and out-of-date, low-tech projects. Su's plan continued the army-centric defense strategy as a predominantly the product of a land-oriented military hierarchy. Liu Huaqing could not sleep for a few days and finally decided to write directly to Deng Xiaoping and Mao Zedong to challenge Su's plan. He took a huge political and career risk since he ignored the chain of command and went around the naval leaders to get to the high command. There was a parallel between Sergey Gorshkov and Liu Huaqing, who challenged a traditional land-centric strategy in their national defense and required a larger role of the navy in their armed forces.

On September 3, 1975, Liu submitted his letter to Deng Xiaoping and Mao Zedong. He wrote directly to the top leaders without permission from the naval chief or defense minister. His letter included an exhaustive (more than 10,000 characters) list of grievances, titled "Naval Shipbuilding and Equipment Development Should Pay Attention to Quality and Improve Technology."[75] Commodore Shi described the report as Liu's policy statement for the Chinese navy's future.[76]

Liu Huaqing's report criticized the naval leadership as a problem and argued that Su Zhenhua failed to comprehend the high command's strategic shift from a land-based army defense to a naval defense at seas. Su's Ten-Year Plan did not provide a new direction for the PLAN to take on the new challenges of the near future. Among the criticisms of Su's report, Liu Huaqing claimed that "the naval leadership lacked careful research and preparation for future naval warfare and strategic tasks. The PLAN Command did not have a good understanding of the chairman's strategic thoughts and campaign tactics since they ignored characteristics, advances, and trends of potential enemy navies and their technologies."[77] With the recent Battle of the Paracel Islands in 1974, he was able to demonstrate the PLAN's many problems and difficulties and necessary changes needed to make in the next ten years. Having expressed his grievances, Liu Huaqing then proposed a new direction for the navy's modernization and for China's sea power.

Liu Huaqing began his statement as the naval shipbuilding chief that "naval shipbuilding and equipment manufacturing are an important strategic issue. . . . The Ten-Year Plan should significantly improve the current backwardness of our naval capability and technology." He posited that Su's plan failed to address major strategic issues and "will not reach the goal" of naval modernization. According to Liu, Su's Ten-Year Plan (1975–1985) seemed out of date and relegated the Chinese navy to remain small, weak, and incapable of facing the new challenges in the Pacific.[78] He highlighted major problems in the Su's plan and provided four counterpoints for a new and strong naval force: big navy vs. small navy, new technology vs. old equipment, far seas warfare vs. coastal defense, and a navy as a strategic, independent force vs. an auxiliary service to the army and air force.

First, Liu Huaqing argued that "our country will launch a large-scale economic construction, which will develop unprecedented oversea trade and depend on importation of important strategic materials. Our navy must take heavy responsibilities of securing ocean-going transportation and protecting oceanic resources."[79] He advocated that China as a large country needed a powerful naval force to support and protect its global economy and international trade. According to Liu's new strategic outlook, the Chinese navy would assume tremendous responsibilities in operating and fighting in distant water to protect Chinese maritime interests. He had successful experience in protecting the country's commercial fishing when he served as deputy commander of the North Sea Fleet in the late 1950s. From his observations, Liu argued that the world's successful navies operated increasingly further from their coasts, and that international trade would become more and more important to China's economy. As a result, China's industrialization and growth should help build a strong navy, which reflected the country's industrial prowess and national achievements in economic advancements. Liu Huaqing believed it was time for the Chinese navy to escalate its modernization since the top CCP leader had indicated clearly that China needed a strong navy. Liu predicted that it was only a matter of time before the Chinese navy would have to engage in operations to protect China's sea lines of communications (SLOCs).[80] Again, both Liu Huaqing and Gorshkov considered a capable naval force as necessary for their national security and economic development.

Second, it was time for China to build a strong navy with big warships. Therefore, China would immediately discontinue the manufacturing of small ships. "If [we] want to build a strong navy, we cannot waste our main resources on manufacturing small ships. The enemy won't be afraid of the little ships." Liu Huaqing juxtaposed this to Su Zhenhua's plan of "manufacturing a large number of various small boats in the next ten years." Among the others in Su's plan were torpedo boats, missile boats, frigates, minesweepers, and submarine chasers, about 78 percent of total shipbuilding from 1975 to 1985. "This means our naval capability will stay as the same ten years later as what we are today without much improvement, except doubling the number of the same small boats. . . . These small ships cannot operate in middle or far seas for strategic missions since they are designed for coastal and offshore operations."[81]

Throughout his report, Liu Huaqing quoted Mao Zedong nine times, including Mao's frustrated comments on China's small and weak navy on May 3 and 23, 1975. Beside constant repetition of ideological themes, Liu Huaqing believed that Chinese leaders were ready and determined to utilize the country's resources and develop its sea power. The high command proposed construction of an aircraft carrier in the early 1970s. After Lin Biao's death, the program was called into question, and then his carrier plan was canceled. Liu suggested that China should now concentrate financial and technological resources to build its own aircraft carriers and large, far sea operational warships. He proposed developing and manufacturing 40,000-ton aircraft carrier, 4,000-ton destroyers, and 2,000-ton frigates.[82] It was the second time for Liu to propose the construction of China's aircraft carrier after his first plan in 1970. The parallels between Liu Huaqing and Gorshkov included the requirement of a large fleet, appreciation of new technology, and preparation of new naval battles in near or even far seas.

Third, Liu Huaqing proposed manufacturing new warships and nuclear submarines with new tech weapon systems. Thereby, the naval development should be led by research and development. Liu opposed Su's

Ten-Year Plan for "manufacturing a large number of out-of-date conventional torpedo submarines, which were imitated Russian models from the 1940s and 1950s . . . slow speed, short submerge time, noisy, and backward technology."[83] He also suggested the immediate termination of producing Type 21 speed boats, minesweepers, and other old ships. "They were all the 1940s or 1950s Russian-models, out-of-date, lack of new technology, no use in future naval warfare." As a perceptive strategic thinker, Liu identified that modern warships and nuclear submarines with the latest technology would change the art of naval warfare. He demanded the application of China's nuclear power to submarine propulsion. He argued that the navy's war preparation and "weapon development should be determined by its future tasks and future warfare. We should design, develop, and manufacture better weapons and equipment. We should have whatever the enemy has. We should even have better ones than the enemy's. . . . We should learn from our own experience and learn from our lessons. [We] cannot repeat the huge learning curve in the next ten years, not even a small learning curve. [We] should never go back to the old path."[84]

Fourth, Liu Huaqing designed new strategy and tactics for the next naval war that included engagements in near sea defense and far sea attacks from the 1980s to the 2000s. He clarified in his report that the PLAN should initiate a new era as China's strategic force. The navy "must significantly improve its current backward situation in equipment, weaponry, and technology. As an independent force, the navy should not only increase its numbers and enlarge its size, but also achieve its combat capability and effectiveness in modern naval warfare. . . . It is really inspiring and exciting that Chairman Mao and the Party Center have determined to escalate naval development. A new plan should bring about a strong navy."[85] He believed that, although naval strategy was part of national defense, it should be an independent strategy rather than serving an army-centric, land-based defense. He predicted the navy's new mission in his report. "Since the Navy also follows active defense strategy, it will operate and destroy the enemy in the near seas as well in the far seas."[86] Liu emphasized joint naval operations, integrated command and control, far sea logistics, and carrier-based air defense. Liu concluded that "the next ten years will be a defining decade for naval modernization. How to make the next move is a strategic step for the country. It is a turning point about how to end the past and open a brand-new path for the Navy's future. A strong navy should have both quantity and quality."[87]

Liu Huaqing began to advocate China's sea power as an indispensable force of its national defense. His vision and plan for the PLAN's development impressed Deng Xiaoping, who believed the future of the PLA lay in a large naval force. On September 4, 1975, the day after receiving Liu's report, Deng forwarded it to Admiral Su Zhenhua, then to the PLAN chiefs and political commissars, with his instruction to "take this report into consideration. Some points deserve our attention."[88] Though bedridden in a hospital, Mao Zedong approved Liu's shipbuilding plan.[89] Liu Huaqing, thereafter, joined Deng Xiaoping as one of the earliest military reformers in modern PLA history.

In 1975, Marshal Nie Rongzhen asked Liu Huaqing to serve as a member of the Core Leadership Group of China Academy of Sciences (CAS). Liu left the navy for a second time and worked directly under Hu Yaobang in CAS. Hu Yaobang was one of China's leading reformers next to Deng Xiaoping and became the CCP's top leader (secretary general) in 1981. In 1975, Premier Zhou Enlai called for China's four modernizations of industry, agriculture, science and technology, and defense. In response to Zhou's call, Deng Xiaoping sent a reform team to CAS for rectification, rehabilitation, and reorganization since he believed that China's modernization should start with science and technology. In 1975, Deng Xiaoping chaired a State Council conference and passed the Core Leadership Group's "Report Outline of Some Major Issues in Science and Technology Development" (known as the "Report Outline"). However, Maoist leaders in Beijing, including Mao's wife Jiang Qing, criticized the Report Outline, arguing that Deng's reform efforts would restore old bourgeoisie lines and return China to rightist ways prior to the Cultural Revolution. In April 1976, Mao supported his wife, accused Deng of criticizing the Cultural Revolution, and dismissed him for a second time from the party, government, and military. Soon a nationwide movement began to criticize Deng's reform policy as "rightist policy." Nevertheless, Mao kept Marshal Ye Jianying's command of China's armed forces.[90] On September 9, 1976, Mao Zedong died.

## REFORM AND OPENING: THE PLAN GOES TO THE PACIFIC

After Mao's death, a new power struggle erupted between the "Gang of Four," including Mao's wife Jiang Qing, and the PLA marshals. During the showdown on October 6, 1976, Mao's successor, Hua Guofeng, along with Marshal Ye Jianying, arrested the "Gang of Four" and Mao's cousin, Mao Yuanxin, in a bloodless military coup.[91] In 1977, Deng Xiaoping staged his third return to Beijing. He ended the Cultural Revolution, started new reform policies, and represented a new generation of Chinese leadership.[92] In 1978, Deng Xiaoping opened China to the outside world for international support for the Four Modernizations, including defense modernization.[93]

In March 1978, CMC and the State Council established the National Commission of Science and Technology of Armament to lead China's defense modernization with Liu Huaqing as the administrative chief. In April, Deng Xiaoping told Liu he needed a comprehensive picture of current military modernization, defense industry, and PLA technology. Deng wanted "to know what kind of equipment the army, navy, and air force have, what new technology to be developed in the future, especially the equipment of the Air Force and Navy. I need to talk to them one by one." From April to August, Liu Huaqing organized and coordinated six high-level arms conferences on military science, technology, and industry, including the Third, Fourth, Sixth, Seventh, and Eighth Machinery Ministries and Air Force and Navy. The ministers and chiefs briefed Deng Xiaoping one by one on their R&D, equipment, production, and plans.[94] Thereafter, Liu continued to oversee PLA equipment and technology and became one of the reform leaders in China's defense modernization from the 1970s to 1990s

After Mao's death, PRC conventional security concerns and the PLA's focus on a ground defense were called into question. China is a great land power, spanning the Asian continent. From the early Red Army's revolutionary wars to the PLA's seizing the mainland, the army always played a dominant role in China's defense policymaking through the Cold War. From 1978, however, Deng Xiaoping's emphasis on international trade "shifted China's economic center of gravity to the coast."[95] Chinese trade with other nations has steadily expanded and affected some 60–70 percent of China's annual revenues. Deng focused more on the navy's development as China opened up to the global market. He provided some guiding thoughts for Chinese maritime strategy beyond the PLAN's traditional role as a coastal defense force. Deng believed Chinese maritime interests should develop the country's maritime economy, protect China's maritime sovereignty over territorial waters, and sustain the ocean environment. While the navy struggled to find its new place in post-Mao China, Liu Huaqing's 1975 report cemented a new direction for naval modernization. The CCP Central Committee accepted Liu's plan and shifted its focus of the defense modernization to naval construction during Deng's economic reform.

The 1970s became the turning point in Chinese naval development and modernization, when the navy received more than 20 percent of an annual defense budget. The PLAN began to change its development direction toward becoming a blue-water navy. In 1978, Deng chaired two naval development conferences on shipbuilding, missile technology, and navigation equipment. The Sixth Machinery Ministry, China's shipbuilding ministry, briefed Deng and other military leaders about issues of guided-missile destroyer manufacturing and nuclear submarine technology. Deng instructed the Sixth Machinery Ministry and the navy to collaborate and solve the issues that year, or the next.[96] In June, the PLAN reported its progress on the guided-missile destroyer's development and manufacturing. Deng instructed the navy to "concentrate the resources and overcome the key problems of building the missile destroyer. We must solve the problems. If not this year, [we must] solve [them] next year."[97]

In December 1978, a national team including CSTIND, the navy, and the State Council formed to improve shipbuilding and naval construction. The State Council mobilized the First, Second, Fourth, Fifth, and Eighth Machinery Ministries to provide assistance and resources for naval modernization. In January 1979, the naval development conference was held at Qingdao and included 240 naval units, ministry offices, shipbuilding enterprises, and companies.[98] On February 7, PLAN political commissar Su Zhenhua had a heart attack and died in Shanghai. Deng Xiaoping appointed General Ye Fei as the navy's new chief on February 12. General Ye was then appointed PLAN commander in 1980 after Fleet Admiral Xiao Jinguang retired.[99]

From July 20 to 31, 1979, the PLAN's Party Committee convened at NSF Qingdao Naval Base. Deng Xiaoping met with naval leaders on July 29 and talked to the admirals about the importance of solving the navy's factional problems. "It will be very difficult to do so by the next generation," Deng said.[100] On the same day, Deng visited the NSF airfield, reviewed the Chinese-made seaplanes, and met with the pilots.[101] On August 2, Deng boarded the first Chinese-manufactured missile destroyer 105 at Yantai and met all the officers and sailors. Deng proclaimed to the captain and his officers that China wanted to be a rich country, which required entering the world, sailing its oceans, and not only building near sea defense, but also far sea operation. During his six-hour sailing tour, Deng inspected weapon controls, communications, engine rooms, and other parts of the new warship. He inscribed a statement in calligraphy on the warship: "Build a strong navy able to fight a modern war!"[102]

Deng Xiaoping removed Hua Guofeng as chairman of the CMC and made himself chief of the PLA General Staff. In February 1979, Liu Huaqing was appointed as the assistant to Deng Xiaoping at the General Chief Headquarters. After China established diplomatic relations with the United States on January 1, 1979, Deng visited Washington, DC, as the first Chinese Communist leader to ever do so. The Sino-U.S. normalization led to the rapid creation of an institutional and legal framework for expanded economic cooperation.[103] Deng's drive to improve relations with the United States paid off. In July 1979, the United States granted Most Favored Nation trading status to China and gradually loosened trade restrictions, shifting the PRC to the category of "friendly, non-allied" country in May 1983.[104]

After normalization of diplomatic relations with Washington, Deng Xiaoping sought to punish Vietnam in February 1979. As a warning to neighboring countries of China's reassuming its power status in Asia-Pacific region, China sent 220,000 PLA troops to invade Vietnam. Deng Xiaoping, however, was disappointed by the PLA's poor discipline, low morale, combat ineffectiveness, and the high casualties in the Sino-Vietnam Border War. The Sino-Vietnamese border conflict continued into the mid-1980s. The 1979 Vietnam incursion exposed the PLA's weaknesses, indicating they were not ready for such a "local war." Deng Xiaoping planned a new military reform in the wake of the 1979 Sino-Vietnamese

Border War and established a "Military System Reform Leading Group" in February 1982.[105]

As Deng's assistant at the PLA's General Chief Headquarters, Liu Huaqing continued developing and manufacturing new combat warships, submarines, and large support vessels for oceangoing operations from 1978 to 1982. The PLAN received new guided missile destroyers, fighter-bombers, antisubmarine helicopters, and other high-performance equipment and weapons. The missile-carrying warships increased from 20 to 200 by the end of the 1980s. With new warships and technology, the PLAN expanded its operations from the near shore (brown water) to near sea (green water). The South Sea Fleet (SSF) dispatched 794 vessels and 262 aircraft between July 1980 and the end of 1982, for patrol, surveillance, and other tasks, and ensured the security of fisheries, the Paracel Islands, and drilling platforms in the Gulf of Tonkin. On November 8, 1980, the PLAN Air Force sent two H-6 bombers to patrol the Spratly Islands in the South China Sea for the first time. Then, the PLANAF began its regular patrols in the area.[106] Those oceangoing voyages convinced Liu Huaqing and Chinese naval officers that the PLAN had new capabilities to reach deep waters (or blue waters, far sea) as a modern navy. For joint operations and amphibious campaigns, the navy also developed a modern equipment framework to carry out maritime combat operations, sea-based nuclear counterattack with near-shore combat as a focus and operational and tactical maneuvers as a complement. In October 1982, the PLAN launched its first ballistic missile, Julang-1, from a Type 31 conventional submarine.

On May 18, 1980, China successfully tested an intercontinental ballistic missile (ICBM), from its own territory to an ocean area, about 4,350 miles northwest of the Fiji islands in the South Pacific. The long-range rocket navigated the Southern and Northern Hemispheres and splashed down as hoped. Throughout testing, a PLAN convoy safeguarded the rocket's flight and landing for 35 days, covering 8,733 nautical miles. The PLA high command and the navy established a task force to retrieve the long-range missile's data bin. From April to July 1980, the Task Force Formation crossed the equator and sailed to the South Pacific for the test.[107] The fleet had eighteen ships, including six destroyers (their hull numbers were 106, 107, 108, 131, 132, and 162), two auxiliary vessels (X 615 and X 950), two ocean salvage and rescue vessels (J 302 and J 506), two marine survey ships

(*Xiangyanghong* 5 and *Xiangyanghong* 10), four ocean tug ships (T 154, T 710, T 830, and *Deyue*), and two main scientific survey ships (*Yuanwang* 1 and *Yuanwang* 2).[108]

After Deng Xiaoping resigned as the PLA general chief of the staff, Liu Huaqing was promoted to deputy chief of the general staff in January 1981. Liu continued to work with Marshal Nie Rongzhen and pushed several major naval projects through research and development in the 1970s, including strategic nuclear submarines, guided-missile frigates, guided-missile destroyers, diesel-powered conventional submarines, anti-ship missiles, attack submarines, and submarine chasers. The appointment of Liu Huaqing as the navy's commander in August 1982 marked a new era in PLAN history since he was the first naval officer to lead the Chinese navy, a then-sizable regional power with nearly all types of warships. Its underwater fleet had SSBNs and SSNs.[109] Its surface warship fleet included missile destroyers, missile frigates, corvettes, minesweepers, minelayers, missile boats, torpedo boats, landing ships, and auxiliary vessels. Its aviation fleet was equipped with medium and light bombers, fighters, attack aircraft, ship-based helicopters, and reconnaissance/surveillance planes, assisted by a radar network that covered all of China's coasts. Its offshore defense force had replaced coastal cannons with anti-ship missiles, and the navy established three new marine brigades.

# CHAPTER 4

# THE COMMANDER

## *New Strategy for a Blue-Water Navy*

The appointment of Rear Admiral Liu Huaqing as the navy's commander in August 1982 marked a new era in PLAN history. When Mao Zedong determined to make China a continental power in East Asia during the 1950s–1970s, the PLAN was the least prioritized service, intended to play only an auxiliary role to the army in a total land war against foreign threats. After Deng Xiaoping resolved to bring China into the global community in 1978, the PLAN found new reasons to update its technology and a new place in post-Mao China, which required a daunting overhaul. Commander Liu Huaqing was the first naval officer to lead the Chinese navy; both predecessors, Xiao Jinguang and Ye Fei, were from the army. Trusted by Deng, Liu carried out Deng's reform policy, developed a new naval strategy, and focused on new technology and large shipbuilding. In 1988, Liu was promoted to admiral. By the early 1990s, Admiral Liu Huaqing became China's top military leader next to Jiang Zemin (as the top leader from 1990 to 2002).[1] Xi Jinping praised Liu's success in "building a strong navy, developing a new naval strategy, enhancing national maritime consciousness, and proactively defending China's maritime rights and resources."[2]

In 1985, Liu Huaqing reconceptualized China's sea power and shifted naval strategy from near-shore defense (近岸防御 *jin'an fangyu*) to near sea defense (近海防御 *jinhai fangyu*). Xi Jinping commented that Liu "actively searched and successfully constructed a new naval strategic theory."[3] Liu Huaqing's strategic thinking broadened the country's maritime interests, redirected China's oceangoing development, and built a blue-water navy capable of near sea defense and far sea protection. Lan Bo argued that "this naval strategy, under Deng Xiaoping's macro influence and announced by PLAN Commander Liu Huaqing in 1985, had a significant impact on domestic policymaking and international relations. [The] Chinese navy adopted the new strategy in the mid-1980s and [continues] to follow it today."[4] Liu's new strategy led the PLAN's development of key combat warships and high-tech weapon systems. Tian Tian of the PLAN Institute of Military Science Research concluded that Liu "established a complete naval strategy with [the] Chinese Navy's characteristics and shaped the framework for today's naval development."[5]

From 1982 to 1988, navy commander Liu Huaqing was determined to pragmatically implement Deng Xiaoping's military reform. Liu repeatedly said, "There is no future for the country without the reform; and there is no future for the PLA without the reform. . . . [We] must escalate and deepen the military reform."[6] Liu Huaqing launched naval reform in all areas. His well-designed plans, resolute actions, solutions, and positive results pushed the military reforms into other PLA services. Xi Jinping recognized that Liu's reform focus was on PLA institutions and the Chinese military system. Liu knew his changes were historically significant as he told his admirals, "No matter what, cannot delay any longer to fix military organizational and structural problems. If not now, it would be much more difficult to deal with it ten years later."[7] Xi Jinping concluded that "he [Liu] led China's military reform in person and moved the PLA forward into a new future."[8]

Under Liu Huaqing's command, the PLAN grew from a coastal fleet into a maritime force of considerable size, supported by China's domestic industry and newly developed reform systems. In 1984, he persuaded admirals to draft two documents, titled the "Seventh Five-Year Plan for the PLAN" and "The Navy in 2000." According to "The Navy in 2000," Liu developed a three-step plan for China's blue-water navy by penetrating three "island chains" in the early twenty-first century.[9] He pursued his dream of a "great China with a strong navy" (see photo 5).

Admiral Liu Huaqing was promoted to deputy secretary general of the CMC in 1987 and CMC vice chairman in 1988 as the third top military leader in China. Although he vacated his PLAN command in 1988, Liu continued his navy dream in naval development and modernization with his top position in the high command. As a result, China's shipbuilding industry, aviation technology research and imports, and naval training and education systems backed its impressive naval development throughout the entire 1980s and continued into the 1990s. Liu shifted the PLAN from

PHOTO 5. Navy commander Liu Huaqing salutes his fleet at a naval parade off Yantai, Shandong, in September 1988. 党史周刊 [*CPC News Weekly*], no. 19, 2013

brown-water operations to blue-water development through reconstruction, qualitative improvement, higher educational standards for personnel, and new Western technology. However, when Deng Xiaoping's reform caused new issues and led to student demonstrations in cities in the summer of 1989, Liu Huaqing, as a trusted top military leader, commanded Chinese armed forces to open fire on student and worker protesters in Beijing when he was appointed as the commander in chief of the PLA Capital Martial Law Forces in May–July 1989.

## NAVAL STRATEGY AND OCEANGOING INITIATIVES

After assuming the PLAN's command in 1982, Liu Huaqing developed and finalized a new naval strategy against three island chains to expand Chinese influence into the Pacific. Liu's new strategy emphasized China's maritime interests, sea power, oceangoing development, and global strategy by building a modern and capable navy. Liu Xinbo claimed that Liu's strategic theory drew critically from Sergey Gorshkov's maritime strategies, including modern naval force, sea control, and naval warfare theories. The new Chinese naval commander borrowed Soviet sea power theories and strategies to format China's maritime strategy to guide the country's oceangoing development and naval modernization and break American maritime containment policy toward the end of the Cold War.[10] As Gorshkov took the Soviet Navy to sea, Liu would take the Chinese navy to the Pacific Ocean.

On February 27, 1983, Liu Huaqing discussed the PLAN reform with officers of the SSF in Guangdong. The navy commander pointed out that "naval reform is imperative. However, it doesn't matter what kind of changes [we] are going to make, [we] must follow naval strategic principles and warfighting tasks. These are 'active defense and near sea warfare.'"[11] For the first time, Liu specifically talked about a new naval strategy. For the PLAN, its traditional strategy focused on a coastal defense to cover twelve to forty nautical miles offshore. Liu's new strategy extended the Chinese navy's capabilities from the coast to the near sea, hundreds or even a thousand of miles from shore. The new naval commander argued that "to build a modern navy, [we] must establish a guidance position of the naval strategy."[12] Liu went beyond the naval chief's role as an advocate of sea power, and as a national strategic thinker he explored the major change of China's next war from ground defense to naval warfare. To defend the country and win the next war, Liu required a new fleet large and strong enough to stop or even defeat a hostile navy in the near or far seas.

After the founding of the PLAN in 1949 and establishment of its headquarters in Beijing in early 1950, the Chinese navy created its first strategy on April 14, 1950. As the PLAN's inaugural commander, Fleet Admiral Xiao Jinguang described the new navy as a "self-defensive" force operating "near coast and around the many islands." "There are many favorable conditions for our naval warfare. . . . We are not going to have a huge naval force, and instead [need] to build a light fleet."[13] From August 11 to 30, Commander Xiao Jinguang held the first PLAN high command conference to discuss the "near-shore or off-coast defense" (近岸防御 *jin'an fangyu*) strategy. All twenty-three naval leaders supported the near coast defensive strategy, by which the PLAN maintained its operations along the shore and no farther than the near offshore areas (about forty miles into the waters from the shore).[14] Early naval leaders also agreed to build a light, small navy with practical and effective means like airplanes, submarines, and torpedo boats for immediate and capable operations from

1950 to 1953. This light navy developed its "air, sub, and speed" (空 *kong*, 潜 *qian*, 快 *kui*) capacities of coast defense, landing assistance, and offshore guerrilla attacks to destroy enemy ships (*haishang youji poxizhan* 海上游击破袭战). The three priorities included the establishment of naval aviation, submarine force, and torpedo fleets from 1950 to 1953.[15]

China's coastal defensive strategy and light naval force could not challenge the U.S. island-chain strategy to contain the newly founded people's republic and the Soviet Union. During the early stage of the Korean War (1950–1953), John Foster Dulles and General Douglas MacArthur made a strategic plan to contain China and Russia in the Pacific through three island chains. The first island chain linked major Pacific islands, including Japan's Ryukyu Islands, Taiwan, the Philippines, and Borneo. The second island chain in the middle of the West Pacific included the island of Guam, the Caroline Islands, and New Guinea. It served as a second strategic defense line for the United States. The third island chain ran from the Aleutian Islands in the north across the Pacific through the American Samoa and Fiji to New Zealand in the south.[16] During the Cold War, the PLAN never broke through the first island chain while Xiao Jinguang served as the PLAN commander from 1950 to 1980. Commodore Wu Dianqing of the PLAN's Political Tasks Department believes that the offshore defense and light navy strategy "became the foundation of the PLAN's development for the next three decades" from 1950 to 1983, rather than for just three years.[17] That is to say, the short-term, quick-fix plan handicapped the PLAN's future development for more than thirty years.

When he launched China's economic reform and opening-up movement, Deng Xiaoping outlined a major change in naval strategic thinking and maritime view. He told admirals and state officials in 1978 that "our strategy is always defensive, and it will be strategic defense even after twenty years. It includes nuclear submarines as strategic defensive weapons, and Vladivostok, the Tsushima Strait, and Strait of Malacca are also for [our] defense."[18] Deng's new perception of China's naval defense tremendously extended the defensive perimeter and reached over three thousand nautical miles (the sea route distance from Hainan to the Strait of Malacca). According to Admiral Yang Huaiqing, while Deng still considered the PLAN as a defensive force, he believed that the Chinese navy should engage in both near and far seas.[19]

Liu Huaqing aligned with Deng's strategic thinking that culminated in a pragmatic naval strategy with a new mission, detailed objectives, available means, and assessment. In 1983, Liu replaced the old coastal defense mission with his new offshore and near sea defense concepts. In October, the navy organized a study seminar for high-ranking officers to discuss near sea defense and reach a consensus among the admirals. Liu provided an exhaustive speech explaining the near sea defense strategy.[20] He also organized his staff, experts, and planners to work on policy reviews, historical research, comparative studies with foreign navies, and strategic analysis to demonstrate the new strategy's necessity and feasibility.[21] He chaired several major conferences, national symposiums, and research meetings to discuss China's maritime interests, oceanic sovereignty, and naval defense capability. Within three years, Liu Huaqing published quite a few articles in *PLAN Magazine* and *People's Navy* to promote the new strategy among the naval officers and sailors. Bernard Cole pointed out that although Deng Xiaoping and Liu Huaqing continued Maoist active defense strategy, they made significant changes "because [of] Liu's emphasis on moving China's maritime defense seaward."[22]

On December 20, 1985, Liu Huaqing presented his naval strategy at the closing meeting of a naval exercise. His new strategy was known as the "near sea defense" (近海防御 *jinhai fangyu*). He explained,

> Near sea defense is an active defense rather than a passive defense. It employs active naval offensive actions to achieve a strategic defense goal. It requires active attacks against the enemy not only in the near sea areas, but also deep in the far seas under favorable conditions with adequate naval force. Under the current condition of our navy, these actions are necessary and possible, including cutting off enemy sea transportation and communication to undermine enemy national capability and coordinate strategically with our ground operations. When our naval force grows and becomes stronger in the future, it is possible to destroy the enemy in naval war to protect our country from a foreign invasion from the seas.[23]

Admirals Wu Shenli and Liu Xiaojiang point out that it was Liu who declared that China "must establish its naval theory, strategy, tactics to complete a smooth transition from coastal defense to near sea warfare and plan and conduct ocean-based operations and battles."[24]

Although Liu continued the PLA's traditional strategy of "active defense" (积极防御 *jiji fangyu*), he drastically extended China's defensive zone into nearly 100 million square miles at sea. According to the naval commander, his new strategy was principally defensive, and its nature was local control, or area denial at sea, known as "anti-access/area denial" (A2/AD).[25] Liu's key contribution was shifting the PLAN's coastal defense to near sea defense along the first island chain. Since 1949, the PLAN had maintained defensive operations along the shore and offshore areas, not including Taiwan and disputed islands in the South China Sea. In 1985, his new strategy proclaimed these areas impenetrable and warned foreign navies to keep out. Moreover, Liu argued that, based on then-current PLAN capability and responsibility, the near sea defense should be along and around the first island chain and include 3 million square kilometers of China's territorial waters in the East and South China Seas. Most areas of the first island chain were claimed by the PRC government as the new naval strategy effectively served the country's maritime interests. David Shambaugh considers it a "principal shift" in China's security and PLA's defense "from continental to maritime and national to regional definitions."[26]

Moreover, Liu Huaqing did not limit the "near seas," even rejecting the traditional concept as "near sea" with a distance of two hundred nautical miles from the shore. Instead, Liu argued that "the 'near sea' should include the Yellow Sea, East China Sea, South China Sea, Spratly Islands, Taiwan, waters around Okinawa island-chain, and northern region of the Pacific. What is beyond the 'near sea' belongs to the 'middle and far seas'" (see map 9).[27] Liu's new concept extended China's near sea margin significantly. The East China Sea extended 360 nautical miles from the Chinese coast into the Pacific. The Yellow Sea covered 430 nautical miles between the Chinese shore in the west and the Korean Peninsula in the east. The most southern Chinese territorial claims in the South China Sea extended to the Zengmu Reefs (James Shoal), about 1,250 nautical miles away from the Chinese mainland. Liu Huaqing stated that the near sea "includes the Japanese Archipelago, Ryukyu Islands, and the vast sea areas west of the Philippine Islands. I believe this the way to define the scale of the near

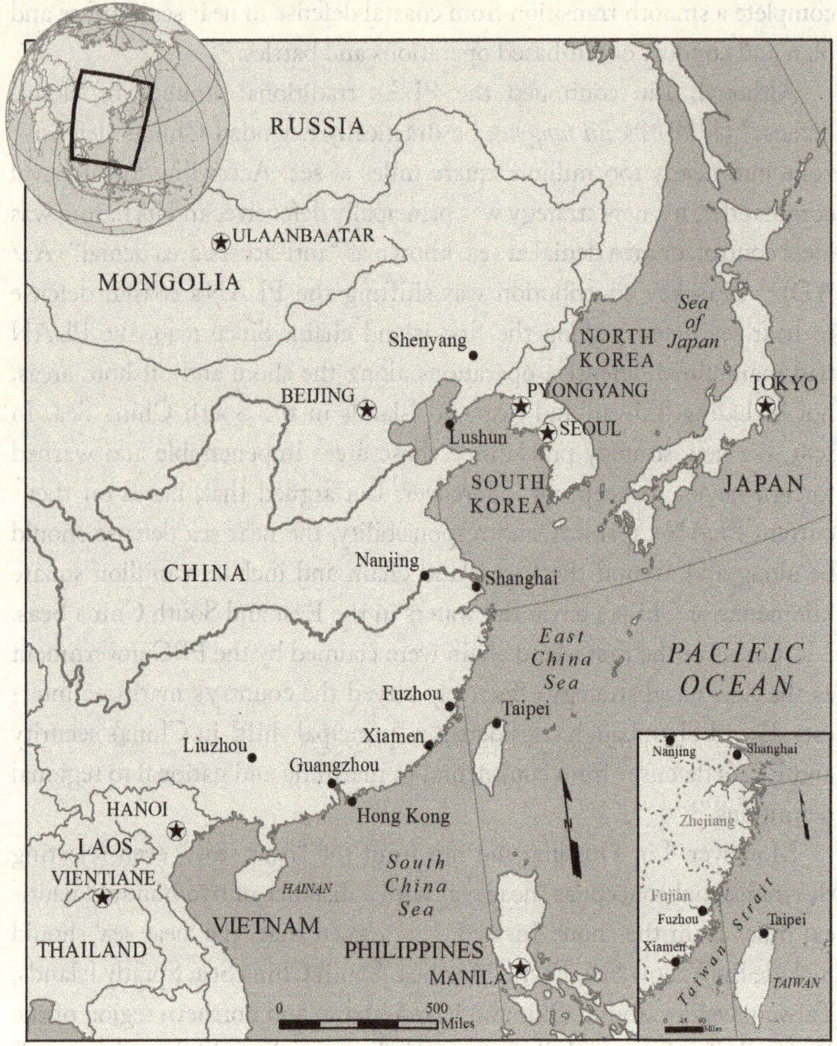


**MAP 9.** Taiwan, East China Sea, and the Pacific Ocean

sea, including all the maritime territory authorized by the International Convention on the Law of the Sea under China's sovereignty and also including the Paracel, Spratly, Dongsha, and Zhongsha Islands in these sea areas, which must belong to our country."[28]

Liu Huaqing continued to employ one of the PLA's traditional concepts of "weak force" theory that envisioned the Chinese army's defense against a superior opponent in the next war. Therefore, his new naval strategy adopted two new engagement formats, near sea battles (近海作战 *jinhai zuozhan*) and far sea attacks (远海作战 *yuanhai zuozhan*) for the Chinese navy against a technologically superior enemy navy. The admiral argued that active defense at sea differed from that on the ground, even though both required defensive depth and luring the enemy deeper. "While the enemy army advanced, we retreat on the ground; [when] the enemy navy advance[s]; we must also advance at sea to attack the enemy both at near sea and at far sea behind the line."[29] He explained this later in his speech at the PLA National Defense University: "Since our current naval force was not the most advanced, we must concentrate a superior force at each battle and at one location. Then, [we] launch a quick and decisive strike behind the line to attack a part of the enemy force and try to annihilate it all. Thus, we are a stronger force in this area, we can attack and win that battle."[30] His strategy was designed to defeat enemy navies in long-range areas at sea.

After his strategic speech in December 1985, Liu Huaqing launched an extensive persuasion campaign promoting his new naval strategy. On January 25, 1986, Liu spoke at an enlarged meeting of the PLAN Headquarters Party Committee and asked all admirals to "comprehend the new naval strategy." Liu explained the unique features of naval defense, coordination, communication, and logistics. The characteristics of modern naval warfare required a "relative independent strategic position" of the PLAN in national defense.[31] In November, the navy held the "Symposium on Naval Development Strategy" and invited admirals, strategists, and naval policymakers to discuss the naval strategy. Lieutenant General Qin Tian and Rear Admiral Huo Xiaoyong stated that "this was the first time for the PLA to use strategic theory to conceptualize comprehensive naval strategic thinking. It indicated that Chinese sea power has become mature."[32] From then on, Liu's new strategy was popularly accepted doctrine in the navy. Rear Admiral Huo Xiaoyong offered classes on Liu's naval strategy and wrote a book, 海军战略学 [Study of the naval strategy], to interpret Liu's strategic thought when Huo Xiaoyang served as the vice provost of the PLA National Defense University.[33]

The naval commander also promoted his naval strategy in the PLA. In May 1984, Liu Huaqing further explained his near sea strategy in guest lectures at the PLA Academy of Military Science (AMS) and Military

Institute (PLA MI). On April 29, 1986, Liu gave more interpretation to the new strategy in his lecture on "Naval Strategy and Future Naval Warfare" at the PLA National Defense University.[34] His lecture was well received by PLA officers from all the services. From 1983 to 1986, Liu published fourteen articles and gave numerous interviews to military journals like *Military Science* (by PLA AMS) and *Military Education*. Shi observed that all of Liu's lengthy articles centered six words: oceanic sovereignty, sea defense, and modern navy, aiming at promoting the public awareness of China's maritime interests and mobilizing public support of China's new naval strategy.[35]

From 1983 to 1986, Liu Huaqing promoted his sea power campaign by publishing articles in national newspapers, mainstream magazines, and popular journals. The naval commander called for a public awareness of China's naval history, oceanic sovereignty, and maritime adventures. Liu pointed out the contributions that the navy had made to Chinese history, and that China was once a great maritime power in the fifteenth century with more advanced navigation and shipbuilding technology than that of medieval and early Renaissance Europe. The historical peak of China's maritime power was in the early Ming dynasty, when Emperor Yongle (r. 1403–1424) expanded the tribute system and dispatched massive overseas missions. Zheng He's expeditions carried goods to build tribute relationships between the Ming and kingdoms in Southeast Asia, South Asia, and Eastern Africa. Between 1405 and 1433, Admiral Zheng He made seven voyages to the western seas, and more than a thousand ships were built under his command, including a hundred "treasure ships," approximately 370–440 feet in length and 150–80 feet abeam, five times bigger and advanced compared to Christopher Columbus's four ships. Moreover, it would be sixty-one years before Columbus set sail.

In his articles, Liu Huaqing blamed palace politics and corrupted bureaucrats for the fateful abrupt turn of Ming's maritime power and then a long period of continentalization of the country's sentiment through the Qing dynasty (1644–1911). The lack of maritime interests and sea power placed China in a powerless position to defend itself when Western colonial powers arrived and attacked and invaded China from the sea 470 times. He was not hesitant to connect China's "Century of Humiliation" to its governments' failures to appreciate the value of sea power. The admiral asked Chinese people "never forget the bloody lesson in modern history."[36] Liu's interpretation of Chinese history indicated his views with regard to the roles of the Chinese navy in the world. He firmly believed in a "rich country and a strong navy" as the ultimate goals of PLA reforms.

In his public speeches, publications, and media interviews, Admiral Liu emphasized China's maritime interests, naval modernization, and sea defense. On November 24, 1984, Liu wrote an article, "Build a Strong Navy and Develop National Maritime Undertakings," for the CCP mouthpiece *People's Daily*. He justified a strong naval defense of "three million square kilometers of jurisdictional waters and more than six thousand islands. . . . Oceanic development and exploitation became strategically significant for our country."[37] On August 5, 1985, another article was published on the front page of the *PLA Daily*, titled "Shoulder the Main Responsibilities of National Defense and National Construction." Liu described new maritime concepts like nationalistic spirit and great country ideals, in his portrayal of a modern naval force with new technology, self-sacrifices, and successful defense at seas.[38] His article "The Talents as the Key to Build a Strong and Modern Navy" was published in the CCP Central Committee's journal, *Red Flag*, on January 16, 1986.[39] Shi Changxue considered maritime consciousness and oceanic awareness as an important part of Chinese nationalism. Naval strategy "is not only the soul of the Navy, but also the soul of the military and the soul of the country."[40] Rear Admiral Li Tiemin of the Naval Command University argued that the new strategy "drastically increased our defensive depth at seas and provided indispensable strategic condition for the Navy to defend the country and protect our maritime interests and resources."[41]In 1986, Liu's naval strategy was finalized after several revisions and adjustments.[42]

On February 13, 1987, Liu Huaqing and Li Yaowen cosigned their report, "The Clarification of the Naval Strategy," and submitted it to the CMC. On March 21, upon request of the PLA General Staff, the naval chiefs submitted their second report, "Brief Explanations of the Naval Strategic Issues," to the high command.[43] For the first time in PLA history, Liu argued that the navy as a strategic force was key in China's national defense, including strategic deterrence and nuclear strike. He confirmed that naval warfare at sea would be the next war between China and its enemies, including potential hostile navies in the Pacific. On April 1, the high command discussed and accepted the new naval strategy as an important part of the PLA's war strategy. In the same month, CMC chairman Deng Xiaoping and PRC president Yang Shangkun approved Liu's naval strategy.[44]

To put his strategic thinking into a strategic plan, Liu Huaqing drafted "The Navy in 2000" from 1985 to 1988.[45] According to Liu's long-term plan, the Chinese navy would break through the three island chains by 2050. When the Soviet Union declined and China rose from the 1980s to 1990s, the island chain containment strategy became an important part of the U.S. military's policy against the PLAN in the Pacific. However, Cole questioned Liu's emphasis on island chains and labeled the admiral as a "continentalist," whose perspective "violates the central tenet of classic maritime strategy . . . there is no 'terrain' at sea."[46] Cole linked Liu's army background and Chinese geostrategic outlook of centuries of continental mindset to the naval strategic thinking of a "terrain" in the map and instead of "water" in a nautical sense.

According to Liu Huaqing's plan, the PLAN would establish its presence in the first island chain, spanning from Okinawa, Japan, to Taiwan, to the Philippines, by 2010. His goal for the Chinese navy's establishment in the second chain from Sakhalin to the islands of the southwestern Pacific Ocean was targeted for 2025. At that time, "with increased new naval power, the areas of our naval warfare will gradually expand into the northern Pacific and the second island chain."[47] The PLAN would become present along the third island chain from the Aleutian Islands in the north to Antarctica in the south of the Pacific by 2050. In one of his articles, "Never Forget the Pacific's Peace," published in September 1985, Liu focused on the history of the Pacific War with emphasis on the economic reasons for the war, prewar naval races, surprise attack and deception, and the nature of World War II in the Pacific from 1941 to 1945.[48] He warned the nation and the PLA that "the Pacific was never peaceful" since the end of the Pacific War, and that "if a superpower navy starts a war today, it will likely use surprise attack as what happened in the Pacific War. . . . [We] must effectively defeat enemy surprise attack and achieve the victory at the early stage of the war." The commander asked his navy "to shoulder more responsibilities than ever before either during wartime or peacetime."[49]

To serve the three-step goals, Liu developed near sea warfighting strategy. Then-current naval capabilities included independent battles against the enemy with or without PLAAF support, countering enemy attack, and long-distance attack against enemy transportation and communication behind the lines. The near sea war plans covered landing in Taiwan and naval attacks on the Senkaku (Diaoyu) Islands. These offensive operations became defensive since they were in near sea areas. Liu summarized his war strategy as "near sea mobile warfare," which "would make a decisive impact on a surface naval war." However, he still mentioned that "the Navy would engage in frequent small group, guerrilla style, quick attacks against separated enemy ships."[50] Shambaugh points out, Liu's plan and "the operational task would be to establish a 'sea' or 'area denial' capacity in a progressively phase[d] fashion."[51] Liu's naval war plan emphasized surface combat capability, offensive attacks, area denial operations, joint campaigns, submarine warfare, and amphibious landings.

According to the "The Navy in 2000" plan, China would build a modern, blue-water naval force by 2025 with aircraft carriers and new high-tech warships. Liu Huaqing's strategy envisioned the Chinese navy with capabilities in the Pacific and Indian Oceans. His new strategy pushed the research, development, and manufacturing of new warships, as well as medium- and long-range missiles and an attack-focused weapons system, all of which would modernize the navy from the 1980s to the twenty-first century. Rear Admiral Li Tiemin concluded that Liu's naval strategy "unquestionably provided a theoretic[al] foundation for the People's Navy's development and operations, clearly showed the new direction for its modernization and professionalism, and established the basic principle and guidance for the naval war readiness."[52]

## NEW TECHNOLOGY: A BIG LEAP FORWARD

In Liu Huaqing's new strategy, a capable naval force was the core element of China's near sea defense. The navy required sophisticated anti-access and area denial technology. Liu promised the party and the country to "build a modern maritime force with combat winning capabilities."[53] To achieve his strategic goal, the naval commander spent most of his time and energy on naval equipment and technological development. Although the PLAN still lacked the power to deny a superior foreign navy, Liu tried to build a navy with denial technology in certain areas like the Taiwan Strait and East China Sea in the early twenty-first century and new capabilities in the South China Sea by the middle of the century. Shi considered Liu's "most important contribution to Chinese naval development was that he creatively and systematically made an overall, long-term strategic plan for PLAN modernization."[54] Liu's strategic thinking, war objectives, oceangoing orientation, and long-term missions helped prepare for naval technological improvement.

First, Liu Huaqing bypassed centralized planning limits, breaking with the PRC and PLA's traditional five-year planning circle long implemented since 1950. He created a new naval development pattern of fifteen years. In 1982, Liu Huaqing began outlining the "Navy's Plan for Reconstruction and Modernization." He combined three five-year plans in drafting the "PLAN Seventh Five-Year Plan (1985–1990)." He argued that complicated and sophisticated naval technology demanded a longer research, development, and manufacturing period, and that it took ten to twenty years for a warship or submarine's research, design, finalization, production, testing, and commissioning. In 1985, Liu made three important plans for the navy's technological improvements, the "PLAN Equipment Improvement Plan, 1985–2000," "Naval Development and Projects before 2000 and the Seventh Fifth-Year Plan," and "The Navy in 2000." The three plans "with historical guidance power" were designed to serve Liu's long-term development strategy for "a big leap forward." He described his plans as "making three steps into one and jumping a big step forward in fifteen years."[55] They still guide the PLAN in the twenty-first century.

Thereby, Liu Huaqing directed research to skip the 1980s' projects, and instead work on the late 1990s and early 2000s' naval R&D projects. Naval research avoided out-of-date programs, reduced its baggage, and the PLAN began researching aircraft carriers and new strategic nuclear submarines. On February 2, 1987, the navy submitted the "PLAN Equipment Improvement Plan, 1985–2000" and "Naval Development and Projects before 2000 and the Seventh Fifth-Year Plan" to the CMC, PLA General Chiefs, and State Council. According to Liu, "This fifteen-year plan merely serves a short-term goal, our navy should reach the world-class level by the middle of the twenty-first century."[56] His dream for a strong navy included "three big steps" to match his steps to break through the three island chains. The first big step was to have a naval force capable of near sea defense along the first island chain by 2000. The development goal for the second step was to build new naval capabilities in operations and far sea attacks toward the second island chain by 2025. The third goal was to have a high-quality, world-class navy to be present in and operate along the third island chain. Shi argued that "the most significant leadership role of Liu Huaqing in naval modernization was that he creatively made a long-term strategic, cross-century, and overall development plan for the Chinese Navy."[57]

Second, Liu Huaqing aimed to build a blue-water navy with advanced technology in the late twentieth century. Xi Jinping identified two shifts in Liu's guiding principles of naval research, development, manufacturing, and technological improvements in the 1980s. In the first case, Liu shifted China's naval building from a "quantity-focused" manufacture to a "quality-focused" development emphasizing new technology, top grade weapons, and cutting-edge equipment. In the second case, he shifted PLAN modernization's focus from a "coastal navy" to a "near sea navy." The two shifts "tremendously improved naval equipment and their combat capability."[58] In Liu's "Navy's Plan for Reconstruction and Modernization" in 1985, the PLAN would cease manufacturing small warships for coastal defense and would instead produce large- and medium-size warships for near sea defense and far sea operations. Liu shifted the naval building doctrine from a "quantity navy" to a "quality navy." He called the shift a "transformation from the PLAN's first-generation warships to its second-generation modern warships."[59] Developing and finalizing the navy's new strategic thinking helped plan a strong, blue-water navy with better equipment and high technology toward the end of the twentieth century.

Liu Huaqing's strategic "big leap forward" endeavored to build a navy capable of near sea defense and winning the next naval war. According to Liu, "PLAN will extend its combined and effective combat radius from current near shoreline to the first island chain. . . . [It will] deploy highly effective mobile forces deep into the oceans beyond China's seas for combat and other operational missions. . . . Our navy will have an exciting and encouraging change by the end of the century."[60] Liu Huaqing's plans included building three groups of new surface warships. The first group had new destroyers with a displacement of 3,000 tons, and then built more destroyers with 5,000–6,000 ton displacements. The second group included new frigates with displacements of 2,000–3,000 tons. The third group consisted of guided missile frigates with displacements of 500–1,000 tons.[61]

Third, Admiral Liu Huaqing continued focusing on key research for Chinese naval development through the 1980s. In October 1982, he submitted a request to the CMC for the PLAN's "Research and Assessment Center for Naval Equipment." The center was designed as a think tank for the navy and high command's top talent. In January 1983, the naval command planned the center's mission, tasks, organization, personnel, and logistics. On February 13, the PLA's Department of General Staff approved Liu's proposal to establish the first high-level advisory, strategic thinking, and decision-making institute of the PLA. Thereafter, Liu also founded the Commission of the Naval Military Science Research, the National Committee of Naval Science and Technology, and the Commission for Naval Science, Education, and Cultural Development. They served as advisory organizations and think tanks for naval planners.

On January 11, 1984, Liu Huaqing talked to participants at the naval equipment and technology conference and crafted justifications for the PLAN's technological improvement. He first argued that new research and development should serve the PLAN's new near sea defense strategy. To expand naval warfare into blue water required developing new warships, the battle radius of naval warplanes, and PLANAF air fueling. Then, he argued, naval development should focus on combined and joint operations in the near sea by improving communication, electronic system, early warning, and cooperative weapon systems on surface warships, especially on frigates and destroyers. Last, Liu demanded a new strategic position of the PLAN in the next major war that emphasized submarine development, especially new strategic weapons for nuclear submarines. They would play an important role in a nuclear showdown with deterrence and second-strike capability. In May 1985, Liu retired many old warships and airplanes and discontinued outdated equipment and weapons.[62]

Nevertheless, 1985 proved a bad year for naval development as Deng Xiaoping downsized the PLA and reduced it by 1 million troops over the next two years. From May 23 to June 6, 1985, the CMC held a landmark conference that became the starting point of Deng's 1980s military reform.

The mid-1980s reform then followed Deng's new doctrines of fighting "limited, local war" and emphasized the development and employment of new technology and improvement in PLA weaponry. Theoretically, the money saved from troop reduction would be diverted to upgrading defense technology.[63] However, the PLA received neither a bigger budget nor new technology. According to Deng, the PLA had to wait for national economic growth as a prerequisite for its technological improvement. Deng emphasized that "only when we have a good economic foundation will it be possible for us to modernize the army's equipment. Thus, we must wait patiently for a few years."[64] Deng Xiaoping believed that defense building must be subordinated to serve national economic development and that the two causes should be promoted in a coordinated manner.

With limited resources and facing troop and budget reductions, Liu Huaqing was forced to provide solutions for naval technological development from 1985 to 1990. First, he shortened development lines, prioritized key projects, focused on new technological research, and escalated renewal and remodeling in accordance with the high command's orders. Although hindered by limited manufacture and production capabilities, his practical approach prioritized new submarines, special maritime airplanes, and landing craft. Liu then worked on improving warship equipment and weapon systems to increase near sea operational capability and combat effectiveness by the turn of the century. The new electronic and digital equipment improved warship firepower, communications, reconnaissance, combined and joint operations, antisubmarine capability, and long-distance attacks.

From 1983 to 1988, Liu Huaqing combined PLAN research and development with imported foreign technology to produce China's second-generation destroyers. In 1983, Liu led design evaluation and manufacture planning of missile destroyers. As the second generation, the new destroyer had anti-air and anti-ship missiles, antisubmarine helicopters, integrated combat systems, and a long endurance. Although the navy approved the missile destroyer's development, there were different opinions from the high command against the plan. After Liu's repeated arguments, firm insistence, and strong defense, most military leaders accepted the new warship production plan generally, but two issues remained, specifically on shipboard helicopters and anti-air missile system. Liu again worked with research institutes and the defense industry and decided on the Chinese-made Type Z-9 as the solution.[65] In 1984, the CMC approved the proposal and prioritized the new destroyer as one of the four major battle projects for national defense. In 1987, the PLA high command approved Liu's plan to manufacture Z-9 helicopters for the new destroyers.

Meanwhile, Liu Huaqing suggested importing foreign-made AIM-9 Sidewinder missiles as the anti-air system. He used his successful experience in importation and imitation from Russian naval technology from the 1960s to the 1970s. He also seized the momentum of China's opening-up policy and acquired new technologies and know-how from the Western countries. The admiral said that "introduction [to] and learning from Western technology will help our own research and shorten the distance between us and them. . . . We are not only buying new tech, but also buying our time. We cannot stay behind [the Western navies] too long."[66] His suggestion was accepted by the high command. In 1987, the PLAN signed a purchase contract for Sidewinder missiles. At that time, Liu also imported diesel engines and gas turbines to replace Chinese steam powered engines for the new destroyers. In 1989, China began building its second-generation destroyers.[67]

Admiral Liu Huaqing continued his effort on conventional missile submarine research and manufacturing. On October 12, 1982, he observed a successful launch of an underwater ballistic missile from a submarine, after its first test failed five days before.[68] He told scientists, experts, researchers, and engineers at the Naval Technological Development Conference in January 1984 that "for the defensive battles in the near sea, submarines still have much promise."[69] In 1987, Liu retired imitated Russian-type conventional submarines and shifted national resources to the improvement of Chinese-designed submarines from the 1970s to the 1980s. After the high command approved Liu's plan, China began manufacturing its improved conventional submarines in 1988 and delivered the new submarines to the navy in 1991. In the late 1990s, Liu's underwater fleet had Chinese-made SSBNs, SSNs, and conventionally powered submarines.[70]

Admiral Liu recalled his long career and continued efforts in developing China's nuclear submarines. "I began to participate and lead nuclear submarines' research and development in 1961. Thereafter, it doesn't matter where I worked or what I did, I was always involved in submarine projects for more than thirty years. I was there for all of its successes and setbacks."[71] After becoming the navy's commander, Liu continued to learn nuclear technology and nuclear submarine development from the West. On December 19, 1982, he hosted a banquet for U.S. admiral Hyman G. Rickover in Beijing and accompanied him to meet Hu Yaobang, CCP secretary general, the next day. Admiral Rickover was known as the "Father of the Nuclear Navy" and served in U.S. Navy for thirty-two years (see photo 6).

In November 1984, Liu Huaqing visited the British Royal Navy's HMNB Clyde in central Scotland as the home of British nuclear deterrence. The Chinese naval delegate observed British nuclear submarine training, exercise, and rescue practice. Liu Huaqing was impressed by the British nuclear submarine fleet's safety routines and emergency measures.[72] After his return, Liu strengthened safety management on Chinese nuclear submarines. When the Chernobyl nuclear disaster happened in the Soviet Union, Liu chaired the Naval Nuclear Safety Conference in Beijing on September 26, 1987, and updated nuclear safety regulations, crew examinations, and safety training procedures. In 1988, Liu established the Bureau of Nuclear Safety in the PLAN headquarters.[73]

As naval commander, Liu Huaqing emphasized nuclear submarine testing, operation, maintenance, and training. In the 1980s, the PLAN improved the Type 091 *Han*-class nuclear submarine (SSN). In March 1983, Liu was briefed by the NSF commander on nuclear submarine bases, crews, and logistics at NSF. In that year, his nuclear submarine *Long March-1* embarked on a monthlong voyage. In August 1984, Liu Huaqing commissioned China's first missile-bearing nuclear submarine, a Type 092 *Xia*-class SSBN. In 1985, Liu ordered his nuclear submarine 403 to embark on a long-distance voyage from November 20 to February 18, 1986. In the same year, the navy received two *Xia*-class SSBNs armed with twelve CSS-N-3 missiles, and three *Han*-class SSNs armed with six SY-2 cruise missiles. In September 1988, the successful underwater launch of a ballistic missile by a nuclear submarine demonstrated the PLAN's capability to provide underwater strategic deterrence and limited nuclear counterattack.[74] Under Liu's leadership in the high command and the Party Center, the PLAN continued nuclear submarine development after the admiral left the navy and became CMC vice chairman in 1988 and Politburo

**PHOTO 6.** Admiral James A. Lyons Jr., USN, congratulates Admiral Liu Huaqing, commander of the Chinese navy, after presenting him with a U.S. Navy surface warfare breast insignia during a ceremony aboard the USS *Reeves* (CG 24) in Qingdao, China, in 1986. U.S. Naval Institute photo archive

Standing Committee member from 1992 to 1998. Liu's lifetime efforts contributed to China's next SSN and SSBN projects, including the Type 093 *Shang*-class in 2006 and Type 094 *Jin*-class in 2007.

By the mid-1980s, the sizable Chinese navy fielded nearly all types of warships and became a regional naval power. Its surface warship fleet included destroyers, frigates, corvettes, minesweepers, minelayers, missile boats, torpedo boats, landing ships, and auxiliary vessels.[75] Its aviation fleet was equipped with medium and light bombers, fighters, attack planes, ship-based helicopters, and reconnaissance/surveillance planes, assisted by a radar network that covered all of China's coasts. Its offshore defense force replaced coastal cannons with anti-ship missiles. Its overall technological level became competitive with other global navies. The tactics and technological performance of the Chinese-made naval equipment improved a great deal. The main surface combat warships greatly improved in terms of being fitted with missiles, integration between command and control, and implementation of stereoscopic combat zones. In the late 1980s, the PLAN was equipped with new guided missile destroyers, fighter-bombers, anti-submarine helicopters, and high-performance equipment and weapons. The PLAN Air Force began testing a newly developed jet fighter, the JH-7 "Flying Leopard" (the FBC-1 is the export version), in 1988. The JH-7 attacking fighter filled the need for a long-range (1,600 kilometers) strike aircraft for the navy. While the PLA Air Force adopted the Russian-made Su-27 fighters, the naval air force adopted the JH-7 as its main strike aircraft in the 1990s. By 1987, the PLAN became the third largest navy in the world with 350,000 sailors and 1,000 ships, including 350 oceangoing warships.[76]

On November 18, 1987, Deng Xiaoping invited Liu Huaqing to meet at his home with CMC vice chairmen Zhao Ziyang and Yang Shangkun and General Hong Xuezhi, chief of the PLA Department of General Logistics (DGL). As the CMC chairman, Deng Xiaoping informed Liu and Hong that the high command had decided to appoint both as deputy secretaries general of the CMC. Deng pointed to Liu and explained it to the others, "With this appointment, he will work on [PLA] modernization and equipment." Then, Deng emphasized it again to Liu. "To transfer you to the CMC is to promote military modernization. It is you who is mostly familiar with miliary R&D in the entire PLA. Your new appointment is for [military] equipment and technology."[77] In 1987, Liu was promoted to serve as deputy secretary general and vice chairman of the CCP Central Military Commission (CMC). In 1988, he was made a full admiral.

Although he left the PLAN's commander post in 1988, Liu continued efforts in naval development and modernization. From 1988 to 1992, he oversaw the PLA's development of military science and technology, and made new plans for naval technology improvement, including naval aviation technology. He continued his research-led naval modernization efforts against any questions, suspicions, and oppositions. He knew what challenges the PLAN faced and what kind of new warships and technology were needed to win the next naval war. As a result, China's shipbuilding industry, navigation technology research and imports, and naval training and education systems supported impressive naval developments in the 1980s. Liu Huaqing transformed the PLAN from green-water operations to a blue-water development through reconstruction, qualitative improvement, higher educational standard for personnel, and new Western technology. Richard A. Bitzinger and other scholars point out that "prior to the 1989 Western arms embargo, China had secured valuable access to key foreign technologies to help kick-start indigenous naval S&T (science and technology). . . . European naval technologies enabled China to institute its new-con warship programs, best manifested in the *Luhu*, *Jiangwei*, *Houjian*, and *Song* series, which served as testbeds for subsequent designs."[78] By the late 1980s, the PLAN was ready for new operations and combat in the Pacific and South China Sea.

## BLUE-WATER TRAINING AND OPERATIONS

Admiral Liu Huaqing's near sea defense strategy required new blue-water operational capabilities. First, the new naval strategy demanded the PLAN's gaining and maintaining control of strategic areas in the near sea for a certain period. Second, the navy should effectively control key near sea routes connecting China with other oceans when necessary. Third, the Chinese navy should be able to fight against other navies in the connected seas. Fourth, the PLAN should have a strong nuclear power for second strike responses.[79] Liu promised Chinese people to "build a modern maritime force with combat winning capabilities."[80] Naval technological improvement provided new blue-water capability for the Chinese navy.

One of the naval strategy's objectives involved breaking the first island chain to reach the second island chain in the Western Pacific.

The naval commander told his captains repeatedly that "the PLAN is not a coast guard," and that it should sail to the oceans.[81] From 1982 to 1988, Liu Huaqing opened new oceangoing training facilities, set up captain and officer evaluation systems, and sent the Chinese navy to the Pacific. Liu stated at the National Defense University in 1986 that "the Pacific region will be the center of global economic development in the next century. Because of this change, global political and military center of gravity will definitely shift into this region."[82]

In January 1983, Liu Huaqing organized a training squadron to sail to the Western Pacific. He worked with Vice Admiral Zhang Xusan, PLAN deputy chief of staff, and submitted their plan on February 23 to the high command. On May 16, the squadron commanded by Zhang Xusan left the Zhanjiang Naval Base with more than 150 captains and young officers aboard. The squadron sailed straight south through the Paracel Islands, Spratly Islands, and then James Shoal in the South China Sea. It was the PLAN's first time to arrive at China's southernmost claimed oceanic territory.[83] On May 25–26, Zhang's squadron traveled northeast, crossing the Balintang Channel between Batanes and Babuyan Islands, and entered the Western Pacific. When the squadron reached Iwo Jima, they received a severe weather warning from Beijing and Liu Huaqing ordered Zhang Xusan to cut the voyage short and return to safety. The squadron then sailed west through the Osumi Strait to the East China Sea. Zhang sailed southwest through the Taiwan Strait and returned to Zhanjiang on June 14, having sailed 6,721 nautical miles.[84]

Thereafter, all three fleets organized oceanic training and exercises in 1984. The number of participating warships increased 2.4 times more than that in 1983, and the number of participating airplanes increased 4.3 times. Both NSF and ESF training squadrons sailed into the Sea of Japan. In early 1986, Liu Huaqing instructed Vice Admiral Ma Xinchun, NSF commander, to organize a joint fast-response exercise to improve combat capability outside the first island chain in the Western Pacific.[85] In May, Commander Ma led the exercise squadron and sailed toward the Pacific. The squadron included three missile destroyers, two submarines, two helicopters, a large supply ship, and a deep-water rescue ship. After they crossed the Osumi

Strait and entered the training area, east of Okinawa and north of Iwo Jima, several bombers and fighters joined the exercise. Ma launched air bombings, anti-ship missiles, submarine attacks, and practiced long-range shooting. He also organized a joint night attack, guided helicopter shooting, rescue operations, and replenishment-at-sea. The exercise lasted fifteen days, accomplishing forty training objectives, while sailing more than four thousand nautical miles in the Western Pacific.[86]

By 1987, all naval war simulation exercises were transferred from electronic to digital systems at naval headquarters, fleet commands, aviation units, institutes, and college levels.[87] Liu Huaqing also implemented maritime laser electronics simulation systems for naval combat training, tactical confrontation, anti-ship missile attack, antisubmarine operation, and digital warfare at sea. From July to August, he commanded the North Sea Fleet to conduct four large-scale laser exercises for combat tactics and joint operation in the Yellow Sea. CCP leaders, PLA chiefs, and top PRC officials observed the exercises and were all impressed by how close the exercises were to real battle situations and how accurate the evaluations could be on the results between the two confronting naval teams.[88] Liu recalled years later that "this exercise opened a new path for our staff and officers' planning and training in a modern and high-tech way. . . . The assessment result indicated that the laser electronic simulators provided much better information and calculations on battle capability, ship location and conditions, combat support, and problem solving. It improved [our] fast response capability."[89] In 1987, the naval logistical ship *Fengcang* began supplying fuel and food to Chinese missile destroyers and missile frigates in the Pacific, which solved the last of the Chinese Navy's three problems for ocean voyages, including long-distance communication, ocean sailing guidance, and replenishment-at-seas.[90]

Liu Huaqing's technological improvement and far-sea training exercises served the PLAN well and prepared it for oceangoing missions and combat in the 1980s. In 1984, after gaining approval from the State Council and CMC, the PLAN launched an Antarctic expedition to establish China's "Great Wall Research Station" at the South Pole. Admiral Hu Yanlin justifies the Chinese exploitation, "with the rapid economic development and population growth, [our] land resources consumed tremendously, it is an inevitable trend [for China] to demand new resources and new living space from the oceans. Therefore, to explore oceanic resources and to maintain [our] sea power are critical to the existence and development of Chinese people."[91] On November 22, 1984, the Antarctic Expedition Formation left Shanghai and included the PLAN J 121 rescue ship with 308 naval sailors commanded by Vice Admiral Zhao Guochen, PLAN chief of staff. After almost one month's sail, the Chinese expedition passed Cape Horn and arrived at Ushuaia, Argentina. It was the first time the Chinese navy crossed the Pacific Ocean and reached the South American continent. Around 2 a.m. on December 26, the expeditionary squadron arrived at the South Pole. Naval personnel worked with more than two hundred scientists, researchers, engineers, and technicians to build China's first station at the South Pole. On February 14, 1985, Zhao Guochen reported to Liu Huaqing in Beijing that the "Great Wall South Pole Research Station" was completed.[92] Commander Zhao's squadron returned to Shanghai on April 10 after a voyage of 40,000 nautical miles.

Starting in 1985, Liu Huaqing sent his fleet formations on diplomatic goodwill visits to other continents and the PLAN began participating in joint military exercises with warships from many countries. On November 16, 1985, Vice Admiral Nie Kuiju, ESF commander, left Shanghai with the missile destroyer 132 and supply ship X 615 for a friendly trip to three Southeast Asian countries. After sixteen days' sail, the Chinese squadron arrived first at Karachi, the largest city of Pakistan. From December 18 to 25, Commander Nie and his squadron visited Colombo, Sri Lanka. His last stop was Chittagong, Bangladesh, from December 26 to 30. The Chinese squadron traveled 15,000 nautical miles in 65 days and made the PLAN's inaugural voyage to the Indian Ocean (see photos 7 and 8).[93]

Moreover, Liu Huaqing's new naval strategy included an operational principle of near sea combats and far sea attacks to serve the strategic goal of A2/AD. The Battle of the Spratly Islands became a case in point for the PLAN to gain control and defend the disputed islands in the South China Sea. As soon as he became PLAN commander, Liu ordered SSF to send a patrol squadron to the Paracel and Spratly Islands. From 1982 to 1988, he personally visited the Paracels three times to inspect construction of the Yongxing airstrip and harbor. In early 1988, China did not have control of any island or reef of the Spratly Islands. Xi Jinping argued that it was Liu who "led to draft the original policy and operational plans of the fight

PHOTO 7. Admiral James D. Watkins escorts Admiral Liu Huaqing to arrival ceremonies at the Washington Navy Yard on November 13, 1985. U.S. Naval Institute photo archive

over the Spratly Islands and led to complete construction of the Yongshu Maritime Observatory Station. He was one of the leaders to command the defense of the Spratly Islands."[94]

While the Sino-Vietnamese border conflict continued through the 1980s, Liu reinforced SSF and instructed the fleet to be prepared for a possible conflict against the Vietnamese navy over the disputed islands. Meanwhile, Liu Huaqing ordered SSF to conduct marine and seaway surveys of the South China Sea. SSF assigned Wu Buyun as chief of the survey squadron in early 1986. Wu Buyun led his squadron throughout the South China Sea, visiting more than 2,000 islands and reefs, mapping navigation conditions, and drawing marine charts. They also conducted surveys on more than 230 islands and reefs in the Spratly Islands. In April, PLAN intelligence reported that the Vietnamese navy deployed a warship to capture Wu and his team as they conducted a survey of the Gulf of Tonkin. The PLAN immediately requested Wu's return to Yulin Naval

**PHOTO 8.** Admiral Liu Huaqing, commander of the People's Liberation Army Navy, receives honors at the Washington Navy Yard on November 13, 1985. U.S. Naval Institute photo archive

Base in Hainan but he remained on the survey mission and completed his tasks while escaping the Vietnamese ship.[95]

From March 7 to April 1, 1987, UNESCO's Intergovernmental Oceanographic Commission (IOC) met in Paris, including more than three hundred official representatives from eighty-seven countries. As IOC's fourteenth international conference, the commission discussed the issues and status of more than 200 Global Sea Level Observing System posts over the world. IOC asked China to build a new station, No. 74 Marine Observatory, in the Spratly Islands. When Yan Hongmo, China maritime bureau chief and head of the Chinese delegation to the conference, told Liu Huaqing about the commission's decision, Liu believed that "the historical moment is coming for us to change the situation on the Spratly Islands!"[96] At that time, China did not have any actual territorial control of the Spratly Islands, even though the PRC government claimed the sovereignty. The Spratly (Nansha) Islands lie over 550 nautical miles from

China, cover a water area of 61,775 square miles, and include 230 islands and reefs. Among them, Vietnam controlled twenty-nine, the Philippines nine, Malaysia nine, and Taiwan occupied one. Then, Admiral Liu Huaqing saw the opportunity for China to enter the Spratly Islands and claim its sovereign rights.[97]

On April 23, 1987, Liu Huaqing ordered SSF commander Vice Admiral Chen Mingshan to send a battle formation to Spratly to claim China's maritime sovereignty, present the PLAN's naval power in the area, and improve SSF combat readiness in the South China Sea.[98] On May 8, a combat squadron, including one missile destroyer, five missile frigates, and four supply ships, left for the Spratly Islands under the command of SSF chief of staff Rear Admiral Li Shuwen. Meanwhile, maritime bureau chief Yan Hongmo sent his maritime research team, consisting of 159 oceanic scientists, geologists, marine experts, environmentalists, construction engineers, and ecologists, to Spratly. After their site search and geographic survey, the team chose the Yongshu (Fiery Cross) Reef as the location for the 74th Marine Observatory post. The bottom of the Yongshu Reef was about sixteen miles long and four miles wide. During high tide, only a small portion of the reef was visible above sea level.[99] On August 7, Liu and Yan Hongmo requested the State Council and CMC's approval of building a marine observation post at Yongshu Reef. On November 6, China announced plans to establish No. 74 Marine Observatory in the Spratly Islands. The CMC and State Council assigned the navy as main construction force for the observatory station.[100]

After receiving approval from the high command, Admiral Liu Huaqing chaired a naval planning conference and appointed PLAN deputy commander Vice Admiral Zhang Lianzhong as the Yongshu observatory construction task force's chief. Although Admiral Liu was promoted to deputy secretary general of the CMC on November 21, 1987, and left the navy on January 29, 1988, he continued focusing on the Yongshu marine observation post's construction. In early January, he called several meetings with CMC vice chairmen, general chiefs, and defense minister to discuss naval war preparations in the South China Sea. The admiral convinced the PLA chiefs that time was of the essence for claiming the Spratly Islands. If China did not occupy the Spratly Islands immediately, the country would never have a foothold in the South China Sea. Chinese leaders could not lose the maritime territory inherited from their ancestors. Other countries did not want to negotiate with Beijing about Spratly because the PRC did not have any leverage, and China did not have any island or reef in the Spratly chain. The more reefs the PLAN occupied, the more initiative the PRC would have.[101]

In January 1988, Liu Huaqing summoned Zhang Lianzhong and Li Yaowen, PLAN political commissar, to plan a possible international conflict at the Spratly Islands.[102] After Vice Admiral Zhang Lianzhong became the navy's commander, his agenda prioritized preparation for a naval battle against the Vietnamese navy over the Spratly Islands. He learned a lesson from the 1974 Battle of the Paracel Islands and issued a pre-active order to SSF commander Vice Admiral Chen Mingshan to send a squadron to the Spratlys before the observatory construction commenced.

On January 11, Chen Mingshan ordered SSF chief of staff Rear Admiral Li Shuwen to lead the 520 Squadron to Spratly, including the missile destroyer *Nanning* 162 and five frigates. Among the frigates were Type 065 *Jiangnan*-class *Nanchong* 502 with a displacement of 1,400 tons and three 100mm cannons and two 37mm AAA guns; Type 053H1 *Jianghu-II* class *Xiangtan* 556 with a displacement of 1,925 tons and four 100mm cannons and two 37mm AAA guns; and *Xichang* 508, 503, and 531 frigates. After the squadron arrived, Li Shuwen deployed two frigates, 531 and 556, to patrol the Yongshu Reef, at the designated construction site, while *Nanchong* 502 and frigate 503 secured the reef by building several high outposts. During the nineteen days of preconstruction patrol, Li Shuwen received several intel warnings that the Vietnamese navy would attack soon.[103] Vietnam already occupied twenty-nine islands and reefs in the Spratly Islands.

On January 31, 1988, two Vietnamese warships approached the Yongshu Reef. Li Shuwen ordered frigates to intercept them and prevent their reaching Yongshu. After several attempts, the Vietnamese failed to land and retreated. Li sent six officers and sailors from *Xichang* 508 to land at the Yongshu Reef. It became the first reef in the Spratly Islands occupied by the Chinese. They raised the Chinese flag at 4 p.m. signifying China's claim over the reef. After receiving Li's engagement report, Admiral Liu Huaqing ordered construction of the 74th Marine Observatory as soon as possible. Admiral Hu Yanlin describes Yongshu from then on as the front line for China's southern frontier.[104]

On February 3, Commander Zhang Lianzhong organized his construction fleet at SSF Zhanjiang Naval Base, including seven warships, four submarines, four landing crafts, eight construction vessels, and eleven supply ships.[105] On February 7, the first group of eleven ships arrived at Yongshu and built stilt houses. Vietnamese warships tried to reach Yongshu but SSF sent more warships to protect the engineering, research survey, construction, and logistical ships around the reef. On the 16th, after the first stilt house was completed, Li sent five seamen to remain there for Yongshu's defense. However, from February 10 to 16, Vietnamese troops occupied five reefs around Yongshu, and the total of the Vietnamese-held islands and reefs increased to thirty-four.

Liu Huaqing realized that his seamen could not hold Yonghsu alone if the Vietnamese occupied other reefs around it. He ordered the SSF to "occupy more reefs whenever you can and defend all of them after you have control!" SSF headquarters passed on Liu's order to Li Shuwen, who dispatched his warships to the reefs around Yongshu.[106] Soon skirmishes between the Chinese and Vietnamese navies broke out over those reefs (see map 10).

On February 17, the destroyer *Nanning* 162 and frigate *Xichang* 508 escorted tug ship *Nantuo* 147 to the Huayang (Cuarteron) Reef. In the early evening, *Nantuo* 147 met Vietnamese minesweeper HQ 851 and transport ship HQ 614 on their way Huayang. The Chinese maneuvered *Nantuo* 147 and tried blocking the Vietnamese landing at the reef. The destroyer *Nanning* 162 also aimed at the Vietnamese ships but maintained the "do not shoot first" policy. During the standoff, the Vietnamese sent dinghies with armed personnel to the reef. Li Shuwen ordered the 162 and 147 captains to send teams to occupy Huayang before the Vietnamese. The race ensued and the Chinese motorboat from the tug ship 147 reached the reef first where six armed workers hoisted the flag up on a steel bracing to signify Chinese sovereignty. The Vietnamese stopped about 100 yards out as they faced a machine gun and several automatic weapons. After Chinese reinforcements arrived at the reef, the Vietnamese returned to their ships. Within three days, Chinese construction workers built a shelter on Huayang Reef, making it the second reef after Yongshu occupied by the PLAN in southern Spratly.[107] Li Shuwen stationed twenty-four seamen for

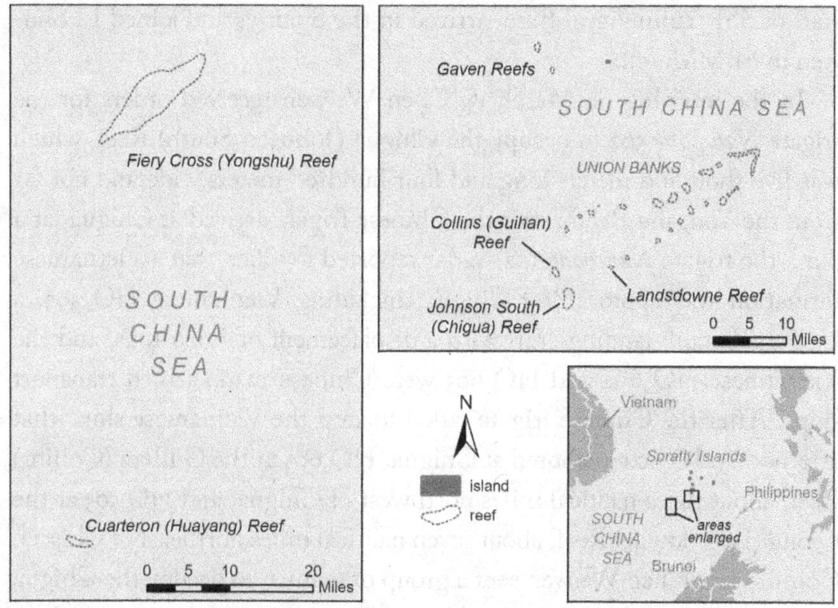


MAP 10. The Battle of the Spratly Islands, 1988

the reef's defense. On February 25, the Chinese occupied two more reefs, the Zhenghe Reef group and Nanxun Reef.

On February 12 and 26, Liu Huaqing briefed Zhao Ziyang, CCP secretary general and the first vice chairman of the CMC, twice on the naval conflict situations at Spratly. Admiral Liu argued that "the Battle of Spratly is inevitable, and it is strategically and historically significant. . . . Moreover, it provides a good opportunity for our naval force to improve its war readiness and increase its combat capability." Satisfied with Liu's briefing, Zhao Ziyang asked him to forward the report to Deng Xiaoping. On February 29, Deng Xiaoping read Liu's report with approval, "Agree!"[108] On March 10, Liu and the CMC briefed the Politburo Standing Committee on the battle situation at Spratly and emphasized that "we must stop any intervention or aggression against China's sovereignty in the South China Sea. The conflict of Spratly will continue for a long time, we must keep our forces in the area to show the Chinese military presence."[109] The PLAN sent reinforcement from SSF and ESF to the Spratly Islands. The SSF 520 Squadron commanded by Commodore Chen Weiwen, chief of staff of SSF Yulin Naval Base, arrived in the Spratlys and joined Li Shuwen in early March.

In the morning on March 13, Chen Weiwen received orders for the frigate *Nanchong* 502 to occupy the Chigua (Johnson South) Reef, which was five thousand meters long and four hundred meters wide and not far from the Yongshu Reef. After the Chinese frigate arrived at Chigua, at 4 p.m., the frigate *Nanchong* 502's radar reported to Chen that a Vietnamese formation was approaching Chigua, including Vietnamese HQ 505, a U.S.-made tank landing craft with a displacement of 4,080 tons, and the Vietnamese HQ 604 and HQ 605 were Chinese-made armed transport ships. After the Chinese frigate failed to stop the Vietnamese ships that afternoon, HQ 604 anchored at Chigua; HQ 605 at the Guihan (Collins) Reef, about three nautical miles northwest of Chigua; and HQ 505 at the Qiong (Lensdowne) Reef, about seven nautical miles northeast of Chigua. Commodore Chen Weiwen sent a group of seamen to occupy the Chigua Reef at 10 p.m. and called in his frigates *Xiangtan* 531 and 556 to reinforce *Nanchong* 502.[110]

The "3–14 Battle of the Chigua Reef" (or the Johnson South Reef Skirmish) started in the early morning. On March 14, HQ 604 landed Vietnamese troops and armed workers at the Chigua Reef. Chen Weiwen sent more sailors to the reef after his frigates *Xiangtan* 531 and 556 arrived to support *Nanchong* 502. By 7:29 a.m., there were forty-three Vietnamese soldiers and fifty-eight Chinese sailors on the Chigua Reef under the command of *Nanchong* 502's political commissar Li Chuqun. Both sides shouted and moved carefully toward each other. Li Chuqun shouted in Vietnamese, asking the Vietnamese to leave the reef, while the Vietnamese asked the Chinese to return to their ships in Chinese. At 8:30 a.m., when both sides met in the middle of the reef, a Chinese sailor grasped the Vietnamese flag. The Vietnamese flag holder jumped out and tried to recover the flag. Eventually, someone opened fire and the first round from the Vietnamese wounded Deputy Gunnery Officer Yang Zhiling in his left arm. Accounts conflict on who fired the first shot.[111]

After the gunfight broke out on Chigua, Chen Weiwen ordered frigate *Nanchong* 502 to shell Vietnamese HQ 604, *Xiangtan* 531 to concentrate fire on landing ship HQ 505, and frigate 556 to fire on HQ 605. Soon Vietnamese HQ 604 was hit, caught fire, and sank around 9 a.m.

on March 14. Then, Chinese frigate *Nanchong* 502 joined *Xiangtan* 531 and fired on the landing ship HQ-505, which was the Vietnamese flagship, armed with eight 40mm guns. After suffering heavy damage, the Vietnamese ship fled Chigua and ran aground on the Guihan Reef. Meanwhile, Vietnamese HQ 605 was also severely damaged and sank near the Qiong Reef that evening. According to the Vietnamese statistics, sixty-four Vietnamese soldiers were killed and nine were captured by the Chinese on Chigua Reef.[112]

The PLAN won the 3–14 Battle of Chigua Reef by sinking one Vietnamese ship and damaging another two. The Chinese navy's victory elated Liu Huaqing at the Naval Operational Commanding Center in Beijing. He still remembered the strong feeling he had at that moment many years later. "All the sudden, the resentful feeling, being bullied by others and contained by others, which had been stuck deeply in my heart for many years, was gone! Now the Chinese Navy is nothing like it was before that it could only stay at the doorstep to defend the coast. Although Chigua was merely a small battle, it indicated the power of the Chinese Navy."[113]

Under Liu Huaqing's order, the Chinese navy occupied the Dongmen Reef of the Jiuzhang Reef Group on March 15, and Zhubi Reef of the Zhongye Reef Group in the north on the 25th. To control the Spratlys, they established a regular garrison with permanent bunkers and defense works at six reefs and atolls. On March 31, at the celebration of the 3–14 Battle of the Chigua Reef at Zhanjiang Naval Base, Commodore Chen Weiwen and his staff were awarded by the PLAN, and Yang Zhiliang became the battle's hero. During his hospitalization in Beijing, Yang Shangkun, China's vice president, Chi Haotian, PLA chief of general staff, and Admiral Li Yaowen, the navy's political commissar, visited Yang Zhiliang. A year later, Yang Zhiliang got married and Admiral Liu Huaqing and PLAN political commissar Li Yaowen attended his wedding ceremony.

On August 1, 1988, the No. 74 Marine Observatory Station became operational on Yongshu. It was built on an artificial island and included a seaport, airstrip, naval facilities, radar and warning system, island defense, and living quarters. The station's main building has two floors with a length of 80 meters, and its harbor can moor a 5,000-ton ship.[114] In April 1988, Liu Huaqing began efforts in air refueling technology to provide effective air support to defend the Spratly Islands and to protect other Chinese-held islands in the South China Sea. He made two trips to the Paracel Islands and worked on the airport construction from October 1988 to April 1990. The airport was built on Yongxing Island, about 200 km from Hainan Island in the north and 800 km to Yongshu Reef in the south. In May 1990, the airport became operational and the PLAN Air Force deployed its jet fighters in the Paracel Islands.[115] On September 2, 1991, China released the nine Vietnamese POWs taken during the Battle of Chigua Reef.

## CORRUPTION, RECTIFICATION, AND THE TIANANMEN SQUARE INCIDENT

After taking office in August 1982, Admiral Liu continued his predecessor Ye Fei's reorganization and rehabilitation of the navy by addressing personnel problems from the Cultural Revolution, reducing factional and regional differences, and training the officer corps in modern naval war concepts. Although he enthusiastically carried out Deng Xiaoping's military reform agenda, he strengthened the navy throughout Deng's downsizing the PLA by 1 million troops from 1985 to 1987.

Deng Xiaoping held a landmark military conference from May 23 to June 6, 1985 that became the starting point of his 1980s military reform. Deng told the Chinese generals and admirals that peace and development were the two leading trends in international affairs. The PLA needed to contemplate a new and different international environment and must participate in China's ongoing reforms.[116] First, the Chinese armed forces should expect a "local war" or a "limited war" rather than a "total war" or a "nuclear war" in the future. Second, the next "local war" or "limited war" needed a professional force with modern technology.[117] This was another strategic transition from Mao's "people's war" doctrine to a new "people's war under modern condition" doctrine.[118] The PLA reform followed Deng's new doctrine and emphasized the development of new military technology. Theoretically, the money saved from troop reduction would be allocated to upgrading defense technology.[119] However, the PLA did not get what it wanted in terms of a bigger budget. According to Deng, the PLA had to wait for national economic growth as prerequisite for its technology improvement. Deng emphasized that "only when we have a good economic foundation will it be possible for us to modernize the army's equipment. So we must wait patiently for a few years."[120] He believed that defense building must be subordinated to serve national economic development and that the two causes should be promoted in a coordinated manner.

Liu Huaqing followed Deng's new doctrine and began naval rectification and reforms by emphasizing standard evaluation, officer regulations, and naval professionalism. He organized the design and drafting of the "Naval Officers Training Manual," the "Captains Training Outlines," and the "Training Handbook for the Officers above the Divisional Level in the Navy."[121] The new guidelines and regulations further defined the duties and responsibilities of naval officers and improved the chain of command. He also removed some of the aging admirals and rebalanced the ratio between officers and seamen. In 1985, Liu approved the establishment of the "Legal Consultant Office of the Naval Headquarters," and then upgraded to the "Naval Office of the Legal Consultation" in 1987. Liu also established legal consultants at all the naval fleets, bases, and aviation. There were legal consultants at the army and division commands and paralegal representatives at the regimental and battalion levels. The Naval Legal Consultation Office became the first of its kind to uphold military law in the PLA. In 1988, all PLA services, regional commands, group armies, and military establishments began to create their own legal consultant offices and law firms.[122] Through the 1980s, the PLAN grew into a maritime force of considerable size, supported by China's indigenous industry and education systems.

During the reforms, Liu Huaqing reorganized the navy headquarters institutionally and professionally. He established detention rooms at the headquarters to punish those who ignored the new orders and remained undisciplined, slack, lazy, and lacking in military professionalism. After a few months, the headquarters changed its complex environment by replacing the poor, messy, and dirty appearances with clean, healthy, and decent working conditions.[123] His reform efforts received full support from his political commissar Li Yaowen. Li joined the CCP in 1937 and became an infantry company political instructor, then a regiment and brigade political commissar in World War II. He was a PLA division and army political commissar in the civil war. Li Yaowen participated in the

Battle of Chosin Reservoir in Korea as the CPVF 26th Army's political commissar. After his return, he was made a major general in 1955. Li was promoted to the Ji'nan Military Region's political commissar in 1965. Approved by Premier Zhou Enlai, Li Yaowen became vice minister of the PRC's Ministry of Foreign Affairs in 1970. He was then appointed as China's ambassador to Tanzania in 1972, the first Chinese ambassador to Madagascar in 1975, and ambassador to the Soviet Union in 1976. He worked with Liu Huaqing after he became CSTIND political commissar in 1977. After Ye Fei's retirement, Li Yaowen was appointed the navy's political commissar in October 1980. He was ranked admiral in September 1988.[124] Li Yaowen supported Liu Huaqing's reorganizations, rectification, and changes through the 1980s, including the PLAN's commercialization since 1985.

However, the PLA admirals and generals described Deng Xiaoping's economic reform as a "double-edged sword." "It [globalization] plays a positive role in promoting world economic development. However, one must not underestimate its negative impact as it may pose more challenges to under-developed countries."[125] While reducing 2 million troops, Deng also reduced the defense budget in the mid-1980s military reform to generate desperately needed resources for national economic reconstruction. China's annual defense budget was reduced from 17.4 percent of the national governmental expenses in 1975 to 10.4 percent of the national budget in 1985, and to 8 percent in 1995.[126] The PLAN suffered a gradual reduction of annual military budgets. The East Sea Fleet requested construction of a naval base on Chongming Island, a strategic point at the mouth of the Yangzi River, but the high command rejected it due to defense budget cuts. Zhoushan Naval Base lacked financial resources and could not solve its issues with potable water, leading to serious conflicts over fresh water with the island's local fishermen. With industrialization and shifting to a market economy, PLAN recruitment declined, and seamen morale was low. A naval officer earned only about half the salary of an average urban worker.[127]

To ease the defense budget crisis, on May 4, 1985, the Party Center and CMC allowed PLA units to engage in commercial manufacturing, business activities, and foreign trade.[128] Some generals opposed PLA-run business policy and argued that the military participation in business would certainly create interest groups and power-capital establishments as the foundations for corruption and power abuse.[129] Nevertheless, most naval officers welcomed the new policy and readied themselves to enter the business world and make money.

Although as confused as other admirals, Liu Huaqing retained his loyalty and firmly supported the high command's decision by engaging the PLAN in the market economy. The navy soon established the Songhai Corporation in Shanghai and Xinghai Corporation in Guangzhou as international commercial shipping companies that used hundreds of naval transit vessels for river and oceanic commercial shipping.[130] The latter included a dozen Hong Kong–based container freighters with a 400,000-ton capacity. The PLAN opened and leased twenty-nine naval bases, ports, and facilities for business and commercial purposes.[131] Some naval bases and PLAN Air Force airfields ran department stores, office buildings, hotels, golf clubs, nightclubs, KTVs, brothels, and underground casinos. Many squadrons owned supermarkets, restaurants, gas stations, and convenient stores. The East Sea Fleet opened a substantial shopping mall in Shanghai with hundreds of stores selling imported luxuries, name-brand apparel, electrical appliances, and furniture. A naval base commander leased an anti-aircraft artillery regiment, including all AAA cannons, radar system, equipment, vehicles, and facilities, and the base to a Hong Kong film company for a monthlong production.

Many PLAN conglomerates were controlled by naval "princelings"—children of high-ranking naval officers. Admiral Liu Huaqing's daughter, Lieutenant Colonel Liu Chaoying (Helen Liu), deputy chief of the Fifth Division of the Intelligence Department of the PLA General Staff, concurrently served as one of Baoli CEOs. The Baoli (Poly) Corporation was established by the PLA's Department of General Staff and involved in manufacturing, energy production, defense industry, and international trade. The military entrepreneurial empire had total assets of over $1 billion, including a $700 million real estate portfolio, steel mills, power plants, and a large portion of China's arms sales trade. Later, she became an executive at China Aerospace International Holdings and China Aerospace Science and Technology Corporation. In July 1996, Liu Chaoying was introduced to Bill Clinton at a Los Angeles fundraising party. It was reported thereafter that Liu wired $300,000 to her Marswell Investment firm in Los Angeles, and some of the money went to the DNC in August. It became the 1996 U.S. presidential campaign financial controversy.

Then, corruption, power abuse, and mismanagement soon swept like wildfire throughout the navy. Admiral Sun Jinmei, deputy commander of the NSF Air Force, received bribes when he was charged with enlarging the Liuting Airport in the late 1980s. Vice Admiral Wang Shouye, navy deputy commander, embezzled 160 million yuan ($27 million) of military funds from the 1990s. Some naval officers accepted bribes, kickbacks, and commissions, just as the other branches had, and used naval facilities, equipment, and warships to make profits easily. Captains and sailors used their warships for smuggling to avoid port inspections and custom searches. Island patrol troops engaged in drug trafficking along the coastline. High-ranking officers sold military secrets to Taiwanese and American intelligence. Some PLAN air force bases, equipment warehouses, military hospitals, and defense facilities became available for rent or sale. Some PLAN units resorted to arms sales, human trafficking, and other criminal activities.

Some generals and admirals became millionaires themselves; their children studied in Western countries and Japan, their wives and parents purchased expensive houses, and they bought permanent residency (or a green card) and citizenship in foreign countries like the United States, Canada, England, France, Australia, and Singapore.[132] Consequently, power-interest groups gradually spread from high-ranking officers to middle-ranking officers, as demonstrated by the high percentage of income not accounted for by traditional means. Senior Colonel Liu Mingfu, professor at China's National Defense University, warned the PLA in his book, "The most dangerous enemy the PLA faces today is its own corruption."[133] In his studies on China under Deng Xiaoping, Maurice Meisner argues that the "crown princes and princesses" or children of top military leaders took advantage of their privileges in benefiting themselves. They become "the most prominent symbols of the official profiteering and corruption that overwhelmed the Communist bureaucracy in the late 1980s." Official corruption in the 1990s was so rampant that its scope and scale "shocked even the most hardened of political cynics." For Meisner, corruption was one of the "unintended consequences" of Deng's economic reform. Unfortunately, Deng's own children conducting lucrative businesses and his policy response to the rampant corruption was "confused, contradictory, and above all, ambiguous."[134] Therefore, rapid economic development coupled with an absence of effective legal and social supervising mechanisms, and official corruption, that the 1989 Tiananmen demonstration targeted, exacerbated, and expanded to more industries and governments.[135]

The PLA was involved in the June 4 Tiananmen Square incident from the very beginning. After former CCP chairman Hu Yaobang as a party reforming leader died on April 15, 1989, college students mourning on their Beijing campus soon became a city-wide and then a nationwide pro-democracy demonstration asking for political reforms across the country while protesting corruption and power abuse. The Party Center and PLA high command deployed nearly 10,000 troops from the 38th Army to the Tiananmen Square, Beijing's center, when Hu Yaobang's funeral was held on April 22. Although the CCP and PRC government denounced the movement as a riot on April 26, hundreds of thousands of students and citizens joined together and continued demonstrating at Tiananmen Square in May.[136] Soon the demonstrations spread to 116 cities across the country.[137] Meanwhile, the 38th Army sent another 5,100 troops as reinforcements to the Capital Security Force.[138]

Although Deng Xiaoping disliked the urban demonstrations, he was extremely disappointed by the party and government's soft attitude and impotent policy, which failed to slow down, if not stop, widely spread student pro-democracy movements. He summoned Yang Shangkun, China's president and secretary general of the Central Military Commission (CMC), on May 11 and suggested "decisive actions" to stop the student demonstrations. When Zhao Ziyang, CCP secretary general, reported students' hunger strike at the Tiananmen Square on May 13, Deng could not tolerate the situation getting any worse, and asked for a Politburo emergency meeting. The five standing committee members of the Politburo met in the evening of the 16th and agreed a direct communication with the student representatives. When they reported their decision at Deng's home on May 17, Deng Xiaoping believed that it was time to stop it once for all without any negotiation or compromise, and that they should order martial law immediately. When the five leaders voted, however, the Politburo split with two supporters, two vetoes, and one abstaining.

The next morning, the Politburo met again at Deng's home by including PLA leaders Admiral Liu Huaqing, General Qin Jiwei, defense minister, and General Hong Xuezhi. With Zhao Ziyang's abstention, the meeting decided to start martial law in Beijing at zero hour on May 21 and form PLA Capital Martial Law Forces to reinforce martial law. On May 19, the high command established the Command of the Martial Law Forces and appointed Admiral Liu Huaqing, CMC vice chairman, as the commander in chief of the Capital Martial Law Forces to command the army, navy, marines, and air force in the military suppression in Beijing. The PLA high command also appointed General Chi Haotian, chief of the PLA General Staff, and General Zhou Yibing, commander of Beijing Military Region, as the deputy commanders under Liu.[139]

That afternoon, the Party Center enforced martial law in Beijing. Admiral Liu Huaqing deployed twenty-two infantry divisions from thirteen armies into the capital. He also ordered the 15th Army Airborne from the air force to stand by under the command of the PLA Martial Law Forces. Many people, including PLA officers, asked questions then and now about why Admiral Liu did not send the PLAN Marine Corps or any naval troops to Tiananmen Square during the suppression. It was said that some naval admirals, including Admiral Li Yaowen, the navy's political commissar, opposed the dispatch of troops to Beijing against the student demonstration. During the crisis, infantry troops were sent to guard (or watch) PLAN HQs in Beijing as the high command held doubts about the navy's loyalty and control.

From May 20, the 250,000–300,000 martial law troops commanded by Liu Huaqing moved toward Beijing. As the Party Center divided, the deployment reflected the Party Elders' uncertainty and anxiety. However, many PLA divisions were stopped in the suburbs by crowds and roadblocks. All martial law troops failed to reach their destinations in the capital as planned.[140] Most generals knew nothing of the movement and the order came as a surprise. A group of generals, including Zhang Aiping and Ye Fei, signed a letter to Deng Xiaoping: "We request that troops not enter the city and that martial law not be carried out in Beijing."[141]

Martial law, however, was ineffective as students remained in Tiananmen Square and the demonstration on May 23 was the largest since its declaration. By the end of May, the Party Center prepared for a final "crackdown." On June 3, the Politburo instructed Admiral Liu Huaqing to put down the "counterrevolutionary riot" by force in Beijing.[142] Liu established two subcommands, including the City Forward Command and Square Clearing Command, to carry out the Party Center's order. He deployed divisions from the 28th, 38th, and 63rd Armies to move into the capital from the west, and divisions from the 15th, 20th, 26th, and 54th Armies from the south. He ordered the Capital First Division and 39th Army to move toward Tiananmen from the east, and the 40th and 64th Armies from the north. All infantry soldiers received two hundred rounds of ammunition.[143] Liu also sent several helicopters over Tiananmen Square, demanding immediate evacuation through loudspeakers and warning of possible "counterattacks."

Some PLA officers questioned the high command's decision and refused to carry out Liu Huaqing's orders. The 38th Army commander, Xu Qinxian, returned to the hospital to avoid commanding his troops against the demonstrators in Beijing.[144] Although he was arrested immediately, his disobedience shocked his troops and other armies. Rumors soon spread that they would fight against the rebellious 38th Army in Beijing. Commander of the 116th Division, 39th Army, Xu Feng refused to move his troops into the capital by creating communication problems, remaining in the eastern suburbs, and delaying his troop movement into the city.[145]

After 9 p.m., PLA troops forced their way through the streets and opened fire on the protesters at 10 p.m. at West Chang'an Street, about six miles from Tiananmen Square. The protesters and local residents burned public trollies on the street to halt, or at least slow down, the 38th's advance. The troops shot their way through the roadblock and fired on residential buildings along both sides of the street. It was reported that by 10:30 p.m., more than forty people were killed on West Chang'an Street.[146] Around 10:30 p.m., the 15th Airborne Army fired on protesters to the south. The protesters tried to burn out the military trucks by throwing Molotov cocktails and using fiery blankets. During the bloody clash, at least seven hundred civilians were killed, while the 15th Army counted couple of dozen casualties.[147] When 70,000–80,000 protesting students remained in the square in the early morning on June 4, the 15th's tanks and armored vehicles forced their way into Tiananmen Square by 1:30 a.m. The troops continued firing on the students. Both the 15th and 38th Armies boasted the "most kills." Around 5 a.m., PLA troops eventually ended the protest at Tiananmen Square.[148]

After the Tiananmen Square incident, the PLA conducted investigations on 3,500 officers. Of these, 111 were punished because they "breached discipline in a serious way." Meanwhile, 1,400 soldiers were court-martialed since they "shed their weapons and ran away."[149] The incident negatively impacted the PLA, especially the navy. PLAN political commissar Admiral Li Yaowen lost his position and was forced to retire from the navy in April 1990. Nevertheless, Deng Xiaoping continued to insist on his "Four Cardinal Principles," including keeping to the socialist road, upholding the people's democratic dictatorship, sticking to the CCP's leadership, and adhering to Marxism-Leninism and Maoist thought. He believed that the country's door must remain open to the world and stressed stability and unity. To guarantee stability, the Communist Party must be in control. However, health problems soon reduced his active political role, as Parkinson's disease, lung ailments, and other problems eventually made him almost blind and deaf by the mid-1990s. Deng Xiaoping died in Beijing on February 28, 1997.[150]

CHAPTER 5

# A NATIONAL LEADER

## *Maritime Interests and Sea Power*

After his promotion to CMC deputy secretary general and then CMC vice chairman in 1988, Admiral Liu Huaqing continued his efforts to build a strong navy as China's strategic force. In October 1992, at the age of seventy-six, Liu was elected as one of seven members on the CCP Politburo's Standing Committee and became one of the top national leaders as he helped consolidate Jiang Zemin's control of the PLA after the Tiananmen incident. Serving from 1992 to 1998 as the CMC's first vice chairman next to Jiang Zeming, Liu administrated the PLA's daily operations, managed China's defense budget, and continued naval development. With the military's support in 1996, Jiang Zemin called for the PLA's "two transformations." First, from an army to fight "local war under ordinary conditions" to an armed forces prepared to fight and win "local wars under modern high-tech conditions." And second from an army based on quantity to an armed force based on quality.[1]

To carry out Jiang's vision for future wars, the high command made a grand three-step plan for the PLA in 1997. It became the PLA's new guideline to prepare for "local wars under modern high-tech conditions" from 1998 to 2040. Admiral Liu Huaqing told the chiefs that China's next war would be a naval conflict in near sea locations like the Taiwan Strait or South China Sea.[2] Thereafter, the PLA moved away from traditional ground war preparation, and instead focused on new naval warfare. According to Liu, the grand plan prioritized the PLA Navy's modernization under the third-generation command and new efforts in reorganization, institutional reform, and improving sustainability systems. To further their interests, Liu and the PLA high command protected Jiang's new leadership based upon a coalition of key political institutions. Jiang earned the PLA's political support and, as such, his position went unchallenged from 1990 to 2002.

Jiang Zemin supported Liu Huaqing's endeavor to build a modern, blue-water naval force by the 2000s. Liu's persistent efforts in aircraft carrier development eventually led to the completion of China's first aircraft carrier in 2011. His continuing efforts in nuclear submarine manufacturing and improvement resulted in the commission of the PLAN's third generation of nuclear submarines with second nuclear strike capability. Although Admiral Liu retired in 1998, his strategy envisioned the Chinese navy with capabilities in the Pacific and Indian Oceans by the end of the twentieth century. His near sea defense and far sea protection concepts became PLAN strategy in the twenty-first century. His sea power theory laid the foundation for China's oceanic sovereignty, maritime policy, and international diplomacy in the Indo-Pacific region. After Jiang left office, new Chinese leader Hu Jintao (2002–2012) launched a nationwide campaign to promote China's maritime interest and fully support naval development. By 2010, the PLAN totaled 300,000 personnel and more than 400 warships, including an aircraft carrier and nuclear submarines. The Chinese navy flew an air arm of 430 warplanes with 35,000 personnel, and commanded China's 12,000-strong marine corps. The Chinese navy evolved and became one of the world naval powers by 2012.

## JIANG'S SUPPORT AND TAIWAN STRAIT CRISIS

After the Tiananmen incident in 1989, both reformers and conservatives in Beijing accepted Deng's choice of successor, former mayor of Shanghai Jiang Zemin, as the CCP chairman and PRC president in November 1989. Deng, however, worried about Jiang as the CCP's first civilian leader without any military background or war experience. Deng Xiaoping continued to serve as the CMC chairman until 1992. In 1990, the PLA expected "reimbursement" from the Party Center after their suppression of the Tiananmen crisis. Some high-ranking officers claimed that they were victims of Deng's reform, forcing Jiang's uncertainty about the military's attitude toward his new leadership, and turned to the old guard conservatives for political support. As CMC chairman, Deng Xiaoping appointed military reformers Admiral Liu Huaqing and General Zhang Zhen, president of the PLA National Defense University, as CMC vice chairmen in 1989 to keep Jiang in the reform and help him establish his new leadership and reputation as the PLA's commander in chief.[3] Although the Soviet

**PHOTO 9.** Deng Xiaoping meets Liu Huaqing at the Great Hall of the People in Beijing during the CCP 14th National Congress on October 14, 1992. 文汇报 [*Wenhui Daily*]

Union dissolved in 1991, Jiang's government stayed the course, continuing to promote Deng Xiaoping's modernization policy and reform agenda through the last decade of the twentieth century (see photo 9).

With Admiral Liu Huaqing and General Zhang Zhen's support, the new Party Center purged generals and officers who disobeyed the Capital Martial Law Force's commander Liu's orders during the Tiananmen Square incident. Jiang Zemin established a moderate, collective leadership willing and able to share power with the military and others through a bureaucratic institution.[4] He developed his own theoretical principles for the party, military, and state as the "Three Represents."[5] In 1992, Deng retired from the CMC and Jiang became the CMC chairman.

Before his retirement, Deng Xiaoping wrote a letter on October 6, 1992, to the Politburo and recommended Liu Huaqing and Zhang Zhen continue to serve as CMC vice chairmen. "As far as I know, Comrades Liu Huaqing and Zhang Zhen were the best of knowing the military. The future task of selecting successors should be charged by those who are familiar with the PLA," Deng wrote in his letter.[6] Liu was surprised when he heard Deng's recommendation since he was seventy-six years old and ready for his own retirement. Instead, Liu was promoted and became one of the nation's top seven leaders to serve as a Standing Committee member of the Politburo in 1992. He was the last active military leader who served in the Politburo Standing Committee. From 1992 to 1998, Admiral Liu was the first CMC vice chairman next to Jiang Zemin. After 1995, the PLA gained more representation in the Politburo from none at the Fourteenth CCP National Congress to two out of eleven members at the Fifteenth National Congress in 1997.

With Liu Huaqing next to him in the Party Center, Jiang Zemin made a concerted effort to befriend the PLA, leading to the military's eventual acceptance of his leadership.[7] In the early 1990s, Jiang granted the PLA high-level autonomy so that PLA interests took priority and throughout the decade, he campaigned vigorously for enlarging the military. From 1990 to 2002, the government doubled its annual defense budget with a GNP growth rate of 8.6 percent. You Ji points out that "although the military is never satisfied with the amount of money it receives each year, the double-digit growth of the military budget does distinguish the period of Jiang's leadership in the 1990s from that of Deng in the 1980s."[8] The PLA was able to act as a fairly autonomous "interest group" for the first time in its history. You Ji also argues, "The rise of cohesive corporate spirit and professionalism nurtures China's new brand of technocrat/officers who are forward looking, ready to learn Western military science and technology, and increasingly indifferent to the party's factional politics, though not immune from the nationalist drive."[9] Jiang's administration believed in a "rich country and a strong military" as the ultimate goal for their economic and military reforms.

Liu Huaqing continued military reforms favoring the navy. Jiang Zemin endorsed Liu's perception of China's maritime interests, sea power, naval war readiness, and sovereignty over the disputed islands. In his early years, Jiang promoted a pragmatic nationalism to emphasize China's unity, sovereignty, strength, and prosperity and gradually shifted the party's ideology from radical communism to moderate nationalism as an ideology to save the state at the end of the Cold War, bringing in one more source of legitimacy for the CCP as the country's ruling party. As Jiang shifted the party's political goals, he faced new challenges such as Taiwan and the East China and South China Seas' disputed islands. In 1992, under Jiang's

**PHOTO 10.** Admiral Liu Huaqing, vice chairman of the Central Military Commission, talks to President Jiang Zemin at the CCP 14th National Congress on October 17, 1992, after Liu is elected a standing committee member of the Politburo and becomes one of the seven top party leaders. *CPC News*

leadership, the National People's Congress (NPC) passed China's First Maritime Law that codified Liu's conception of "sea as territory," including the country's "sovereignty" over 3 million square kilometers of ocean and seas (see photo 10). From that point, China considered the oceans and seas as new frontiers. General Chi Haotian, China's defense minister (1993–2003) and CMC's vice chairman (1995–2003), supported Jiang Zemin's claims of sea power and "oceanic territory." He believes "the country's rise and fall depends on its role in the oceans." The Chinese navy should be a blue-water navy and "going to the four oceans" is its strategic choice.[10]

On April 7, 1990, Jiang Zemin attended a PLAN commissioning ceremony for a new model of a Chinese-made submarine. Liu Huaqing accompanied Jiang Zemin's visit to the nuclear submarine base, testing site, and sub-building yard. The newly elected CCP chairman observed the nuclear submarine fleet's exercise. Liu complained to Jiang about the limited defense budget and lack of naval orders that threatened the nuclear submarine's research and manufacturing. Jiang Zemin understood and promised his support to the nuclear submarine's development. After his visit, Jiang approved Liu's request to continue the production of nuclear submarines.[11] During his visit to the submarine base, Jiang Zemin prescribed for the PLAN submarine program: "Strengthen nuclear submarine force to strengthen our national pride and our military power."[12] At lunch that day, Jiang sat with submarine sailors and learned how the new technology worked underwater. The new president stated, "We must recognize the oceans from a strategic point of view and promote a strong sea perspective of all the Chinese people." On June 23, Jiang visited a South Sea Fleet training base and told SSF commanders, "since building a strong naval force is a very complicated task, we need to train the best naval officers first." On April 18, 1993, Jiang Zemin visited SSF Hainan Naval Base and met the officers and sailors of a submarine squadron. He told the seamen, "This is the foremost front of China's sea defense."[13] At the base, he inscribed in calligraphy, "Prepare for war all the time to defend our southern frontier." Jiang considered the South China Sea as China's new frontier.

On April 29, 1994, Jiang Zemin attended a commissioning ceremony in Shanghai for a new Chinese-made guided missile destroyer *Harbin* 112, touring its missile launchers, weapon systems, and new engine technology. Jiang told Captain Wu Hongle at the bridge, "This is China's new modern warship. You are the pioneers of our new naval operations." Jiang asked sailor Yang Chunsheng what was new about the warship. Yang demonstrated to the president four new features, including its anti-air missiles, new engine, antisubmarine helicopters, and a digital warfare system. Jiang was satisfied by the sailor's answer.[14]

A year later, from October 15 to 19, 1995, Jiang Zemin and Liu Huaqing led all Chinese military leaders to observe a large-scale naval exercise in the Yellow Sea that included nuclear submarines, missile destroyers, missile frigates, fighters, bombers, and helicopters. Jiang told the CMC standing members, "We must prioritize the naval construction and escalate its modernization to safeguard China's sea security and accomplish the great task of national unification."[15] After the naval exercise, Jiang revisited the flagship, *Harbin* 112 missile destroyer, and received Captain Wu's report on the destroyer's operations, sailor training, and fire system exercises from the previous year. Thereafter, *Harbin* 112 continued its drills, operations, and routine patrols.[16] In February 1997, the destroyer 112 led a PLAN fleet, as its flagship, and visited the United States, Mexico, Peru, and Chile for more than 100 days and sailed 24,000 nautical miles.[17] From 1989 to 1993, the PLA sent its warships to visit the United States, Thailand, Bangladesh, and India.

During his military reform, Jiang Zemin assessed the PLA's command and control, combat readiness, and crisis management during the Taiwan Strait missile crisis. Lasting from June 1995 to March 1996, the Third Taiwan Strait Crisis erupted when ROC president Lee Teng-hui (Li Denghui) visited his alma mater Cornell University in the United States. The PLA responded with missile tests and landing exercises. In opposition to Washington's permission for Lee Teng-hui's visit, a violation to the "One China" policy, Beijing delayed Defense Minister Chi Haotian's visit to the United States in June 1995 and recalled the Chinese ambassador from Washington. General Chi Haotian convincingly suggested to Jiang Zemin the necessity of employing military forces to stop further distortion of Sino-American relations.[18] Jiang accepted Chi's proposal and decided on a show of force that summer. The PLA high command conducted its first round of missile tests from July 21 to 28, 1995, in an area thirty-six miles north of Taiwan. At 1 a.m. on July 21, the PLA's Second Artillery Force (SAF, strategic force or the rocket force) launched two short-range ballistic *Dongfeng* (DF)-15 (M-9) surface-to-surface missiles from Jiangxi at about seventy nautical miles from Taiwan's coast. At 12 a.m. and 2 a.m. on July 22, the SAF fired two DF-15 missiles and hit an area within forty miles north of Taiwan. Two more missiles launched on July 24 and hit the same area.[19]

Simultaneously, the PLA concentrated large naval and landing forces and launched one wave after another of military exercises, including a joint amphibious landing exercise in the Taiwan Strait.[20] From August 15 to 25, the ESF deployed 59 warships and naval vessels for a large-scale naval attack and amphibious landing exercise. The PLAN Air Force launched 192 sorties and scrambled its fighters and bombers during the naval attack exercise. From October 31 to November 23, the PLA launched another joint amphibious landing campaign on Dongshan Island off the Fujian coast.

The navy deployed 63 warships, landing crafts, and support vessels. The army's 91st Infantry Division conducted landing and beachhead defense. The PLAAF sent fifty fighters, bombers, and other planes to the joint amphibious landing campaign.[21] By the late fall, Beijing's military aggression caused the most serious international crisis since militarily engaging Taipei over the islands of Jinmen and Mazu in 1958. Nevertheless, Admiral Liu Huaqing told PLA officers, "It proved that [we] could not unify [our country] peacefully without a fully military readiness. Whenever Taiwan makes a major turn and threatens national unification, we must respond to it militarily."[22]

Before the year's end, cross-strait tensions rose drastically. Taiwan's military remained on high alert and declared that it had made all necessary preparations to deal with a possible PLA invasion of the island. In December 1995, the Clinton administration sent the aircraft carrier *Nimitz* to pass through the Taiwan Strait in response to PLA activities. With Liu's support, Jiang Zemin remained resolute in continuing missile tests and landing exercises. Between January and February 1996, the PLA concentrated 100,000 troops along the coast across the strait from Taiwan and launched another large-scale landing exercise to send a stronger signal to both Taipei and Washington. Through the winter of 1995–1996, tensions remained heightened in the strait.[23]

In early 1996, Taiwan prepared for its first general election since 1949. Lee Teng-hui ran on the KMT ticket. To discourage Taiwanese voters from supporting him, Jiang Zemin conducted new set of missile tests, accompanied by live fire and naval exercises. He used the military to threaten Taiwanese voters. On March 8, 1996, the PLA conducted more missile tests by firing three DF-15 surface-to-surface missiles just twelve miles off Kaohsiung and about twenty-nine nautical miles off Keelung.[24] On the same day, the United States announced the deployment of the *Independence* carrier battle group to international waters near Taiwan. On March 11, the *Nimitz* carrier battle group joined the *Independence* in the Taiwan area as the largest U.S. naval movement in the Asia-Pacific region since the Vietnam War. In response to U.S. naval deployments, China announced more live-fire exercises near Penghu, an ROC-held island group near Taiwan. From March 18 to 25, the PLA deployed 300 airplanes, guided missile destroyers, and submarines in the joint exercise at Pingtan Island with

150,000 troops, about 70 nautical miles from the Taiwanese-held islands. The exercise included amphibious landings, paratroopers, and mountain assaults. Meanwhile, several nuclear submarines departed from their base at Qingdao. Without identifying the Chinese nuclear submarines' locations, the *Nimitz* remained 350 miles away from the strait.[25]

The Third Taiwan Strait Crisis ended with Lee Teng-hui's election as Taiwan's president on March 23, 1996. China's intimidation was counterproductive and boosted Lee 5 percent in the polls, earning him a majority of the voters. Beijing continued criticizing Lee as "the general representative of Taiwan's separatist forces, a saboteur of the stability of the Taiwan Straits, a stumbling-block preventing the development of relations between China and the United States, and a troublemaker for the peace and stability of the Asian-Pacific region."[26] Scobell considers "hawkish" as "the most accurate term to use to describe the words and deeds" of Chinese military during the crisis. Nevertheless, Beijing "achieved most of its goals without resorting to actual warfare: its actions got Taipei and Washington to take China's warnings seriously and resulted in a more chastened and less boisterous Taiwanese independence movement."[27] Worthing adds, "In the interests of reducing tensions in the Straits, the United States scaled back its arms sales, restricted Taiwanese officials to transit visas, and urged Lee Teng-hui to avoid action that might upset the status quo."[28] Robert Ross states that Beijing and Washington tried to protect their strategic positions through the crisis, and both reached their goals with certain strategic benefits.[29] Nevertheless, Liu Huaqing angrily observed China's incapable response to the arrival of the U.S. aircraft carriers in China's near sea during the 1996 Taiwan Strait missile crisis. He convinced the PLA high command that China needed aircraft carriers for the sake of national defense, Taiwan, and the South China Sea.[30]

## LIU'S NEW WARSHIPS AND CARRIER PROJECT

From 1992 to 1998, Liu Huaqing continued promoting naval development. The admiral prioritized research, development, and manufacturing of nuclear submarines, larger warships, and naval planes.[31] In concurrence with Liu's focus on the navy's development, the PLAN received the lion's share of Jiang Zemin's new defense budget. Jiang told PLA leaders, "We must prioritize the naval construction."[32]

In 1994, Jiang Zemin and CMC approved Liu Huaqing's plan to begin the research and development of China's second-generation nuclear submarines. Admiral Liu believed in nuclear submarines as instruments of national strategic deterrence and indicators of China's magnitude of comprehensive national power. While first-generation Type 091 *Han*-class nuclear submarines (SSNs), launched in the 1970s, continued their service, the PLAN received more new Type 092 *Xia*-class SSBNs in the late 1980s.[33] Then, Liu's second generation included Type 093 *Shang*-class nuclear submarines and Type 094 *Jin*-class with *Julang*-2 ballistic missiles. Both classes of SSBNs replaced old PWR systems with new HTGR nuclear reactors for their propulsion systems and reduced the "loud noise" of Type 091 and Type 092. In the 2010s, China continued its efforts to reduce the noise when the Type 093A and Type 093B were launched. Then, two nuclear ballistic missile submarines, the Type 094, were constructed.[34] The PLAN claimed new Type 094 nuclear submarines were equivalent to the U.S. SSN-688 *Los Angeles*-class and the Russian *Akula*-class. Meanwhile, a new domestic, conventionally powered submarine emerged as Type 039 on May 18, 1994, as the first improved Chinese submarine was commissioned. According to Liu's plans, three *Song*-class conventionally powered submarines were also constructed in the 2000s.

In the 1990s, the PLAN added more than twenty warships to its force with upgraded electronic countermeasures, radar and sonar, and fire-control systems. China manufactured Type 052 and Type 054 missile destroyers and Type 053H2G and Type 053H3 missile frigates. The Type 052 destroyers have upgraded anti-aircraft, anti-ship, and electronic combat capabilities. They gained fame as the "Chinese Shield."[35] The Type 052C *Luoyang-II* destroyers were equipped with a phased-array radar for their HQ-9 surface-to-air missile (SAM) systems. (The HQ-9 is comparable to U.S. *Patriot* missiles.) The Type 054A *Jiangkai-II* frigates were equipped with the HQ-16 SAM system and displaced between 3,600 and 5,500 tons with a speed between 18 and 32 knots. All the new warships and submarines were blue-water capable.[36] The navy sent out second-generation destroyers and frigates to visit four countries in the Americas. From 1993 to 1996, the Chinese warships visited Vladivostok and other Russian seaports. New missiles and electronic warfare systems were manufactured as main battle equipment. The new missiles were used in the 1995–1996 Taiwan Strait Crisis by the Jiang administration.

During the 1990s, the Chinese navy was sizable, boasting nearly all types of warships, and became a regional naval power under Liu's leadership. The underwater fleet had SSBNs, SSNs, and nuclear-powered submarines. The surface warship fleet included destroyers, frigates, corvettes, minesweepers, minelayers, missile boats, torpedo boasts, landing ships, and auxiliary vessels. The aviation fleet was equipped with medium and light bombers, fighters, attackers, ship-based helicopters, and reconnaissance/surveillance planes, assisted by a radar network that covered all of China's coasts. The offshore defense force replaced coastal cannons with anti-ship missiles. Thus, by the 1990s, the PLAN's overall technological level competed with other global navies. To show off China's new warships and naval technology, from 1995 to 2001 the PLAN's task groups visited ports in Indonesia, Australia, the Philippines, South Africa, the United States, Canada, France, Italy, Germany, and Britain. From February to May 1997, PLAN deputy commander Vice Admiral He Pengfei and SSF commander Vice Admiral Wang Yonguo led the missile destroyer *Zhuhai* 166 and the replenishment oiler *Nancang* 953 with 789 sailors and officers to complete a circumnavigation of the Pacific Ocean for ninety-eight days, including port visits to the United States, Mexico, Peru, and Chile. The PLAN convoy crossed the International Date Line and entered the Western Hemisphere for the first time. At American naval bases in Hawaii and San Diego, He and Wang visited the U.S. Pacific Command and Naval Pacific Fleet HQs.[37]

Meanwhile, Admiral Liu Huaqing purchased new weaponry and imported advanced naval technology from Russia and the West, thereby narrowing the Chinese navy's technological gap with its major Western competitors. Liu purchased two *Sovremenny*-class destroyers (*DDG*) and four *Kilo*-class diesel electric submarines from Russia. Russians built the 8,000-ton destroyers in St. Petersburg for the Chinese and sold the first one for $840 million in 1996 and the second one for $1 billion in November 1997. The first Russian destroyer arrived at Zhoushan, Zhejiang, in February 2000, named *Hangzhou*; the second arrived in January 2001, named *Fuzhou*. The PLAN Air Force continued to purchase Su-30 and Su-32 strike fighters from Russia in the 2000s. The Su-30MK2 has a maximum speed of 1,305 mph, an altitude ceiling of 56,800 feet, and a flying range of 1,900 miles. Meanwhile, the PLAN introduced its new JH series of fighter-bombers to improve its aerial maritime strike capability. The H-6 twin-engine bombers were a new version of the Russian Tu-16 *Badger*. The JH-7/FBC-1, nicknamed *Flying Leopard*, carries four YJ-82 anti-ship cruise missiles and air-to-air missiles with a cruising speed of 528 mph. The new planes and weapon systems provided China more firepower over its territorial waters. China also manufactured its SH-5 seaplanes, Z-8, and Z-9 helicopters. From 1997 to 2001, the PLAN expedited its modernization by developing better technology and purchasing more Russian equipment, including the purchase of a Soviet semi-manufactured aircraft carrier.

To establish China's modern and capable principal surface combatant fleet in the near sea defense, Liu Huaqing vigorously sought for the development of China's aircraft carrier. In the 1990s, Admiral Liu became a national leader for the carrier's research and development. He believed that aircraft carriers were instrumental as national strategic deference and indicators of China's magnitude of comprehensive national power. He initiated a long journey of PLAN's race for a credible carrier battle group in 1985, continued his efforts in the 1990s, and supported the PLAN's carrier project in the 2000s after his retirement in 1998. Admiral Liu earned the title "the father of the Chinese aircraft carrier."

As far back as his service as the PLAN's commander from 1982 to 1987, Liu Huaqing thought about China's aircraft carrier and convinced his admirals and experts that the PLAN should plan for its research and development. On January 11, 1984, Liu spoke to scientists, experts, and engineers at the First PLAN Equipment and Technology Convention, concluding that the navy should focus on its aviation development, including new fighters, bombers, ship-borne helicopters, and air refueling technology. Then, he called for the carrier's research and development: "It has been a long time for the Navy to think about developing its aircraft carrier. It seems impossible [to do it] before the 1990s due to the country's weak economy. However, [we] must produce our aircraft carrier. Currently, [we] should research how to send the land-based planes to the sea and maximize their combat capabilities."[38]

In the summer of 1985, Commander Liu Huaqing sent experts and engineers to Guangzhou to research and evaluate Australia's HMAS *Melbourne* (R21) aircraft carrier since Australia declined Chinese request for the blueprint of the steam catapult system. The 20,000-ton carrier was retired in 1982 and purchased by a Chinese scrapping company at $30 million in 1984. After towing the *Melbourne* from Australia to Huangpu Harbor, Guangdong, the ship's scrapping was delayed until 2002 as Chinese naval engineers and designers surprisingly found key equipment and operational systems untouched and used them for research purposes, including the flight deck, steam catapult system, and Optical Landing System (OLS).[39] Nanda Avalist considers the purchase of *Melbourne* as "the beginning of decades-long vigorous endeavors by China to acquire either samples of blueprints of aircraft carriers and their associated onboard systems to accumulate the national technological know-how in the intricacies of the aircraft carriers as a complex system."[40]

In February 1986, Commander Liu Huaqing told all top naval officers at a technology briefing that "the aircraft carrier will be produced soon or later. [We] must consider the aircraft carrier by 2000. Its research and development may not include its model, and instead work on pre-research. . . . The Navy should start with flexibility research, while informing and coordinating with our superiors and defense industry to work together."[41] In April and June 1986, when PLAN deputy commander Vice Admiral Li Jing and chief of PLAN Equipment and Technology Department Rear Admiral Zheng Ming were invited to visit France and Italy, Liu asked them to learn more about French and Italian carrier technology during their visits.[42]

On August 28, 1986, chiefs of the PLAN Center for Equipment and Technology Tasks reported to naval leaders that the aircraft carrier's research was included as the key project in their Seventh Five-Year Plan (1985–1990). Liu Huaqing was delighted to know the carrier's research and development had begun and instructed, "[The design] depends on our strategic needs, cannot be small, but not too big over the budget, and has a battle radius of 1,000 nautical miles. Think about a long-term, [we] must develop our aircraft carrier."[43] From November 18 to 20, Liu chaired a naval strategy symposium, including PLA leaders, top diplomats, strategists, and government officials. Many of the participants argued that the navy should have its own aircraft carrier for national unification, protection of China's oceanic sovereignty, and maritime interests.[44] On November 27, Liu spoke at the annual naval science and technology conference's closing ceremony. The admiral explained the PLAN's necessity for aircraft carriers. "[We] must do a big, strategic calculation! If so, the result should show a need for aircraft carrier. We must have it, and it doesn't matter how much it will cost. It has strategic significance for the South China Sea and Taiwan. . . . If not, we will be guilty in history."[45]

In January 1987, Liu Huaqing talked to chiefs of the PLA and CSTIND, who were invited to the Fourth Naval Equipment and Technology Development Conference, about China's aircraft carrier. The admiral said, "[We] should start our research and design to make sure our aircraft carrier will fit to the needs of future war. . . . Although we are currently facing many difficulties in terms of finance and technology, we have to begin right now to consider it as a long-term plan. We would still face many difficulties, if we start it ten years later. I am asking its research and development as soon as possible."[46]

On March 31, 1987, Liu Huaqing briefed the CMC on two pressing issues for the navy's development strategy, first, aircraft carriers; second, nuclear submarines. He argued that the PLAN's fleet operations needed air coverage and support. The current coast-based planes could not serve the operational needs of future naval warfare. Liu suggested the PLA start carrier research and development in the Eighth Five-Year Plan (1990–1995) and begin its design in 2000. He also emphasized the deterrent potential of an aircraft carrier in his report. Both aircraft carrier and nuclear submarines' manufacturing "were not only for war, but also for 'show,' a show has its deterrent power."[47] For Liu's naval war preparation, the navy would first fight in the near sea, including the northern and northwestern Pacific with the aircraft carrier. Second, the PLAN prepared to protect itself against its major enemy. Third, it should extend its strategic defense depth. "Its first step should reach the first island chain and include all our islands. We must defend our 200 miles of exclusive economic zones, 3 million square miles of our sovereign waters, and 11,000 miles of coastal lines."[48]

In May and June 1987, the PLAN Center for Equipment and Technology Development held two aircraft carrier research conferences in Beijing.

In July, Liu Huaqing designed a training program for aircraft carrier captains. In September, the first training class of carrier captains commenced at the Guangzhou Naval Academy with ten captains. Liu approved the list of the captain candidates, and the training program required a comprehensive examination for graduation. Admiral Zhang Lianzhong, the fourth PLAN commander (1988–1996) after Liu, recalled that "Liu's training program deeply inspired the younger generation. . . . This training class prepared the future captains for China's aircraft carriers."[49] Among the trainees, Captain Li Xiaoyan was first on the list, and in 2010, Li Xiaoyan became captain of the *Liaoning*, China's first aircraft carrier. In November 1987, Deng Xiaoping appointed Liu Huaqing as the CMC deputy secretary general and then CMC vice chairman. After Liu left the navy for the PLA high command, he continued working on aircraft carrier research and development from 1988 to 1998. Liu said to his staff that he "could not die with eyes closed without seeing China's development of its own carrier."[50]

After the Battle of the Spratly Islands in early 1988, Liu noted the Chinese navy's weakness in lacking air support and coverage in the South China Sea. He firmly considered the carrier as the only effective means to support distant fleet maneuvers and operations. The admiral said, "In today's world, an aircraft carrier is not only the core of naval wars at seas, but also a powerful strategic deterrence. It indicates the level of national strength and reflects our international status in the world. To modernize national defense and establish a comprehensive naval system, [we] must consider the carrier's development." Xi Jinping appreciated Liu's endless effort in developing China's aircraft carrier and agreed with Liu that "an aircraft carrier signifies the comprehensive strength of our country and provides a core strength of our joint branches to fight combined battles at seas."[51] Meanwhile, there were exchanges of proposals for carrier development between China and Spain and France. The latter offered carrier designs, blueprints, and even a surplus French aircraft carrier, *Clemenceau*, though an agreement regarding the latter was never reached.

After Liu Huaqing became the CMC vice chairman, Admiral Zhang Lianzhong was appointed as the navy's commander from January 1988 to November 1996. Liu knew Zhang very well when the latter served as the commander of the Lüshun Naval Base from 1980 to 1985. Then PLAN commander Liu was impressed by Zhang's leadership style, organizational skills, and technology training at the Lüshun Naval Base where Liu had served as deputy commander and commander from 1958–1962. Liu promoted Zhang to commander of the North Sea Fleet in 1982 and deputy commander of the PLAN in 1985. As Liu recommended to the CMC, Zhang was appointed as the commander of the Chinese navy in 1988, promoted to vice admiral in September 1988, and then admiral in May 1993.

During his tenure as the naval commander, Admiral Zhang Lianzhong made significant efforts in aircraft carrier research and development. In February 1988, Commander Zhang prioritized carrier development to improve naval technology and strengthen combat effectiveness. "The core of naval warfighting capability will depend on aircraft carrier battle groups and strategic nuclear submarines."[52] As naval commander, Zhang visited carriers in the United States, Great Britain, and France. He reported to PLA chiefs that China could build two or three new and modern armies, but it would not change China's strategic place in the world. If China built one aircraft carrier, it would raise their global strategic status immediately. From 1988 to 1996, Admiral Zhang organized research conferences, conducted flexibility debates, and continuously worked on the purchase of *Varyag* (or *Voyage*) from Ukraine.[53]

China's first aircraft carrier—Type 01 *Liaoning*, CV-16—was laid down as the *Varyag*, a Soviet-designed *Kuznetsov*-class 55,000-ton aircraft carrier. It was built at the Black Sea Naval Shipyard and was about 68 percent complete in late December 1991, when the Soviet Union collapsed. A Chinese visiting professor from Harbin Ship Engineering College, studying at Ukraine Shipbuilding Academy, sent the information back home.[54] Soon Vice Admiral Zheng Ming, chief of the PLAN Equipment and Technology Department, received the information and shared it with Pan Zengxi, chairman of China's National Shipbuilding Engineering Association. Pan invited the professor to Beijing to brief Admiral Liu and shipbuilding chiefs in early 1992. CMC vice chairman Liu Huaqing sent a civilian business delegation to Ukraine to inspect *Varyag* for possible purchase.[55] In March, the Chinese delegation, including Vice Admiral Zheng Ming and headed by the vice president of the Seventh Research Institute, arrived at the Black Sea Naval Shipyard. After their return to Beijing, the delegation gave eight briefings and three reports to the high command from 1992 to 1994 about purchasing the *Varyag*.[56] However, for unknown reasons, Jiang

Zemin and the high command failed to approve financial support for the purchase of *Varyag*.

CMC vice chairman Liu Huaqing persisted and in April 1995, he instructed Commander Zhang Lianzhong to organize another carrier development conference that focused on the *Varyag*'s importation. Liu invited all PLA chiefs, State Council ministers, and industry leaders to attend the carrier conference. Thereafter, the navy submitted another request to the high command for the *Varyag*'s purchase. In May, Liu asked Huang Pingtao, president of the China National Shipbuilding Corporation, to examine *Varyag* again. After his return from Ukraine, Huang briefed General Cao Gangchuan, deputy chief of the PLA General Staff, and Vice Admiral He Pengfei, deputy commander of the PLAN.[57] However, by the end of 1995, Jiang Zemin decided not to launch the carrier's project.[58]

There were several factors in the mid-1990s working against China's carrier development. One of He Pengfei's staff said that "it takes four conditions for China to develop its aircraft carrier: national strategic need, top leader's willingness, comprehensive national strength, and technology. Any one of them is indispensable. It was because of the lack of the four elements that China did not have an aircraft carrier in the past forty years."[59] The author of *China's Aircraft Carrier* argued that "after the Soviet Union collapsed, China was released from Cold War security threats and began to adopt a relaxed international environment and accepted a 'new concept of security.' Purchasing the *Varyag* seemed misaligned with the Party Center's new diplomacy."[60] The others indicated some shipbuilding offices calculated the cost of *Varyag*'s remodeling as too expensive.

Moreover, Jiang Zemin held grievances toward Liu Huaqing in 1995. Jiang used the carrier's initiative to leverage Liu's political support. During his second term, Jiang Zemin offered special promotions to young and supportive generals. He also considered selecting his own successor instead of Hu Jintao, whom Deng Xiaoping had chosen for him. From his powerful position as a member of the Politburo Standing Committee and the first CMC vice chairman, Admiral Liu disagreed with Jiang's personnel rearrangement and insisted on staying with Deng's transition plan. Although he was not happy, Jiang Zemin stopped his replacement attempt and continued supporting Hu Jintao as his successor.

In November 1996, Vice Admiral Shi Yunsheng became the navy's new commander (1996–2003). As a navy pilot, Commander Shi prioritized aircraft carrier research and development than anyone else in the navy headquarters. After his graduation from the Air Force Academy, Shi became a jet fighter pilot of the navy air force in 1962. He served as a squadron commander, wing deputy commander, and regiment deputy commander from 1964 to 1978. Then, Shi enrolled in the Naval Command University. He became an air force division commander in 1981 and South Sea Fleet air force commander in 1983. Ranked rear admiral in 1988, Shi was promoted to the navy aviation deputy commander in 1990 and PLAN deputy commander in 1992. He was made vice admiral in 1994 and admiral in June 2000. During his tenure as PLAN commander, Shi made tremendous efforts in developing Liu Huaqing's aircraft carrier projects and training carrier pilots.[61]

With Commander Shi Yunsheng's support, PLAN vice commander He Pengfei suggested in 1996 a new approach to purchase *Varyag*, which the Ukrainians wanted to sell for scrap after removing all weaponry and electronic systems from the carrier. Vice Admiral He Pengfei told business owners and investors from Hong Kong and Macao that if they purchased *Varyag*, they could receive loans and financial support from Chinese security or credit companies as "a government's project through private deals." The naval deputy commander considered it China's last chance and would never have forgiven himself if the opportunity was lost.[62]

Meanwhile, China purchased two more former Soviet cruisers/aircraft carriers, *Kiev* and *Minsk*, in 1996 and 1998; both were aviation capable. Russian cruiser/aircraft carrier *Kiev* served in the Soviet and then Russian navy from 1975 to 1993 with a displacement of 41,000 tons (loaded), a top speed of 32 knots, and able to carry 32 warplanes and 20 helicopters. A Chinese private company purchased *Kiev* and turned it into an amusement park in Tianjin, Hebei, in 2000. China also purchased another former Soviet cruiser/carrier, *Minsk*, which, as the second *Kiev*-class carrier with similar operational characteristics, served in the Soviet and the Russian navy from 1978 to 1994. A Chinese state-owned ship dismantling company purchased *Minsk* in 1998 and sold it for $4.3 million to an entertainment company, which transformed the carrier into the Shenzhen Minsk Military World, a naval theme park, in Shenzhen, Guangdong.

In 1997, Deng Xiaoping died. Jiang Zemin removed Admiral Liu Huaqing in 1998 from his posts because of his criticism. In 1999, Liu's daughter, Lieutenant Colonel Liu Chaoying, was arrested at the Beijing International Airport and his daughter-in-law was also arrested in Beijing. General Zhang Wannian, chief of the PLA General Staff, became the designated successor to Liu Huaqing and the candidate to enter the next Politburo. Zhang Wannian voiced his firm support for Jiang Zemin's September 1995 speech on politics. Zhang's endorsement on behalf of the PLA exerted great weight in China's political arena where Jiang's speech on politics was compared to Deng's historical speech on the "truth discussion" in 1979.[63]

Despite his retirement at the age of eighty-two, Liu Huaqing remained active in naval research, development, and production, and continued efforts to purchase the *Varyag*. In 1998, with naval support, a Macao-based Chinese firm purchased *Varyag* for $20 million. In July 2000, the company towed the carrier from Ukraine to China. However, the Turkish government denied the ship's passage through the Bosphorus Strait, citing concerns about its blockage of the strait during high wind and the *Varyag* had to turn back and remained in the Black Sea for sixteen months.[64] Beijing negotiated with the Turkish government from mid-2000 to mid-2001. In July 2001, China invited the chief of the Turkish General Staff of the Armed Force General Huseyin Krvnkoglu to Beijing. Jiang Zemin met the Turkish chief and promised arms sales and other favorable conditions. In August, the Turkish government agreed to allow *Varyag* to pass. On November 1, the carrier passed through the Bosphorus, and then later through the Strait of Malacca. By February 20, 2002, *Varyag* arrived at the Dalian Naval Shipyard for structural studies.[65] Although it took three years and $5 million to tow the *Varyag* from Ukraine to Dalian Shipyard, Liu Huaqing's carrier dream became reality.

## HU AND NEW NAVAL DEVELOPMENT

After Jiang Zemin retired from the CMC chairmanship in 2002, new leader Hu Jintao continued China's aircraft carrier's development. At a Politburo meeting in April 2004, Hu Jintao and the top leaders decided on conversion of the *Varyag* carrier. On February 3, 2005, PLAN commander Zhang Dingfa and political commissar Hu Yanlin visited Admiral Liu

Huaqing at home. Commander Zhang told Liu the great news that "your dream will become reality soon!" Then, Hu Yanlin explained, "The Party Center has decided to develop our aircraft carrier!" Happy and excited, Liu gave a thumbs-up and said, "Great! Great! Great!" The retired admiral told the new naval leaders that "starting the development now, it may take ten years to launch and commission it; it will take another ten years to gain real combat capabilities." Admirals Zhang and Hu appreciated Liu's lifetime effort in pushing China's carrier development and said, "You have done a great deal for our carrier's research and development, all naval officers and sailors will remember it forever!"[66] On July 27, 2011, the PRC Defense Ministry announced, "China is now remodeling a worn-out aircraft carrier for scientific research, experiment and training."[67] On September 25, 2012, Hu personally commissioned China's first aircraft carrier, the Type 01 *Liaoning* (CV 16), and gained a new public profile as achieving significant success in the navy's modernization.[68]

Hu Jintao appreciated Liu Huaqing's opposition to Jiang's attempt at terminating his succession status after Deng's death in 1997. During his tenure from 2002 to 2012, Hu Jintao supported Liu's naval strategy and launched a national campaign to promote China's maritime interests and oceanic sovereignty. Hu Jintao became the party's chairman at the CCP Sixteenth National Congress after Jiang retired in November 2002. Hu was elected president of the PRC at the Sixth National People's Congress (NPC) the following March. In September 2004, Jiang left command of the Chinese military, and Hu Jintao became the new civilian commander in chief of the twenty-first-century PLA. Diversity grew within CMC leadership and competing factions became dynamically interdependent under Hu Jintao. Several political groups of younger, ambitious, and capable leaders aggressively fought political battles for control of the government and military.[69] Hu tried maintaining a balance in Beijing by emphasizing political and social harmony and nurturing working relations among the different military groups, while he emphasized the importance of continuing naval development. He supported the military professionalism and merit-based system of officer promotion and stressed that the PLA officers should have college degrees and formal overseas training (see photo 11). By 2005, all naval pilots and commanders of warships had college educations.[70]

PHOTO 11. President Hu Jintao (*left*) visits Liu Huaqing at home during the Chinese Lunar New Year on January 26, 2008. 光明日报 [*Guangming Daily*]

After taking over as commander in chief, Hu Jintao deliberately maintained successful naval reforms. He continued promoting Liu Huaqing's concepts of sea power, oceanic territory, maritime sovereignty, and naval modernization. Hu Jintao told PLA leaders that "China is a big oceanic country. The Chinese Navy plays a crucial role in defending our country's sovereignty, security, marine interests, and sea power. It is a glorious mission."[71] With naval power rapidly increasing, at the CCP Sixteenth National Congress in 2002, the Party Center for the first time called for "implementing the maritime development" and "developing the maritime economy" as one of the party's new tasks in the twenty-first century. In August 2004, Hu chaired a Politburo meeting to mobilize national resources and promote naval modernization. Hu escalated efforts for naval transformation and combat readiness. In December 2006, Hu met the representatives of the PLAN Tenth Party Committee Conference and told naval leaders to "build a modern, professional, and strong navy to meet China's new demands and development in the new century."[72] At the CCP's Seventeenth National Congress in 2007, Hu Jintao discussed the "growth of maritime economy" and made plans to develop China's maritime interests. During Hu's administration, the navy improved its equipment and weapon systems and received scores of new warships.

Since 2000, the Chinese navy has commissioned more than thirty new submarines, including sixteen Chinese-manufactured *Song*-class submarines and twelve *Kilo*-class submarines purchased from Russia. Meanwhile, the PLAN designed, manufactured, and completed four *Yuan*-class submarines with an air-independent propulsion (AIP) system to reduce their vulnerability. The navy received new missile destroyers like the Type 051C *Shijiazhuan*, with a displacement of 7,000 tons and speed over 30 knots, in 2005. The PLAN also received missile frigates like *Wenzhou*, commissioned in September 2005, with a displacement of 4,000 tons. The PLAN commissioned sixty Type 022 *Houbei* missile-armed catamarans after 2007, equipped with sea-skimming YJ-082 supersonic anti-ship cruise missiles. The Chinese navy is armed with wire-guided, wake-homing torpedoes and ship-borne air defense. The PLAN, however, had only limited indigenous technological capabilities. It remained as a "learner" rather than an "innovator" in many areas of naval technology in the 2010s.

Hu Jintao appointed Admiral Zhang Dingfa as the new navy commander in June 2003 after Shi Yunsheng retired. Zhang started his naval career as a submarine torpedo officer after college, and then a staff member at the Nuclear Submarine Office in PLAN HQ. From 1973, Zhang Dingfa became a submarine deputy captain and captain. In 1980, he studied at the Naval Command University. In January 1985, Zhang became an assistant chief of the North Sea Fleet, and the chief staff of the Qingdao Naval Base. He enrolled in the graduate curriculum at the National Defense University in 1988. After 1993, Zhang served as the NSF chief staff, deputy commander, and commander. He became PLAN deputy commander in 2000 and president of the PLA Academy of Military Science in 2002 before he became PLAN commander.

During his tenure from 2003 to 2006, Commander Zhang Dingfa increased PLAN joint exercises with foreign navies. In October 2003, Chinese warships, seaplanes, and helicopters hosted a joint military exercise with the Pakistani destroyer *Babur* and the comprehensive depot ship *Nasr* in the near water off Shanghai. From March 12 to 16, 2004, Chinese missile destroyer *Harbin* and depot ship *Hongzehu* held a joint exercise with the French navy's antisubmarine destroyer *Latouche-Treville* and frigate *Commandant Birot* in the Yellow Sea. From August 15 to 24, 2005, the Chinese and Russian navies launched a joint exercise, code-named *Peace Mission 2005*.[73] The first U.S.-Chinese naval exercise took place on September 20, 2006, off the California coast. The Chinese missile destroyer *Qingdao* worked with USS *Shoup* and Seahawk helicopters in a joint maritime search-and-rescue exercise. After the U.S.-China joint naval exercise, Rear Admiral Wang Fushan, commander of the Chinese visiting formation, cabled Admiral Gary Roughead: "The commanding skills and professional quality of the U.S. Pacific Fleet impressed us deeply."[74]

In 2004, the navy edited Liu Huaqing's military work from his early career in World War II to his retirement in 1998. In 2007, after the Party Center and CMC's approvals, the PLA Press published *Selected Military Papers of Liu Huaqing* in two volumes, totaling 850,000 words. It declassified more than 200 of Liu's reports, speeches, articles, instructions, and letters since he became a Red Army officer. The first volume had 109 pieces of Liu's military work from September 1939 to January 1988, and the second volume included 104 pieces of his naval papers from February 1988 to September 1997 when he became top PLA leader and worked in the Party Center. These primary materials became fundamental sources for understanding Liu's strategic thinking and examining his naval development.

In the same year, the PLA Press published Liu Huaqing's autobiography *Memoir of Liu Huaqing*. The admiral spent four years (2003–2007) and provided a historical perspective of seventy years of his entire military career and naval development in great details for the first time. His memoir totaled 520,000 words and included 68 historical photos. Liu Huaqing concluded his life in three sentences: "As a citizen, I spent my lifetime doing the best for our country and people with all my heart and intelligence. As a service man, I continued fighting battles and never allowed my uniform to be stained. As one of his subordinates, I have accomplished the great missions assigned by Deng Xiaoping. I won't sweat if I would brief him in the future."[75] Navy headquarters hosted news conferences and book launches for both of Liu's works. China's mainstream media described him as a "commoner admiral" (*buyi jiangjun*).[76] Liu Huaqing remained active to promote China's maritime interests and sea power. Invited by national TV stations, he served as military advisor or consultant from 2000 to

2008 for several TV series, documentaries, and educational programs on the PLAN's development, China's oceanic sovereignty, and maritime strategy.

China's rapid increase in overseas trade made the oceans more important to national economic growth. By 2003, China's maritime industry contributed 1 trillion yuan (about $167 billion) to the national economy, a huge increase from 10 billion yuan ($1.7 billion) in 1978.[77] Cole believes that the Chinese have "the idea that a great country should have a great Navy." He links Chinese naval efforts to "the nation's economic development" and to "dependence on overseas trade," which have been principally overlooked by other works in the field.[78] In 2010, China's total energy consumption surpassed the United States for the first time ever, making it the world's largest energy consumer. China's economy faces more challenges and pressures than ever, and the export-oriented manufacturing that relied especially on energy resources is no longer sustainable. Therefore, the 12th Five-Year Plan period became crucial in that China entered a period of reforming the energy economy.

In the later 2000s, China had the second largest economy in the world, following only the United States. The country became more dependent on overseas trade. Its energy production and consumption taken together signifies how the national economy operates. China ranked fifth in world oil production with more than 4 million barrels a day in 2011, about 51 percent of the Asia-Pacific total oil production.[79] In the meantime, Beijing shifted its strategic priorities from a land power to maritime power. China's maritime economic interests, as a net energy importer, are supported by increasing regional and global sea lines of communication (SLOCs).

After Admiral Zhang's sudden death in June 2006, Wu Shengli was appointed as navy commander from 2006 to 2016. Wu majored in marine survey at the PLA Institute of Surveying and Mapping. After his graduation, Wu Shengli worked as navigation officer and deputy captain on four different frigates and destroyers. He served as a frigate and then a destroyer captain for eight years. In July 1994, he achieved the rank of rear admiral. Wu was then promoted to a fleet captain, naval base chief of staff, president of the PLA Dalian Warship Academy, ESF deputy commander, and SSF commander. He was promoted to vice admiral in July 2003. Wu became the PLA deputy chief of the General Staff in April 2004 and the navy's commander in August 2006. He was promoted to admiral on June 20, 2007. Commander Wu held the Peace Mission 2007 joint maritime training exercise in the Arabian Sea with seven foreign navies. In September 2007, he conducted a joint exercise with the British navy in the Atlantic. British aircraft carrier *Ark Royal* and Chinese missile destroyer *Guangzhou* and comprehensive depot ship *Weishanhu* conducted emergency communication, joint command, and search-and-rescue exercises. Under Wu's command, the Chinese navy had several joint naval exercises with the Russian navy in 2005, 2009, and 2012. From April 22 to 27, 2012, the Chinese navy held a joint exercise with the Russian navy on the Yellow Sea. Twenty-three warships, two submarines, thirteen fixed-wing aircraft, nine helicopters, and two special combat units participated in the exercise from both navies.

Hu Jintao visited the South Sea Fleet on April 9, 2008. He proclaimed the Chinese navy was a "strategic, comprehensive, and international force, which plays a pivot[al] role in defending our oceanic territory, maintaining our sea power, and developing our national maritime interests."[80] Hu attended the naval parade at Qingdao on April 23, 2009, to celebrate the navy's sixtieth birthday. Hu Jintao inspected naval forces and warships. More than thirty destroyers, frigates, and submarines participated in the parade, plus thirty-one warplanes. Most of the warships and planes were designed and manufactured under the command of Admiral Liu Huaqing.[81] Something new at the largest parade in PLAN history was the invitation and attendance of twenty-one foreign warships from fourteen countries, including the United States, Russia, France, Canada, Mexico, and India. Before the parade, Hu met foreign naval delegations from twenty-nine countries.[82]

In 2008, Commander Wu Shengli ordered the South Sea Fleet to prepare for international anti-piracy operations off the coast of Somalia to protect Chinese commercial shipping. From January to November 2008, Chinese commercial ships made 1,265 navigations of the Gulf of Aden, about three to five ships every day. Eighty-four Chinese ships, about 20 percent of the total victimized, were attacked, robbed, or kidnapped by Somali pirates.[83] At the time, China was the fourth largest international shipping nation in the world and needed the PLAN's protection. This was the first time the Chinese navy sent naval combat forces overseas for international humanitarian operations. In November, SSF Command launched three anti-piracy exercises that involved destroyers, helicopters, naval special forces, and marines. On December 19, China announced it would send its naval fleet to fight pirates along the Somali coast. The SSF Command dispatched the missile destroyers Type 052C *Wuhan* and 052B *Haikou* (hull number 171, flagship) with *Weishanhu* 887, PLAN's largest supply ship, as the First Group Convoy Formation under the command of Rear Admiral Du Jingchen, SSF deputy commander. During its four-month operations, Rear Admiral Du and his fleet responded to all requests and escorted 212 Chinese and international commercial ships. Du used his helicopters as the "forward eyes" to patrol and report any suspicious pirate activities. Occasionally, the helicopters proved sufficient enough to stop pirate threats.

From December 2008 to February 2011, the PLAN sent ten group formations to the Gulf of Aden and African coast against the pirates, including 25 warships, 18 airplanes and helicopters, totaling 8,400 sailors, marines, and naval special forces. They escorted 4,411 Chinese and international commercial ships and rescued 51 cargo ships. The special force troops launched 22 rescue operations on 33 commercial ships and successfully rescued Chinese and foreign sailors without casualties. It was the first time for the Chinese navy to conduct joint operations in defending national strategic interests in the far sea. It was also the first time for the PLAN to continue its transoceanic military missions for an extended period of time. On November 30, 2011, the spokesman for China's Defense Ministry announced, "China will continue to dispatch naval convoy formations to the waters of the Gulf of Aden and Somalia for escort work and to further carry out international convoy cooperation."[84]

In 2010, China became the largest shipbuilder in the world after its total building tonnage exceeded the longtime leader South Korea. Chinese news agency *Xinhua News* reported, "China built ships with a total deadweight capacity of 65.5 million tons, accounting for 43 percent of the deadweight capacity of ships built in the world."[85] The PLAN was ready to improve its logistical support system for longtime maritime missions by providing better fleet trains. The *China's National Defense White Paper in 2010* indicated the accelerated construction of "large support vessels."[86] You Ji examines the PLAN's transformation in the 2000s–2010s when it was "extending its operations from coastal defense to far-seas power projection."[87]

With new naval development, Hu Jintao continued his nationalistic foreign policy and engaged Japan in the Senkaku Island disputes. The Diaoyu/Senkaku Islands become a testing ground for the Chinese public to judge the military strength, political toughness, and diplomatic skills of the new leadership. As China's oil and gas industries shifted to deep water exploration, international tensions increased between China and Japan over the sovereignty of areas along the median line in the East China Sea. Tokyo asked Beijing to stop drilling and building gas exploration platforms close to disputed waters. In June 2008, Chinese coast guard vessels accompanied Taiwanese activists approaching the Diaoyu Dao/Uotsurishima Island.[88] The disputed islands became the Chinese government's demonstration of strong nationalistic stands against foreign threats that involved territorial integrity and naval strength. Any compromise over the islands currently seems exceedingly difficult, if not impossible.

Chinese naval leaders certainly felt pressured, or even threatened, by U.S. naval activities in East Asia. They believed that the United States "has increased its strategic attention to and input in the Asia-Pacific region, further consolidating its military alliances, adjusting its military development, and enhancing its military capabilities."[89] China insists that UNCLOS (United Nations Convention on the Law of the Sea) gives coastal states the right to regulate not only economic activities, but also foreign military activities, in their EEZs (exclusive economic zones). It has been the root cause of various contentious physical encounters between U.S. and PRC vessels, both military and civilian, in the past. In 2006, a Chinese submarine surfaced near the USS *Kitty Hawk*. In 2007, China denied safe harbor to two small U.S. Navy minesweepers caught in the midst of dangerous weather. In 2009, Secretary of State Hillary Clinton told the Japanese foreign minister that the Treaty of Mutual Cooperation and Security between the United States and Japan covers the disputed areas; meaning that the Obama administration may commit the U.S. armed forces to

Japanese defense of these islands.[90] On March 8, 2009, a U.S. Navy survey vessel, *Impeccable*, was confronted by five Chinese navy ships. According to the American accounts, the Chinese ships surrounded and harassed the USS *Impeccable*, which conducted surveillance in an area over which Beijing claimed jurisdiction, but other countries consider international waters. The Chinese tried to block the ship and snag its cables with hooks. The Americans used a fire hose to spray water at the Chinese. The chief American intelligence officer called it the "most serious" military incident with China since 2001. On March 12, 2009, when President Barack Obama met China's foreign minister Yang Jiechi, he told the Chinese foreign minister that the two countries need to raise "the level and frequency" of military dialogue "in order to avoid future incidents" like the high sea confrontation.[91] The East China Sea gained importance as China significantly and urgently focused on building its maritime power. As Liu Huaqing predicted it became one of the major sources of international tension in the Pacific region in the twenty-first century.[92]

On October 1, 2009, Liu Huaqing was invited to the top of the Tiananmen Tower in his uniform to review the Grand Military Parade of the Sixtieth National Day with Hu Jintao and other national leaders. Hu told Chinese military leaders at a conference in December 2011 that the navy should "accelerate its transformation and modernization in a sturdy way and make extended preparations for warfare in order to make greater contributions to safeguard national security."[93] Nan Li emphasizes Hu Jintao's two contributions to China's naval strategy and capability developments. First, Hu requested the PLA "to safeguard China's newly emerging overseas interests, which defines PLAN's far-seas missions." Second, Hu "endorsed the concept of information-based system of systems operations, which impacts how PLAN conducts operations."[94]

On January 14, 2011, Admiral Liu Huaqing died in the hospital at the age of ninety-five. Hu Jintao and all top Chinese leaders, PLA chiefs, and naval officers attended his funeral on January 24 in Beijing. General Liu Yazhou praised the admiral who "did not forget Deng Xiaoping's great trust nor disappoint the expectations of the party and people."[95] Rear Admiral Yang Yi told a reporter that "Comrade Liu Huaqing made historical contribution to the People's Navy. It was because of him that we have a great navy today."[96] Admirals Wu Shengli and Liu Xiaojiang promised that Chinese naval officers and sailors "won't forget his hearty efforts to develop a new navy and his precious strategic wealth for a naval power."[97] Chinese mainstream media described Liu Huaqing as the "father of [the] modern Chinese navy." Moreover, when Commodore Shi Changxue published his official biography of Liu Huaqing in 2013, official blogs and social media in China referred to Liu as "China's Gorshkov."[98]

# CONCLUSION

## *Liu's Legacy and Xi's Navy*

This historical overview shows Admiral Liu Huaqing's strong impact on the PLAN's development in the twenty-first century. It took four decades from the 1970s to the 2010s to transform the Chinese navy from a brown-water fleet to a blue-water modern navy. The diachronic discussions here have explained the needs for naval reforms and the results of Liu's efforts. His story indicated successive generations of Chinese naval officers and sailors with modernization as the central theme and patterns of the naval development. In 2010, China became the largest shipbuilder in the world.[1] In 2020, the global shipbuilding industry estimated that China's shipbuilding capacity is the largest, making up around 45 percent of global capacity. By 2020, the PLAN had 240,000 naval officers and sailors with an overall battle force of 350 surface ships and submarines—the U.S. Navy had 293 warships at that time.

This biography of Liu Huaqing provides a historical analysis of how the admiral designed, planned, and executed his naval development and operations through the Cold War. His political experience in the PLA helped his maritime ideas become naval strategy and practical policy for sea power. He took advantage of CCP power transitions from one generation to the next when the changes or reforms became necessary and were an important component for the party's survival and transformation. In 1975, the last year of Mao's life, Liu questioned and criticized PLA traditional land-based defense and ignorance of naval technology, opening the door for Deng Xiaoping's military reform. In 1991, the last year of Deng's political career, Liu finalized his new naval strategy and prepared China for an oceangoing development, providing new opportunities for Jiang Zemin's globalization and naval-centric national defense. Liu's military career proved that he loyally served the party's agenda and supported the PRC's policies.

Therefore, Liu rejected the Western military experts' comments that he was the "Chinese Mahan."[2] China's unique civil-military characteristics influence naval reforms and changes amid political loyalty to the Party Center and especially to the top leaders like Mao Zedong, Deng Xiaoping, Jiang Zemin, and now Xi Jinping. In return, Deng Xiaoping trusted Liu Huaqing and Xi Jinping trusts the navy.

Political loyalty and trust became the fundamental characteristic of Liu Huaqing's naval career and China's military reform. Both became necessary and available during Liu's efforts in PLAN modernization from 1975 to 1998. In return, a developing navy and a centralized PLA high command facilitated two power transitions: first, from Mao Zedong to Deng Xiaoping in 1976–1978; second, from Deng Xiaoping to Jiang Zemin in 1989–1991. Liu Huaqing played an important supportive role during the two power transitions, including his commanding role in the Tiananmen Square incident in 1989. As Sergey Gorshkov said, "The sole agent waging armed struggle has always been the army and the fleet which even in peace time continued to serve as an instrument or tool of policy of state."[3] Liu's political experience and naval career seemed quite similar with what Gorshkov described here.

Although Liu Huaqing's theory and practice sometimes resembled or overlapped with parts of Mahanian theory, the findings in the work did not provide enough evidence to show Mahan's influence on the Chinese admiral. One of the reasons is that Mahanian theory may include universal truths about the nature of maritime strategy. These truths are accessible to theorists and practitioners regardless of whether they have read Mahan or not. Meanwhile, Liu's fundamental understanding of maritime theory and naval force-building was derived from the same intellectual roots as Gorshkov's maritime theory and naval-building. The Chinese admiral shared the similar institutional framework and organizational system with the Soviet naval commander. Therefore, Liu Huaqing was more like China's Gorshkov than "Red Mahan."[4]

Liu Huaqing became Chinese naval commander when the PLAN was at a historical moment. He had to overcome formidable obstacles before his military reform and naval building to achieve his design and plans. The way Liu both carried on long-standing traditions while made remarkable changes was crucial to building a "rich country with a strong navy." The PLAN plays an increasingly important role on the international stage and is now well on its way to becoming a world-class naval power and a military juggernaut. To celebrate the one hundredth anniversary of Liu's birthday, China's national TV station, CCTV (China Central TV), broadcasted the nine-episode documentary *Liu Huaqing* in the fall of 2016. It received a positive nationwide reaction. Holmes and Yoshihara suggested that "Western observers should monitor the commentary over Liu's life and legacy, monitoring which schools of thought lay claim to his ideas and how they interpret and seek to apply these ideas."[5]

Xi Jinping was convinced that Liu Huaqing's achievement and contribution "would inspire the whole party, whole country, and all the Chinese people to work very hard to realize the great goals of the 'Two One-hundred Years' and realize China's Dream of the great rejuvenation of the Chinese nation."[6] You Ji examines the PLAN's transformation in the 2000s–2010s when it was "extending its operations from coastal defense to far-seas power projection."[7] Cole concludes that Chinese maritime strategy attempts to "achieve near-term national security objective and long-term regional maritime dominance."[8]

The biographical analysis provided an understanding of how the PLAN continued reorganization, modernization, professionalization, and digitalization, which were started by Liu Huaqing in the late twentieth century and define the PLAN's characteristics in the twenty-first century. Since Xi Jinping became China's commander in chief in 2012, he emphasized Liu's sea power doctrine and expanded China's maritime policy beyond that of either Jiang Zemin or Hu Jintao. Xi Jinping reaffirms Jiang Zemin's post–Cold War doctrine and continues to employ nationalism as an ideology to unite the country and fight for its superpower status, perhaps resulting in one more source of legitimacy for the CCP as the country's ruling party. In April 2013, Beijing announced in its annual *Defense White Paper* that it is a strategic task of China's modernization drive as well as a strong guarantee for China's development to build a strong national defense and powerful armed forces, which are commensurate with China's international standing and meet the needs of its security and development interests. China's naval force must meet the new requirement of China's national development and security strategy.[9] Xi repositioned China as the Asia-Pacific regional epicenter, despite experiencing unprecedented demands and facing new challenges.

Xi, however, tried to surpass Deng Xiaoping and Liu Huaqing's maritime interests in the Pacific Ocean, and instead target the Indian and Atlantic Oceans. Liu's strong naval strategy became part of Xi's grand strategy. Xi Jinping believed the current Asian-Pacific trade system under the U.S. leadership limited China's maritime interests. With geostrategic ambitions and political confidence, Xi Jinping launched his global plan "New Silk Road and Economic Belt" in 2013. The official name for the Belt and Road Initiative (BRI) is the "Silk Road Economic Belt and Twenty-First-Century Maritime Silk Road Development Strategy."

According to the official reference, the "road" is short for the Twenty-First-Century Maritime Silk Road. In 2013, Xi Jinping announced China's intention to create the new maritime silk road during his state visit to Jakarta, Indonesia. It is a sea trading route from the Pacific to Indian Ocean through Southeast Asia to South Asia, the Middle East, and Africa, representing the maritime dimension of China's global geostrategic ambitions. The BRI brought massive trade, finance, transportation, communication, infrastructure, and energy programs, by both sea and land routes, from Chinese coasts to other continents. It was designed to establish a China-centric global system excluding America. In October 2017, the Party Center adopted the BRI into the constitution of the CCP at the Nineteenth National Congress in Beijing. By early 2024, the PRC government had recruited about 140 countries into the BRI project. Xi Jinping promised the party and the country that the BRI would accomplish by 2049, the centennial of the PRC's founding.

Xi Jinping carried on Deng Xiaoping's active defense and enhanced Liu Huaqing's naval strategy of near sea defense. However, Xi's new military transformation in 2012–2022 certainly affects such areas as strategy, doctrine, operational concepts, and combat techniques. For example, an important ongoing change in the PLA doctrine moves away from the traditional defense principle of "never open fire first" in war as Deng Xiaoping's active defensive and Liu Huaqing's naval doctrines in the battles of the South China Sea. The new doctrine dismisses the timing issue and instead justifies the war efforts as defensive in nature even though Chinese warships may have to open fire first. The new strategy and transformations require the PLAN to build a combat fleet capable of winning naval battles in the near and far seas. It requires the Chinese navy to prepare itself for defensive and offensive operations under the most difficult and complex circumstances at sea.

In near sea operations, the PLAN would employ aircraft carriers, landing ships, land-based missiles, surface warships, and conventional submarines. Moreover, during the 2010s–2020s, Beijing strengthened multi-agent naval services, including the China Coast Guard (CCG) and Chinese maritime militia. The PLAN closely coordinated with its sister services for the similar strategic goals in near seas. In the recent years, as a "law enforcement" naval force, the CCG maintains regular patrol around Taiwan's islands like Jinmen in the Taiwan Strait. It also played an important role in some incidents against the Filipino ships near Ren'ai Reefs (the Second Thomas Shoal) of the Spratly Islands in the South China Sea in March 2024. Avalist argues that "China may have become the pioneer of the deliberate and well-calculated revivalism of the oldest naval tactics known to humankind, that is, ramming and shouldering, in reminiscence of the Greek trireme of Thucydides' contemporaries during the classical antiquities."[10]

Xi Jinping shifted China's strategic position in the Pacific with an emphasis of far sea protection. For the protections in far seas, the Chinese navy could use anti-aircraft carrier weapons, ship-based A2/AD systems, anti-ship ballistic missiles (ASBM), and nuclear submarines. In line with the strategic requirements of mobile operations and multidimensional offense and defense, the PLAN has reoriented from near sea defense to transoceanic mobility. You Ji points out that the PLAN has transformed itself "from a tactical homeland defensive force to one that is capable of strategic offensive missions beyond national borders . . . as a credible fighting force globally."[11] The Chinese navy also expanded its amphibious assault capabilities by building more landing ships, including amphibious transport docks.[12] In the 2020s, China operates ninety maritime installations, thirteen of which are owned by the PRC and ten of which are suitable for a naval base, after the PLA established its first naval facility in Djibouti in 2017.[13]

Since he believed that the United States is in decline, Xi changed China's strategic role from supporting the United States in the Asia-Pacific to challenging the United States in the region, despite experiencing unprecedented demands and facing new challenges. As he shifted his maritime strategy, Xi took the challenge and made new aggressive initiatives in the East China Sea. In November 2013, Beijing began using "China's East Sea" (*Zhongguo Donghai*), rather than the traditional term of East China Sea, to define the area and claimed the establishment of an Air Defense Identification Zone (ADIZ), including the disputed Diaoyu/Senkaku Islands.[14] Thereafter, the PLAAF regularly patrolled the zones to strengthen the effective control over the zone. Shen Jinke, spokesman for the PRC Defense Ministry, said that the PLAAF would conduct routine air drills in the zone for dealing with any emergency situations.[15] In 2016, the territorial conflict escalated to naval confrontation involving naval vessels, coast guard gunboats, and fighters in the East China Sea's disputed areas, promoting more worries from the international community. The East China Sea has become one of the most worrisome flash points in Asia, an important source of insecurity in the Western Pacific, and possibly a point of contention between the U.S. Navy against the PLAN in East Asia.

In 2015, Chinese warplanes began patrolling the South China Sea, including the disputed Paracel and Spratly Islands. The PLAN's outposts in the South China Sea extend the air force's possible operating areas. Deployments of Chinese warplanes from Spratly Island outposts can extend range and loiter time over the South China Sea and even reach the Indian Ocean. The PLAAF's medium-range H-6K bombers carry up to six precision-guided CJ-20 air-launched cruise missiles (ALCMs) each, giving it the ability to engage U.S. armed forces as far away as the islands of Guam and Okinawa. The Southern Theater Command Air Force (TCAF) was the first to receive the H-6J maritime strike bombers. Thereafter, confrontation between Chinese and American naval and air forces in the South China Sea has aroused serious concerns about security and stability in the Asia-Pacific region. The United States continues to fly military aircraft in the ADIZ without informing China, defying

China's declaration that the region falls into a Chinese airspace defense zone. In December 2019, Beijing commissioned its newly manufactured aircraft carrier, Type 02 *Shandong*, into service at Hainan Island's Yulin Naval Base in the South China Sea.

Taiwan has emerged as the most dangerous flash point in the growing U.S.-China rivalry. Chinese attacks on Taiwan, to protect Beijing's so called "core interests," is in China's strategy. Taiwan plays important strategic and political roles in the security and stability of the South China Sea subregion. During Liu Huaqing's era, Chinese leaders blamed their failure in Taiwan's liberation on the naval technological gap between the PLAN and the U.S. Navy. During the post-Liu era since 2012, China began to claim its maritime interests and oceanic sovereignty in both the South and East China Seas. However, with Taiwan in the middle, China finds it difficult to project its sea power over the South China Sea and challenge the U.S. dominance in the region. Taiwan's safety and security fit into U.S. Asian-Pacific policy to deal with China's rising and contain Beijing's aggressive behavior since it is a key link in the "first island chain" against China. Taiwan has become the testing ground for U.S. determination to contain the "China threat" in the South China Sea region. A failed defense of Taiwan would undermine the subregional countries' trust and confidence in the U.S. commitments and responsibilities.

From 2018 to 2024, the United States shifted its policy toward Taiwan from an "ambiguous strategy" to a "clear strategy" by clarifying its commitment to the island's defense.[16] Then, the PLA has significantly escalated its military activities directed at Taiwan, including air patrols in the Taiwan Strait, joint exercises to simulate landing campaigns, and anti-ship missile exercises aimed largely at American intervention against possible PLA attacks on Taiwan. In June 2021, the PLA conducted an amphibious landing exercise in waters near Taiwan amid renewed tensions between Beijing and Washington. The navy expanded its amphibious assault capabilities by building more landing ships, including amphibious transport docks.[17] Among its most publicized development is a growing Chinese carrier fleet with several conventional takeoff/barrier landing carriers. In August 2022, the PLA launched its largest military exercise ever by sending 140 fighters and bombers, deploying 10 destroyers, and firing 12 missiles around Taiwan, after two U.S. congressional delegations visited the

ROC.[18] Western nations were shocked and wondering how the United States would respond if Chinese armed forces conducted an amphibious invasion of Taiwan. After consolidating his perpetual power at the CCP's Twentieth National Congress in October, Xi Jinping emphasized that the CCP "will never promise not to use force" to liberate Taiwan and unify the country.[19]

During Xi Jinping's third term, Beijing's defense strategy against such backdrop included deterrence and defeat of foreign invasion, protection of China's three layers of political, state, and people's security, containment and defeat of "Taiwan independence," safeguard of national sovereignty, unity, and territorial integrity, protection of the country's maritime rights and interests, oversea interests, and sustainable national development. It divides naval defense in two main zones of near seas and far seas with different goals, or near sea defense and far sea protection.[20] Although Liu Huaqing categorized the East China Sea and South China Sea as near seas, the PLAN has developed much mature strategic thinking by the 2010s. While Liu defined his strategic goals by the three lines of island chains, the admirals under Xi Jinping have expanded their doctrinal tendency of new mentality and understanding of maritime conception. In 2017, Admiral Jiang Weilie, commander of PLAN South Sea Fleet, had an interview after his fleet's sixteen-day exercise in the Western Pacific and through the first chain of islands. The PLAN admirals said that the purpose of the exercise was to test long-distance operations, antimissile capabilities, and antisubmarine attacks as well as coordination among battleships and fighter jets. They treated the exercise as a real war.[21]

To match China's economic superpower status, the Chinese navy acquired more ships, improved its technology, and conducted frequent naval exercises. In April 2013, Beijing announced in its annual *Defense White Paper* that it is the navy's strategic task to meet the new requirement of China's national interests and security needs.[22] After Wu Shengli retired, Shen Jinlong became the PLAN commander from 2017 to 2021. Admiral Shen made it clear that the PLAN became more prominent since the turn of the century due to a change in China's economic growth, international status, new security concerns, and global strategic priorities. China is developing a blue-water navy. In 2019, the PLAN's tonnage totaled 1.82 million tons as the second largest navy in the world, only after the U.S. Navy.

Beijing remained its close military relations with Moscow. Xi Jinping made eight trips to Moscow between 2012 and 2020 with the purpose of strengthening strategic support to China. By 2014, the two nations announced a new era of military collaboration as part of an enhanced strategic partnership. In a long-term view, the PLAN's investment in Soviet technology and advisory assistance in 1950–1960 paid significant dividends during Liu Huaqing's naval modernization in the 1970s-2000s. The partnership between the PRC and Russian Federation naval forces continues growing through collaborative engagement launched in the 2010s. This raises serious questions over the future of American security, and whether the United States has anything to fear from a potential naval superpower of Communist China. In May 2015, the Chinese and Russian forces conducted a joint naval exercise, code-named Joint Sea 2015, in the Mediterranean Sea. In August, a larger scale operation, Joint Sea II, was held in international waters, about 250 miles from Japan, and involved twenty-two warships and twenty aircraft. Vice Admiral Aleksandr Fedotenkov, deputy commander of the Russian navy, was satisfied with the joint training's results, which "showed that Russian and Chinese forces can effectively fulfill tasks in such a difficult region."[23] In the same year, the PLA conducted three large-scale naval exercises in the East China Sea. The third live-fire exercise from August 24 to 28 involved more than one hundred naval vessels, dozens of aircraft, and information warfare units. Chinese warships fired nearly one hundred various missiles.[24]

In the 2010s, the PLAN continued the efforts in nuclear submarines development when the Type 093A and Type 093B *Shang*-class were launched. They received some improvements in terms of quieting technologies from Russia and were considered as "quiet." Then, Type 094 *Jin*-class SSBNs were launched after 2018 with new reactors for their propulsion systems. Some Chinese naval scholars compared Type 093 *Shang* and Type 094 *Jin* with Russian *971 Akula*-class and early U.S. SSN 688 *Los Angeles*–class SSBNs. Another important transition took place in 2021 when China's principal surface combatants entered the fifth generation with bigger and better Type 055 *Renhai* DDGs (guided missile destroyers). The U.S. Department of Defense categorized Chinese DDGs, Type 055 *Renhai*-class, as guided missile cruisers (CGs). Since 2021, the PLAN has received two new Type-055 destroyers every year. The Chinese navy has also expanded its ballistic missile submarine fleet, including Type 094 *Jin*-class SSBNs and long-range *JL-2* SLBMs.[25] The Chinese navy also has 15,000 marines and 26,000 naval aviation personnel with 690 aircraft.

Among its most publicized development is a growing Chinese aircraft carrier fleet. Under the command of Xi Jinping, Liu Huaqing's dreams of China's aircraft carriers and a blue-water navy became realities. In August 2013, Xi Jinping visited the aircraft carrier *Liaoning*, commenting that China should build an even stronger naval force.[26] In November, China began construction of its second aircraft carrier. On April 26, 2017, the PLAN launched its new aircraft carrier Type 02 *Shandong* at the Dalian Shipyard. Xi Jinping commissioned it into service on December 17, 2019. As a modified version of the *Liaoning* (Russian *Kuznetsov*) design, Type 02 adopted better 346A S-band phased radar arrays than the Type 01's radar arrays. Type 02 uses a ski-jump takeoff method for its J-15 fighters. Then, China built its third aircraft carrier, Type 03 *Fujian*, which launched on June 17, 2022, and started sea trials in May 2024. Type 03 is China's first indigenously designed carrier with its first capable of catapult-assisted takeoffs (CATOBAR). It has a full load displacement of 80,000–85,000 tons and forty fixed-wing aircraft, including J-15 and FC-31 fighters, and twelve helicopters. Since 2022, the PLAN began to establish its carrier battle groups (CVBGs) with the *Liaoning*. PLAN Commander Admiral Shen Jinlong made it clear that the PLAN became more prominent since the turn of the century due to a change in China's economic growth, international status, new security concerns, and global strategic priorities.

The maritime competition in the Pacific became clearly more visible in recent years from the nature of the United States' responses. The U.S. Department of Defense pointed out, "The pace and scope of China's military transformation have increased in recent years, fueled by acquisition of advanced foreign weapons, continued high rates of investment in its domestic defense and science and technology industries, and far-reaching organizational and doctrinal reforms of the armed forces."[27] One of the major U.S. policy moves was the establishment of the Quadrilateral Security Dialogue (QSD, or the Quad) with Japan, Australia, and India in

2016. Meanwhile, the U.S. Pacific Command (USPACOM) continued its expansion and by far remains the largest of all U.S. combatant fleets in the world. In 2021, President Joe Biden declared a joint high-tech cooperation, AUKUS, with Britain and Australia. AUKUS provides Australia with access to nuclear propulsion technology for submarines, artificial intelligence (AI), quantum mechanics technologies, and cyber applications for military purposes.

The Chinese navy's new mission is to strengthen its combat readiness and effectiveness and make innovative efforts to protect the national security at seas. According to Chinese experts, the ocean means a great deal to China as it is the international communication waterway and holds strategic resources for the world's sustainable development. China has its own strategic interests from the oceans. Many estimate that at some point, China's major threat will come from its surrounding waters. Expanding the battlefield to the seas could greatly change the international military balance of power, and create serious challenges for Indo-Pacific region's safety and stability. The time period from 2025 to 2049 is the most important for China's rejuvenation as well as when the PLAN will reach three milestones as a world-class navy. According to the navy's plan, the PLAN will integrate its mechanization and informatization by 2027; complete the modernization of surface combatants and submarine force by 2035; and fully transform the PLAN into a "world-class navy" by 2049. Due to all the aforementioned challenges, the PLAN has an arduous task to safeguard China's national unification, oceanic territory, and maritime interests. The Chinese naval force will continue to fulfill its mission while evolving through adaptation and improvement for informatization and intelligentization. Through its operational experience in the Taiwan Strait, East China Sea, and the South China Sea, the PLAN confronts the same key issues as Liu Huaqing always did, planning, learning, changing, and political control. The Taiwan Landing Campaign and naval battles over the disputed islands are still the most prominent and foremost of PLAN operations.

# NOTES

## INTRODUCTION

1. Jeffery B. Goldman, "China's Mahan," U.S. Naval Institute *Proceedings* 122, no. 3 (March 1996), https://www.usni.org/magazines/proceedings/1996/march/chinas-mahan.
2. 吴胜利上将 [Admiral Wu Shengli]、刘晓江上将 [Admiral Liu Xiaojiang], 海军发展壮大是他一生的牵挂 ["He Spent Whole Life on a Strong Navy"], in 海军司令刘华清 [*Naval Commander Liu Huaqing*], 施昌学大校 [by Commodore Shi Changxue] (Beijing: Long March Press, 2013), iii. Wu Shengli (1945– ) was PLA Navy commander from 2008 to 2017. Liu Xiaojiang (1949– ) was PLAN political commissar from 2008 to 2014.
3. Beijing considered a U.S. cold war "island chain" defensive strategy as a security challenge to isolate and encircle China in the Pacific. In the early 1950s, U.S. officials made a strategic plan to contain China and Russia in the Pacific through three island chains. The first island chain linked Japan's Ryukyu Island, Taiwan, the Philippines, and Borneo. Toshi Yoshihara, "China's Vision of Its Seascape: The First Island Chain and Chinese Sea-Power," *Asian Politics and Policy* 4, no. 3 (July 2012): 239–314.
4. 施昌学大校 [Commodore Shi Changxue], 海军司令刘华清 [*Naval Commander Liu Huaqing*], 134. Shi Changxue (1957– ) worked at the PLAN Department of Political Tasks from 1992 to 2012, and he began to write the biography of Liu Huaqing in 1999. Hereafter cited as 施 [Shi], 刘华清 [*Liu Huaqing*].
5. 习近平 [Xi Jinping], 在纪念刘华清同志诞辰100 周年座谈会上的讲话 ["Speech at the Symposium to Commemorate the 100th Anniversary of the Birth of Comrade Liu Huaqing"], September 28, 2016, 新华社 [*New China News Agency*], www.english.cctv.com/2016/09/29/ARTISzfc7wHez510m6JcAHnE160929.shtml.
6. 杨舟 [Yang Zhou], 中国的戈尔什科夫: 红色马汉刘华清 ["China's Gorshkov and 'Red Mahan': Liu Huaqing"], 新华网 [Xinhua Net], July 2013, www.xinhuanet.com/book/xinshu/201307/.
7. John Keegan, *The American Civil War* (New York: Knopf Doubleday, 2010), 272.
8. Other important works include *The Influence of Sea Power upon the French Revolution and Empire, 1793–1812* (1892), *The Interest of America in Sea Power; Present and Future* (1897), and *Sea Power in Relation to the War of 1812* (1905).
9. John H. Maurer, "Alfred Thayer Mahan and the Strategy of Sea Power," in *The New Makers of Modern Strategy: From the Ancient World to the Digital Age*, ed. Hal Brands (Princeton, NJ: Princeton University Press, 2023), 169–92.

10. Philip A. Crowl, "Alfred Thayer Mahan: The Naval Historian," in *Makers of Modern Strategy: From Machiavelli to the Nuclear Age*, ed. Peter Paret (Princeton, NJ: Princeton University Press, 1986), 451, 460.
11. 胡俊修 [Hu Junxiu], 近代国人海权观念的演变 ["Chinese Evolution of Sea Power Concept in Modern China"], 光明日报 [*Guangming Daily*], February 8, 2021, 14.
12. In 1906, the first group of 22 Chinese students were sent to study naval technology in Japan from Yantai Naval School. From 1904 to 1909, China sent 149 naval students to study overseas, including 44 to Great Britain and 105 to Japan. See 吴杰章少将 [Rear Admiral Wu Jiezhang]、苏小东 [Su Xiaodong]、程志发 [Cheng Zhifa], 中国近代海军史 [*A History of the Modern Chinese Navy*] (Beijing: PLA Press, 1989), 160, 161. Wu Jiezhang (1931– ) served as the director of the Department of Political Tasks at the PLA Naval Aviation Engineering University from 1987 to 1996.
13. 周益锋 [Zhou Yifeng], "'海权论'东渐及其影响" ["'Sea Power Theory' in the East and Its Impact"], 历史月刊 [*History Monthly*], no. 4 (2006): 3, www.aisixiang.com/data/30517.html.
14. 赵建国 [Zhao Jianguo], 清季报刊对海权论的传播 ["The Spread of Concept Sea Power Theory on Press in Late Qing Period"], 学术月刊 [*Academic Monthly*] 55, no. 6 (2023): 195.
15. 周益锋 [Zhou Yifeng], "海权论的传入和晚清海权思想" ["Translations of Sea Power Theory and Sea Power Thought in Late Qing"], 唐都学刊 [*Academic Journal of Tangdu*], no. 4 (2005): 12–15.
16. It is an ongoing debate on whether Chinese intellectuals, officials, and the public had their own conceptions of "sea power" before Mahan's theory was introduced to China in the late nineteenth and early twentieth centuries.
17. 梁启超 [Liang Qichao], 论太平洋海权及中国的前途 ["On Sea Power in the Pacific and the Future of China"], 新民丛报 [*New People's Voices*], no. 26 (1903): 2.
18. 杨德昌大校 [Commodore Yang Dechang], 海权! 中华海权! [*Sea Power! China's Sea Power!*] (Beijing: Three Alliance Publishing House, 2022), 416. Yang Dechang (1946– ) was the inaugural director of PLA Navy Shanghai Museum in the early 1990s and then the designer and director of PLA Navy Qingdao Museum in the 2000s.
19. The report quoted in 周益锋 [Zhou Yifeng], "'海权论'东渐及其影响" ["'Sea Power Theory' in the East and Its Impact"], 4.
20. Governor Zhang Renjun's suggestion quoted in 周益锋 [Zhou Yifeng], "'海权论'东渐及其影响" ["'Sea Power Theory' in the East and Its Impact"], 6.
21. Li Hongzhang's quote in 刘子明 [Liu Ziming], 中国近代军事思想史 [*History of Military Thoughts in Modern China*] (Nanchang: Jiangxi People's Press, 1997), 357.
22. John K. Fairbank, Edwin O. Reischauer, and Albert M. Craig, *East Asian: Transition and Transformation*, rev. ed. (Boston: Houghton Mifflin, 1989), 222–23; Bruce A. Elleman, *Modern Chinese Warfare, 1795–1989* (London: Routledge, 2001), 141.

23. The 1900 Boxer Rebellion was a mass movement against foreign missionaries and establishments in North China. As the Boxers struck against the Westerners without mercy, eight powers—Russia, Britain, Germany, France, the United States, Japan, Italy, and Austria—formed an alliance to launch a war against the Boxers as well as the Qing regime, which decided to use the movement's anti-missionary policy to seize popular leadership and had declared that the movement was legal. For more details, see Frederic Wakeman Jr., *The Fall of Imperial China* (New York: Free Press, 1977), 216–20.
24. 杨德昌 [Yang Dechang], 海权！中华海权！ [*Sea Power! China's Sea Power!*], 419–20.
25. 唐宝镐 [Tang Baogao], 海上权力之要素 ["The Key Elements of Sea Power"], 海军期刊 [*Journal of Naval Force*], vol. 1 (no. 6–12, 1927) and vol. 2 (no. 1–8, 1928).
26. 杨德昌 [Yang Dechang], 海权！中华海权！ [*Sea Power! China's Sea Power!*], 422.
27. 高晓星编 [Gao Xiaoxing, ed.], 陈绍宽文集 [*Collected Papers of Chen Shaokuan*] (Beijing: Ocean Waves Publishing House, 1994), 4.
28. 抗日战争纪念网 [Anti-Japanese War Memorial Network], 中国航母第一人：陈绍宽的未竟航母梦 ["China's First Aircraft Carrier: Chen Shaokuan's Unfulfilled Carrier Dream"]（2018–10–6）, https://www.krzzjn.com/show-1475-82630.html.
29. 陈绍宽大将 [Fleet Admiral Chen Shaokuan], 对于国防上之感想 ["Some Thoughts on National Defense"], 东方杂志 [*Oriental Magazine*] 33, no. 1 (1936): 2–3.
30. The statistics from 吴杰章 [Wu Jiezhang]、苏小东 [Su Xiaodong]、程志发 [Cheng Zhifa] 主编，中国近代海军史 [*A History of the Modern Chinese Navy*], 372–73.
31. Edward L. Dreyer, *China at War, 1901–1949* (New York: Longman, 1995), 7.
32. 施 [Shi], 刘华清 [*Liu Huaqing*], 336.
33. 杨德昌 [Yang Dechang], 海权！中华海权！ [*Sea Power! China's Sea Power!*], 458–59.
34. 杨国宇少将 [Rear Admiral Yang Guoyu], 当代中国海军 [*Contemporary Chinese Navy*] (Beijing: China's Social Science Press, 1987), 17. Yang Guoyu (1914–2000) served as PLAN chief of staff from 1975 to 1982 and deputy commander from 1978 to 1985.
35. 杨国宇 [Yang Guoyu], 当代中国海军 [*Contemporary Chinese Navy*], 16.
36. When Mao met the former KMT admirals in Beijing, the CCP chairman told them that "our new [PLA] navy must learn from you. The new and old [revolted KMT] navies must learn from each other." Mao's words are quoted in 杨国宇 [Yang Guoyu], 当代中国海军 [*Contemporary Chinese Navy*], 33–34.
37. For example, Professor Zhou Qingyi returned from America. Many instructors served in the ROC Navy before they transferred to the Dalian Naval Academy. See 刘华清上将 [Admiral Liu Huaqing], 怀念肖劲光同志在兼任大连海校校长的日子里 ["The Years When Comrade Xiao Jinguang Served as the President of Dalian Naval School"], in 一代元戎 [*Heros of Their General*], 王祖尧编 [ed. Wang Zuyao] (Beijing: PLA Press, 1991), 14. Wang Zuyao (1931–2022) served as deputy chief of PLA General Staff from 1988 to 1996.
38. Some Chinese naval strategists argued that Mahan's theory was based upon the colonial period's experience and applied to imperialist power struggles and warfare. World War II, however, ended the global colonial system, to which Mahan's theory had belonged. See 胡波 [Hu Bo], 后马汉时代的中国海权 [*China's Sea Power in*

*the Post-Mahan Era*] (Beijing: Ocean Waves Publishing House, 2018); 陈海宏 [Chen Haihong], 马汉和他的海权论 ["Mahan and His Sea Power Theory"], 山东师范大学学报（人文社会科学版） [*Journal of Shandong Normal University (Humanities and Social Sciences Edition)*] 56, no. 5 (2011): 101–5. Moreover, some scholars were critical and argued that Mahan's sea power theory was not applicable to China. For example, 高月 [Gao Yue], 近代中国海权思想浅析 ["Modern China's Sea Power Thoughts"], 浙江学刊 [*Academic Journal of Zhejiang*], no. 6 (2013): 1–2.

39. 刘华清上将 [Admiral Liu Huaqing], 刘华清回忆录 [*Memoir of Liu Huaqing*] (Beijing: PLA Press, 2004), 439. Hereafter cited as 刘回忆录 [*Liu's Memoir*].
40. Norman C. Polmar, Thomas A. Brooks, and George E. Fedoroff, *Admiral Gorshkov: The Man Who Challenged the U.S. Navy* (Annapolis, MD: Naval Institute Press, 2019), chapter 13.
41. 刘回忆录 [*Liu's Memoir*], 266.
42. You Ji, "The Soviet Model and the Breakdown of the Military Alliance," in *China Learns from the Soviet Union, 1949–Present*, eds. Thomas P. Bernstein and Hua-yu Li (Lanham, MD: Lexington Books, 2010), 132–33, 135.
43. Mao, "A Single Spark Can Start a Prairie Fire," in *Selected Works of Mao Tse-tung* (Beijing: Foreign Languages Press, 1977), 1:117–28.
44. Mao made it clear that "our principle is that the Party commands the gun, and that the gun must never be allowed to command the Party." Mao, "Problems of War and Strategy," in *Selected Works of Mao Tse-tung*, 2:224; Dreyer, *China at War*, 5.
45. 《星火燎原》编辑部 [*Xinghuo liaoyuan* Composition Department], 中国人民解放军将帅名录 [*PLA Marshals and Generals*] (Beijing: PLA Press, 1992), 2:301. Hereafter cited as 将帅名录 [*PLA Marshals and Generals*].
46. 刘回忆录 [*Liu's Memoir*], 308.
47. 刘回忆录 [*Liu's Memoir*], 358.
48. 刘回忆录 [*Liu's Memoir*], 350.
49. Rear Admiral Michael A. McDevitt, *China as a Twenty-First Century Naval Power: Theory, Practice, and Implications* (Annapolis, MD: Naval Institute Press, 2020), x.
50. McDevitt, *China as a Twenty-First Century Naval Power*, 55, 129–31, 172.
51. McDevitt, *China as a Twenty-First Century Naval Power*, vii.
52. Bernard D. Cole, *The Great Wall at Sea: China's Navy in the Twenty-First Century*, 2nd ed. (Annapolis, MD: Naval Institute Press, 2010), 190.
53. Cole, *Great Wall at Sea*, 42.
54. James C. Bussert and Bruce A. Elleman, *People's Liberation Army Navy: Combat Systems Technology, 1949–2010* (Annapolis, MD: Naval Institute Press, 2011), x.
55. Bussert and Elleman, *People's Liberation Army Navy*, 180.
56. Toshi Yoshihara and James R. Holmes, *Red Star over the Pacific: China's Rise and the Challenge to U.S. Maritime Strategy* (Annapolis, MD: Naval Institute Press, 2010), 4.
57. Yoshihara and Holmes, *Red Star over the Pacific*, 18–19.
58. Toshi Yoshihara, *Mao's Army Goes to Sea: The Island Campaigns and the Founding of China's Navy* (Washington, DC: Georgetown University Press, 2022), xi.

59. Andrew S. Erickson, book review on *China's New Navy* and *Mao's Army Goes to Sea*, *Naval War College Review* 77, no. 3 (Summer/Autumn 2024), https://digital-commons.usnwc.edu/nwc-review.
60. Yoshihara, *Mao's Army Goes to Sea*, iv.
61. 刘华清 [Liu Huaqing], 刘华清书法与题词选集 [*Selected Inscriptions and Calligraphy of Liu Huaqing*] (Beijing: Great Wall Publishing House, 2010).
62. Liu's book chapters are in 一代元戎 [*Heroes of Their Generation*] (Beijing: PLA Press, 1991); 共和国祭奠 [*The Republic Pays Homage to Them*] (Beijing: East Publishing, 2015); 历史从这转弯：长征中的重大战略决策 [*History Turns Here: Key Strategic Decisions in the Long March*] (Hong Kong: Heaven and Earth Books, 2017); 星火燎原 [*A Spark Ignites a Prairie Fire*], vol. 9 (Beijing: PLA Press, 2007); 问鼎天下 [*Aim for World Domination*] (Beijing: East Publishing, 2011). Among his journal articles are 刘华清 [Liu Huaqing], 有关海军战略问题的探讨 ["Discussion about Naval Strategic Issues"], in 海军杂志 [*Navy's Magazine*], no. 7 (1986); and 走向世界 ["March into the World"], in 湖南师大学报 [*Journal of Hunan Normal University*] (January 1999).
63. For example, 刘华清 [Liu Huaqing], 刘华清书法与题词选 [*Selected Inscriptions and Calligraphy of Liu Huaqing*].
64. Chinese leaders' papers and manuscripts include 毛泽东 [Mao Zedong], 建国以来毛泽东文稿，1949–1976 [*Mao Zedong's Manuscripts since the Founding of the State, 1949–1976*] (Beijing: CCP Central Archival and Manuscript Press, 1993), vols. 1–13; 建国以来毛泽东军事文稿 [*Mao Zedong's Military Manuscripts since the Founding of the PRC*] (Beijing: Military Science Press and CCP Central Archival and Manuscript Press, 2010), vols. 1–3; 毛泽东军事文集 [*Collected Military Works of Mao Zedong*] (Beijing: Military Science Press, 1993), vols. 1–6; 毛泽东军事文选（内部版）[*Selected Military Papers of Mao Zedong: Internal Edition*] (Beijing: PLA Soldiers Press], 1981), vols. 1–2; 毛泽东外交文选 [*Selected Diplomatic Papers of Mao Zedong*] (Beijing: CCP Central Archival and Manuscript Press, 1994); 毛泽东文选 [*Collected Works of Mao Zedong*] (Beijing: People's Press, 1999), vols. 1–8; 毛泽东选集 [*Selected Works of Mao Zedong*], five volumes (Beijing: People's Press, 1979); 刘少奇 [Liu Shaoqi], 建国以来刘少奇文稿 [*Liu Shaoqi's Manuscripts since the Founding of the State*] (Beijing: CCP Central Archival and Manuscript Press, 2008), vols. 1–7; 周恩来 [Zhou Enlai], 建国以来周恩来文稿 [*Zhou Enlai's Manuscripts since the Founding of the State, 1949–1950*] (Beijing: CCP Central Archival and Manuscript Press, 2008], vols. 1–3; 周恩来军事文选 [*Selected Military Papers of Zhou Enlai*] (Beijing: People's Press, 1997), vols. 1–4.
65. The PRC government documents include 中国外交部办公厅档案资料部 [Archives Department of the General Office, PRC Foreign Ministry], 中国外交档案 [*China's Foreign Affairs Archives*], 北京 [Beijing]; 新华社 [Xinhua News Agency], 新华社文件资料汇编 [*A Collection of Documentary Materials of Xinhua News Agency*] (Beijing: Xinhua News Agency Publishing House, n.d.).
66. For examples, 前苏联档案 [Former Soviet Archives], "斯大林与中共代表团会谈记录" ["The Meeting Minutes of Stalin's Negotiations with the CCP Delegation"], June 27, 1949, in 有关刘少奇1949 年访苏的俄国档案 [*The Russian Archives of the 1949*

*Liu Shaoqi Visit in the Soviet Union*]; "斯大林与毛泽东会谈记录" ["The Meeting Minutes of Stalin's Conversation with Mao Zedong"], December 16, 1949, in 有关1950年中苏条约谈判的俄国档案 [*The Russian Archives of the 1950 Treaty Negotiations on the Soviet-Chinese Agreement*].

67. For example, Kathryn Weathersby, trans. and ed., "New Russian Documents on the Korean War," *Bulletin: Cold War International History Project* 6–7 (Washington, DC: Woodrow Wilson International Center for Scholars, winter 1995/1996): 30–125.
68. 沈志华主编 [Shen Zhihua, ed.], 苏联历史档案选编 [*Selected Historical Archives of the Soviet Union*] (Beijing: Archives and Manuscripts of Social Science Press, 2002).
69. 沈志华主编 [Shen Zhihua, ed.], 朝鲜战争: 俄国档案馆的解密文件 [*The Korean War: Declassified Documents in the Russian Archives*] (Taipei: Academia Sinica, 2015).
70. 朱德元帅 [Marshal Zhu De], 朱德军事文选 [*Selected Military Writings of Zhu De*] (Beijing: PLA Press, 1986); 彭德怀元帅 [Marshal Peng Dehuai], 彭德怀军事文选 [*Selected Military Writings of Peng Dehuai*] (Beijing: CCP Central Archival and Manuscript Press], 1988); 刘伯承元帅 [Marshal Liu Bocheng], 刘伯承军事文选 [*Selected Military Writings of Liu Bocheng*] (Beijing: PLA Press, 1992); 聂荣臻元帅 [Marshal Nie Rongzhen], 聂荣臻军事文选 [*Selected Military Writings of Nie Rongzhen*] (Beijing: PLA Press, 1992); 徐向前元帅 [Marshal Xu Xiangqian], 徐向前军事文选 [*Selected Military Writings of Xu Xiangqian*] (Beijing: PLA Press, 1992); 贺龙元帅 [Marshal He Long], 贺龙军事文选 [*Selected Military Writings of He Long*] (Beijing: PLA Press, 1989); 陈毅元帅 [Marshal Chen Yi], 陈毅军事文选 [*Selected Military Papers of Chen Yi*] (Beijing: PLA Press, 1996).
71. 肖劲光大将 [Fleet Admiral Xiao Jinguang], 肖劲光军事文选 [*Selected Military Writings of Xiao Jinguang*] (Beijing: PLA Press, 2003); 刘华清上将 [Admiral Liu Huaqing], 刘华清军事文选 [*Selected Military Writings of Liu Huaqing*] (Beijing: PLA Press, 2008). Hereafter cited as 刘军事文选 [*Selected Military Writings of Liu*].
72. Part of the research effort resulted in a translated and edited volume by Xiaobing Li, Allan R. Millett, and Bin Yu, trans. and eds., *Mao's Generals Remember Korea* (Lawrence: University Press of Kansas, 2001).
73. Ma Ying-jeou, *Trouble over Oily Waters: Legal Problems of Seabed Boundaries and Foreign Investment in the East China Sea*, S.J.D. thesis (Harvard Law School, December 1980); 马英九 [Ma Ying-jeou], 从新海洋法论钓鱼台列屿与东海划界问题 [*New Oceanic Regulations: Issues of Senkaku Island and the Border of the East China Sea*] (Taipei: Zhengzhong Books, 1986); 钓鱼台列屿主权争议回顾与展望 [*Disputed Sovereignty of Senkaku Island: The Past and Future*] (Taipei: ROC Government Printing, 1996).
74. For example, 李曙光 [Li Shuguang], 刘华清 [*Liu Huaqing*] (Beijing: Great Wall Publishing House, 2005).
75. For example: 刘新博 [Liu Xinbo], 刘华清海洋战略思想研究 ["Interpretation of Liu Huaqing's Maritime Strategic Thinking"], master's thesis, College of History and Culture, University of Heilongjiang, Harbin (2015); 兰波 [Lan Bo], 改革开放以来中国海权认识演进研究 ["Study of Cognitive Process of China's Sea Rights since Its Reform and Opening Up"], PhD diss., College of History and Culture, University of Shandong, Ji'nan (2017).

## CHAPTER 1. FROM A POLITICAL COMMISSAR TO A REAR ADMIRAL

1. 刘华清 [Liu Huaqing], 怀念肖劲光同志在兼任大连海校校长的日子里 ["The Years When Comrade Xiao Jinguang Served as the President of the Dalian Naval Academy"], 8–9.
2. 肖劲光大将 [Fleet Admiral Xiao Jinguang], 肖劲光回忆录 [*Memoirs of Xiao Jinguang*] (Beijing: PLA Press, 1988), 287–88.
3. 习近平 [Xi Jinping], 在纪念刘华清同志诞辰100 周年座谈会上的讲话 ["Speech at the Symposium to Commemorate the 100th Anniversary of the Birth of Comrade Liu Huaqing"].
4. 《星火燎原》编辑部 [*Xinghuo liaoyuan* Composition Department], 将帅名录 [*PLA Marshals and Generals*], 2:301.
5. Sergey Gorshkov, *The Sea Power of the State* (Annapolis, MD: Naval Institute Press, 1979), xi.
6. 中共中央文献研究室 [CCP Central Archival and Manuscript Research Division], 毛泽东年谱, 1893–1949 [*A Chronological Record of Mao Zedong, 1893–1949*] (Beijing: CCP Central Archival and Manuscript Press, 1993), 1:208. Mao said it again in 1938 that "every Communist must grasp the truth, 'Political power grows out of the barrel of a gun.'" Mao, "Problems of War and Strategy," in *Selected Works of Mao Tse-tung*, 2:224; Mao, "Comments on the Report of the Comintern Representative, August 7, 1927," in *The Rise to Power of the Chinese Communist Party: Documents and Analysis*, ed. Anthony Saich (Armonk, NY: M. E. Sharpe, 1996), 317.
7. 中国人民革命军事博物馆 [National Military Museum of Chinese People's Revolution], 中国战争发展史 [*The Historical Development of Chinese Warfare*] (Beijing: People's Press, 2002), 2:821–22; 中共中央党史研究室 [Party History Research Division, CCP Central Committee], 中国共产党历史大事记, 1919–2009 [*Major Historical Events of the CCP, 1919–2009*] (Beijing: CCP Party History Press, 2013), 51; Jing Chang and Jon Halliday, *Mao: The Unknown Story* (New York: Knopf, 2005), 50–51.
8. 军事科学院军事历史研究部 [Military History Research Division, PLA Academy of Military Science (AMS)], 中国人民解放军的七十年 [*Seventy Years of the Chinese PLA*] (Beijing: Military Science Press, 1997), 33–38.
9. 刘回忆录 [*Liu's Memoir*], 4.
10. 施 [Shi], 刘华清 [*Liu Huaqing*], 12.
11. 徐向前元帅 [Marshal Xu Xiangqian], 历史的回顾 [*Recollection of the History*] (Beijing: PLA Press, 1987), 70–71.
12. 国防大学《战史简编》编写组 [PLA Defense University's *Concise War History* Compilation Team], 中国人民解放军战史简编 [*Concise History of the PLA's Wars*], 4th ed. (Beijing: PLA Press, 2001), 36–37.
13. 刘回忆录 [*Liu's Memoir*], 13–14.
14. 徐向前 [Xu Xiangqian], 历史的回顾 [*Recollection of the History*], 100–10.
15. 军事科学院军事历史研究部 [Military History Research Division, PLA AMS], 中国人民解放军的七十年 [*Seventy Years of the Chinese PLA*], 68.
16. 施 [Shi], 刘华清 [*Liu Huaqing*], 12.
17. 刘回忆录 [*Liu's Memoir*], 24, 28, 29.

18. 刘华清上将 [Admiral Liu Huaqing], 在纪念长征胜利六十周年红军老战士座谈会上的发言 ["Speech at the Red Army Veterans Symposium to Commemorate the 60th Anniversary of the Victory of the Long March"], in 刘华清军事文选 [*Selected Military Writings of Liu Huaqing*] (Beijing: PLA Press, 2008), 2:494. Hereafter cited as 刘军事文选 [*Selected Military Writings of Liu*].
19. 习近平 [Xi Jinping], 在纪念刘华清同志诞辰100 周年座谈会上的讲话 ["Speech at the Symposium to Commemorate the 100th Anniversary of the Birth of Comrade Liu Huaqing"].
20. 习近平 [Xi Jinping], 在纪念刘华清同志诞辰100 周年座谈会上的讲话 ["Speech at the Symposium to Commemorate the 100th Anniversary of the Birth of Comrade Liu Huaqing"].
21. 《星火燎原》编辑部 [*Xinghuo liaoyuan* Composition Department], 将帅名录 [*PLA Marshals and Generals*], 2:301.
22. 刘回忆录 [*Liu's Memoir*], 81.
23. Mao, "Unite All Anti-Japanese Forces and Combat the Anti-Communist Die-Hards," in *Selected Works of Mao Tse-tung*, 2:391–92.
24. 《彭德怀传》编写组 [*Peng Dehuai Biography* Compilation Team], 彭德怀传 [*Biography of Peng Dehuai*], 2nd ed. (Beijing: Contemporary China Press, 2006), 99.
25. 陈冠任 [Chen Guanren], 十大元帅：解放军十大统帅的历史 [*Ten Marshals: History of the Top Ten Leaders of the PLA*] (Beijing: CCP Party History Press, 2020), 133–34.
26. 刘回忆录 [*Liu's Memoir*], 87, 92.
27. 陶汉章少将 [Major General Tao Hanzhang], 孙子兵法概论 [*A Geneal Interpretation of Sun Zi's Art of War*] (Beijing: PLA Press, 1991), 4.
28. 刘伯承元帅 [Marshal Liu Bocheng], 刘伯承军事文选 [*Selected Military Writings of Liu Bocheng*] (Beijing: PLA Press, 1992), 227.
29. 刘华清上将 [Admiral Liu Huaqing], 刘伯承战术思想研究札记 ["Study Notes on Liu Bocheng's Tactical Thinking"], 军事知识 [*Military Knowledge*], no. 2 (1988): 4–5.
30. 彭德怀元帅 [Marshal Peng Dehuai], 彭德怀自述 [*Self-Recollection of Peng Dehuai*] (Beijing: People's Press, 1981), 235.
31. Liu Bocheng's words quoted in 《彭德怀传》编写组 [*Peng Dehuai Biography* Compilation Team], 彭德怀传 [*Biography of Peng Dehuai*], 2nd ed., 123.
32. 李保忠 [Li Baozhong], 中外军事制度比较 [*Comparative Study between Chinese and Foreign Military Systems*] (Beijing: China Commercial Press, 2003), 229.
33. Deng Xiaoping, "In Memory of Liu Bocheng," October 21, 1986, in *Selected Works of Deng Xiaoping* (Beijing: Foreign Languages Press, 1994), 3:186.
34. 国防大学《战史简编》编写组 [PLA Defense University's *Concise War History* Compilation Team], 中国人民解放军战史简编 [*Concise History of the PLA's War*], 484.
35. 钱海皓 [Qian Haihao], 军队组织编制学教程 [*Study of Military Organization and Formation: Graduate Curriculum*] (Beijing: Military Science Press, 2001), 39.
36. 施 [Shi], 刘华清 [*Liu Huaqing*], 12, 17.

37. 古越 [Gu Yue], 邓小平兵法 [*Deng Xiaoping's Art of War*] (Beijing: United Press, 2015), 2.
38. 习近平 [Xi Jinping], 在纪念中国共产党建立100 周年庆祝大会上的讲话 [Speech at the CCP's 100th Anniversary Celebration], *Renmin ribao* [*People's Daily*], July 1, 2021.
39. 习近平 [Xi Jinping], 在纪念刘华清同志诞辰100 周年座谈会上的讲话 ["Speech at the Symposium to Commemorate the 100th Anniversary of the Birth of Comrade Liu Huaqing"].
40. These rules and points later went through some changes until they were finalized in 1947 as follows. The "Three Main Rules of Discipline": (1) obey orders in all your actions; (2) don't take a single needle or piece of thread from the masses; and (3) turn in everything captured. The "Eight Points for Attention": (1) speak politely; (2) pay fairly for what you buy; (3) return everything you borrow; (4) pay for anything you damage; (5) don't hit or swear at people; (6) don't damage crops; (7) don't take liberties with women; and (8) don't ill-treat captives. The PLA General HQ, "Instruction on the Re-issue of the Three Main Rules of Discipline and the Eight Points for Attention," in Mao, *Selected Works of Mao Tse-tung*, 4:155–56.
41. 国防大学《战史简编》编写组 [PLA Defense University's *Concise War History* Compilation Team], 中国人民解放军战史简编 [*Concise History of the PLA's Wars*], 566.
42. Mao's quote from 古越 [Gu Yue], 邓小平兵法 [*Deng Xiaoping's Art of War*], 19.
43. Mao, "Manifesto of the Chinese People's Liberation Army," in *Selected Works of Mao Tse-tung*, 4:150. This political manifesto was drafted by Mao at Shenchuanpao, northern Shaanxi, for the general headquarters of the PLA. It was issued on October 10, 1947, and known as the "October 10 Manifesto."
44. 钱海皓 [Qian Haihao], 军队组织编制学教程 [*Study of Military Organization and Formation: Graduate Curriculum*], 40.
45. The Third Army Group entered Korea in March 1951, including the 12th, 15th, and 60th Armies. For more details of its operations in the Korean War, see Xiaobing Li, *China's Battle for Korea: The 1951 Spring Offensive* (Bloomington: Indiana University Press, 2014), 67–68.
46. 王玉彬 [Wang Yubin], 第二野战军 [*The Second Field Army*] (Beijing: Long March Press, 2012), 465–66.
47. In January 1951, the university was renamed the PLA's Second Advanced Infantry Academy at Chongqing, Sichuan.
48. Xiaobing Li, *Attack at Chosin: The Chinese Second Offensive in Korea* (Norman: University of Oklahoma Press, 2020), 37.
49. Li, *China's Battle for Korea*, 68–69.
50. 聂荣臻元帅 [Marshal Nie Rongzhen], 聂荣臻回忆录 [*Memoir of Nie Rongzhen*] (Beijing: People's Press, 2022), 618; Major General Xu Yan, "Chinese Forces and Their Casualties in the Korean War," trans. Xiaobing Li, *Chinese Historians* 6, no. 2 (Fall 1991): 54; Xiaobing Li, "China's Intervention and the CPVF Experience in the Korean War," in *The Korean War at Fifty: International Perspectives*, ed. Mark F. Wilkinson (Lexington: Virginia Military Institute Press, 2004), 136–37.

51. 刘回忆录 [Liu's Memoir], 252.
52. 中共中央党内指示 [CCP Central Committee's Instruction], 目前形势和党在一九四九年的任务 ["Current Situation and the Party's Tasks in 1949"], drafted by Mao Zedong and passed by the Politburo on January 8, 1949, in 毛泽东军事文集 [*Collected Military Manuscripts of Mao Zedong*] (Beijing: CCP Central Archival and Manuscript Press and Military Science Press, 1993), 5:471–78.
53. Mao, "On the Outrages by British Warships—Statement by the Spokesman of the General Headquarters of the Chinese People's Liberation Army," in *Selected Works of Mao Tse-tung*, 4:402.
54. 东方鹤 [Dong Fanghe], 张爱萍传 [*Biography of Zhang Aiping*] (Beijing: People's Press, 2000), 1:559–60.
55. Mao and Zhu's words quoted in 杨德昌 [Yang Dechang], 海权！中华海权！ [*Sea Power! China's Sea Power!*], 460.
56. 张爱萍上将 [General Zhang Aiping], 中国人民解放军 [*The Chinese People's Liberation Army*] (Beijing: Contemporary China Press, 1994), 2:25. Zhang Aiping (1910–2003) served as deputy chief of the PLA General Staff from 1955 to 1958 and from 1977 to 1980, as China's vice premier from 1980 to 1982, and as defense minister from 1982 to 1987.
57. Gao Xiaoxing et al., *The PLA Navy* (Beijing: China Intercontinental Press, 2012), 40.
58. 中华民国国防部 [Defense Ministry, ROC], 国军后勤史 [*Logistics History of the KMT Armed Forces*] (Taipei: Bureau of Historical and Political Records, Taiwan's Defense Ministry, 1992), 6:277.
59. 毛泽东 [Mao Zedong], 关于兵力部署的意见给林彪的电报 ["My Suggestions on Your Troops, Disposition and Battle Array"], October 31, 1949, in 建国以来毛泽东文稿, 1949–1976 [*Mao Zedong's Manuscripts since the Founding of the State, 1949–1976*] (Beijing: CCP Central Archival and Manuscript Press, 1993), 1:107. Hereafter cited as 毛文稿 [*Mao's Manuscripts*].
60. 中华民国国防部 [Defense Ministry, ROC], 国军后勤史 [*Logistics History of the KMT Armed Forces*], 6:199–200.
61. Bruce A. Elleman, *High Seas Buffer: The Taiwan Patrol Force, 1950–1979* (Newport, RI: Naval War College Press, 2012), 5.
62. 军事科学院军事历史研究部 [Military History Research Division, PLA Academy of Military Sciences (AMS)], 中国人民解放军战史 [*War History of the Chinese People's Liberation Army*] (Beijing: Military Science Press, 1987), 3:359.
63. Xiaobing Li, *A History of the Modern Chinese Army* (Lexington: University Press of Kentucky, 2007), 223.
64. 前苏联档案 [Former Soviet Archives], 斯大林与中共代表团会谈记录 ["The Meeting Minutes of Stalin's Negotiations with the CCP Delegation"], June 27, 1949, in 有关刘少奇1949 年访苏的俄国档案 [*The Russian Archives of 1949 Liu Shaoqi's Visit in the Soviet Union*], 中共党史研究 [*CCP Party History Research*], no. 2 (1998): 15–16.
65. 杨忠义大校 [Commodore Yang Zhongyi], 苏联专家与中国海军航空兵 [*Soviet Experts and Chinese Naval Aviation*] (Beijing: PLA Press, 2013), 10. Commodore Yang

Zhongyi became a naval pilot in 1965 and later served as office chief of the Command Center of the PLAN Air Force.

66. 前苏联档案 [Former Soviet Archives], 斯大林与毛泽东会谈记录 ["The Meeting Minutes of Stalin's Conversation with Mao Zedong"], December 16, 1949, in 有关1950年中苏条约谈判的俄国档案 [*The Russian Archives of the 1950 Treaty Negotiations on the Soviet-Chinese Agreement*], in 党史研究 [*Party History Research*], no. 4 (1998): 4.
67. 杨国宇 [Yang Guoyu], 当代中国海军 [*Contemporary Chinese Navy*], 48, 52.
68. Mao's conversation with Pavel Yudin, Ambassador of the Soviet Union to China on July 22, 1958, in Mao, *Mao Zedong on Diplomacy* (Beijing: Foreign Languages Press, 1998), 255.
69. 中国人民海军总部 [PLAN General Headquarters], 中国人民解放军海军编年史，1949–1983 [*The Chronicle of the PLA Navy, 1949–1983*] (Beijing: PLAN Press, 1995), 24; 刘亮 [Liu Liang], 岸防劲旅：中国人民解放军海军岸防部队 [*Strong Coastal Defense: PLAN Coastal Defense Forces*] (Beijing: Blue Sky Publishing House, 2014), 4.
70. 张爱萍 [Zhang Aiping], 中国人民解放军 [*The Chinese People's Liberation Army*], 2:25–26.
71. 中国人民海军总部 [PLAN General Headquarters], 中国人民解放军海军编年史，1949–1983 [*The Chronicle of the PLA Navy, 1949–1983*], 43.
72. 肖劲光大将 [Fleet Admiral Xiao Jinguang], 肖劲光回忆录（续集） [*Memoir of Xiao Jinguang (Sequel)*] (Beijing: PLA Press, 1989), 2.
73. 吴殿卿大校 [Commodore Wu Dianqing], 组建海军重大决策的历史事实 ["Historical Facts on Important Decisions to Establish the PLA Navy"], 人民海军 [*People's Navy*], no. 9 (October 2002): 4–5. Wu Dianqing (1951– ) served as deputy chief of the Propaganda Division, PLAN's Political Tasks Department, in the 1990s.
74. 吴殿卿大校 [Commodore Wu Dianqing], 毛泽东与肖劲光大将 ["Mao Zedong and Fleet Admiral Xiao Jinguang"], in 毛泽东与海军将领 [*Mao Zedong and Naval Admirals*], 吴殿卿、袁永安、赵小平主编 [ed. Wu Dianqing, Yuan Yong'an, and Zhao Xiaoping] (Beijing: PLA Literature Press, 1999), 25–26.
75. 郑雅茹 [Zheng Yaru], 肖劲光 ["Xiao Jinguaung"], in 中国人民解放军高级将领传 [*Biographies of the PLA's High-Ranking Generals*], 《中国人民解放军高级将领传》编审委员会编著 [ed. PLA *Biographies of the PLA's High-Ranking Generals* Editorial Committee] (Beijing: PLA Press, 2008), 4:477–78.
76. Fleet Admiral Xiao Jinguang (1903–1989) was purged during the Cultural Revolution. For more information on his military career, see 《星火燎原》编辑部 [*Xinghuo liaoyuan* Composition Department], 将帅名录 [*PLA Marshals and Generals*], 1:30–31.
77. 刘华清 [Liu Huaqing], 怀念肖劲光同志在兼任大连海校校长的日子里 ["The Years When Comrade Xiao Jinguang Served as the President of the Dalian Naval Academy"], 10.
78. 杨国宇 [Yang Guoyu], 当代中国海军 [*Contemporary Chinese Navy*], 48–49.
79. When Mao met the former KMT admirals in Beijing, the CCP chairman told them that "our new [PLA] navy must learn from you. The new and old [revolted KMT] navies must learn from each other." Mao's words are quoted in 杨国宇 [Yang Guoyu], 当代中国海军 [*Contemporary Chinese Navy*], 33–34.

80. 刘华清 [Liu Huaqing], 怀念肖劲光同志在兼任大连海校校长的日子里 ["The Years When Comrade Xiao Jinguang Served as the President of the Dalian Naval Academy"], 9.
81. 李东野少将 [Rear Admiral Li Dongye], 忆大连第一海军学校的创建 ["The Founding of the First Naval Academy in Dalian"], in 海军回忆史料 [*The Navy: Memoirs and History Records*] (Classified), 中国人民解放军历史资料丛书海军编审委会 [ed. Navy Compilation Committee, PLA Historical Documents and Collections Series] (Beijing: Ocean Waves Publishing House, 1994), 2:634–37. Li Dongye (1916–2011) worked with Liu Huaqing as the director of the Political Tasks Department at the Dalian Naval Academy in the early 1950s. Then, he served as deputy political commissar of the PLAN East Sea Fleet in the 1960s.
82. Among the 80,000 Soviet advisors sent to China each year in the 1950s, most were military advisors. See 沈志华 [Shen Zhihua], 毛泽东、斯大林与朝鲜战争 [*Mao Zedong, Stalin, and the Korean War*] (Guangzhou: Guangdong People's Press, 2004), 371–72. Shen found the information in the archives of the Second Division, Defense Intelligence Agency, ROC Defense Ministry, in Taiwan. He believes that the numbers collected by the intelligence agents in the 1950s were incomplete.
83. Kecherjin's quotes are in 沈志华 [Shen Zhihua], 苏联专家在中国（1948–1960） [*Soviet Experts in China, 1948–1960*] (Beijing: China International Broadcasting Publishing House, 2003), 146.
84. 杨国宇 [Yang Guoyu], 当代中国海军 [*Contemporary Chinese Navy*], 48–49.
85. Kecherjin's quotes are in 沈志华 [Shen Zhihua], 苏联专家在中国 [*Soviet Experts in China*], 146–47.
86. 罗时叙 [Luo Shixu], 由蜜月到反目: 苏联专家在中国 [*From Honeymoon to Betrayal—Soviet Experts in China*] (Beijing: World Knowledge Press, 1999), 55–57.
87. 杨国宇 [Yang Guoyu], 当代中国海军 [*Contemporary Chinese Navy*], 34.
88. 杨国宇 [Yang Guoyu], 当代中国海军 [*Contemporary Chinese Navy*], 35–36.
89. For example, Professor Zhou Qingyi returned from America. Many instructors served in the ROC Navy before they transferred to the Dalian Naval Academy. See 刘华清 [Liu Huaqing], 怀念肖劲光同志在兼任大连海校校长的日子里 ["The Years When Comrade Xiao Jinguang Served as the President of Dalian Naval School"], 14.
90. 肖劲光 [Xiao Jinguang], 肖劲光回忆录 [*Memoirs of Xiao Jinguang*], 161–62.
91. 苏振兰 [Su Zhenlan], 刘华清主持大连海军学院 ["Liu Huaqing Administrates Dalian Naval Academy"], 党史纵览 [*Review of the Party History*], no. 8 (2014): 13–14.
92. 刘永路 [Liu Yonglu], 刘华清将军与大连舰艇学院 ["Fleet Admiral Liu Huaqing and Dalian Naval Academy"], 党史纵横 [*Overview of the Party History*], no. 3 (2013): 7–8.
93. 刘华清 [Liu Huaqing], 怀念肖劲光同志在兼任大连海校校长的日子里 ["The Years When Comrade Xiao Jinguang Served as the President of the Dalian Naval Academy"], 15.
94. Chen Jian, *Mao's China and the Cold War* (Chapel Hill: University of North Carolina Press, 2001), 60.
95. Mao's speech at the Fourth Plenary of the First Chinese People's Political Consultative Conference (CPPCC) on February 7, 1953, in 毛文稿 [*Mao's Manuscripts since 1949*], 4:45–46.

96. Mao's instruction on General Xiao Xiangrong's report on the PLA officers' relations with the Soviet advisors, in 毛文稿 [*Mao's Manuscripts since 1949*], 4:1–2.
97. Major General Qin Chaoying, interview by the author at the China Society of Strategy and Management (CSSM), Beijing, July 2002.
98. For more details on Vice Admiral Fang Qiang, see 《星火燎原》编辑部 [*Xinghuo liaoyuan* Composition Department], 将帅名录 [*PLA Marshals and Generals*], 1:184–85.
99. For more details on Rear Admiral Zhang Xuesi (1916–1970), see 《星火燎原》编辑部 [*Xinghuo liaoyuan* Composition Department], 将帅名录 [*Marshals and Generals of the PLA*], 3:73–74.
100. 刘回忆录 [*Liu's Memoir*], 314.
101. Sergey Gorshkov, *The Sea Power of the State* (Annapolis, MD: Naval Institute Press, 1979), xi.
102. 施 [Shi], 刘华清 [*Liu Huaqing*], 97.
103. 刘回忆录 [*Liu's Memoir*], 314.
104. Chen Jian, *Zhou Enlai: A Life* (Cambridge, MA: Harvard University Press, 2024), 425–26.
105. 张爱萍 [Zhang Aiping], 中国人民解放军 [*The Chinese People's Liberation Army*], 2:25–26.
106. 刘华清 [Liu Huaqing], 怀念肖劲光同志在兼任大连海校校长的日子里 ["The Years When Comrade Xiao Jinguang Served as the President of the Dalian Naval Academy"], 10.
107. 毛泽东 [Mao Zedong], 建设一支强大的海军 ["Build a Strong Naval Force"], Mao's speech at the CCP Enlarged Politburo meeting on December 4, 1953, in 建国以来毛泽东军事文稿 [*Mao Zedong's Military Manuscripts since the Founding of the PRC*] (Beijing: Military Science Press and CCP Central Archival and Manuscript Press, 2010), 2:192. Hereafter cited as 毛军事文稿 [*Mao's Military Manuscripts since 1949*].
108. 徐焰少将 [Major General Xu Yan], 中国由注重"海防"变为争取"海权" ["China Shifts Its Focus from 'Coastal Defense' to 'Sea Power'"], in 徐焰讲稿自选集 [*Self-Selected Lectures of Xu Yan*] (Beijing: National Defense University Press, 2014), 206.
109. Sherman Xiaogang Lai, "Ensured Loyalty versus Professionalism at Sea: A Historical Review of the PLA Navy, 1949–1982," conference paper at the annual meeting of Chinese Military History Society (CMHS), Ottawa, Ontario, Canada (April 16, 2016): 15.
110. 吴殿卿大校 [Commodore Wu Dianqing], 周恩来、朱德指导制定第一个海军三年建设计划 ["Zhou Enlai and Zhu De Instruct to Make the Navy's First Three-Year Development Plan"], 铁军 [*Iron Force*], no. 3 (2013), 21–22. Commodore Wu Dianqing served as Deputy Chief of the Propaganda Division, PLAN's Political Tasks Department, in the 1990s.
111. 储峰 [Chu Feng], 二十世纪50年代中苏军事关系研究 ["Sino-Soviet Military Relations in the 1950s"], 中共中央党校2006年博士论文 [PhD diss., CCP Central Party University, Beijing, 2006], 71–72.
112. 杨国宇 [Yang Guoyu], 当代中国海军 [*Contemporary Chinese Navy*], 83.
113. 施 [Shi], 刘华清 [*Liu Huaqing*], 21.

## CHAPTER 2. REFORMER OF RUSSIAN MODEL

1. 毛泽东 [Mao Zedong], 在政协一届四次会议上的讲话 [Speech at the Fourth Plenary of the First Chinese People's Political Consultative Conference (CPPCC)], February 7, 1953, in 毛文稿 [*Mao's Manuscripts since 1949*], 4:45–46.
2. 施 [Shi], 刘华清 [*Liu Huaqing*], 23.
3. 聂荣臻 [Nie Rongzhen], 聂荣臻回忆录 [*Memoir of Nie Rongzhen*], 2:653.
4. 李安东上将 [General Li Andong], 刘华清领导我军武器装备建设两三事 ["Liu Huaqing's Leadership in Development of the Weapons and Equipment of Our Armed Forces"], 《百年潮》 [*Hundred Year Tide*], no. 1 (January 2012): 41–43. Li Andong (1946– ) served as director of the Equipment Development Division of the Scientific Research Department of the PLAAF from 1983 to 1985, deputy director and director of the Comprehensive Planning Division of the Equipment Department of the PLA General Staff from 1988 to 1992, and director of the General Planning Bureau of the Equipment Department of PLA General Staff from 1992 to 1993, under Liu Huaqing.
5. Ming-Yen Tsai, *From Adversaries to Partners: Chinese and Russian Military Cooperation after the Cold War* (Westport, CT: Praeger, 2003), 25–27.
6. 刘回忆录 [*Liu's Memoir*], 274–75.
7. 刘华清 [Liu Huaqing], 编写海军条令条例要坚持以我为主 ["The Compilation of Naval Regulations Must Stick to Ourselves (Chinese Navy)-Centric"], in 刘军事文选 [*Selected Military Works of Liu*], 1:41.
8. 刘回忆录 [*Liu's Memoir*], 278.
9. 中国人民解放军历史资料丛书编审委员会 [The Editorial Board of Collected Historical Documents of the PLA], 海军历史资料 [*Historical Documents of the Navy*] (Beijing: PLA Press, 2006), 147–55.
10. 储峰 [Chu Feng], 二十世纪50年代中苏军事关系研究 ["Sino-Soviet Military Relations in the 1950s"], 88–89.
11. 杨国宇 [Yang Guoyu], 当代中国海军 [*Contemporary Chinese Navy*], 83.
12. 沈志华 [Shen Zhihua], 苏联专家在中国 [*Soviet Experts in China*], 407.
13. 张爱萍 [Zhang Aiping], 中国人民解放军 [*The Chinese People's Liberation Army*], 1:540.
14. 郭海云少校 [Major Guo Haiyun], interviews by the author in Chengde, Hebei, in July 2006. Guo Haiyun served as the chief of staff of the 2nd Battalion, 611th Regiment, 64th AAA Division in 1967–69. See also 军事科学院军事历史研究部 [Military History Research Division, PLA AMS], 中国人民解放军的七十年 [*Seventy Years of the Chinese PLA*], 455, 461.
15. 毛泽东 [Mao Zedong], 海空军强大起来了就能够收复台湾 ["Strong Naval and Air Forces Can Take over Taiwan"], in 毛军事文稿 [*Mao's Military Manuscripts since 1949*], 2:227–28.
16. Mao, "Speech at the Moscow Conference of Communist and Workers' Parties, November 16, 1957," in 毛文稿 [*Mao's Manuscripts since 1949*], 5:625–44.
17. Chen, *Mao's China and the Cold War*, 71.

18. Chen Jian and Xiaobing Li, "China and the End of the Cold War," in *The Cold War: From Détente to the Soviet Collapse*, ed. Malcolm Muir Jr. (Lexington: Virginia Military Institute Press, 2006), 121–22.
19. For example, Premier Zhou said on April 29, 1968, that the Soviet Union [like America] was apparently circulating and containing China. Zhou's words quoted in 李丹慧 [Li Danhui], 中苏在援越抗美问题上的矛盾与冲突（1965–1972）["Conflicts between China and the Soviet Union in Their Efforts to Aid Vietnam and Resist America"], in 冷战与中国 [*The Cold War and China*], 章百家、牛军主编 [ed. Zhang Baijia and Niu Jun] (Beijing: World Knowledge Publishing, 2002), 373n1.
20. Former Soviet major (Red Army, ret.) and KGB agents, interviews by the author in 2004 and 2009. See also Major T., "Russian Missile Officers in Vietnam" and Russian Agent (KGB), "Russian Spies in Hanoi," in Xiaobing Li, *Voices from the Vietnam War: Stories from American, Asian, and Russian Veterans* (Lexington: University Press of Kentucky, 2010), 65–72, 93–100.
21. 杨奎松 [Yang Kuisong], 美苏冷战的起源对中国革命的影响 ["Origins of the U.S.-Soviet Cold War and Its Impact on China's Revolution"], in 冷战与中国 [*The Cold War and China*], 章百家、牛军主编 [ed. Zhang Baijia and Niu Jun] (Beijing: Global Knowledge Publishing, 2002), 51–88.
22. 聂荣臻 [Nie Rongzhen], 聂荣臻回忆录 [*Memoir of Nie Rongzhen*], 2:806; 唐秀颖 [Tang Xiue], 锷刺长天: 记火箭技术专家屠守锷 ["A Sword Thrusts the Sky: Story of Rocket Expert Tu Shoue"], in 两弹一星—- 共和国丰碑 [*The Bomb, Missile, and Satellite: The Monuments of the Republic*] 解放军总装备部政治部编 [ed. Department of Political Tasks, PLA General Armament Department] (Beijing: Nine Continents Press, 2001), 366.
23. Mark A. Ryan, David M. Finkelstein, and Michael A. McDevitt, "Introduction: Patterns of PLA Warfighting," in *Chinese Warfighting: The PLA Experience since 1949*, ed. Ryan, Finkelstein, and McDevitt (Armonk, NY: M. E. Sharpe, 2003), 15.
24. 《彭德怀传》编写组 [*Peng Dehuai Biography* Compilation Team], 一个真正的人: 彭德怀 [*A Real Man: Peng Dehuai*] (Beijing: People's Press, 1994), 243–46; Ellis Joffe, *Party and Army: Professionalism and Political Control in the Chinese Officer Corps, 1948–1964* (Cambridge, MA: Harvard University Press, 1967), 102–5.
25. 刘回忆录 [*Liu's Memoir*], 281–82.
26. 刘华清 [Liu Huaqing], 编写海军条令条例要坚持以我为主 ["The Compilation of Naval Regulations Must Stick to Ourselves (Chinese Navy)-Centric"], in 刘军事文选 [*Selected Military Works of Liu*], 1:42–43.
27. 刘回忆录 [*Liu's Memoir of Liu*], 281.
28. 刘华清 [Liu Huaqing], 训练工作的几点意见 ["A Few Points on the Training Operation"], in 刘军事文选 [*Selected Military Works of Liu*], 1:58–61.
29. 刘回忆录 [*Liu's Memoir*], 279–80.
30. 中共中央党史研究室 [Party History Research Division, CCP Central Committee]. 中国共产党政治工作七十年, 1927–1997 [*Seventy Years of the CCP Political Tasks, 1927–1997*] (Beijing: CCP Central Archival and Manuscript Press, 1998), 5:238.

31. Ellis Joffe, *The Chinese Army after Mao* (Cambridge, MA: Harvard University Press, 1987), 16.
32. 李作鹏中将 [Vice Admiral Li Zuopeng], 关于海军工作情况的汇报材料 ["Investigation Report on the Current Situations of the Navy"], in 李作鹏回忆录 [*Memoir of Li Zuopeng*] (Hong Kong: Beixing Publishing House, 2011), 509–10. Li Zuopeng (1914–2009) served as PLAN deputy commander from 1962 to 1967 and ranked vice admiral in 1963. He was PLAN political commissar from 1967 to 1971 and deputy chief of the PLA General Staff from 1968 to 1971.
33. 李作鹏 [Li Zuopeng], 关于海军工作情况的汇报材料 ["Investigation Report on the Current Situations of the Navy"], 510.
34. Vice Admiral Li Zuopeng was purged as a member of Lin Biao's clique after Lin was killed in a plane crash in 1971. Li was arrested in late September 1971, dismissed from all his military positions in 1972, and expelled from the CCP in August 1973. He was sentenced to seventeen years in prison by the PRC Supreme Court on January 25, 1981, because of his involvement in Lin's plot against Mao Zedong and the Party Center as one of the leading members. For more information on his military and political career, see 《星火燎原》编辑部 [*Xinghuo liaoyuan* Composition Department], 将帅名录 [*PLA Marshals and Generals*], 1:274–75.
35. 郑雅茹 [Zheng Yaru], 肖劲光 ["Xiao Jinguaung"], 4:529.
36. Lai, "Ensured Loyalty versus Professionalism at Sea: A Historical Review of the PLA Navy, 1949–1982," 23.
37. Chen, *Zhou Enlai*, 515.
38. 钱三强 [Qian Sanqiang], 老一辈革命家关心中国原子核科学发展 ["The Revolutionary Leaders Took Care of China's Nuclear Research and Development"], in 两弹一星—- 共和国丰碑 [*The Bomb, Missile, and Satellite: The Monuments of the Republic*], 解放军总装备部政治部编 [ed. Department of Political Tasks, PLA General Armament Department], (Beijing: Nine Continents Press, 2001), 81. Qian Sanqiang (1913–1992) was the founder of China's nuclear program, head of the first nuclear institute, and vice president of China Academy of Science in the 1970s.
39. 彭继超大校 [Senior Colonel Peng Jichao], 东方巨响: 中国核武器试验纪实 [*Thunderbolt from the East: Historical Facts of China's Development of Nuclear Weapons*], 2nd ed. (Beijing: CCP Central Party University Press, 2005), 76–77. Peng Jichao (1952– ) worked at the Department of Political Tasks, PLA General Armament Department from the 1970s through the 1980s.
40. 聂荣臻 [Nie Rongzhen], 聂荣臻回忆录 [*Memoir of Nie Rongzhen*], 2:819; 刘柏罗 [Liu Bailuo], 中央专委会与"两弹一星" ["The 'Special Commission' of the Central Committee for Nuclear Bomb, Missile, and Satellite"], in 两弹一星—- 共和国丰碑 [*The Bomb, Missile, and Satellite: The Monuments of the Republic*], 解放军总装备部政治部编 [ed. Department of Political Tasks, PLA General Armament Department] (Beijing: Nine Continents Press, 2001), 96–97. Liu Bailuo (1917–2004) served as deputy secretary and deputy department chief of CSTIND from the 1960s through the 1970s.
41. 聂荣臻 [Nie Rongzhen], 聂荣臻回忆录 [*Memoir of Nie Rongzhen*], 1:38–39.

42. On April 11, 1948, Mao, CCP Central Committee, and the high command removed from Yan'an, the remote Communist capital in the northwest, to Chengnanzhuan, Fuping, Hebei, North China, closer to the civil war battleground. In late April, two KMT spies inside the PLA regional command HQ found out Mao's residence. They passed the information to the KMT army. In early May, the KMT Air Force sent two B-25 bombers to Chengnanzhuan and raided Mao's residence. When Mao refused to leave his bedroom, Nie ordered his guards to carry Mao into the shelter. The B-25s dropped five bombs, one of which exploded in Mao's yard. Several days later, Nie moved Mao from Chengnanzhuan to Xibaipo. For more details, see 聂荣臻 [Nie Rongzhen], 聂荣臻回忆录 [*Memoir of Nie Rongzhen*], 2:676–80.
43. 《聂荣臻传》编写组 [*Nie Rongzhen Biography* Compilation Team], 聂荣臻传 [*Biography of Nie Rongzhen*], 2nd ed. (Beijing: Contemporary China Press, 2006), 271–72.
44. 《星火燎原》编辑部 [*Xinghuo liaoyuan* Composition Department], 将帅名录 [*PLA Marshals and Generals*], 1:18.
45. John Lewis and Xue Lewis, *China Builds the Bomb* (Stanford, CA: Stanford University Press, 1991), 47.
46. 聂荣臻 [Nie Rongzhen], 聂荣臻回忆录 [*Memoir of Nie Rongzhen*], 2:765, 785.
47. 施 [Shi], 刘华清 [*Liu Huaqing*], 23.
48. Liu called the Party Center's support as "*Shangfang baojian*" (the sword of the state), in 刘回忆录 [*Liu's Memoir*], 283, 286.
49. 刘回忆录 [*Liu's Memoir*], 292.
50. 刘华清 [Liu Huaqing], 舰船科研工作和体系建设问题 ["The Issues on the Mission, System, and Tasks of Ship Research"], in 刘军事文选 [*Selected Military Works of Liu*], 1:74, 76.
51. 刘华清 [Liu Huaqing], 舰船科研工作和体系建设问题 ["The Issues on the Mission, System, and Tasks of Ship Research"], in 刘军事文选 [*Selected Military Works of Liu*], 1:74, 76.
52. 刘回忆录 [*Liu's Memoir*], 281.
53. 刘回忆录 [*Liu's Memoir*], 292.
54. 李可、郝生章 [Li Ke and Hao Shengzhang], 文化大革命中的人民解放军 [*The PLA in the Cultural Revolution*] (Beijing: CCP Party Historical Materials Press, 1989), 283.
55. 刘回忆录 [*Liu's Memoir*], 291.
56. For more details on the 1959–62 "natural disaster," see John K. Fairbanks and Merle Goldman, *China: A New History*, enlarged ed. (New York: Belknap Press, 1998), 372–82; Jonathan D. Spence, *The Search for Modern China*, 4th ed. (New York: W. W. Norton, 2025), 552–53.
57. Mao's quote is from 《当代中国》编辑委员会 [*Contemporary China* Compilation Committee], 当代中国的国防科技事业 [*Technology and Science of National Defense in Contemporary China*] (Beijing: Contemporary China Press, 1992), 1:45.
58. 聂荣臻 [Nie Rongzhen], 聂荣臻回忆录 [*Memoir of Nie Rongzhen*], 2:812; You Ji, *The Armed Forces of China* (New York: I. B. Tauris, 1999), 85.

59. Interview with Huang Liqun, senior fellow at the Center for Research and Information, Space and Navigation Ministry, in Beijing in July 2004.
60. 刘回忆录 [*Liu's Memoir*], 294.
61. 储峰 [Chu Feng], 二十世纪50年代中苏军事关系研究 ["Sino-Soviet Military Relations in the 1950s"], 88–89.
62. 刘华清 [Liu Huaqing], 关于仿制为主的方针问题 ["The Policy Issue on the Imitation as the First Priority"], in 刘军事文选 [*Selected Military Works of Liu*], 1:62.
63. 刘回忆录 [*Liu's Memoir*], 298.
64. 刘华清 [Liu Huaqing], 舰船科研工作和体系建设问题 ["The Issues on the Mission, System, and Tasks of Ship Research"], 1:68.
65. 李可、郝生章 [Li Ke and Hao Shengzhang], 文化大革命中的人民解放军 [*The PLA in the Cultural Revolution*], 301.
66. 徐焰 [Xu Yan], 中国由注重"海防"变为争取"海权" ["China Shifts Its Focus from 'Coastal Defense' to 'Sea Power'"], 207.
67. Mao's words quoted in 赵小平 [Zhao Xiaoping], 毛泽东与吴瑞林中将 ["Mao Zedong and Lieutenant General Wu Ruilin"], in 毛泽东与海军将领 [*Mao Zedong and His Admirals and Generals*], 吴殿卿、袁永安、赵小平主编 [ed. Wu Dianqing, Yuan Yong'an, and Zhao Xiaoping] (Beijing: PLA Literature Press, 1999), 206.
68. 韩怀智 [Han Huaizhi], 当代中国军队的军事工作 [*Military Affairs of Contemporary China's Armed Forces*], 1:351.
69. 军事科学院军事历史研究部 [Military History Research Division, PLA AMS], 中国人民解放军的七十年 [*Seventy Years of the PLA*], 533.
70. 杨国宇 [Yang Guoyu], 当代中国海军 [*Contemporary Chinese Navy*], 386.
71. 毛泽东 [Mao Zedong], 对击沉国民党"剑门"、"章江"两舰战斗经验总结报告的批语 ["Instructions on the Battle Report on Combat Experience in Sinking Two KMT Warships of *Jianmen* and *Zhangjiang*"], August 15, 1965, in 毛军事文稿 [*Mao's Military Manuscripts since 1949*], 3:325.
72. 刘广凯上将 [Admiral Liu Guangkai (ROC Navy)], 刘广凯将军报国忆往 [*Admiral Liu Guangkai's Recollection of Defending the Country*] (Taipei: Institute of Modern China, Academia Sinica, 1994), 268–69.
73. 杨国宇 [Yang Guoyu], 当代中国海军 [*Contemporary Chinese Navy*], 387.
74. 胡彦林上将 [Admiral Hu Yanlin], 威震海疆：人民海军征战纪实 [*Shocking the Sea: Records of the People's Navy's Battles*] (Beijing: National Defense University Press, 1996), 345. Hu Yanlin (1943– ) served as the political commissar of the PLAN from 2003 to 2009 and was ranked admiral in 2004.
75. Elleman, *High Sea Buffer*, 115.
76. 胡彦林 [Hu Yanlin], 威震海疆 [*Shocking the Sea*], 303.
77. Gao Xiaoxing et al., *The PLA Navy* (Beijing: China Intercontinental Press, 2012), 40.
78. 钟坚 [Zhong Jian], 导读: 英雄不回头 ["Introduction: The Hero No Return"], in 看不见的屏障: 决定台湾命运的第七舰队 [*Invisible Shell: The Seventh Fleet and Taiwan's Fate*], 布鲁斯. 艾里曼 [by Bruce A. Elleman], 吴润睿译 [trans. Wu Runrui] (Xinbei, Taiwan: Eight Banner Culture Publishing, 2017), 21.

79. 刘华清 [Liu Huaqing], 对院部合并的意见 ["My Points on the Emerge of the Ministries and Institutes"], in 刘军事文选 [*Selected Military Works of Liu*], 1:95–96.
80. 《聂荣臻传》编写组 [*Nie Rongzhen Biography* Compilation Team], 聂荣臻传 [*Biography of Nie Rongzhen*], 2nd ed. (Beijing: Contemporary China Publishing House, 2006), 318–19.
81. Lewis and Xue, *China Builds the Bomb*, 46–47, 219, 236.
82. 施 [Shi], 刘华清 [*Liu Huaqing*], 171.
83. 刘回忆录 [*Liu's Memoir*], 314.
84. Bussert and Elleman, *People's Liberation Army Navy*, 19.
85. 李琼 [Li Qiong], 海上长城: 中国人民解放军海军六十年 [*The Great Wall at Sea: Sixty Years of the PLA Navy*] (Jilin: Jilin Publishing Group, 2011), 53.
86. 吴本湘 [Wu Benxiang], 037 型反潜护卫舰的设计和生产 ["The Design and Manufacturing of *Type-037* Submarine Chaser"], in 中国人民解放军历史资料丛书: 海军回忆史料 [*PLA Historical Sources Series: The Navy's Memoirs and Records*] (Classified), 海军编审委员会 [ed. Navy Editorial Committee] (Beijing: Ocean Wave Publishing, 1994], 2:1060. Wu Benxiang was an engineer worked in the First Institute of the Seventh Research Institute and participated in the design and manufacturing of Type-037 submarine chaser.
87. 刘回忆录 [*Liu's Memoir*], 300.
88. 吴本湘 [Wu Benxiang], 037 型反潜护卫舰的设计和生产 ["The Design and Manufacturing of *Type-037* Submarine Chaser"], 2:1062–63.
89. Bussert and Elleman, *People's Liberation Army Navy*, 66.
90. Gao, *PLA Navy*, 81.
91. 刘回忆录 [*Liu's Memoir*], 300.
92. 刘华清 [Liu Huaqing], 迅速搞好国防科研体制调整工作 ["Chang and Improve National Defense Research Structure Soon"], in 刘军事文选 [*Selected Military Works of Liu*], 1:99.
93. 张毅民 [Zhang Yimin], 舰对舰导弹的试制 ["Testing the Ship-to-Ship Missile"], in 中国人民解放军历史资料丛书: 海军回忆史料 [*PLA Historical Sources Series: The Navy's Memoirs and Records*] (Classified), 海军编审委员会 [ed. Navy Editorial Committee] (Beijing: Ocean Wave Publishing, 1994], 2:1076.
94. 李可、郝生章 [Li Ke and Hao Shengzhang], 文化大革命中的人民解放军 [*The PLA in the Cultural Revolution*], 304.
95. The quote of the "May 16 Circular" is from Fang Zhu, *Gun Barrel Politics: Party-Army Relations in Mao's China* (Boulder, CO: Westview Press, 1998), 116.
96. 崔向华、陈大鹏 [Cui Xianghua and Chen Dapeng], 陶勇将军传 [*Biography of Vice Admiral Tao Yong*] (Beijing: PLA Press, 1989), 448.
97. Captain Zhou Baoshan (CPVF), "China's Crouching Dragon," in *Voices of the Korean War: Personal Stories of American, Korean, and Chinese Soldiers*, by Richard Peters and Xiaobing Li (Lexington: University Press of Kentucky, 2004), 93. Zhou Baoshan was captain of the Fourth Company, Second Battalion, 347th Regiment, 116th Division, 39th Army, CPVF in the Korean War.

98. 《聂荣臻传》编写组 [*Nie Rongzhen Biography* Compilation Team], 聂荣臻传 [*Biography of Nie Rongzhen*], 370–71.
99. 徐长友少将 [Rear Admiral Xu Changyou], interview by the author in Shanghai, April 26, 2000. Xu Changyou served as vice political commissar of the East Sea Fleet Air Force of the PLAN in 1999–2004 and deputy secretary general of the CMC in 1995–99.
100. 刘回忆录 [*Liu's Memoir*], 301.
101. 刘华清 [Liu Huaqing], 关于核潜艇工程的几点看法和建议 ["Our Stand and Suggestions on the Nuclear Submarine Project"], in 刘军事文选 [*Selected Military Works of Liu*], 1:85.
102. 陈右铭 [Chen Youming], 第一代核潜艇的诞生 ["The Birth of the First Nuclear Submarine"], in 中国人民解放军历史资料丛书: 海军回忆史料 [*PLA Historical Sources Series: The Navy's Memoirs and Records*] (Classified), 海军编审委员会 [ed. Navy Editorial Committee] (Beijing: Ocean Wave Publishing, 1994), 2:1080.
103. 《周恩来军事活动记事》编写组编著 [Compilation Team of *Chronicle of Zhou Enlai's Military Affairs*], 周恩来军事活动记事 [*Chronicle of Zhou Enlai's Military Affairs*] (Beijing: CCP Central Archival and Manuscript Press, 2000), 2:611.
104. Cole, *Great Wall at Sea*, 2nd ed., 12.
105. 陈右铭 [Chen Youming], 第一代核潜艇的诞生 ["The Birth of the First Nuclear Submarine"], 2:1080–81.
106. 刘回忆录 [*Liu's Memoir*], 316.

### CHAPTER 3. NAVY BUILDER

1. 杨奎松 [Yang Kuisong], 从珍宝岛事件到中美关系缓和 ["From the Zhenboa Island Incident to Sino-American Rapprochement"], 党史研究资料 [*Party History Research Sources*], no. 12 (1997), 7–8; Thomas Robinson, "The Sino-Soviet Border Conflicts of 1969; New Evidence Three Decades Later," in *Chinese Warfighting: The PLA Experience since 1949*, ed. Mark A. Ryan, David M. Finkelstein, and Michael A. McDevitt (Armonk, NY: M. E. Sharpe, 2003): 198–216.
2. 刘回忆录 [*Liu's Memoir*], 358.
3. Lin's speech quoted in 杨贵华 [Yang Guihua], 准备"早打、大打、打核战争"的历史回顾—— 全国大备战史末 ["A Historical Reflection on Preparing an Early, Large-Scale, and Nuclear War—The Whole Story of Nationwide War Mobilization"], in 军事科学院军事历史研究部 [Military History Research Division, PLA Academy of Military Science (AMS)], 军旗飘飘: 新中国五十年军事大事述实 [*PLA Flag Fluttering: The Facts about China's Major Military Events in the Past Fifty Years*] (Beijing: PLA Press, 1999), 2:572.
4. 徐焰少将 [Major General Xu Yan], 中苏为何从"蜜月"走向敌对 ["Why Did Sino-Soviet Relations Change from 'Honeymoon' to Hostility"], in 徐焰讲稿自选集 [*Self-Selected Lecture Notes of Xu Yan*] (Beijing: National Defense University Press, 2014), 265–66.
5. Chen, *Zhou Enlai*, 618.

6. For example, Premier Zhou said on April 29, 1968, that the Soviet Union (like America) was apparently circulating and containing China. 李丹慧 [Li Danhui], 中苏在援越抗美问题上的矛盾与冲突（1965–1972） ["Conflicts between China and the Soviet Union in Their Efforts to Aid Vietnam and Resist America, 1965–1972"], 373n1.
7. Nicholas Khoo, *Collateral Damage: Sino-Soviet Rivalry and the Termination of the Sino-Vietnamese Alliance* (New York: Columbia University Press, 2011), 3.
8. Chen Jian and Xiaobing Li, "China and the End of the Cold War," 122–23.
9. Chen, *Zhou Enlai*, 617.
10. Richard Nixon, *The Memoirs of Richard Nixon* (New York: Grosset & Dunlap, 1978), 390; Charles Freeman Jr., "The Process of Rapprochement: Achievements and Problems," in *Sino-American Normalization and Its Policy Implications*, ed. Gene T. Hsiao and Michael Witunsky (New York: Praeger, 1983), 2–3, 10–14.
11. 施 [Shi], 刘华清 [*Liu Huaqing*], 357.
12. Mao's words quoted in Gao, *PLA Navy*, 121.
13. 李可、郝生章 [Li Ke and Hao Shengzhang], 文化大革命中的人民解放军 [*The PLA in the Cultural Revolution*], 304.
14. 李可、郝生章 [Li Ke and Hao Shengzhang], 文化大革命中的人民解放军 [*The PLA in the Cultural Revolution*], 301–2.
15. 刘子庚舰长 [Captain Liu Zigeng], 新型导弹驱逐舰试航 [The Trial Voyage of the New Missile Destroyer], in 中国人民解放军历史资料丛书: 海军回忆史料 [*PLA Historical Sources Series: The Navy's Memoirs and Records*] (Classified), 海军编审委员会 [ed. Navy Editorial Committee] (Beijing: Ocean Wave Publishing House, 1994], 2:1111–12. Liu was the captain of the destroyer *105* from 1970 to 1979.
16. 陆其明 [Lu Qiming], 加速人民海军建设: 朱德委员长视察海军新型舰艇纪实 ["Accelerate the Naval Construction: Report on Congressional Chairman Zhu De's Visit of New Warship"], in 共和国领袖与海军 [*National Leaders and China's Navy*], 吴殿卿、袁永安、赵小平主编 [ed. Wu Dianqing, Yuan Yong'an, and Zhao Xiaoping] (Beijing: Ocean Waves Publishing House, 2000), 192–96.
17. Bussert and Elleman, *People's Liberation Army Navy*, 19.
18. Bussert and Elleman, *People's Liberation Army Navy*, 66.
19. In the U.S. Cold War containment policy against the Communists, Secretary of State John Foster Dulles and General Douglas MacArthur designed an island-chain strategy against the USSR and PRC in the Pacific through three island chains. The first island chain linked Japan's Ryukyu Island, Taiwan, the Philippines, and Borneo. The second island chain, in the middle of the Western Pacific, included the Island of Guam, the Caroline Islands, and New Guinea. Toshi Yoshihara, "China's Vision of Its Seascape: The First Island Chain and Chinese Sea-Power," *Asian Politics and Policy* 4, no. 3 (July 2012): 239–314.
20. 陈右铭 [Chen Youming], 第一代核潜艇的诞生 ["The Birth of the First Nuclear Submarine"], 2:1098.
21. 陈右铭 [Chen Youming], 第一代核潜艇的诞生 ["The Birth of the First Nuclear Submarine"], 2:1100.

22. 李作鹏 [Li Zuoping], 李作鹏回忆录 [*Memoir of Li Zuoping*], chapter 29.
23. Liu's report quoted in 施 [Shi], 刘华清 [*Liu Huaqing*], 359–61.
24. 郑明少将 [Rear Admiral Zheng Ming], 难忘的回忆与珍贵的启迪 ["Unforgettable Memory and Valuable"], 现代舰船 [*Modern Ships*], no. 3 (2005): 4. Zheng Ming (1933–2018) served as deputy chief (1983–85) and chief of the PLAN's Department of Equipment and Technology from 1985 to 1992.
25. 施 [Shi], 刘华清 [*Liu Huaqing*], 362–63.
26. 郑明 [Zheng Ming], 难忘的回忆与珍贵的启迪 ["Unforgettable Memory and Valuable"], 6–7.
27. 施 [Shi], 刘华清 [*Liu Huaqing*], 363.
28. Zhu, *Gun Barrel Politics*, 181.
29. There have been several speculations about the crash of Lin Biao's plane, including a Chinese missile attack, running out of fuel, or simply an accident. See 高文谦 [Gao Wenqian], 晚年周恩来 [*Zhou Enlai's Later Years*] (Hong Kong: Mingjing Publishing, 2003), 350–55; 黄耀、严敬棠 [Huang Yao and Yan Jingtang], 林彪一生 [*The Life of Lin Biao*] (Beijing: PLA Literature Press, 2004), 490–507; 叶永烈 [Ye Yonglie], 高层较量 [*Power Struggle at the Top*] (Urumqi: Xinjiang People's Press, 2004), 369–76.
30. 军事科学院军事历史研究部 [Military History Research Division, PLA AMS], 中国人民解放军的七十年 [*Seventy Years of the Chinese PLA*], 566.
31. 中共中央党史研究室 [Party History Research Division, CCP Central Committee], 中国共产党历史大事记，1919–2009 [*Major Historical Events of the CCP, 1919–2009*], 309.
32. For the last phase of the Cultural Revolution, see 高皋、严家其 [Gao Gao and Yan Jiaqi], 文化大革命十年史，1966–1976 [*Ten-Year History of the Cultural Revolution, 1966–1976*] (Tianjin: Tianjin People's Press, 1986), chapters 6–7; 李可、郝生章 [Li Ke and Hao Shengzhang], 文化大革命中的人民解放军 [*The PLA in the Cultural Revolution*]; Maurice Meisner, *Mao's China and After: A History of the People's Republic* (New York: Free Press, 1999), chapter 20.
33. Mao's new political campaign to "Criticize Lin and Confucius" (批林批孔) purged most of Lin's generals and eliminated his military programs in 1972–1973. By September 1973, 75 percent of the PLA officers had gone through the "reeducation" program. For details, see 军事科学院军事历史研究部 [Military History Research Division, PLA AMS], 中国人民解放军的七十年 [*Seventy Years of the Chinese PLA*], 566–68.
34. Zhou's words quoted in 施 [Shi], 刘华清 [*Liu Huaqing*], 364.
35. For more details on Admiral Su Zhenhua (1912–79), see 《星火燎原》编辑部 [*Xinghuo liaoyuan* Composition Department], 解放军将帅名录 [*PLA Marshals and Generals*], 1:72–73.
36. 李琼 [Li Qiong], 海上长城 [*The Great Wall at Sea*], 53.
37. Gao, *PLA Navy*, 86–87.
38. Xiaobing Li, "China's Support to the Vietnamese Communists," in *The Brown Water War at 50: A Retrospective on the Coastal and Riverine Conflict in Vietnam*, ed.

Thomas J. Cutler and Edward J. Marolda (Annapolis, MD: Naval Institute Press, 2023), 192–200.

39. Colonel Yan Guitang, interviews by the author in Xi'an, Shaanxi, on July 29–30, 2006. Yan Guitang served as a staff member at the PLA Department of General Staff.
40. Yan Guitang, interviews by the author in Xi'an on July 29–30, 2006.
41. 张世鸿、张炎平、吴迪 [Zhang Shihong, Zhang Yanping, and Wu Di], 胡志明小道上的701天: 越战见闻录 [*701 Days through the Ho Chi Minh Trail: Vietnam War in My Eyes*] (Beijing: PLA Literature Press, 2007), 2–4.
42. 李宝祥 [Li Baoxiang], 援越扫雷的技术保障工作 ["Technological Assistance in Helping Vietnam's Mine-Sweepings"], in 援越抗美— 中国支援部队在越南 [*Aid Vietnam and Resist the U.S.: Chinese Supporting Forces in Vietnam*], 曲爱国少将、鲍明荣、肖祖跃 [ed. Major General Qu Aiguo, Bao Mingrong, and Xiao Zuyue] (Beijing: Military Science Press, 1995), 301. Li Baoxiang was the senior engineer of the PLA Naval Research Institute in 1965–1973.
43. 李宝祥 [Li Baoxiang], 援越扫雷的技术保障工作 ["Technological Assistance in Helping Vietnam's Mine-Sweepings"], 301–2.
44. For more details on Operation Linebacker I, see Spencer C. Tucker, *Vietnam* (Lexington: University Press of Kentucky, 1999), 170–71.
45. 来光祖 [Lai Guangzu], 周总理运筹援越扫雷 ["Premier Zhou Organizes the Mine-Sweepings in Vietnam"], in 援越抗美 [*Aid Vietnam and Resist the U.S.*], 曲爱国、鲍明荣、肖祖跃 [ed. Qu Aiguo, Bao Mingrong, and Xiao Zuyue], 299.
46. 刘回忆录 [*Liu's Memoir*], 346–47.
47. 萧石忠 [Xiao Shizhong], 扑灭印度支那战火的一次重要军事行动 ["An Important Military Operation to Put Out War Flames in Indochina"], in 军旗飘飘: 新中国五十年军事大事述实 [*PLA Flag Fluttering: The Facts about China's Major Military Events in the Past Fifty Years*], 军事科学院军事历史研究部 [by Military History Research Division, PLA Academy of Military Science (AMS)] (Beijing: PLA Press, 1999), 2:461.
48. 郭保兰 [Guo Baolan], 援越扫雷 ["Assist Vietnam in Mine-Sweepings"], in 中国人民解放军历史资料丛书: 海军回忆史料 [*PLA Historical Sources Series: The Navy's Memoirs and Records*] (Classified), 海军编审委员会 [ed. Navy Editorial Committee] (Beijing: Ocean Waves Publishing House, 1994], 2:1168. Guo Baolan served as political commissar of the PLAN mine-sweepings survey team that entered North Vietnam on May 29, 1972.
49. 张寿瀛 [Zhang Shouying], 赴越扫雷的回顾 ["Reflection of Mine-Sweeping Experience in Vietnam"], in 援越抗美 [*Aid Vietnam and Resist the U.S.*], 曲爱国、鲍明荣、肖祖跃 [ed. Qu Aiguo, Bao Mingrong, and Xiao Zuyue], 306–7. Zhang Shouying served as political commissar of the PLAN mine-sweepings survey team that entered North Vietnam on May 29, 1972.
50. 杨国宇 [Yang Guoyu], 当代中国海军 [*Contemporary Chinese Navy*], 423–24.
51. 张寿瀛 [Zhang Shouying], 赴越扫雷的回顾 ["Reflection of Mine-Sweeping Experience in Vietnam"], 306.

52. 萧石忠 [Xiao Shizhong], 扑灭印度支那战火的一次重要军事行动 ["An Important Military Operation to Put Out War Flames in Indochina"], 2:461.
53. 郭保兰 [Guo Baolan], 援越扫雷 ["Assist Vietnam in Mine-Sweepings"], 2:1171.
54. 胡彦林 [Hu Yanlin], 威震海疆 [*Shocking the Sea*], 368–69.
55. 田铭、夏三保、陈康明 [Tian Ming, Xia Sanbao, and Chen Kangming], 越南人民的功臣 ["A Hero for the Vietnamese People"], in 援越抗美 [*Aid Vietnam and Resist the U.S.*], 曲爱国, 鲍明荣, 肖祖跃 [ed. Qu Aiguo, Bao Mingrong, and Xiao Zuyue], 313. Tian Ming was captain of the *PLAN 312–05* minesweeper in 1972–73.
56. The announcement of the PRC Foreign Ministry is quoted in 郭明 [Guo Ming], 中越关系演变四十年 [*Deterioration of the Sino-Vietnam Relations in the Past Forty Years*] (Nanning: Guangxi People's Press, 1992), 151–52.
57. 胡彦林 [Hu Yanlin], 威震海疆 [*Shocking the Sea*], 387–88.
58. 赵小平 [Zhao Xiaoping], 坐镇总参谋部, 决胜南中国海—— 叶剑英副主席指挥西沙海战纪实 ["Command in the DGS and Victory in the South China Sea—Records of Vice Chairman Ye Jianying's Commanding the Battle of Paracel"], in 共和国领袖与海军 [*PRC National Leaders and the Navy*], 吴殿卿、袁永安、赵小平主编 [ed. Wu Dianqing, Yuan Yong'an, and Zhao Xiaoping] (Beijing: Ocean Wave Publishing House, 2000), 187–88.
59. Li Ruyi was the charge-man on PLAN *274*. His memoir was quoted in Gao, *PLA Navy*, 66.
60. 杨国宇 [Yang Guoyu], 当代中国海军 [*Contemporary Chinese Navy*], 397.
61. 胡彦林 [Hu Yanlin], 威震海疆 [*Shocking the Sea*], 395.
62. 杨国宇 [Yang Guoyu], 当代中国海军 [*Contemporary Chinese Navy*], 398.
63. Xinhua News Agency, *China's Foreign Relations: A Chronology of Events, 1949–1988* (Beijing: Foreign Languages Press, 1989), 461–67.
64. After the Soviet invasion of Czechoslovakia in 1968, Moscow reinforced its border forces from seventeen divisions to twenty-seven divisions in 1969 along the Russo-Chinese borders. See Xiaobing Li, "Sino-Soviet Border Disputes," in *Magill's Guide to Military History*, ed. John Powell (Amenia, NY: Salem Press, 2001), 4:1423.
65. Lin's speech quoted in 杨贵华 [Yang Guihua], 准备"早打、大打、打核战争"的历史回顾—— 全国大备战史末 ["A Historical Reflection on Preparing an Early, Large-Scale, and Nuclear War—The Whole Story of Nationwide War Mobilization"], 2:572.
66. Li, "Sino-Soviet Border Disputes," 4:1424.
67. For the last phase of the Cultural Revolution, see 高皋、严家其 [Gao Gao and Yan Jiaqi], 文化大革命十年史, 1966–1976 [*Ten-Year History of the Cultural Revolution, 1966–1976*], chapters 6–7; 李可、郝生章 [Li Ke and Hao Shengzhang], 文化大革命中的人民解放军 [*The PLA in the Cultural Revolution*].
68. 毛泽东 [Mao Zedong], 要研究海军落后的原因 ["Must Study the Reasons of Naval Backwardness"], in 毛军事文稿, *Mao's Military Manuscripts since 1949*, 3:369.
69. 毛泽东 [Mao Zedong], 关于海上作战等问题 ["Issues on Naval Combat and the Others"], in 毛军事文稿, *Mao's Military Manuscripts since 1949*, 3:370–71.

70. For more details of Deng Xiaoping's life during the Cultural Revolution, see Deng Rong, *Deng Xiaoping and the Cultural Revolution—A Daughter Recalls the Critical Years*, trans. Sidney Shapiro (Beijing: Foreign Languages Press, 2002), chapter 17, "Early Days in Jiangxi," and chapter 18, "Working Life."
71. 丁伟 [Ding Wei], 拨乱反正的先声——1975 年军委扩大会议的召开 ["The Prelude of Bringing Order out of Chaos—The 1975 CMC Enlarged Meeting"], in 军旗飘飘: 新中国五十年军事大事述实 [*PLA Flag Fluttering: The Facts about China's Major Military Events in the Past Fifty Years*], 军事科学院军事历史研究部 [by Military History Research Division, PLA Academy of Military Science (AMS)] (Beijing: PLA Press, 1999), 2:591; Merle Goldman and Roderick MacFarquhar, "Dynamic Economy, Declining Party-State," in *The Paradox of China's Post-Mao Reforms*, ed. Goldman and MacFarquhar (Cambridge, MA: Harvard University Press, 1999), 4.
72. Joffe, *Chinese Army after Mao*, 22.
73. Deng, "The Army Needs to be Consolidated, January 25, 1975," speech at a meeting of officers of regimental level and above at the PLA Department of General Staff, in *Selected Works of Deng Xiaoping*, 2:13–15.
74. Mao's words quoted in 杨肇林大校 [Commodore Yang Zhaolin], 毛泽东与苏振华上将 ["Mao Zedong and Admiral Su Zhenhua"], in 毛泽东与海军将领 [*Mao Zedong and His Admirals*], 吴殿卿、袁永安、赵小平主编 [ed. Wu Dianqing, Yuan Yong'an, and Zhao Xiaoping] (Beijing: PLA Literature Publishing, 1999), 82.
75. 刘华清 [Liu Huaqing], 海军装备建设应注意质量，提高水平 ["Naval Shipbuilding and Equipment Development Should Pay Attention to Quality and Improve Technology"], in 刘军事文选 [*Selected Military Papers of Liu*], 1:103–14.
76. 施 [Shi], 刘华清 [*Liu Huaqing*], 38.
77. 刘华清 [Liu Huaqing], 海军装备建设应注意质量，提高水平 ["Naval Shipbuilding and Equipment Development Should Pay Attention to Quality and Improve Technology"], 1:113.
78. 刘回忆录 [*Liu's Memoir*], 350.
79. 刘回忆录 [*Liu's Memoir*], 356, 358.
80. 施 [Shi], 刘华清 [*Liu Huaqing*], 38, 40–41.
81. 施 [Shi], 刘华清 [*Liu Huaqing*], 39–40.
82. 刘回忆录 [*Liu's Memoir*], 358.
83. 刘回忆录 [*Liu's Memoir*], 351.
84. 刘华清 [Liu Huaqing], 海军装备建设应注意质量，提高水平 ["Naval Shipbuilding and Equipment Development Should Pay Attention to Quality and Improve Technology"], 1:112.
85. 刘华清 [Liu Huaqing], 海军装备建设应注意质量，提高水平 ["Naval Shipbuilding and Equipment Development Should Pay Attention to Quality and Improve Technology"], 1:110–11.
86. 刘回忆录 [*Liu's Memoir*], 356, 358.
87. 施 [Shi], 刘华清 [*Liu Huaqing*], 40–42.
88. 刘回忆录 [*Liu's Memoir*], 350.

89. 徐焰 [Xu Yan], 中国由注重"海防"变为争取"海权" ["China Shifts Its Focus from 'Coastal Defense' to 'Sea Power'"], 231.
90. 丁伟 [Ding Wei], 拨乱反正的先声 ["The Prelude of Bringing Order out of Chaos"], 2:604.
91. For the details of arresting the "Gang of Four," see Deng Rong, *Deng Xiaoping and the Cultural Revolution*, 436–43.
92. Deng became the second generation of the CCP political and military leadership. See Cheng Li, *China's Leaders: The New Generation* (Lanham, MD: Rowman & Littlefield, 2001), 7–9.
93. Among the English accounts on the Sino-American rapprochement are William Burr, ed., *The Kissinger Transcripts: The Top-Secret Talks with Beijing and Moscow* (New York: New Press, 1999); Jim Mann, *About Face: A History of America's Curious Relationship with China, from Nixon to Clinton* (New York: Knopf, 1999); Rosemary Foot, *The Practice of Power: U.S. Relations with China since 1949* (Oxford: Oxford University Press, 1997); Robert Ross, *Negotiating Cooperation: The United States and China, 1969–1989* (Stanford, CA: Stanford University Press, 1995).
94. 刘回忆录 [*Liu's Memoir*], 379–80.
95. Dean Chen, "Sea Power and the Chinese State: China's Maritime Ambitions," *Heritage Foundation*, July 11, 2011, www.heritage.org/asia/report/sea-power-and-the-chinese-state-maritime-ambitions.
96. 杨国宇 [Yang Guoyu], 当代中国海军 [*Contemporary Chinese Navy*], 437–38.
97. Deng's words quoted in 杨国宇 [Yang Guoyu], 当代中国海军 [*Contemporary Chinese Navy*], 438.
98. 吴瑞虎 [Wu Ruihu], 三代驱逐舰启程中南海—— 党和国家领导人关心驱逐舰部队建设记事 ["Three Generations of Destroyers Started from Zhongnanhai: History Shows How CCP and PRC Leaders Cared about Construction of the Destroyer Fleet"], in 共和国领袖与海军 [*National Leaders and China's Navy*], 吴殿卿、袁永安、赵小平主编 [ed. Wu Dianqing, Yuan Yong'an, and Zhao Xiaoping] (Beijing: Ocean Waves Publishing House, 2000), 289.
99. For more details on General Ye Fei (1914–99), see 《星火燎原》编辑部 [*Xinghuo liaoyuan* Composition Department], 将帅名录 [*PLA Marshals and Generals*], 1:58–59.
100. Deng, "The Organizational Line Guarantees the Implementation of the Ideological and Political Lines," a speech to attendees at an enlarged meeting of the standing committee of the PLAN Party Committee on July 29, 1979, in *Selected Works of Deng Xiaoping*, 2:198.
101. 叶飞上将 [General Ye Fei], 叶飞回忆录 [*Memoir of Ye Fei*] (Beijing: PLA Press, 1988), 832.
102. 吴殿卿 [Wu Dianqing], 乘长风破万里浪 ["Ride a Long Wind and Thousands of Miles of Waves"], in 共和国领袖与海军 [*National Leaders and China's Navy*], 吴殿卿、袁永安、赵小平主编 [ed. Wu Dianqing, Yuan Yong'an, and Zhao Xiaoping] (Beijing: Ocean Waves Publishing House, 2000), 232.

103. Warren I. Cohen, *America's Response to China: A History of Sino-American Relations*, 6th ed. (New York: Columbia University Press, 2019), 206
104. Cohen, *America's Response to China*, 207.
105. As General Xiong Guangkai, deputy chief of the General Staff, states, "Promoting RMA (Revolution of Military Affairs) with Chinese characteristics purports that we need to study and draw on the experience as well as lessons of RMA in other countries and of each hi-tech local war. Yet we cannot copy the entire mode of RMA of other countries." Xiong, "On Revolution in Military Affairs," a conference presentation at the "Chinese Scientists' Forum on Humanities" on April 16, 2003, in Xiong, *International Strategy and Revolution in Military Affairs* (Beijing: Tsinghua University Press, 2003), 183.
106. 杨国宇 [Yang Guoyu], 当代中国海军 [*Contemporary Chinese Navy*], 481–82.
107. Gao, *PLA Navy*, 86.
108. 杨国宇少将 [Rear Admiral Yang Guoyu], 天涯迎飞舟 ["Receiving the Rocket on the Other Side of the World"], in 中国海军走向深蓝, *1980–2020* [*The Chinese Navy Goes to Blue Water, 1980–2010*], 左津玲主编 [ed. Zuo Jinling] (Beijing: PLA Press, 2014), 1:16.
109. 陈右铭 [Chen Youming], 第一代核潜艇的诞生 ["The Birth of the First Nuclear Submarine"], 2:1100.

## CHAPTER 4. THE COMMANDER

1. 刘回忆录 [*Liu's Memoir*], 342–44.
2. 习近平 [Xi Jinping], 在纪念刘华清同志诞辰100 周年座谈会上的讲话 ["Speech at the Symposium to Commemorate the 100th Anniversary of the Birth of Comrade Liu Huaqing."
3. 习近平 [Xi Jinping], 在纪念刘华清同志诞辰100 周年座谈会上的讲话 ["Speech at the Symposium to Commemorate the 100th Anniversary of the Birth of Comrade Liu Huaqing."
4. 兰波 [Lan Bo], 改革开放以来中国海权认识演进研究 ["Study of Cognitive Process of China's Sea Right since the Reform and Opening Up"], 69.
5. 田甜 [Tian Tian], 刘华清海权思想与近海防御战略 ["Liu Huaqing's Thought of Sea Power and the Strategy of Near Sea Defense"], 军事思想史研究 [*History Studies of Military Thoughts*], no. 4 (2017): 65. Tian Tian was a research fellow at the PLAN Military Science Institute from 2015 to 2020.
6. 刘华清 [Liu Huaqing], 在军委扩大会议上的讲话 ["Speech at the CMC Enlarged Conference"], in 刘军事文选 [*Selected Military Papers of Liu*], 2:208.
7. Liu's words quoted in 习近平 [Xi Jinping], 在纪念刘华清同志诞辰100 周年座谈会上的讲话 ["Speech at the Symposium to Commemorate the 100th Anniversary of the Birth of Comrade Liu Huaqing"].
8. 习近平 [Xi Jinping], 在纪念刘华清同志诞辰100 周年座谈会上的讲话 ["Speech at the Symposium to Commemorate the 100th Anniversary of the Birth of Comrade Liu Huaqing"].

9. 刘华清 [Liu Huaqing], 新时期海军装备建设的几个问题 ["Major Issues in Naval Technology Improvement during the New Reform Era"], in 刘军事文选 [*Selected Military Papers of Liu*], 1:417–18.
10. 刘新博 [Liu Xinbo], 刘华清海洋战略思想研究 ["Study of Liu Huaqing's Maritime Strategic Thinking"], 12, 16.
11. 刘华清 [Liu Huaqing], 在南海舰队科以上干部会议上的讲话 ["Speech at the SSF Conference of the Officers at the Battalion and above Levels"], in 刘军事文选 [*Selected Military Papers of Liu*], 1:228.
12. 施 [Shi], 刘华清 [*Liu Huaqing*], 86.
13. Xiao Jinguang's words quoted in 施 [Shi], 刘华清 [*Liu Huaqing*], 123.
14. 石家铸 [Shi Jiazhu], 海权与中国 [*Sea Power and China*] (Beijing: Three Unions Books, 2008), 215.
15. 张爱萍 [Zhang Aiping], 中国人民解放军 [*The Chinese People's Liberation Army*], 2:25–26.
16. Yoshihara, "China's Vision of Its Seascape: The First Island Chain and Chinese Sea-Power," 239–314.
17. 吴殿卿 [Wu Dianqing], 周恩来、朱德指导制定第一个海军三年建设计划 ["Zhou Enlai and Zhu De Instruct to Make the Navy's First Three-Year Development Plan"], 21–22.
18. 邓小平 [Deng Xiaoping], 在听取海军和六机部汇报时的讲话, 1978 年6 月29 日 ["Deng Xiaoping's Speech during the Navy and the Sixth Machinery Ministry's Briefing, June 29, 1978"], in 邓小平关于新时期军队建设论述选编 [*Selected Xiaoping's Writings and Speeches on Military Reconstruction during the New Era*] (Beijing: August First Publishing House, 1993), 43.
19. 杨怀庆上将 [Admiral Yang Huaiqing], 回忆邓小平 [*Remembering Deng Xiaoping*] (Beijing: CCP Central Archival and Manuscript Press, 1998), 443. Admiral Yang Huaiqing served as the PLAN political commissar from 1995 to 2003.
20. 刘华清 [Liu Huaqing], 关于海军贯彻积极防御战略方针的几个问题 ["Several Issues on How the Navy Carries out the Strategy of Active Defense"], in 刘回忆录 [*Liu's Memoir*], 434.
21. 田甜 [Tian Tian], 刘华清海权思想与近海防御战略 ["Liu Huaqing's Thought of Sea Power and the Strategy of Near Sea Defense"], 65.
22. Cole, *Great Wall at Sea*, 176.
23. 刘华清 [Liu Huaqing], 应加强海军战略问题的研究 ["Strengthen the Research on Naval Strategic Issues"], in 刘军事文选 [*Selected Military Papers of Liu*], 1:412.
24. 吴胜利 [Wu Shengli]、刘晓江 [Liu Xiaojiang], 海军发展壮大是他一生的牵挂 ["He Spent Whole Life on a Strong Navy"], iii.
25. 刘华清 [Liu Huaqing], 海军战略与未来海上作战 ["Naval Strategy and Naval Warfare in the Future"], in 刘军事文选 [*Selected Military Papers of Liu*], 1:462. Liu's speech at the PLA National Defense University on April 29, 1986.
26. David Shambaugh, *Modernizing China's Military: Progress, Problems, and Prospects* (Berkeley: University of California Press, 2002), 67.
27. Liu's speech quoted in 施 [Shi], 刘华清 [*Liu Huaqing*], 112.

28. 刘华清 [Liu Huaqing], 海军战略与未来海上作战 ["Naval Strategy and Naval Warfare in the Future"], in 刘军事文选 [*Selected Military Papers of Liu*], 1:467.
29. 刘华清 [Liu Huaqing], 海军装备建设应注意质量，提高水平 ["Naval Shipbuilding and Equipment Development Should Pay Attention to Quality and Improve Technology"], 1:110.
30. 刘华清 [Liu Huaqing], 海军战略与未来海上作战 ["Naval Strategy and Naval Warfare in the Future"], 1:481.
31. 刘华清 [Liu Huaqing], 努力建设一支精干顶用的具有现代战斗能力的人民海军 ["Build a People's Navy Capable of Fighting Modern Warfare"], in 刘军事文选 [*Selected Military Papers of Liu*], 1:429–41.
32. 秦天中将、霍小勇少将 [Lieutenant General Qin Tian and Rear Admiral Huo Xiaoyong], 悠悠深蓝: 中华海权史 [*Deep Blue: A History of Chinese Sea Power*] (Beijing: New China Press, 2013), 207. Lieutenant General Qin Tian was vice president of PLA Academy of Military Science from 2015 to 2017 and deputy commander of the People's Armed Police from 2017 to 2023. Rear Admiral Huo Xiaoyong served as the director of the research division, PLA National Defense University, from 2016 to 2022.
33. 霍小勇少将 [Rear Admiral Huo Xiaoyong], 海军战略学 [*Study of the Naval Strategy*] (Beijing: PLA National Defense University, 2006).
34. 刘华清 [Liu Huaqing], 海军战略与未来海上作战 ["Naval Strategy and Naval Warfare in the Future"], 1:456–88.
35. 施 [Shi], 刘华清 [*Liu Huaqing*], 102.
36. 刘华清 [Liu Huaqing], 前言 ["Introduction"], in 中国近代海军史 [*A History of the Modern Chinese Navy*], 吴杰章、苏小东、程志发主编 [ed. Wu Jiezhang, Su Xiaodong, and Cheng Zhifa] (Beijing: PLA Press, 1989), 2.
37. 刘华清 [Liu Huaqing], 建设一支强大的海军，发展我国的海洋事业 ["Build a Strong Navy and Develop National Maritime Undertakings"], 人民日报 [*People's Daily*], November 24, 1984. See also 刘军事文选 [*Selected Military Papers of Liu*], 1:369.
38. 刘华清 [Liu Huaqing], 肩负起保卫祖国建设祖国的重任 ["Shoulder the Main Responsibilities of National Defense and National Construction"], 解放军报 [*PLA Daily*], August 5, 1985. See also 刘军事文选 [*Selected Military Papers of Liu*], 1:397–99.
39. 刘华清 [Liu Huaqing], 建设强大的现代化海军关键在人才 ["The Talents as the Key to Build a Strong and Modern Navy"], 红旗杂志 [*Red Flag Magazine*], January 16, 1986. See also 刘军事文选 [*Selected Military Papers of Liu*], 1:422–28.
40. 施 [Shi], 刘华清 [*Liu Huaqing*], 103.
41. 李铁民少将 [Rear Admiral Li Tiemin], 邓小平海军建设思想研究 [*Studies on Deng Xiaoping's Thought of Naval Development*] (Beijing: National Defense University, 1997), 8. Rear Admiral Li Tiemin served as vice president of the PLA Naval Command University from 1995 to 2001.
42. 兰波 [Lan Bo], 改革开放以来中国海权认识演进研究 ["Study of Cognitive Process of China's Sea Right since the Reform and Opening Up"], 70.
43. 刘回忆录 [*Liu's Memoir*], 439.
44. 施 [Shi], 刘华清 [*Liu Huaqing*], 133.

45. 刘回忆录 [*Liu's Memoir*], 469.
46. Cole, *The Great Wall at Sea*, 177.
47. 刘回忆录 [*Liu's Memoir*], 437.
48. 刘华清 [Liu Huaqing], 时刻想着太平洋的太平 ["Never Forget the Pacific's Peace"], 瞭望周刊 [*Outlook Weekly*], September 1985. See also 刘军事文选 [*Selected Military Papers of Liu*], 1:404–8.
49. 刘华清 [Liu Huaqing], 时刻想着太平洋的太平 ["Never Forget the Pacific's Peace"], 1:407.
50. 刘华清 [Liu Huaqing], 论海上作战形式 ["On the Way of Naval Battles"], in 刘军事文选 [*Selected Military Papers of Liu*], 1:292–93.
51. Shambaugh, *Modernizing China's Military*, 68.
52. 李铁民 [Li Tiemin], 邓小平海军建设思想研究 [*Studies on Deng Xiaoping's Thought of Naval Development*], 9.
53. 刘华清 [Liu Huaqing], 时刻想着太平洋的太平 ["Never Forget the Pacific's Peace"], 1:404–8.
54. 施 [Shi], 刘华清 [*Liu Huaqing*], 171.
55. 刘华清 [Liu Huaqing], 海军战略与未来海上作战 ["Naval Strategy and Naval Warfare in the Future"], 1:473.
56. 刘回忆录 [*Liu's Memoir*], 470.
57. 施 [Shi], 刘华清 [*Liu Huaqing*], 171.
58. 习近平 [Xi Jinping], 在纪念刘华清同志诞辰100 周年座谈会上的讲话 ["Speech at the Symposium to Commemorate the 100th Anniversary of the Birth of Comrade Liu Huaqing."]
59. 刘回忆录 [*Liu's Memoir*], 468.
60. Liu's words quoted in 施 [Shi], 刘华清 [*Liu Huaqing*], 172–73.
61. 刘回忆录 [*Liu's Memoir*], 471.
62. 李安东 [Li Andong], 刘华清领导我军武器装备建设二三事 ["A Few Memories of Liu Huaqing's Leadership in PLA Equipment and Technological Modernization"], 39.
63. Deng, "Speech at an Enlarged Meeting of the CMC, June 4, 1985," in *Selected Works of Deng Xiaoping*, 3:131.
64. Deng, "Speech at an Enlarged Meeting of the CMC, June 4, 1985," 3:133.
65. 施 [Shi], 刘华清 [*Liu Huaqing*], 184–85.
66. Liu's words quoted in 施 [Shi], 刘华清 [*Liu Huaqing*], 186–87.
67. 新华社 [New China News Agency], 人民海军已发展成为合成军种，近海作战力量初具现代化规模 ["The PLAN Developed into a Combined Branch, Achieving Near Sea Combat Capability in Modern Warfare"], 人民日报 [*People's Daily*], April 24, 1989, 1.
68. 杨国宇 [Yang Guoyu], 当代中国海军 [*Contemporary Chinese Navy*], 712.
69. 施 [Shi], 刘华清 [*Liu Huaqing*], 195.
70. 陈右铭 [Chen Youming], 第一代核潜艇的诞生 ["The Birth of the First Generation of Nuclear Submarines"], 2:1100.
71. 刘回忆录 [*Liu's Memoir*], 474.
72. 刘回忆录 [*Liu's Memoir*], 512–13.

73. 施 [Shi], 刘华清 [*Liu Huaqing*], 314, 348–49.
74. 中国人民解放军军兵种历史丛书海军史编委 [Naval History Compilation Committee, PLA Services History Series], 海军史 [*History of the Navy*] (Beijing: PLA Press, 1989), 219–20.
75. 中国人民解放军军兵种历史丛书海军史编委 [Naval History Compilation Committee, PLA Services History Series], 海军史 [*History of the Navy*], 219.
76. 新华社 [New China News Agency], 人民海军已发展成为合成军种，近海作战力量初具现代化规模 ["The PLAN Developed into a Combined Branch, Achieving Near Sea Combat Capability in Modern Warfare"], 1.
77. 刘回忆录 [*Liu's Memoir*], 527–28.
78. Richard A. Bitzinger, Michael Raska, Collin Koh Swee Lean, and Kelvin Wong Ka Weng, "Locating China's Place in the Global Defense Economy," in *Forging China's Military Might: A New Framework for Assessing Innovation*, ed. Tai Ming Cheung (Baltimore, MD: Johns Hopkins University Press, 2014), 180.
79. 刘回忆录 [*Liu's Memoir*], 438.
80. 刘华清 [Liu Huaqing], 时刻想着太平洋的太平 ["Never Forget the Pacific's Peace"], 1:404–8.
81. 施 [Shi], 刘华清 [*Liu Huaqing*], 235, 265.
82. 刘华清 [Liu Huaqing], 海军战略与未来海上作战 ["Naval Strategy and Naval Warfare in the Future"], 1:462.
83. 张序三中将 [Vice Admiral Zhang Xusan], 忆海军舰艇远航航海实习 ["Recollection of a Naval Oceanic Training Sail"], in 中国海军走向深蓝，1980–2020 [*The Chinese Navy Goes to Blue Water, 1980–2010*], 左津玲主编 [ed. Zuo Jinling] (Beijing: PLA Press, 2014), 1:28.
84. 张序三 [Zhang Xusan], 忆海军舰艇远航航海实习 ["Recollection of a Naval Oceanic Training Sail"], 1:33.
85. 刘回忆录 [*Liu's Memoir*], 493.
86. 施 [Shi], 刘华清 [*Liu Huaqing*], 266–67.
87. 张爱萍 [Zhang Aiping], 中国人民解放军 [*The Chinese People's Liberation Army*], 2:39–40.
88. 施 [Shi], 刘华清 [*Liu Huaqing*], 271.
89. 刘回忆录 [*Liu's Memoir*], 495–96.
90. 聂奎聚中将 [Vice Admiral Nie Kuiju], 扬帆起航向大洋 ["Set Sail to the Oceans"], in 左津玲主编 [Zuo Jinling, ed.], 中国海军走向深蓝，1980–2020 [*The Chinese Navy Goes to Blue Water, 1980–2010*] (Beijing: PLA Press, 2014), 1:74. Vice Admiral Nie Kuiju (1926–92) was deputy commander of the PLAN from 1982 to 1988 and commander of the East China Sea Fleet from 1985 to 1989.
91. 胡彦林 [Hu Yanlin], 威震海疆 [*Shocking the Sea*], 501.
92. 赵国臣中将 [Vice Admiral Zhao Guochen], 难忘首次南极考察 ["Unforgettable the First Expedition to the South Pole"], in 中国海军走向深蓝，*1980–2020* [*The Chinese Navy Goes to Blue Water, 1980–2010*], 左津玲主编 [ed. Zuo Jinling] (Beijing: PLA Press, 2014), 1:57. Vice Admiral Zhao Guochen (1935–94) was commander of the

Lüshun Naval Base from 1985 to 1990 and chief of staff of the PLAN from 1990 to 1994.

93. 杨德昌 [Yang Dechang], 海权！中华海权！ [*Sea Power! China Sea Power!*], 572.
94. 习近平 [Xi Jinping], 在纪念刘华清同志诞辰100 周年座谈会上的讲话 ["Speech at the Symposium to Commemorate the 100th Anniversary of the Birth of Comrade Liu Huaqing."
95. 胡彦林 [Hu Yanlin], 威震海疆 [*Shocking the Sea*], 550–51.
96. Liu's words quoted in 施 [Shi], 刘华清 [*Liu Huaqing*], 275.
97. 刘回忆录 [*Liu's Memoir*], 538.
98. Liu's orders quoted in 施 [Shi], 刘华清 [*Liu Huaqing*], 277–78.
99. Min Gyo Koo, *Island Disputes and Maritime Regime Building in East Asia* (New York: Springer, 2010), 154.
100. 张驭涛 [Zhang Yutao], 新中国军事大事纪要 [*Chronicle of Major Military Events of China*] (Beijing: Military Science Press, 1998), 485.
101. 施 [Shi], 刘华清 [*Liu Huaqing*], 297–98.
102. 刘回忆录 [*Liu's Memoir*], 539.
103. 张驭涛 [Zhang Yutao], 新中国军事大事纪要 [*Chronicle of Major Military Events of China*], 491.
104. 胡彦林 [Hu Yanlin], 威震海疆 [*Shocking the Sea*], 562.
105. 施 [Shi], 刘华清 [*Liu Huaqing*], 284.
106. Liu's orders quoted in 施 [Shi], 刘华清 [*Liu Huaqing*], 290.
107. 胡彦林 [Hu Yanlin], 威震海疆 [*Shocking the Sea*], 554–59.
108. Deng Xiaoping's word quoted in 刘回忆录 [*Liu's Memoir*], 539.
109. 刘回忆录 [*Liu's Memoir*], 539.
110. 施 [Shi], 刘华清 [*Liu Huaqing*], 292–93.
111. 胡彦林 [Hu Yanlin], 威震海疆 [*Shocking the Sea*], 559–61.
112. 董宝存、李维坤 [Dong Baocun and Li Weikun], 刘华清与西沙设防、南沙夺礁 ["Liu Huaqing's Defense of Paracel and Battle of Spratly"], 党史博览 [*Party Historical Review*] (2012): 9.
113. 刘回忆录 [*Liu's Memoir*], 541.
114. 胡彦林 [Hu Yanlin], 威震海疆 [*Shocking the Sea*], 571.
115. 施 [Shi], 刘华清 [*Liu Huaqing*], 309–10.
116. Deng, "Speech at an Enlarged Meeting of the CMC, June 4, 1985," 3:131–33.
117. Deng, "Streamline the Army and Raise Its Combat Effectiveness," a speech at an enlarged meeting of CMC Standing Committee on March 12, 1980, 2:284–87.
118. Deng, "Streamline the Army and Raise Its Combat Effectiveness," a speech at an enlarged meeting of CMC Standing Committee on March 12, 1980, *Selected Works of Deng Xiaoping*, 2:284–87.
119. Deng, "Speech at an Enlarged Meeting of the CMC, June 4, 1985," 3:131.
120. Deng, "Speech at an Enlarged Meeting of the CMC, June 4, 1985," 3:133.
121. 刘回忆录 [*Liu's Memoir*], 271–76.
122. 施 [Shi], 刘华清 [*Liu Huaqing*], 54–55.

123. 刘华清 [Liu Huaqing], 搞好整顿，加强海军正规化建设 ["Complete the Rectification and Construct Naval Standardization"], in 刘华清军事文选 [*Selected Military Papers of Liu Huaqing*], 1:311.

124. For more information on Admiral Li Yaowen (1918–2018), see 《星火燎原》编辑部 [*Xinghuo liaoyuan* Composition Department], 将帅名录 [*PLA Marshals and Generals*], 2:494.

125. General Xiong Guangkai, "The International Strategic Situation at the Dawn of the New Century." Xiong was interviewed by the staff writer of *Study Times*. The interview article was published by the journal on December 30, 2000, 10–13.

126. 军事科学院军事历史研究部 [Military History Research Division, PLA AMS], 中国人民解放军的七十年 [*Seventy Years of the Chinese PLA*], 662.

127. Senior Colonel Yang Shaojun, interview by the author at the PLA Academy of Logistics in Beijing, July 1994.

128. 张驭涛 [Zhang Yutao], 新中国军事大事纪要 [*Chronicle of Major Military Events of China*], 427.

129. 张胜 [Zhang Sheng], 从战争中走来 [*Coming from the War*] (Beijing: Three Alliances Publishing, 2013), 641–42; 东方鹤 [Dong Fanghe]. 张爱萍传 [*Biography of Zhang Aiping*], 2:1095–96.

130. 军事科学院军事历史研究部 [Military History Research Division, PLA Academy of Military Science (AMS)], 中国人民解放军的八十年 [*Eighty Years of the Chinese People's Liberation Army*] (Beijing: Military Science Press, 2007), 520.

131. 军事科学院军事历史研究部 [Military History Division, PLA AMS], 中国人民解放军的七十年 [*Seventy Years of the Chinese PLA*], 665.

132. R. Keith Schoppa argues that "for many in China, the actions cost the army a huge amount of respect." Schoppa, *Revolution and Its Past: Identities and Change in Modern Chinese History*, 3rd ed. (New York: Prentice Hall, 2011), 422.

133. 刘明福 [Liu Mingfu], 为什么解放军能赢 [*Why the PLA Can Win the Next War*] (Beijing: People's Armed Police [PAP] Press, 2012), 9–11.

134. Meisner, *Mao's China and After*, 475–76; Maurice Meisner, *The Deng Xiaoping Era: An Inquiry into the Fate of Chinese Socialism, 1978–1994* (New York: Hill & Wang, 1996), 304–21.

135. Xiaobing Li, "Introduction: Social-Economic Transition and Cultural Reconstruction in China," in *Social Transition in China*, ed. Jie Zhang and Xiaobing Li (Lanham, MD: University Press of America, 1998), 1–18.

136. Deng's views were reflected in an April 26, 1989, editorial in the *Renmin ribao* [*People's Daily*]. See Zhang Liang, ed., *The Tiananmen Papers: The Chinese Leadership's Decision to Use Force against Their Own People—In Their Own Words* (New York: Public Affairs, 2001), 71–75.

137. Zhang, *Tiananmen Papers*, 121–22.

138. 吴仁华 [Wu Renhua], 六四事件中的戒严部队 [*The Martial Law Forces in the June Fourth Incident*] (Los Angeles: Truth Publishing House, 2009), 86, 432.

139. 美国之音 [Voice of America], 《六四事件中的戒严部队》出版 ["Publication of Martial Law Forces in the June Fourth Incident"], May 29, 2009, https://www.voachinese.com/a/a-21-w2009-05-29-voa31-61399277/1030984.html.
140. Martial Law Troop Command, "Martial Law Situation Report, no. 3, May 19," in Zhang, *Tiananmen Papers*, 227.
141. Zhang Liang's book listed eight generals, while the others had different numbers. For example, seven generals were mentioned in an essay collection edited by Suzanne Ogden, Kathleen Hartford, Lawrence Sullivan, and David Zweig, *China's Search for Democracy: The Student and the Mass Movement of 1989* (Armonk, NY: M. E. Sharpe, 1992), 292.
142. Party Central Office Secretariat, "Minutes of the Politburo Standing Committee Meeting, June 3, 1989," Zhang, *Tiananmen Papers*, 368–70.
143. Louisa Lim, *The People's Republic of Amnesia* (New York: Oxford University Press, 2014). 17.
144. Harlan Jencks, "Civil-Military Relations in China: Tiananmen and After," *Problems of Communism* 40 (May–June 1991): 22.
145. 黄春梅 [Huang Chunmei], 六四戒严军官李晓明: 解放军镇压是犯罪行为 ["Martial Law Officer Li Xiaoming: PLA's Suppression Was War Crime"], 自由亚洲电台 [*Radio Free Asia*], May 28, 2019, https://www.rfa.org/mandarin/yataibaodao/renquanfazhi/hcm-05282019081359.html. Li Xiaoming served a radar station lieutenant of the Second Company, First Battalion, AAA Regiment, 116th Division, 39th Army in Haicheng, Liaoning, in 1989.
146. 吴仁华 [Wu Renhua], 六四事件中的戒严部队 [*Martial Law Troops in the June Fourth Incident*], 131–33, 145–47.
147. The official statistics listed 264 deaths, including twenty-three college students and twenty PLA soldiers and officers. The Beijing Red Cross estimated 2,600 deaths, and China Radio International reported in Beijing on June 4 that "several thousand people, mostly innocent citizens" had been killed by "heavily armed soldiers." Zhang, *Tiananmen Papers*, 385, 389.
148. 黄春梅 [Huang Chunmei], 六四戒严军官李晓明: 解放军镇压是犯罪行为 ["Martial Law Officer Li Xiaoming: PLA's Suppression Was War Crime"], 自由亚洲电台 [*Radio Free Asia*], May 28, 2019.
149. Extracts from military security report are included in a CMC document, dated December 29, 1989.
150. Xiaobing Li, "Reforming the People's Army: Military Modernization in China," *Journal of Southwest Conference on Asian Studies* 5 (2005): 17.

## CHAPTER 5. A NATIONAL LEADER

1. Jiang Zemin's words are quoted in Information Office, the PRC State Council, *White Papers of China's National Defense in 1998* (Beijing: Foreign Languages, 2000), 2:645.
2. 刘华清 [Liu Huaqing], 海军战略与未来海上作战 ["Naval Strategy and Naval Warfare in the Future"], 1:468.

3. 刘回忆录 [*Liu's Memoir*], 575–77.
4. Theoretically, the idea of "collective leadership" was always in place in the CCP. But Mao Zedong and Deng Xiaoping as the first and second generations of the CCP leadership had dominated the party politics and policymaking. Jiang Zemin actually put the "collective leadership" into practice at the Party Center during his tenures. See Jiang, "On Improving the Party's Style of Work," speech at the Fifth Plenary Session of the Fifteenth CCP Central Committee on October 11, 2000, in Jiang Zemin, *On the "Three Represents"* (Beijing: Foreign Languages Press, 2002), 92–95.
5. Jiang's speech, "How Our Party Is to Attain the 'Three Represents' under the New Historical Condition," was delivered during his tour of Guangdong Province on February 25, 2000; see Jiang, *On the "Three Represents,"* 8.
6. Deng's letter quoted in 刘回忆录 [*Liu's Memoir*], 630.
7. Bin Yu, "China's Gun-Control Problem: Jiang vs. Hu?" *PacNet*, no. 40 (Honolulu: Pacific Forum CSIS, September 16, 2004), 2, www.csis.org/pacfor/ccejournal.html.
8. You Ji, "Changing Leadership Consensus: The Democratic Context of War Games," in *Across the Taiwan Strait: Mainland China, Taiwan, and the 1995–1996 Crisis*, ed. Suisheng Zhao (London: Routledge, 1999), 88.
9. You Ji, "Changing Leadership Consensus: The Democratic Context of War Games," 87.
10. 迟浩田上将 [General Chi Haotian], 前言 [Introduction], 中国海军走向深蓝，1980–2020 [*The Chinese Navy Goes to Blue Water, 1980–2010*], in 左津玲主编 [ed. Zuo Jinling] (Beijing: PLA Press, 2014), vii.
11. 新浪新闻 [Sina News], 关键时刻，刘华清干的三件大事 ["Liu Huaqing's Three Big Actions at the Critical Moments"], 新浪 [*Sina*], September 29, 2016, www.news.sina.cn/gn/2016-09-29/detail-ifxwkvys2331162.d.html.
12. Jiang's inscription quoted in 施 [Shi], 刘华清 [*Liu Huaqing*], 352.
13. 陈万军、袁华智、司彦文 [Chen Wanjun, Yuan Huazhi, and Si Yanwen], 春风鼓浪好杨帆—— 江泽民主席关心人民海军现代化建设记事 ["Ride the Spring Wind and Waves: Historical Records of President Jiang Zemin's Efforts in the Modernization of the People's Navy"], in 共和国领袖与海军 [*Chinese Leaders and the Navy*], 吴殿卿、袁永安、赵小平 [ed. Wu Dianqing, Yuan Yong'an, and Zhao Xiaoping] (Beijing: Ocean Waves Publishing House, 2000), 301.
14. 吴瑞虎 [Wu Ruihu], 三代驱逐舰启程中南海 ["Three Generations of Destroyers Started from Zhongnanhai"], 291–92.
15. 新华社 [New China News], 人民海军70 年：党中央关心人民海军建设发展纪实 ["70 Years of the People's Navy: The Historical Facts of the Party Center's Support to Construction and Development of the People's Navy"], 新华社新媒体 [*New China's News Media*], April 22, 2019, www.baijiahao.baidu.com/s?id=1631510382706012l248&wfr.
16. 陈万军、袁华智、司彦文 [Chen Wanjun, Yuan Huazhi, and Si Yanwen], 春风鼓浪好杨帆 ["Ride the Spring Wind and Waves"], 302–4.

17. 王永国中将 [Vice Admiral Wang Yongguo], 横跨太平洋首次出访美洲四国 ["Across the Pacific: The First Voyage to Four Countries in Americas"], in 中国海军走向深蓝，1980–2020 [*The Chinese Navy Goes to Blue Water, 1980–2010*], 左津玲主编 [ed. Zuo Jinling] (Beijing: PLA Press, 2014), 185. Wang Yongguo, ranked rear admiral in 1988 and vice admiral in 1996, was the commander of the South China Sea Fleet and deputy commander of the PLA Guangzhou Military Region from 1994 to 2002.
18. For more discussions on General Chi Haotian's hardline position, see John F. Copper, "The Origins of Conflict across the Taiwan Strait: The Problem of Differences in Perceptions," in *Across the Taiwan Strait: Mainland China, Taiwan, and the 1995–1996 Crisis*, ed. Suisheng Zhao (London: Routledge, 1999), 43; You Ji, "Changing Leadership Consensus: The Domestic Context of War Game," 91–93.
19. 张驭涛 [Zhang Yutao], 新中国军事大事纪要 [*Chronicle of Major Military Events of China*], 608.
20. For a detailed overview of the 1995–96 Taiwan Strait Crisis, see Qimao Chen, "The Taiwan Strait Crisis: Causes, Scenarios, and Solutions," in *Across the Taiwan Strait: Mainland China, Taiwan, and the 1995–1996 Crisis*, ed. Suisheng Zhao (London: Routledge, 1999), 127–62.
21. 张驭涛 [Zhang Yutao], 新中国军事大事纪要 [*Chronicle of Major Military Events of China*], 610.
22. 刘华清 [Liu Huaqing], 加强空降兵部队的建设 ["Strengthen the Buildup of the Airborne Troops"], in 刘军事文选 [*Selected Military Papers of Liu*], 2:420–21.
23. William Perry and Ashton Carter, *Preventive Defense: A New Security for America* (Washington, DC: Brookings Institute, 1999), 92–93.
24. Patric Tyler, *A Great Wall: Six Presidents and China* (New York: Public Affairs, 1999), 33, 195.
25. William Perry, Secretary of U.S. Defense Department, made a public statement on March 11, 1996, about the large U.S. naval maneuver near the Taiwan Strait. For Perry's statement, see *American Forces Press Service*, March 11; the Department of Defense, *News Briefings*, March 12, 14, and 16, 1996.
26. Taiwan Affairs Office and the Information Office, PRC State Council, "The One-China Principle and the Taiwan Issue, February 2000," in *White Papers of the Chinese Government, 2000–2001* (Beijing: Foreign Languages Press, 2003), 29.
27. Andrew Scobell, *China's Use of Military Force: Beyond the Great Wall and the Long March* (Cambridge: Cambridge University Press, 2003), 189.
28. Peter Worthing, *A Military History of Modern China: From the Manchu Conquest to Tiananmen Square* (Westport, CT: Praeger, 2007), 197.
29. Worthing, *Military History of Modern China*, 122.
30. 刘华清 [Liu Huaqing], 科技强军，理论先行 ["Strengthen the Military with Science and Technology: Research Goes First"], in 刘军事文选 [*Selected Military Papers of Liu*], 2:486.

31. 刘华清 [Liu Huaqing], 新时期海军建设的几个问题 ["The Major Issues in Naval Development during the New Period"], in 刘军事文选 [*Selected Military Papers of Liu*], 2:430.
32. 陈万军、袁华智、司彦文 [Chen Wanjun, Yuan Huazhi, and Si Yanwen], 春风鼓浪好杨帆 ["Ride the Spring Wind and Waves"], 300.
33. 陈右铭 [Chen Youming], 第一代核潜艇的诞生 ["The Birth of the First Generation of Nuclear Submarines"], 2:1100.
34. 刘回忆录 [*Liu's Memoir*], 477.
35. Gao, *PLA Navy*, 107.
36. 李琼 [Li Qiong], 海上长城 [*Great Wall at Sea*], 55.
37. 王永国 [Wang Yongguo], 横跨太平洋首次出访美洲四国 ["Across the Pacific: The First Voyage to Four Countries in Americas"], 191.
38. 刘华清 [Liu Huaqing], 为海军武器装备现代化建设打好基础 ["Build a Solid Foundation for Naval Weaponry and Equipment Modernization"], in 刘军事文选 [*Selected Military Papers of Liu*], 1:269–70.
39. 日本海人社编 [Japanese Oceanic Association, ed.], 英国航空母舰史 [*History of British Aircraft Carriers*] (Qingdao: Qingdao Publishing House, 2013), 66–68.
40. Nanda Avalist, "The Naval Dimension of the Great Power Contest for Global Hegemony: A Case of the US-China-Russia Rivalry," PhD diss., Curtin University, Australia (2024), 205.
41. Liu's words quoted in 施 [Shi], 刘华清 [*Liu Huaqing*], 374.
42. 吴殿卿大校 [Commodore Wu Dianqing], 刘华清的航母情结 ["Liu Huaqing's Life and Heart on Aircraft Carrier"], 党史博览 [*Chronicle of the Party's History*], no. 9 (2011): 5.
43. 刘回忆录 [*Liu's Memoir*], 478.
44. 施 [Shi], 刘华清 [*Liu Huaqing*], 374.
45. Liu's words quoted in 施 [Shi], 刘华清 [*Liu Huaqing*], 374–75.
46. 刘华清 [Liu Huaqing], 以海军发展战略指导装备技术研制工作 ["Naval Development Strategy Guides Equipment and Technological Development Tasks"], in 刘军事文选 [*Selected Military Papers of Liu*], 1:522–23.
47. 施 [Shi], 刘华清 [*Liu Huaqing*], 378.
48. 刘华清 [Liu Huaqing], 海军装备规划要从长远考虑 ["Naval Equipment and Technology Development Should Have a Long-Range Plan"], in 刘军事文选 [*Selected Military Papers of Liu*], 1:563, 564.
49. Admiral Zhang Lianzhong's words quoted in 共青团中央 [Central Committee of Communist Youth League], "三航母"时代，告慰刘华清将军 ["The Era of Three Aircraft Carriers: Comfort Liu Huaqing"], January 14, 2023, https://mp.weixin.qq.com/s?__biz=MzA3NTE5MzQzMA==&mid=2656993222&idx=1&sn=f8524289d0e9f202d9c5ab9225498746&chksm=84de92ffb3a91be90715141206016 85d3b56dc92053ceea9eed9cbb97fbef35872663fe3d02e&scene=27.
50. Liu's words quoted in You Ji, *China's Military Transformation: Politics and War Preparation* (Cambridge: Polity, 2016), 194.

51. 习近平 [Xi Jinping], 在纪念刘华清同志诞辰100 周年座谈会上的讲话 ["Speech at the Symposium to Commemorate the 100th Anniversary of the Birth of Comrade Liu Huaqing."
52. Admiral Zhang Lianzhong's words quoted in 施 [Shi], 刘华清 [*Liu Huaqing*], 397.
53. 张召忠少将 [Rear Admiral Zhang Zhaozhong], 百年航母 [*Aircraft Carriers in 100 Years*] (Guangzhou: Guangdong Economy Publishing House, 2011), 2:308–10.
54. 戴旭 [Dai Xu], 中国航母 [*China's Aircraft Carriers*] (Beijing: Chinese Literature Publishing House, 2009), 103–4.
55. 施昌学大校 [Commodore Shi Changxue], 刘华清的航母梦 ["Liu Huaqing's Carrier's Dream"], 中国政协网 [*China CPPCC Net*], May 7, 2020, www.cppcc.gov.cn/zxww/2020/05/08/ARTI1588900134352215.shtml.
56. 李忠效 [Li Zhongxiao], "瓦良格"号航母来中国—中国航母"辽宁舰"前世真相调查 [*Varyag Coming to China: An Investigation of the True Background of Chinese Aircraft Carrier Liaoning*] (Beijing: Aiming Aihua Co., 2019), chapter 1.
57. 施 [Shi], 刘华清 [*Liu Huaqing*], 394–95.
58. 张召忠 [Zhang Zhaozhong], 百年航母 [*Aircraft Carriers in 100 Years*], 2:306–7.
59. The words of He Pengfei's staff member quoted in 李忠效 [Li Zhongxiao], "瓦良格"号航母来中国 [*Varyag Coming to China*], chapter 2.
60. 戴旭 [Dai Xu], 中国航母 [*China's Aircraft Carriers*], xii, 117–18.
61. 戴旭 [Dai Xu], 中国航母 [*China's Aircraft Carriers*], 212–22.
62. 李忠效 [Li Zhongxiao], "瓦良格"号航母来中国 [*Varyag Coming to China*], chapter 5.
63. 江泽民 [Jiang Zemin], 正确处理社会主义现代化建设中的若干重大关系 ["Correctly Deal with the Critical Relations in Socialist Construction for Modernization"], in 江泽民文选 [*Selected Works of Jiang Zemin*] (Beijing: People's Press, 2006), 1:460–75.
64. 李忠效 [Li Zhongxiao], "瓦良格"号航母来中国 [*Varyag Coming to China*], chapter 6.
65. 张召忠 [Zhang Zhaozhong], 百年航母 [*Aircraft Carriers in 100 Years*], 2:306–7.
66. 施昌学 [Shi Changxue], 刘华清的航母梦 ["Liu Huaqing's Carrier's Dream"], 中国政协网 [*China CPPCC Net*], May 7, 2020.
67. 李忠效 [Li Zhongxiao], "瓦良格"号航母来中国 [*Varyag Coming to China*], chapter 11.
68. 施昌学 [Shi Changxue], 刘华清的航母梦 ["Liu Huaqing's Carrier's Dream"], 中国政协网 [*China CPPCC Net*], May 7, 2020.
69. Xiansheng Tian, "When Chongqing Challenges Beijing: The Bo Xilai Case," in *Evolution of Power: China's Struggle, Survival, and Success*, ed. Xiaobing Li and Xiansheng Tian (Lanham, MD: Lexington Books, 2014), 323.
70. Interview with the officer at Langfang, Hebei, on July 28, 2002. The provincial commander sent out a survey form to all of the officers of its regiments in 2003. The survey provides a mixed report on the only-child officers. Liberal and democratic, some emphasize individual competition and equal opportunity, and dislike the political control. For more details, see Xiaobing Li, "The Impact of Social Changes on the PLA: A Chinese Military Perspective," in *Civil-Military Relations in Today's China: Swimming in a New Sea*, ed. David M. Finkelstein and Kristen Gunness (Armonk, NY: M. E. Sharpe, 2007), 26–47.

71. Hu Jintao's words quoted in 迟浩田 [Chi Haotian], 前言 ["Introduction"], in 中国海军走向深蓝，*1980–2020* [*The Chinese Navy Goes to Blue Water, 1980–2010*], viii.
72. 新华社 [New China News], 胡锦涛会见海军代表 ["Hu Jintao Meets Naval Representatives"], 中国新闻网 [*China News*], December 28, 2006, www.chinanews.com.cn/gn/news/2006/12-28.
73. 李琼 [Li Qiong], 海上长城 [*Great Wall at Sea*], 15.
74. Rear Admiral Wang Fushan's telegram quoted in Gao, *PLA Navy*, 195.
75. 刘回忆录 [*Liu's Memoir*], 729.
76. 余玮 [Yu Wei], 布衣将军刘华清 ["'Plain Cloth' Admiral: Liu Huaqing"], 党史博览 [*Chronicle of the Party History*], no. 7 (2004): 3–4.
77. 刘錫贵 [Liu Xigui], 在建设海洋强国的伟大征途中铸就辉煌 ["Achieve Glory during the Great Cause of Building a Strong Country with Sea Power"], 中国海洋报 [*China Maritime News*], July 23, 2014, A-1.
78. Cole, *Great Wall at Sea*, xix, 187, 190.
79. Xiaobing Li, "Sino-Japanese Maritime Conflicts and Security Concerns in the East China Sea," in *Maritime Security in the Indian Ocean and Western Pacific: Heritage and Contemporary Challenges*, ed. Howard M. Hensel and Amit Gupta (London: Routledge, 2018), 249.
80. Hu's words quoted in 李琼 [Li Qiong], 海上长城 [*Great Wall at Sea*], 73.
81. 施 [Shi], 刘华清 [*Liu Huaqing*], 443–44.
82. 新华社 [New China News], 胡锦涛出席庆祝人民海军成立60 周年海上阅兵活动 ["Hu Jintao Attends the Naval Parade to Celebrate the People's Navy's 60th Birthday"], 中国台湾网 [*China's Taiwan News*], www.taiwan.cn/xwzx/jrbd/200904/t20090424_876110.htm.
83. 新华社 [New China News Agency], 中国海军出击亚丁湾 ["The Chinese Navy Dispatched to the Gulf of Aden"], 参考消息 [*Reference News*], December 27, 2008, 1–2.
84. Chinese Defense Ministry's spokesman's announcement quoted in Gao, *PLA Navy*, 148.
85. Wang Guangqun, "China Rises to Top in Ranks of Ship Makers," Xinhua News Agency, May 9, 2011, http://news.xinhuanet.com/english2010/china/2011-05/09/c_13865547.htm.
86. Information Office, PRC State Council, *China's National Defense in 2010* (Beijing: State Council Information Office, 2011), http://www.gov.cn/english/official/2011-03/31/content_1835499.htm.
87. You Ji, *China's Military Transformation*, 181.
88. Hsiu-Chuan Shih and Flora Wang, "Officials Drop Plan to Visit Diaoyutais," *Taipei Times*, June 18, 2008.
89. Information Office, PRC State Council, *White Papers of China's National Defense in 2007* (Beijing: Foreign Languages Press, 2008), 8.
90. Hillary Clinton, "Secretary Clinton Joint Press Availability with Japanese Foreign Minister Seiji Maehara," October 27, 2010, www.state.gov/secretary/rm/2010/10/150110.htm.

91. P. Baker, "Obama Calls for Military Dialogue with China," *New York Times*, March 12, 2009.
92. 刘华清 [Liu Huaqing], 海军战略与未来海上作战 ["Naval Strategy and Naval Warfare in the Future"], 1:468.
93. "Hu Jintao Tells China Navy: Prepare for Warfare," *BBC News*, December 7, 2011, www.bbc.com/news/world-asia-china-16063607.
94. Nan Li, "China's Evolving Naval Strategy and Capabilities in the Hu Jintao Era," in *Assessing the People's Liberation Army in the Hu Jintao Era*, ed. Roy Kamphausen, David Lai, and Travis Tanner (Carlisle, PA: U.S. Army War College, 2014), 257.
95. 刘亚洲大将 [Genera Liu Yazhou], 厚重的人生，炫目的光彩 ["Significant Life with Shining Colors"], 解放军报 [*PLA Daily*], January 6, 2005. General Liu Yazhou served as the political commissar of the PLA National Defense University from 2009 to 2017.
96. 欧阳开宇 [Oyang Kaiyu], 刘华清对海军发展有巨大历史性贡献 ["Liu Huaqing Made Great Historical Contribution to the Navy"], 中国网络电视台 [China Net TV Station], January 14, 2011, www.news.cntv.cn/china/20110114/105861.shtml.
97. 吴胜利 [Wu Shengli]、刘晓江 [Liu Xiaojiang], 海军发展壮大是他一生的牵挂 ["He Spent Whole Life on a Strong Navy"], ix.
98. 杨舟 [Yang Zhou], 中国的戈尔什科夫: 红色马汉刘华清 ["China's Gorshkov and 'Red Mahan': Liu Huaqing"].

## CONCLUSION

1. Wang Guangqun, "China Rises to Top in Ranks of Ship Makers," Xinhua News Agency, May 9, 2011, http://news.xinhuanet.com/english2010/china/2011-05/09/c_13865547.htm.
2. 刘回忆录 [*Liu's Memoir*], 439.
3. Gorshkov, *The Sea Power of the State* (Naval Institute Press, 1979), xi.
4. The paragraph includes several points from Harold Tanner's comments on the manuscript as an invited reviewer by the press, December 15, 2024.
5. James Holms and Toshi Yoshihara, "Liu Huaqing, RIP," *Diplomat*, January 18, 2011, www.thediplomat.com/2011/01/liu-huaqing-rip.
6. 习近平 [Xi Jinping], 在纪念刘华清同志诞辰100 周年座谈会上的讲话 ["Speech at the Symposium to Commemorate the 100th Anniversary of the Birth of Liu Huaqing"], 1.
7. You Ji, *China's Military Transformation*, 181.
8. Cole, *The Great Wall at Sea*, xix, 187, 190.
9. Information Bureau, PRC State Council, *The Diversified Employment of China's Armed Forces* (*China's Defense White Paper*), April 2013, http://www.chinadaily.com.cn/language_tips/news/2013-04/17/content_16414985.htm.
10. Avalist, "The Naval Dimension of the Great Power Contest for Global Hegemony," 198.
11. You Ji, *China's Military Transformation*, 144, 227.

12. U.S. Defense Intelligence Agency, *China Military Power: Modernizing a Force to Fight and Win* (Washington, DC: U.S. Government Printing Office, 2019), 70.
13. Council for Foreign Relations, "Tracking China's Control of Overseas Ports," November 6, 2023, *Asia Program*, Greenberg Center for Geoeconomic Studies, https://www.cfr.org/tracker/china-overseas-ports.
14. You Ji, *China's Military Transformation*, 10, 72, 77–78.
15. *PLA Daily*, "China's Establishment of the Air Defense Identification Zone (ADIZ) in the East China Sea, January 22, 2014," http://eng.chinamil.com.cn/view/2014-01.
16. Dean P. Chen, *U.S.-China Rivalry and Taiwan's Mainland Policy: Security, Nationalism and the 1992 Consensus* (London: Palgrave Macmillan, 2017), 183.
17. U.S. Defense Intelligence Agency, *China Military Power*, 70.
18. Nadia Tsao, "Hong Kong Crackdown Sparks 'Fundamental Change' in U.S. Taiwan Policy: Trump Adviser," *Radio Free Asia*, November 13, 2020, www.rfa.org/english/news/china/crackdown-11132020095826.html.
19. Low De Wei, "Full Text of Xi Jinping's Speech at China's Party Congress," *Bloomberg*, October 18, 2022, www.bloomberg.com/news/article/2022-10-18/full-text-of-xi-jinping-s-speech-at-china-20th-party-congress-2022.
20. Information Bureau, PRC State Council, *China's Defense White Paper 2019*.
21. General Jiang Weilie, quoted interview with a reporter on April 9, 2013, PRC Defense Ministry's website, www.mod.gov.cn.
22. Information Office, the PRC State Council, *The Diversified Employment of China's Armed Forces* (*China's Defense White Paper*), April 2013.
23. Vice Admiral Fedotenkov's praise was quoted in Franz-Stefan Gady, "Russian and China Kick off Naval Exercise in Sea of Japan," *Diplomat*, August 24, 2015, http://thediplomat.com/2015/08/Russian-and-china-kick-off-naval-exercise-in-sea-of-japan.
24. M. Rajagopalan, "China Conducts Air, Sea Drills in East China Sea," *Reuters*, August 27, 2015, 1–2, http://www.reuters.com/articles/us-china-defense-idUSKCN0QW1EX20150827.
25. Dean Cheng, "Assessing Threats to US Vital Interests: China," *The Heritage Foundation*, www.heritage.org/2021-index-us-military-strength/assessing-threats-us-vital-interests/china.
26. C. Huang and T. Ng, "Xi Jinping Sends Signal to Neighbors with High-Profile Tour of Liaoning Aircraft Carrier," *South Chinese Morning Post*, August 31, 2013, 1–3.
27. Office of the U.S. Secretary of Defense, *Annual Report to Congress: Military Power of the People's Republic of China, 2009*, http://www.defenselink.mil/pubs/pdfs/China_Military_Report_09.pdf.

# SELECTED BIBLIOGRAPHY


**CHINESE-LANGUAGE SOURCES [中文资料]**

***Archives, Manuscripts, and Military Papers [档案文稿及军事文件]***

中国外交部办公厅档案资料部 [Archives Department of the General Office, PRC Foreign Ministry]. 中国外交档案 [*China's Foreign Affairs Archives*], 北京 [Beijing].

中共中央档案局 [CCP Central Archives]. 中共中央文件选集，1921–1949 [*Selected Documents of the CCP Central Committee, 1921–1949*]. 18 vols. Beijing: CCP Central Party University Press, 1992.

中共中央档案局、中央文献研究室、中央组织部 [CCP Central Archives, Central Archival and Manuscript Research Division, and CCP Organization Department, comps.]. 中国共产党组织史资料，1921–1997 [*Documents of the CCP Organization's History, 1921–1997*]. 14 vols. Beijing: CCP Central Committee's Party History Press, 2000.

陈绍宽 [Chen Shaokuan]. 对于国防上之感想 ["Some Thoughts on National Defense"]. 东方杂志 [*Oriental Magazine*] 33, no. 1 (1936): 2–3.

陈毅 [Chen Yi]. 陈毅军事文选 [*Selected Military Writings of Chen Yi*]. Beijing: PLA Press, 1996.

邓小平 [Deng Xiaoping]. 邓小平关于新时期军队建设论述选编 [*Selected Deng Xiaoping's Writings and Speeches on Military Reconstruction during the New Era*]. Beijing: August First Publishing House, 1993.

前苏联档案 [Former Soviet Archives]. 斯大林与毛泽东会谈记录 ["The Meeting Minutes of Stalin's Conversation with Mao Zedong"], December 16, 1949. In 有关1950 年中苏条约谈判的俄国档案 [*The Russian Archives of the 1950 Treaty Negotiations on the Soviet-Chinese Agreement*]. 中共党史研究 [*CCP Party History Research*], no. 4 (1998): 1–13.

前苏联档案 [Former Soviet Archives]. 斯大林与中共代表团会谈记录 ["The Meeting Minutes of Stalin's Negotiations with the CCP Delegation"], June 27, 1949. In 有关刘少奇1949 年访苏的俄国档案 [*The Russian Archives of the 1949 Liu Shaoqi Visit in the Soviet Union*]. 中共党史研究 [*CCP Party History Research*], no. 2 (1998): 12–25.

高晓星编 [Gao Xiaoxing, ed.]. 陈绍宽文集 [*Collected Papers of Chen Shaokuan*]. Beijing: Ocean Waves Publishing House, 1994.

江泽民 [Jiang Zemin]. 江泽民文选 [*Selected Works of Jiang Zemin*]. Beijing: People's Press, 2006.

梁启超 [Liang Qichao]. 论太平洋海权及中国的前途 ["On Sea Power in the Pacific and the Future of China"]. 新民丛报 [*New People's Voices*], no. 26 (1903): 2–3.

刘伯承 [Liu Bocheng]. 刘伯承军事文选 [*Selected Military Writings of Liu Bocheng*]. Beijing: PLA Press, 1992.

刘华清 [Liu Huaqing]. 有关海军战略问题的探讨 ["Discussion about Naval Strategic Issues"]. 海军杂志 [*Navy's Magazine*], no. 7 (1986): 1–5.

刘华清 [Liu Huaqing]. 前言 ["Introduction"]. In 中国近代海军史 [*A History of the Modern Chinese Navy*], 吴杰章、苏小东、程志发 [by Wu Jiezhang, Su Xiaodong, and Cheng Zhifa], 1–5. Beijing: PLA Press, 1989.

刘华清 [Liu Huaqing]. 刘华清书法与题词选集 [*Selected Inscriptions and Calligraphy of Liu Huaqing*]. Beijing: Great Wall Publishing House, 2010.

刘华清 [Liu Huaqing]. 刘华清军事文选 [*Selected Military Writings of Liu Huaqing*]. Beijing: PLA Press, 2008.

刘华清 [Liu Huaqing]. 刘伯承战术思想研究札记 ["Study Notes on Liu Bocheng's Tactical Thinking"]. 军事知识 [*Military Knowledge*], no. 2 (1988): 1–6.

刘少奇 [Liu Shaoqi]. 建国以来刘少奇文稿 [*Liu Shaoqi's Manuscripts since the Founding of the State*]. 7 vols. Beijing: CCP Central Archival and Manuscript Press, 2008.

中国人民海军旅顺基地 [Lüshun Naval Command, PLA Navy]. 林彪、李作鹏反党乱军罪行文件汇编 ["Document Collection on Lin Biao and Li Zuopeng's Criminal Activities of Attacking the Party and Betraying the PLA, October 1971"]. In 批林批李资料 [*Political Files against the Lin-Li Group (1971–1972)*]. 旅顺海军基地档案室 [Lüshun Naval Base Archives], Lüshun, Liaoning.

毛泽东 [Mao Zedong]. 毛泽东军事文集 [*Collected Military Manuscripts of Mao Zedong*]. 6 vols. Beijing: CCP Central Archival and Manuscript Press and Military Science Press, 1993.

毛泽东 [Mao Zedong]. 毛泽东文选 [*Collected Works of Mao Zedong*]. 8 vols. Beijing: People's Press, 1999.

毛泽东 [Mao Zedong]. 建国以来毛泽东军事文稿 [*Mao Zedong's Military Manuscripts since the Founding of the PRC*]. 3 vols. Beijing: Military Science Press and CCP Central Archival and Manuscript Press, 2010.

毛泽东 [Mao Zedong]. 建国以来毛泽东文稿，1949–1976 [*Mao Zedong's Manuscripts since the Founding of the State, 1949–1976*]. 13 vols. Beijing: CCP Central Archival and Manuscript Press, 1993.

毛泽东 [Mao Zedong]. 毛泽东外交文选 [*Selected Diplomatic Papers of Mao Zedong*]. Beijing: CCP Central Archival and Manuscript Press, 1994.

毛泽东 [Mao Zedong]. 毛泽东军事文选（内部版）[*Selected Military Papers of Mao Zedong: Internal Edition*]. 2 vols. Beijing: PLA Soldiers Press, 1981.

毛泽东 [Mao Zedong]. 毛泽东选集 [*Selected Works of Mao Zedong*]. 5 vols. Beijing: People's Press, 1979.

马英九 [Ma Ying-jeou]. 钓鱼台列屿主权争议回顾与展望 [*Disputed Sovereignty of Senkaku Island: The Past and Future*]. Taipei: ROC Government Printing, 1996.

马英九 [Ma Ying-jeou]. 从新海洋法论钓鱼台列屿与东海划界问题 [*New Oceanic Regulations: Issues of Senkaku Island and the Border of the East China Sea*]. Taipei: Zhengzhong Books, 1986.

聂荣臻 [Nie Rongzhen]. 聂荣臻军事文选 [*Selected Military Writings of Nie Rongzhen*]. Beijing: PLA Press, 1992.

彭德怀 [Peng Dehuai]. 彭德怀军事文选 [*Selected Military Writings of Peng Dehuai*]. Beijing: CCP Central Archival and Manuscript Press, 1988.

沈志华主编 [Shen Zhihua, ed.]. 朝鲜战争：俄国档案馆的解密文件 [*The Korean War: Declassified Documents in the Russian Archives*]. Taipei: Academia Sinica, 2015.

沈志华主编 [Shen Zhihua, ed.]. 苏联历史档案选编 [*Selected Historical Archives of the Soviet Union*]. Beijing: Archives and Manuscripts of Social Science Press, 2002.

台湾档案管理局 [Taiwan Archival Administration]. 外交部档案 [*Foreign Ministry Archives*], 台北 [Taipei].

唐宝镐 [Tang Baogao]. 海上权力之要素 ["The Key Elements of Sea Power"]. 海军期刊 [*Journal of Naval Force*] 1, no. 6–12 (1927).

唐宝镐 [Tang Baogao]. 海上权力之要素 ["The Key Elements of Sea Power"]. 海军期刊 [*Journal of Naval Force*] 2, no. 1–8 (1928).

习近平 [Xi Jinping]. 在纪念中国共产党建立100 周年庆祝大会上的讲话 [Speech at the CCP's 100th Anniversary Celebration]. *Renmin ribao* [*People's Daily*], July 1, 2021.

肖劲光 [Xiao Jinguang]. 肖劲光军事文选 [*Selected Military Writings of Xiao Jinguang*]. Beijing: PLA Press, 2003.

习近平 [Xi Jinping]. 在纪念刘华清同志诞辰100 周年座谈会上的讲话 ["Speech at the Symposium to Commemorate the 100th Anniversary of the Birth of Comrade Liu Huaqing"], September 28, 2016. 新华社 [*New China News Agency*]. www.english.cctv.com/2016/09/29/ARTISzfc7wHez51om6JcAHnE160929.shtml.

新华社 [Xinhua News Agency]. 新华社文件资料汇编 [*A Collection of Documentary Materials of Xinhua News Agency*]. Beijing: Xinhua News Agency Publishing House, n.d.

徐向前 [Xu Xiangqian]. 徐向前军事文选 [*Selected Military Writings of Xu Xiangqian*]. Beijing: PLA Press, 1992.

周恩来 [Zhou Enlai]. 周恩来军事文选 [*Selected Military Papers of Zhou Enlai*]. 4 vols. Beijing: People's Press, 1997.

周恩来 [Zhou Enlai]. 建国以来周恩来文稿 [*Zhou Enlai's Manuscripts since the Founding of the State, 1949–1950*]. 3 vols. Beijing: CCP Central Archival and Manuscript Press, 2008.

朱德 [Zhu De]. 朱德军事文选 [*Selected Military Writings of Zhu De*]. Beijing: PLA Press, 1986.

### *Official Chronicles, Recollections, and Memoirs* [官方记事及回忆录]

中共中央文献研究室 [CCP Central Archival and Manuscript Research Division]. 毛泽东传，1893–1949 [*Biography of Mao Zedong, 1893–1949*]. 2 vols. Beijing: CCP Central Archival and Manuscript Press, 1996.

中共中央文献研究室 [CCP Central Archival and Manuscript Research Division]. 毛泽东年谱，1893–1949 [*A Chronological Record of Mao Zedong, 1893–1949*]. 3 vols. Beijing: CCP Central Archival and Manuscript Press, 1993.

中共中央文献研究室 [CCP Central Archival and Manuscript Research Division]. 周恩来年谱，1949–1976 [*A Chronological Record of Zhou Enlai, 1949–1976*]. Beijing: CCP Central Archival and Manuscript Press, 1997.

中共中央文献研究室 [CCP Central Archival and Manuscript Research Division]. 朱德年谱, 1886–1976 [*A Chronological Record of Zhu De, 1886–1976*]. Beijing: People's Press, 1986.

陈右铭 [Chen Youming]. 第一代核潜艇的诞生 ["The Birth of the First Nuclear Submarine"]. In 中国人民解放军历史资料丛书: 海军回忆史料 [*PLA Historical Sources Series: The Navy: Memoirs and Historical Records*] (Classified), 海军编审委员会 [edited by Navy Editorial Committee], 2:1076–1102. Beijing: Ocean Waves Publishing House, 1994.

《周恩来军事活动记事》编写组编著 [Compilation Team of *Chronicle of Zhou Enlai's Military Affairs*]. 周恩来军事活动记事 [*Chronicle of Zhou Enlai's Military Affairs*]. Beijing: CCP Central Archival and Manuscript Press, 2000.

中华民国国防部 [Defense Ministry, ROC]. 国军后勤史 [*Logistics History of the KMT Armed Forces*]. 8 vols. Taipei: Bureau of Historical and Political Records, Taiwan Defense Ministry, 1992.

国防部军务局 [Department of Military Affairs, ROC Defense Ministry]. 八二三台海战役 [*The 8-23 Battle of the Taiwan Strait*]. Taipei: Department of Military Affairs, ROC Defense Ministry, 1998.

中国人民解放军历史资料丛书编审委员会 [The Editorial Board of Collected Historical Documents of the PLA]. 海军历史资料 [*Historical Documents of the Navy*]. Beijing: PLA Press, 2006.

郭保兰 [Guo Baolan]. 援越扫雷 ["Assist Vietnam in Mine-Sweepings"]. In 中国人民解放军历史资料丛书: 海军回忆史料 [*PLA Historical Sources Series: The Navy's Memoirs and Records*] (Classified), 海军编审委员会 [edited by Navy Editorial Committee], 2:1166–82. Beijing: Ocean Waves Publishing House, 1994.

国防部史政编译局 [History Compilation and Translation Bureau, ROC Defense Ministry]. 8-23 炮战胜利30 周年纪念文集 [*Recollection for the 30th Anniversary of the Victorious August 23 Artillery Battle*]. Taipei: Defense Department Printing, 1989.

侯向之 [Hou Xiangzhi]. 《二四协定》的签定 ["The Conclusion of February 4 Agreement"]. In 海军回忆史料 [*The Navy: Memoirs and Historical Records*] (Classified), 海军编审委员会编 [edited by Navy Editorial Committee], 2:1046–56. Beijing: Ocean Waves Publishing House, 1994.

胡润民 [Hu Runmin]. 台湾军情局的疯狂岁月 ["The Crazy Era of Taiwan's Military Intelligence Bureau"]. 环球人物 [*Global People*], no. 5 (2011).

胡士弘 [Hu Shihong]. 横槊东海 ["Couching the Lance in the East China Sea"]. In 三军挥戈战东海 [*Combined Forces Wield Spears and Fight in the East China Sea*], 聂凤智等 [edited by Nie Fengzhi et al.], 38–58. Beijing: PLA Press, 1986.

段与衡将军访问记录 ["Interview Records of Major General Duan Yuheng"]. In 尘封的作战计划—— 国光计划—— 口述历史 [*Oral History: Historical Operational Plan—Guoguang Jihua*], 彭大年编 [edited by Peng Danian]. Taipei: Department of Military Affairs, ROC Defense Ministry, 2005.

邢祖援将军访问记录 ["Interview Records of Major General Xing Zuyuan"]. In 尘封的作战计划—— 国光计划—— 口述历史 [*Oral History: Historical Operational Plan—Guoguang Jihua*], 彭大年编 [edited by Peng Danian]. Taipei: Department of Military Affairs, ROC Defense Ministry, 2005.

来光祖 [Lai Guangzu]. 周总理运筹援越扫雷 ["Premier Zhou Organizes the Mine-Sweepings in Vietnam"]. In 援越抗美— 中国支援部队在越南 [*Aid Vietnam and Resist the U.S.: Chinese Supporting Forces in Vietnam*], 曲爱国、鲍明荣、肖祖跃 [edited by Qu Aiguo, Bao Mingrong, and Xiao Zuyue], 296–301. Beijing: Military Science Press, 1995.

李安东 [Li Andong]. 刘华清领导我军武器装备建设两三事 ["Liu Huaqing's Leadership in Development of the Weapons and Equipment of Our Armed Forces"].《百年潮》 [*Hundred Year Tide*], no. 1 (January 2012): 38–47.

李宝祥 [Li Baoxiang]. 援越扫雷的技术保障工作 ["Technological Assistance in Helping Vietnam's Mine-Sweepings"]. In 援越抗美— 中国支援部队在越南 [*Aid Vietnam and Resist the U.S.: Chinese Supporting Forces in Vietnam*], 曲爱国、鲍明荣、肖祖跃 [edited by Qu Aiguo, Bao Mingrong, and Xiao Zuyue], 301–4. Beijing: Military Science Press, 1995.

李东野 [Li Dongye]. 忆大连第一海军学校的创建 ["The Founding of the First Naval Academy in Dalian"]. In 海军回忆史料 [*The Navy: Memoirs and Historical Records*] (Classified), 海军编审委员会编 [edited by Navy Editorial Committee], 2:634–53. Beijing: Ocean Waves Publishing House, 1994.

李作鹏 [Li Zuopeng]. 李作鹏回忆录 [*Memoir of Li Zuopeng*]. Hong Kong: Beixing Publishing House, 2011.

刘柏罗 [Liu Bailuo]. 中央专委会与"两弹一星" ["The 'Special Commission' of the Central Committee for Nuclear Bomb, Missile, and Satellite"]. In 两弹一星—- 共和国丰碑 [*The Bomb, Missile, and Satellite: The Monuments of the Republic*], 解放军总装备部政治部编 [edited by Department of Political Tasks, PLA General Armament Department], 95–116. Beijing: Nine Continents Press, 2001.

刘广凯 [Liu Guangkai]. 刘广凯将军报国忆往 [*Admiral Liu Guangkai's Recollection of Defending the Country*]. Taipei: Institute of Modern China, Academia Sinica, 1994.

刘华清 [Liu Huaqing]. 刘华清回忆录 [*Memoir of Liu Huaqing*]. Beijing: PLA Press, 2004.

刘华清 [Liu Huaqing]. 怀念肖劲光同志在兼任大连海校校长的日子里 ["The Years Comrade Xiao Jinguang Served as the President of Dalian Naval School"]. In 一代元戎 [*Heros of Their General*], 王祖尧编 [edited by Wang Zuyao], 8–16. Beijing: PLA Press, 1991.

刘子庚 [Liu Zigeng]. 新型导弹驱逐舰试航 ["The Trial Voyage of the New Missile Destroyer"]. In 中国人民解放军历史资料丛书: 海军回忆史料 [*PLA Historical Sources Series: The Navy's Memoirs and Records*] (Classified), 海军编审委员会 [edited by the Navy Editorial Committee], 2:1103–13. Beijing: Ocean Wave Publishing House, 1994.

马冠三 [Ma Guansan]. 鏖战东海忆当年 ["Remember the Combat Years in the East China Sea"]. In 三军挥戈战东海 [*Combined Forces Wield Spears and Fight in the East China Sea*], 聂凤智等 [edited by Nie Fengzhi et al.], 26–33. Beijing: PLA Press, 1986.

南平波 [Nan Pingbo]. 潜艇部队初建时期的政治工作 ["The Political Tasks of the Submarine Fleet during Its Formative Years"]. In 海军回忆史料 [*The Navy: Memoirs and History Records*] (Classified), 海军编审委员会编 [edited by Navy Editorial Committee], 2:806–14. Beijing: Ocean Wave Publishing House, 1994.

中国人民解放军历史资料丛书海军编审委会 [Navy Editorial Committee, PLA Historical Documents and Collections Series]. 海军回忆史料 [*The Navy: Memoirs and History Records*] (Classified). Beijing: Ocean Wave Publishing House, 1994.

聂凤智 [Nie Fengzhi]. 海陆空军联合作战解放一江山岛 ["Join Force with the Army and Navy to Liberate the Yijiangshan Island"]. In 中国人民解放军历史资料丛书: 空军回忆史料 [*PLA Historical Source Collection Series: The Air Force: Memoirs and History Records*] (Classified), 空军编审委员会 [edited by Air Force Editorial Committee], 1:231–48. Beijing: PLA Press, 1999.

聂奎聚 [Nie Kuiju]. 扬帆起航向大洋 ["Set Sail to the Oceans"]. In 中国海军走向深蓝, *1980–2020* [*The Chinese Navy Goes to Blue Water, 1980–2010*], 左津玲主编 [edited by Zuo Jinling], 1:60–75. Beijing: PLA Press, 2014.

聂荣臻 [Nie Rongzhen]. 聂荣臻回忆录 [*Memoir of Nie Rongzhen*]. Beijing: People's Press, 2022.

中共中央党史研究室 [Party History Research Division, CCP Central Committee]. 中国共产党历史大事记, 1919–2009 [*Major Historical Events of the CCP, 1919–2009*]. Beijing: CCP Party History Press, 2013.

中共中央党史研究室 [Party History Research Division, CCP Central Committee]. 中国共产党政治工作七十年, 1927–1997 [*Seventy Years of the CCP Political Tasks, 1927–1997*]. Beijing: CCP Central Archival and Manuscript Press, 1998.

彭德怀 [Peng Dehuai]. 彭德怀自述 [*Self-Recollection of Peng Dehuai*]. Beijing: People's Press, 1981.

中国人民解放军历史资料丛书编审委员会 [PLA Historical Documents and Collections Series Compilation Committee]. 解放战争时期国民党军起义投诚（综合册）[*The Revolts and Realignments of the GMD Forces during the War of Liberation*, (Combined Volume)]. Beijing: PLA Press, 1996.

中国人民解放军海军政治部 [PLAN Department of Political Tasks]. 中国人民解放军海军编年史, 1949–1983 [*Chronicle of the PLA Navy, 1949–1983*]. Beijing: PLA Press, 1985.

钱三强 [Qian Sanqiang]. 老一辈革命家关心中国原子核科学发展 ["The Revolutionary Leaders Took Care of China's Nuclear Research and Development"]. In 两弹一星—— 共和国丰碑 [*The Bomb, Missile, and Satellite: The Monuments of the Republic*], 解放军总装备部政治部编 [edited by Department of Political Tasks, PLA General Armament Department], 74–83. Beijing: Nine Continents Press, 2001.

曲爱国、鲍明荣、肖祖跃 [Qu Aiguo, Bao Mingrong, and Xiao Zuyue, eds.]. 援越抗美— 中国支援部队在越南 [*Aid Vietnam and Resist the U.S.: Chinese Supporting Forces in Vietnam*]. Beijing: Military Science Press, 1995.

任秀生 [Ren Xiusheng]. 华东军区海军舰船修造工作的回顾 ["Recollection of ECMR Navy's Shipbuilding and Rebuilt"]. In 海军回忆史料 [*The Navy: Memoirs and History Records*] (Classified), 海军编审委员会编 [edited by Navy Editorial Committee], 2:997–1009. Beijing: Ocean Wave Publishing House, 1994.

田铭、夏三保、陈康明 [Tian Ming, Xia Sanbao, and Chen Kangming]. 越南人民的功臣 ["A Hero for the Vietnamese People"]. In 援越抗美 [*Aid Vietnam and Resist the U.S.*],

曲爱国，鲍明荣，肖祖跃 [edited by Qu Aiguo, Bao Mingrong, and Xiao Zuyue], 313–15. Beijing: Military Science Press, 1995.

王永国 [Wang Yongguo]. 横跨太平洋首次出访美洲四国 ["Across the Pacific: The First Voyage to Four Countries in Americas"]. In 中国海军走向深蓝，1980–2020 [*The Chinese Navy Goes to Blue Water, 1980–2010*], 左津玲主编 [edited by Zuo Jinling], 1:184–201. Beijing: PLA Press, 2014.

王祖尧编 [Wang Zuyao, ed.]. 一代元戎 [*Heros of Their General*]. Beijing: PLA Press, 1991.

吴本湘 [Wu Benxiang]. 037 型反潜护卫舰的设计和生产 ["The Design and Manufacturing of *Type*-037 Submarine Chaser"]. In 中国人民解放军历史资料丛书: 海军回忆史料 [*PLA Historical Sources Series: The Navy's Memoirs and Records*] (Classified), 海军编审委员会 [edited by Navy Editorial Committee], 2:1056–63. Beijing: Ocean Wave Publishing, 1994.

吴瑞林 [Wu Ruilin]. 吴瑞林回忆录 [*Memoirs of Wu Ruilin*]. Beijing: China Archival Publishing, 1995.

夏光 [Xia Guang]. 从华东军区海校到海军联校 ["From East China Military Region's Naval School to PLAN Academy"]. In 海军回忆史料 [*The Navy: Memoirs and History Records*] (Classified), 海军编审委会 [edited by Navy Editorial Committee], 2:621–33. Beijing: Ocean Wave Publishing House, 1994.

肖劲光 [Xiao Jinguang]. 肖劲光回忆录 [*Memoir of Xiao Jinguang*]. Beijing: PLA Press, 1988.

肖劲光 [Xiao Jinguang]. 肖劲光回忆录（续集） [*Memoir of Xiao Jinguang* (Sequel)]. Beijing: PLA Press, 1989.

徐向前 [Xu Xiangqian]. 历史的回顾 [*Recollection of the History*]. Beijing: PLA Press, 1987.

杨国宇 [Yang Guoyu]. 天涯迎飞舟 ["Receiving the Rocket on the Other Side of the World"]. In 中国海军走向深蓝，*1980–2020* [*The Chinese Navy Goes to Blue Water, 1980–2010*], 左津玲主编 [edited by Zuo Jinling], 1:12–23. Beijing: PLA Press, 2014.

杨怀庆 [Yang Huaiqing]. 回忆邓小平 [*Remembering Deng Xiaoping*]. Beijing: CCP Central Archival and Manuscript Press, 1998.

叶飞 [Ye Fei]. 叶飞回忆录 [*Memoirs of Ye Fei*]. Beijing: PLA Press, 1988.

章长蓉 [Zhang Changrong]. 回顾八二三台海战役之海军作战 ["Recollection of the Naval Battles in the 8-23 Battle of the Taiwan Strait"]. 海军学术 [*Naval Studies*] 52, no. 5 (2018): 6–15.

张力等 [Zhang Li et al.]. 徐学海先生访问记录 ["Interview of Vice Admiral Xu Xuehai"]. In 海军人物访问记录 [*Interview Records of Naval Admirals*], 张力、曾金兰编 [edited by Zhang Li and Zeng Jinlan]. Taipei: Institute of Modern China, Academia Sinica, 2002.

张世鸿、张炎平、吴迪 [Zhang Shihong, Zhang Yanping, and Wu Di]. 胡志明小道上的701天: 越战见闻录 [*701 Days through the Ho Chi Minh Trail: Vietnam War in My Eyes*]. Beijing: PLA Literature Press, 2007.

张寿瀛 [Zhang Shouying]. 赴越扫雷的回顾 ["Reflection of Mine-Sweeping Experience in Vietnam"]. In 援越抗美 [*Aid Vietnam and Resist the U.S.*], 曲爱国、鲍明荣、肖祖跃

[edited by Qu Aiguo, Bao Mingrong, and Xiao Zuyue], 305–11. Beijing: Military Science Press, 1995.

张万年 [Zhang Wannian]. 张万年自传 [*Autobiography of Zhang Wannian*]. Beijing: PLA Press, 2011.

张序三 [Zhang Xusan]. 忆海军舰艇远航航海实习 ["Recollection of a Naval Oceanic Training Sail"]. In 中国海军走向深蓝，*1980–2020* [*The Chinese Navy Goes to Blue Water, 1980–2010*], 左津玲主编 [edited by Zuo Jinling], 1:24–33. Beijing: PLA Press, 2014.

张毅民 [Zhang Yimin]. 舰对舰导弹的试制 ["Testing the Ship-to-Ship Missile"]. In 中国人民解放军历史资料丛书: 海军回忆史料 [*PLA Historical Sources Series: The Navy's Memoirs and Records*] (Classified), 海军编审委员会 [edited by Navy Editorial Committee], 2:1064–76. Beijing: Ocean Wave Publishing, 1994

张驭涛 [Zhang Yutao]. 新中国军事大事纪要 [*Chronicle of Major Military Events of China*]. Beijing: Military Science Press, 1998.

赵国臣 [Zhao Guochen]. 难忘首次南极考察 ["Unforgettable the First Expedition to the South Pole"]. In 中国海军走向深蓝，*1980–2020* [*The Chinese Navy Goes to Blue Water, 1980–2010*], 左津玲主编 [edited by Zuo Jinling], 1:34–59. Beijing: PLA Press, 2014.

郑明 [Zheng Ming]. 难忘的回忆与珍贵的启迪 ["Unforgettable Memory and Valuable"]. 现代舰船 [*Modern Ships*], no. 3 (2005): 1–6.

周官英 [Zhou Guan-ying]. 忆往事，话太平: 记太平军舰遇伏始末 ["Remember the History: A Complete Story of How *Taiping* Was Ambushed"]. 海军学刊 [*Journal of the Navy*] 44, no. 1 (February 2010): 106–14.

左津玲主编 [Zuo Jinling, ed.]. 中国海军走向深蓝，*1980–2020* [*The Chinese Navy Goes to Blue Water, 1980–2010*]. Beijing: PLA Press, 2014.

***Books, Articles, and Other Materials [书刊资料]***

抗日战争纪念网 [Anti-Japanese War Memorial Network]. 中国航母第一人: 陈绍宽的未竟航母梦 ["China's First Aircraft Carrier: Chen Shaokuan's Unfulfilled Carrier Dream"]. October 6, 2018. https://www.krzzjn.com/show-1475-82630.html.

陈冠任 [Chen Guanren]. 十大元帅: 解放军十大统帅的历史 [*Ten Marshals: History of the Top Ten Leaders of the PLA*]. Beijing: CCP Party History Press, 2020.

陈海宏 [Chen Haihong]. 马汉和他的海权论 ["Mahan and His Sea Power Theory"]. 山东师范大学学报（人文社会科学版） [*Journal of Shandong Normal University (Humanities and Social Sciences Edition)*] 56, no. 5 (2011): 93–115.

陈万军、袁华智、司彦文 [Chen Wanjun, Yuan Huazhi, and Si Yanwen]. 春风鼓浪好杨帆—— 江泽民主席关心人民海军现代化建设记事 ["Ride the Spring Wind and Waves: Historical Records of President Jiang Zemin's Efforts in the Modernization of the People's Navy"]. In 共和国领袖与海军 [*Chinese Leaders and the Navy*], 吴殿卿、袁永安、and 赵小平编 [edited by Wu Dianqing, Yuan Yong'an, and Zhao Xiaoping], 299–306. Beijing: Ocean Wave Publishing, 2000.

迟浩田 [Chi Haotian]. 前言 ["Introduction"]. In 中国海军走向深蓝，1980–2020 [*The Chinese Navy Goes to Blue Water, 1980–2010*], 左津玲主编[edited by Zuo Jinling], vii–viii. Beijing: PLA Press, 2014.

储峰 [Chu Feng]. 二十世纪50 年代中苏军事关系研究 ["Sino-Soviet Military Relations in the 1950s"]. 中共中央党校2006 年博士论文 [PhD diss., CCP Central Party University, Beijing, 2006].

《当代中国》编辑委员会 [*Contemporary China* Compilation Committee]. 当代中国的国防科技事业 [*Technology and Science of National Defense in Contemporary China*]. Beijing: Contemporary China Press, 1992.

崔向华、陈大鹏 [Cui Xianghua and Chen Dapeng]. 陶勇将军传 [*Biography of Vice Admiral Tao Yong*]. Beijing: PLA Press, 1989.

戴旭 [Dai Xu]. 中国航母 [*China's Aircraft Carriers*]. Beijing: Chinese Literature Publishing House, 2009.

地久、克峰 [Di Jiu and Ke Feng]. 潮涨潮落: 国共角逐台湾海峡纪实 [*Ebb and Flow: Records of the CCP-GMD Confrontations in the Taiwan Strait*]. Beijing: China Industrial and Commercial Publishing House, 1996.

丁伟 [Ding Wei]. 在移动的国土上: 人民海军的创建与发展 ["On the Floating Territory: Creation and Development of the People's Navy"]. In 军旗飘飘: 新中国五十年军事大事述实 [*PLA Flag Fluttering: The Facts about China's Major Military Events in the Past Fifty Years*], 军事科学院军事历史研究部 [by Military History Research Division, PLA Academy of Military Science (AMS)], 1:90–105. Beijing: PLA Press, 1999.

丁伟 [Ding Wei]. 拨乱反正的先声——1975 年军委扩大会议的召开 ["The Prelude of Bringing Order out of Chaos—The 1975 CMC Enlarged Meeting"]. In 军旗飘飘: 新中国五十年军事大事述实 [*PLA Flag Fluttering: The Facts about China's Major Military Events in the Past Fifty Years*], 军事科学院军事历史研究部 [edited by Military History Research Division, PLA Academy of Military Science (AMS)], 2:591–604. Beijing: PLA Press, 1999.

董宝存、李维坤 [Dong Baocun and Li Weikun]. 刘华清与西沙设防、南沙夺礁 ["Liu Huaqing's Defense of Paracel and Battle of Spratly"]. 党史博览 [*Party Historical Review*] (2012): 6–13.

东方鹤 [Dong Fanghe]. 张爱萍传 [*Biography of Zhang Aiping*]. Beijing: People's Press, 2000.

高皋、严家其 [Gao Gao and Yan Jiaqi]. 文化大革命十年史, 1966–1976 [*Ten-Year History of the Cultural Revolution, 1966–1976*]. Tianjin: Tianjin People's Press, 1986.

高文谦 [Gao Wenqian]. 晚年周恩来 [*Zhou Enlai's Later Years*]. Hong Kong: Mingjing Publishing, 2003.

高晓星等 [Gao Xiaoxing et al.]. 中国人民解放军海军 [*The PLA Navy*]. Beijing: China Intercontinental Press, 2012.

高月 [Gao Yue]. 近代中国海权思想浅析 ["Modern China's Sea Power Thoughts"]. 浙江学刊 [*Academic Journal of Zhejiang*], no. 6 (2013): 1–17.

贡力 [Gong Li]. 跨越鸿沟: 1969–1979 年中美关系的演变 [*Bridging the Chasm: The Evolution of Sino-American Relations, 1969–1979*]. Zhengzhou: Henan People's Press, 1992.

古越 [Gu Yue]. 邓小平兵法 [*Deng Xiaoping's Art of War*]. Beijing: United Press, 2015.

郭金炎 [Guo Jinyan]. 大海之子邓兆祥 [*Son of the Sea: Deng Zhaoxiang*]. Beijing: Ocean Publishing House, 2004.

郭明 [Guo Ming]. 中越关系演变四十年 [*Deterioration of the Sino-Vietnam Relations in the Past Forty Years*]. Nanning: Guangxi People's Press, 1992.

韩怀智 [Han Huaizhi]. 当代中国军队的军事工作 [*Military Affairs of Contemporary China's Armed Forces*]. Beijing: China's Social Science Press, 1989.

何迪 [He Di]. 台海危机和中国对金门、马祖政策的形成 ["Taiwan Strait Crisis and China's Policy-Making toward Jinmen and Mazu"]. 美国研究 [*American Studies*] 3, no. 1 (Fall 1988): 19–45.

何森 [He Sen]. 海上较量: 解放军海军取得八六海战与崇武海战胜利 [*Battles at Seas: PLA Navy's Victories of the Battles of the August Sixth and Chongwu*]. Jilin: Jilin Publishing, 2011.

贺茂之 [He Maozhi]. 张爱萍 ["Zhang Aiping"]. In 中国人民解放军高级将领传 [*Biographies of the PLA's High-Ranking Generals*], 中国人民解放军高级将领传编审委员会编著 [edited by PLA *Biographies of the High-Ranking Generals* Editorial Committee], 9:417–52. Beijing: PLA Press, 2007.

黄春梅 [Huang Chunmei]. 六四戒严军官李晓明: 解放军镇压是犯罪行为 ["Martial Law Officer Li Xiaoming: PLA's Suppression Was War Crime"]. 自由亚洲电台 [*Radio Free Asia*], May 28, 2019. https://www.rfa.org/mandarin/yataibaodao/renquanfazhi/hcm-05282019081359.html.

黄耀、严敬棠 [Huang Yao and Yan Jingtang]. 林彪一生 [*Lin Biao: A Life*]. Beijing: PLA Literature Press, 2004.

胡波 [Hu Bo]. 后马汉时代的中国海权 [*China's Sea Power in the Post-Mahan Era*]. Beijing: Ocean Waves Publishing House, 2018.

胡俊修 [Hu Junxiu]. 近代国人海权观念的演变 ["Chinese Evolution of Sea Power Concept in Modern China"]. 光明日报 [*Guangming Daily*], February 8, 2021, 12–14.

霍小勇 [Huo Xiaoyong]. 海军战略学 [*Study of the Naval Strategy*]. Beijing: PLA National Defense University, 2006.

胡彦林 [Hu Yanlin]. 威震海疆: 人民海军征战纪实 [*Shocking the Sea: Records of the People's Navy's Battles*]. Beijing: National Defense University Press, 1996.

日本海人社编 [Japanese Oceanic Association, ed.]. 英国航空母舰史 [*History of British Aircraft Carriers*]. Qingdao: Qingdao Publishing House, 2013.

俊涛 [Jun Tao]. 炮击金门 ["Bombardment of Jinmen"]. 中华传奇 [*Legacy of China*], no. 179 (November 2004): 64–80.

兰波 [Lan Bo]. 改革开放以来中国海权认识演进研究 ["Study of Cognitive Process of China's Sea Rights since Its Reform and Opening Up"]. PhD diss., College of History and Culture, University of Shandong, Ji'nan, 2017.

雷华建、王冀城 [Lei Huajian and Wang Jicheng]. 新中国海战内幕 [*Inside Story of New China's Naval Warfare*]. Beijing: China International Translations and Publishing House, 1993.

李保忠 [Li Baozhong]. 中外军事制度比较 [*Comparative Study between Chinese and Foreign Military Systems*]. Beijing: China Commercial Press, 2003.

李丹慧 [Li Danhui]. 中苏在援越抗美问题上的矛盾与冲突（1965–1972） ["Conflicts between China and the Soviet Union in Their Efforts to Aid Vietnam and Resist America,

1965–1972"]. In 冷战与中国 [*The Cold War and China*], 章百家、牛军主编 [edited by Zhang Baijia and Niu Jun], 372–414. Beijing: World Knowledge Publishing, 2002.

李健 [Li Jian]. 台海两岸战事回顾 [*History of the Military Conflicts over the Taiwan Strait*]. Beijing: China Literature Publishing, 1996.

李可、郝生章 [Li Ke and Hao Shengzhang]. 文化大革命中的人民解放军 [*The PLA in the Cultural Revolution*]. Beijing: CCP Party Historical Materials Press, 1989.

李琼 [Li Qiong]. 海上长城：中国人民解放军海军六十年 [*The Great Wall at Sea: Sixty Years of the PLA Navy*]. Jilin: Jilin Publishing Group, 2011.

李曙光 [Li Shuguang]. 刘华清 [*Liu Huaqing*]. Beijing: Great Wall Publishing, 2005.

李铁民 [Li Tiemin]. 邓小平海军建设思想研究 [*Studies on Deng Xiaoping's Thought of Naval Development*]. Beijing: National Defense University, 1997.

李忠效 [Li Zhongxiao]. "瓦良格"号航母来中国— 中国航母"辽宁舰"前世真相调查 [*Varyag Coming to China: An Investigation of the True Background of Chinese Aircraft Carrier Liaoning*]. Beijing: Aiming Aihua Co., 2019.

刘亮 [Liu Liang]. 岸防劲旅：中国人民解放军海军岸防部队 [*Strong Coastal Defense: PLAN Coastal Defense Forces*]. Beijing: Blue Sky Publishing House, 2014.

刘明福 [Liu Mingfu]. 为什么解放军能赢 [*Why the PLA Can Win*]. Beijing: PAP Press, 2012.

刘錫贵 [Liu Xigui]. 在建设海洋强国的伟大征途中铸就辉煌 ["Achieve Glory during the Great Cause of Building a Strong Country with Sea Power"]. 中国海洋报 [*China Maritime News*], July 23, 2014, A-1.

刘新博 [Liu Xinbo]. 刘华清海洋战略思想研究 ["Interpretation of Liu Huaqing's Maritime Strategic Thinking"]. Master's thesis, College of History and Culture, University of Heilongjiang, Harbin, 2015.

刘亚洲 [Liu Yazhou]. 厚重的人生，炫目的光彩 ["Significant Life with Shining Colors"]. 解放军报 [*PLA Daily*], January 6, 2005.

刘子明 [Liu Ziming]. 中国近代军事思想史 [*History of Military Thoughts in Modern China*]. Nanchang: Jiangxi People's Press, 1997.

刘永路 [Liu Yonglu]. 刘华清将军与大连舰艇学院 [Fleet Admiral Liu Huaqing and Dalian Naval Academy]. 党史纵横 [*Overview of the Party History*], no. 3 (2013): 7–8.

卢辉 [Lu Hui]. 三军战一江 [*Joint Operation against Yijiangshan*]. Beijing: China United Literature Publishing House, 2014.

罗时叙 [Luo Shixu]. 由蜜月到反目：苏联专家在中国 [*From Honeymoon to Betrayal—Soviet Experts in China*]. Beijing: World Knowledge Press, 1999.

罗选优 [Luo Xuanyou]. 中越台海战争征战纪实 [*Battle Records of the Sino-Vietnam and Taiwan Strait Wars*]. Urumqi: Xinjiang People's Press, 2004.

陆其明 [Lu Qiming]. 加速人民海军建设：朱德委员长视察海军新型舰艇纪实 [Accelerate the Naval Construction: Report on Congressional Chairman Zhu De's Visit of New Warship]. In 共和国领袖与海军 [*National Leaders and China's Navy*], 吴殿卿、袁永安、赵小平主编 [edited by Wu Dianqing, Yuan Yong'an, and Zhao Xiaoping], 191–96. Beijing: Ocean Waves Publishing House, 2000

陆其明 [Lu Qiming]. 奇袭太平号：人民海军鱼雷快艇首次海战纪实 ["Ambush Taiping: The Story of the First Battle of the PLAN Torpedo Boats"]. In 三军挥戈战东海 [*Combined*

*Forces Wield Spears and Fight in the East China Sea*], 聂凤智等 [edited by Nie Fengzhi et al.], 194–202. Beijing: PLA Press, 1985.

军事科学院军事历史研究部 [Military History Research Division, PLA Academy of Military Science (AMS)]. 军旗飘飘: 新中国五十年军事大事述实 [*PLA Flag Fluttering: The Facts about China's Major Military Events in the Past Fifty Years*]. Beijing: PLA Press, 1999.

军事科学院军事历史研究部 [Military History Research Division, PLA AMS]. 中国人民解放军的八十年 [*Eighty Years of the Chinese PLA*]. Beijing: Military Science Press, 2007.

军事科学院军事历史研究部 [Military History Research Division, PLA AMS]. 中国人民解放军全国解放战争史 [*History of the PLA in the Chinese Liberation War*]. Beijing: Military Science Press, 1997.

军事科学院军事历史研究部 [Military History Research Division, PLA AMS]. 中国人民解放军的七十年 [*Seventy Years of the Chinese PLA*]. Beijing: Military Science Press, 1997.

军事科学院军事历史研究部 [Military History Research Division, PLA AMS]. 中国人民解放军战史 [*War History of the Chinese People's Liberation Army*]. Beijing: Military Science Press, 1987.

中国人民革命军事博物馆 [National Military Museum of Chinese People's Revolution]. 中国战争发展史 [*The Historical Development of Chinese Warfare*]. Beijing: People's Press, 2002.

中国人民解放军军兵种历史丛书海军史编委 [Naval History Compilation Committee, PLA Services History Series]. 海军史 [*History of the Navy*]. Beijing: PLA Press, 1989.

新华社 [New China News]. 胡锦涛会见海军代表 ["Hu Jintao Meets Naval Representatives"]. 中国新闻网 [*China News*], December 28, 2006. www.chinanews.com.cn/gn/news/2006/12-28.

新华社 [New China News Agency]. 人民海军已发展成为合成军种, 近海作战力量初具现代化规模 ["The PLAN Developed into a Combined Branch, Achieving Near Sea Combat Capability in Modern Warfare"]. 人民日报 [*People's Daily*], April 24, 1989, 1.

《聂荣臻传》编写组 [*Nie Rongzhen Biography* Compilation Team]. 聂荣臻传 [*Biography of Nie Rongzhen*]. 2nd ed. Beijing: Contemporary China Press, 2006.

欧阳开宇 [Oyang Kaiyu]. 刘华清对海军发展有巨大历史性贡献 ["Liu Huaqing Made Great Historical Contribution to the Navy"]. 中国网络电视台 [China Net TV Station], January 14, 2011. www.news.cntv.cn/china/20110114/105861.shtml.

《彭德怀传》编写组[*Peng Dehuai Biography* Compilation Team]. 彭德怀传 [*Biography of Peng Dehuai*]. 2nd ed. Beijing: Contemporary China Press, 2006.

《彭德怀传》编写组 [*Peng Dehuai Biography* Compilation Team]. 一个真正的人: 彭德怀 [*A Real Man: Peng Dehuai*]. Beijing: People's Press, 1994.

彭继超 [Peng Jichao]. 东方巨响: 中国核武器试验纪实 [*Thunderbolt from the East: Historical Facts of China's Development of Nuclear Weapons*]. 2nd ed. Beijing: CCP Central Party University Press, 2005.

中国人民解放军高级将领传编审委员会编著 [PLA *Biographies of the High-Ranking Generals* Editorial Committee, ed.]. 中国人民解放军高级将领传 [*Biographies of the PLA's High-Ranking Generals*]. Beijing: PLA Press, 2008.

国防大学《战史简编》编写组 [PLA Defense University's *Concise War History* Compilation Team]. 中国人民解放军战史简编 [*Concise History of the PLA's Wars*]. 4th ed. Beijing: PLA Press, 2001.

中国人民海军总部 [PLAN General Headquarters]. 中国人民解放军海军编年史，1949–1983 [*The Chronicle of the PLA Navy, 1949–1983*]. Beijing: PLAN Press, 1995.

钱海皓 [Qian Haihao]. 军队组织编制学教程 [*Study of Military Organization and Formation: Graduate Curriculum*]. Beijing: Military Science Press, 2001.

秦天、霍小勇 [Qin Tian and Huo Xiaoyong]. 悠悠深蓝：中华海权史 [*Deep Blue: A History of Chinese Sea Power*]. Beijing: New China Press, 2013.

沈卫平 [Shen Weiping]. 8.23 炮击金门 [*The August 23 Bombardment of Jinmen*]. Beijing: Huayi Publishing House, 1999.

沈志华 [Shen Zhihua]. 毛泽东、斯大林与朝鲜战争 [*Mao Zedong, Stalin, and the Korean War*]. Guangzhou: Guangdong People's Press, 2004.

沈志华 [Shen Zhihua]. 苏联专家在中国（1948–1960） [*Soviet Experts in China, 1948–1960*]. Beijing: China International Broadcasting Publishing House, 2003.

施昌学 [Shi Changxue]. 刘华清的航母梦 ["Liu Huaqing's Carrier's Dream"]. 中国政协网 [*China CPPCC Net*], May 7, 2020. www.cppcc.gov.cn/zxww/2020/05/08/ARTI1588900134352215.shtml.

施昌学 [Shi Changxue]. 海军司令刘华清 [*Naval Commander Liu Huaqing*]. Beijing: Long March Press, 2013.

石家铸 [Shi Jiazhu]. 海权与中国 [*Sea Power and China*]. Beijing: Three Unions Books, 2008.

新浪新闻 [Sina News]. 关键时刻，刘华清干的三件大事 ["Liu Huaqing's Three Big Actions at the Critical Moments"]. 新浪 [*Sina*], September 29, 2016. www.news.sina.cn/gn/2016-09-29/detail-ifxwkvys2331162.d.html.

宋万贤 [Song Wanxian]. 毛泽东与张爱萍上将 ["Mao Zedong and General Zhang Aiping"]. In 毛泽东与海军将领 [*Mao Zedong and Naval Admirals*], 吴殿卿等 [edited by Wu Dianqing et al.], 85–98. Beijing: PLA Literature Press, 1999.

苏振兰 [Su Zhenlan]. 刘华清主持大连海军学院 ["Liu Huaqing Administrates Dalian Naval Academy"]. 党史纵览 [*Review of the Party History*], no. 8 (2014): 10–16.

唐秀颖 [Tang Xiue]. 锷刺长天：记火箭技术专家屠守锷 ["A Sword Thrusts the Sky: Story of Rocket Expert Tu Shoue"]. In 两弹一星—— 共和国丰碑 [*The Bomb, Missile, and Satellite: The Monuments of the Republic*], 解放军总装备部政治部编 [edited by Department of Political Tasks, PLA General Armament Department], 361–72. Beijing: Nine Continents Press, 2001.

陶汉章 [Tao Hanzhang]. 孙子兵法概论 [*A General Interpretation of Sunzi's Art of War*]. Beijing: PLA Press, 1991.

田甜 [Tian Tian]. 刘华清海权思想与近海防御战略 ["Liu Huaqing's Thought of Sea Power and the Strategy of Near Sea Defense"]. 军事思想史研究 [*History Studies of Military Thoughts*], no. 4 (2017): 64–73.

美国之音 [Voice of America]. 《六四事件中的戒严部队》出版 ["Publication of Martial Law Forces in the June Fourth Incident"], May 29, 2009. https://www.voachinese.com/a/a-21-w2009-05-29-voa31-61399277/1030984.html.

王成志 [Wang Chengzhi]. 潮涨潮落：打击海上窜扰之敌 ["Ebb and Flow: Defeat the Enemy Force at Seas"]. In 军旗飘飘：新中国五十年军事大事述实 [*PLA Flag Fluttering: The Facts about China's Major Military Events in the Past Fifty Years*], 军事科学院军事历史研究部编 [edited by Military History Research Division, PLA Academy of Military Science (AMS)], 2:427–44. Beijing: PLA Press, 1999.

王蜀宁 [Wang Shuning]. 八六海战评析 ["Analysis of the August 6 Naval Battle"]. 海军学术 [*Naval Studies*] 42, no. 6 (December 2008): 26–38.

王太平 [Wang Taiping]. 中华人民共和国外交史，1970–1978 [*Diplomatic History of the People's Republic of China, 1970–1978*]. Beijing: World Knowledge Press, 1999.

王焰 [Wang Yan]. 彭德怀传 [*Biography of Peng Dehuai*]. Beijing: Contemporary China Press, 1993.

王玉彬 [Wang Yubin]. 第二野战军 [*The Second Field Army*]. Beijing: Long March Press, 2012.

吴殿卿 [Wu Dianqing]. 蓝色档案：新中国海军大事纪实 [*Blue Archives: The Major Events of the Chinese Navy*]. Taiyuan: Shanxi Publishing Group, 2015.

吴殿卿 [Wu Dianqing]. 组建海军重大决策的历史事实 ["Historical Facts on Important Decisions to Establish the PLA Navy"]. 人民海军 [*People's Navy*], no. 9 (October 2002): 1–13.

吴殿卿 [Wu Dianqing]. 刘华清的航母情结 ["Liu Huaqing's Life and Heart on Aircraft Carrier"]. 党史博览 [*Chronicle of the Party's History*], no. 9 (2011): 1–6.

吴殿卿 [Wu Dianqing]. 毛泽东与肖劲光大将 ["Mao Zedong and Fleet Admiral Xiao Jinguang"]. In 毛泽东与海军将领 [*Mao Zedong and Naval Admirals*], 吴殿卿、袁永安、赵小平主编 [edited by Wu Dianqing, Yuan Yong'an, and Zhao Xiaoping], 1–35. Beijing: PLA Literature Press, 1999.

吴殿卿 [Wu Dianqing]. 总司令的"海军月" ["The 'Naval Month' of the Commander in Chief"]. In 共和国领袖与海军 [*PRC National Leaders and the Navy*], 吴殿卿、袁永安、赵小平主编 [edited by Wu Dianqing, Yuan Yong'an, and Zhao Xiaoping], 27–33. Beijing: Ocean Wave Publishing House, 2000.

吴殿卿 [Wu Dianqing]. 乘长风破万里浪 ["Ride a Long Wind and Thousands of Miles of Waves"]. In 共和国领袖与海军 [*National Leaders and China's Navy*], 吴殿卿、袁永安、赵小平主编 [edited by Wu Dianqing, Yuan Yong'an, and Zhao Xiaoping], 222–34. Beijing: Ocean Waves Publishing House, 2000.

吴殿卿 [Wu Dianqing]. 叶飞 ["Ye Fei"]. In 中国人民解放军高级将领传 [*Biographies of the Leading Generals of the Chinese People's Liberation Army*], 《中国人民解放军高级将领传》编审委员会编著 [edited by *Biographies of the PLA's High-Ranking Generals* Editorial Committee. Beijing: PLA Press, 2007.

吴殿卿 [Wu Dianqing]. 周恩来、朱德指导制定第一个海军三年建设计划 ["Zhou Enlai and Zhu De Instruct to Make the Navy's First Three-Year Development Plan"]. 铁军 [*Iron Force*], no. 3 (2013): 18–29.

吴殿卿、袁永安、赵小平主编 [Wu Dianqing, Yuan Yong'an, and Zhao Xiaoping, eds.]. 毛泽东与海军将领 [*Mao Zedong and Naval Admirals*]. Beijing: PLA Literature Press, 1999.

吴殿卿、袁永安、赵小平主编 [Wu Dianqing, Yuan Yong'an, and Zhao Xiaoping, eds.]. 共和国领袖与海军 [*PRC National Leaders and the Navy*]. Beijing: Ocean Wave Publishing House, 2000.

吴杰章、苏小东、程志发 [Wu Jiezhang, Su Xiaodong, and Cheng Zhifa]. 中国近代海军史 [*A History of the Modern Chinese Navy*]. Beijing: PLA Press, 1989.

吴仁华 [Wu Renhua]. 六四事件中的戒严部队 [*The Martial Law Forces in the June Fourth Incident*]. Los Angeles: Truth Publishing House, 2009.

吴瑞虎 [Wu Ruihu]. 三代驱逐舰启程中南海—— 党和国家领导人关心驱逐舰部队建设记事 ["Three Generations of Destroyers Started from Zhongnanhai: History Shows How CCP and PRC Leaders Cared about Construction of the Destroyer Fleet"]. In 共和国领袖与海军 [*National Leaders and China's Navy*], 吴殿卿、袁永安、赵小平主编 [edited by Wu Dianqing, Yuan Yong'an, and Zhao Xiaoping], 285–92. Beijing: Ocean Waves Publishing House, 2000.

吴胜利、刘晓江 [Wu Shengli and Liu Xiaojiang]. 海军发展壮大是他一生的牵挂 ["He Spent Whole Life on a Strong Navy"]. In 海军司令刘华清 [*Naval Commander Liu Huaqing*], 施昌学 [by Shi Changxue], 1–9. Beijing: Long March Press, 2013.

萧石忠 [Xiao Shizhong]. 扑灭印度支那战火的一次重要军事行动 ["An Important Military Operation to Put Out War Flames in Indochina"]. In 军旗飘飘：新中国五十年军事大事述实 [*PLA Flag Fluttering: The Facts about China's Major Military Events in the Past Fifty Years*], 军事科学院军事历史研究部 [edited by Military History Research Division, PLA Academy of Military Science (AMS)], 2:445–62. Beijing: PLA Press, 1999.

《星火燎原》编辑部 [*Xinghuo liaoyuan* Composition Department]. 中国人民解放军将帅名录 [*PLA Marshals and Generals*]. Beijing: PLA Press, 1992.

新华社 [Xinhua News Agency]. 中国海军出击亚丁湾 ["The Chinese Navy Dispatched to the Gulf of Aden"], 参考消息 [*Reference News*], December 27, 2008.

新华社 [Xinhua News Agency]. 胡锦涛出席庆祝人民海军成立60 周年海上阅兵活动 ["Hu Jintao Attends the Naval Parade to Celebrate the People's Navy's 60th Birthday"]. 中国台湾网 [*China's Taiwan News*], April 24, 2009. ww.taiwan.cn/xwzx/jrbd/200904/t20090424_876110.htm.

新华社 [Xinhua News Agency]. 人民海军七十年：党中央关心人民海军建设发展纪实 ["Seventy Years of the People's Navy: The Historical Facts of the Party Center's Support to Construction and Development of the People's Navy"]. 新华社新媒体 [*New China's News Media*], April 22, 2019. www.baijiahao.baidu.com/s?id=1631510382706012124&wfr.

许峰源 [Xu Feng-Yuan]. 迁台初期台湾对沿海岛屿的防御策略调整（1950–1955 ） ["Adjustment of Taiwan's Outer Islands Defense Strategy (1950–1955)"]. 档案半年刊 [*Archives Semiannual*] 21, no. 1 (June 2022): 28–43.

徐焰 [Xu Yan]. 金门之战 [*The Battle of Jinmen*]. Beijing: China's Radio and Television Publishing House, 1992.

徐焰 [Xu Yan]. 中国由注重"海防"变为争取"海权" ["China Shifts Its Focus from 'Coastal Defense' to 'Sea Power'"]. In 徐焰讲稿自选集 [*Self-Selected Lectures of Xu Yan*], 203–11. Beijing: National Defense University Press, 2014.

徐焰 [Xu Yan]. 徐焰讲稿自选集 [*Self-Selected Lectures of Xu Yan*]. Beijing: National Defense University Press, 2014.

徐焰 [Xu Yan]. 中苏为何从"蜜月"走向敌对 ["Why Did Sino-Soviet Relations Change from 'Honeymoon' to Hostility"]. In 徐焰讲稿自选集 [*Self-Selected Lectures of Xu Yan*], 259–72. Beijing: National Defense University Press, 2014.

杨德昌 [Yang Dechang]. 海权！中华海权！ [*Sea Power! China's Sea Power!*]. Beijing: Three Alliance Publishing House, 2022.

杨贵华 [Yang Guihua]. 准备"早打、大打、打核战争"的历史回顾—— 全国大备战史末 ["A Historical Reflection on Preparing an Early, Large-Scale, and Nuclear War—the Whole Story of Nationwide War Mobilization"]. In 军旗飘飘： 新中国五十年军事大事述实 [*PLA Flag Fluttering: The Facts about China's Major Military Events in the Past Fifty Years*], 军事科学院军事历史研究部 [edited by Military History Research Division, PLA Academy of Military Science (AMS)], 2:559–78. Beijing: PLA Press, 1999.

杨国宇 [Yang Guoyu]. 当代中国海军 [*Contemporary Chinese Navy*]. Beijing: China's Social Science Press, 1987.

杨奎松 [Yang Kuisong]. 从珍宝岛事件到中美关系缓和 ["From the Zhenboa Island Incident to Sino-American Rapprochement"]. 党史研究资料 [*Party History Research Sources*], no. 12 (1997): 1–9.

杨奎松 [Yang Kuisong]. 美苏冷战的起源对中国革命的影响 ["Origins of the U.S.-Soviet Cold War and Its Impact on China's Revolution]. In 冷战与中国 [*The Cold War and China*], 章百家、牛军主编 [edited by Zhang Baijia and Niu Jun], 51–88. Beijing: World Knowledge Publishing, 2002.

杨肇林 [Yang Zhaolin]. 毛泽东与苏振华上将 ["Mao Zedong and Admiral Su Zhenhua"]. In 毛泽东与海军将领 [*Mao Zedong and His Admirals*], 吴殿卿、袁永安、赵小平主编 [edited by Wu Dianqing, Yuan Yong'an, and Zhao Xiaoping], 65–84. Beijing: PLA Literature Publishing, 1999.

杨忠义 [Yang Zhongyi]. 苏联专家与中国海军航空兵 [*Soviet Experts and Chinese Naval Aviation*]. Beijing: PLA Press, 2013.

杨舟 [Yang Zhou]. 中国的戈尔什科夫: 红色马汉刘华清 ["China's Gorshkov and 'Red Mahan': Liu Huaqing"]. 新华网 [Xinhua Net], July 2013. www.xinhuanet.com/book/xinshu/201307/.

叶永烈 [Ye Yonglie]. 高层较量 [*Power Struggle at the Top*]. Urumqi: Xinjiang People's Press, 2004.

余玮 [Yu Wei]. 布衣将军刘华清 ["Commoner Admiral: Liu Huaqing"]. 党史博览 [*Chronicle of the Party History*], no. 7 (2004): 1–5.

张爱萍 [Zhang Aiping]. 中国人民解放军 [*The Chinese People's Liberation Army*]. Beijing: Contemporary China Press, 1994.

章百家、牛军主编 [Zhang Baijia and Niu Jun, eds.]. 冷战与中国 [*The Cold War and China*]. Beijing: World Knowledge Publishing, 2002.

张胜 [Zhang Sheng]. 从战争中走来 [*Coming from the War*]. Beijing: Three Alliances Publishing, 2013.

张驭涛 [Zhang Yutao]. 新中国军事大事纪要 [*Chronicle of Major Military Events of China*]. Beijing: Military Science Press, 1998.

张召忠 [Zhang Zhaozhong]. 百年航母 [*Aircraft Carriers in 100 Years*]. Guangzhou: Guangdong Economy Publishing House, 2011.

赵建国 [Zhao Jianguo]. 清季报刊对海权论的传播 ["The Spread of Concept Sea Power Theory on Press in Late Qing Period"]. 学术月刊 [*Academic Monthly*] 55, no. 6 (2023): 193–205.

赵小平 [Zhao Xiaoping]. 坐镇总参谋部，决胜南中国海—— 叶剑英副主席指挥西沙海战纪实 ["Command in the DGS and Victory in the South China Sea—Records of Vice Chairman Ye Jianying's Commanding the Battle of Paracel"]. In 共和国领袖与海军 [*PRC National Leaders and the Navy*], 吴殿卿、袁永安、赵小平主编 [edited by Wu Dianqing, Yuan Yong'an, and Zhao Xiaoping], 183–90. Beijing: Ocean Wave Publishing House, 2000.

赵小平 [Zhao Xiaoping]. 毛泽东与吴瑞林中将 ["Mao Zedong and Lieutenant General Wu Ruilin"]. In 毛泽东与海军将领 [*Mao Zedong and His Admirals and Generals*], 吴殿卿、袁永安、赵小平主编 [edited by Wu Dianqing, Yuan Yong'an, and Zhao Xiaoping], 179–208. Beijing: PLA Literature Press, 1999.

郑雅茹 [Zheng Yaru]. 肖劲光 ["Xiao Jinguaung"]. In 中国人民解放军高级将领传 [*Biographies of the PLA's High-Ranking Generals*], 《中国人民解放军高级将领传》编审委员会编著 [edited by PLA *Biographies of the High-Ranking Generals* Editorial Committee], 4:465–81. Beijing: PLA Press, 2008.

钟坚 [Zhong Jian]. 导读: 英雄不回头 ["Introduction: The Hero No Return"]. In 看不见的屏障: 决定台湾命运的第七舰队 [*Invisible Shell: The Seventh Fleet and Taiwan's Fate*], 布鲁斯. 艾里曼 [by Bruce A. Elleman], 吴润睿译 [translated by Wu Runrui]. Xinbei, Taiwan: Eight Banner Culture Publishing, 2017.

周益锋 [Zhou Yifeng]. "海权论"东渐及其影响 ["'Sea Power Theory' in the East and Its Impact"]. 历史月刊 [*History Monthly*], no. 4 (2006): 3. www.aisixiang.com/data/30517.html

周益锋 [Zhou Yifeng]. "海权论的传入和晚清海权思想" ["Translations of Sea Power Theory and Sea Power Thought in Late Qing"]. 唐都学刊 [*Academic Journal of Tangdu*], no. 4 (2005): 8–17.

## ENGLISH-LANGUAGE SOURCES

### *Governmental Documents and Personal Papers*

CCP Central Committee. *Selected Documents of the Fifteenth CCP National Congress.* Beijing: New Star Publishing House, 1997.

Deng Xiaoping. *Selected Works of Deng Xiaoping.* 3 vols. Beijing: Foreign Languages Press, 1994.

"Document No. 1: The First Conversation of N. S. Khrushchev with Mao Zedong, Hall of Huaizhentang, Beijing, July 31, 1958; The Mao-Khrushchev Conversation, July 31–August 3, 1958 and October 2, 1959." In "New Evidence on the Cold War in Asia," translated by Vladislav M. Zubok. In *Cold War International History Project*

*Bulletin No. 12/13 (Fall/Winter 2001): The End of the Cold War*, edited by Christian F. Ostermann, 243–72. Washington, DC: Wilson International Center for Scholars.

*Important Documents concerning the Question of Taiwan*. Beijing: Foreign Languages Press, 1955.

Information Office, PRC State Council. *China's National Defense in 2010*. Beijing: State Council Information Office, 2011. http://www.gov.cn/english/official/2011-03/31/content_1835499.htm.

Information Office, PRC State Council. *The Diversified Employment of China's Armed Forces* (*China's Defense White Paper*). April 2013. http://www.chinadaily.com.cn/language_tips/news/2013-04/17/content_16414985.htm.

Information Office, PRC State Council. "The Security Situation." In *White Papers of China's National Defense in 2008*. http://English.people.com.cn/90001/90776/90785/6578688.html.

Information Office, PRC State Council. *White Papers of China's National Defense in 1998*. Beijing: Foreign Languages Press, 2000.

Information Office, PRC State Council. *White Papers of China's National Defense in 2007*. Beijing: Foreign Languages Press, 2008.

Jiang Weilie. Interview by a reporter on April 9, 2013. PRC Defense Ministry website. www.mod.gov.cn.

Jiang Zemin. *On the "Three Represents."* Beijing: Foreign Languages Press, 2002.

Li, Xiaobing, Chen Jian, and David L. Wilson, trans. and eds. "Mao Zedong's Handling of the Taiwan Strait Crisis of 1958: Chinese Recollections and Documents." In *Cold War International History Project Bulletin No. 6/7 (Winter 1995): The Cold War in Asia*, edited by James G. Hershberg, 208–27. Washington, DC: Wilson International Center for Scholars.

Ma Ying-jeou. "Trouble over Oily Waters: Legal Problems of Seabed Boundaries and Foreign Investment in the East China Sea." S.J.D. thesis, Harvard Law School, 1980.

Major T. "Russian Missile Officers in Vietnam." In *Voices from the Vietnam War: Stories from American, Asian, and Russian Veterans*, by Xiaobing Li, 65–72. Lexington: University Press of Kentucky, 2010.

Mao Zedong. *Mao Zedong on Diplomacy*. Beijing: Foreign Languages Press, 1998.

Mao Zedong. *Selected Works of Mao Tse-tung*. 4 vols. Beijing: Foreign Languages Press, 1977.

National Defense Authorization Act for Fiscal Year 2013. Pub. L. No. 112–239. 126 Stat. 1632.

Perry, William. Public statement of the U.S. Secretary of Defense, March 11, 1996. American Forces Press Service, March 11; the Department of Defense, *News Briefings*, March 12, 14, and 16, 1996.

Research Department of Party Literature, CCP Central Committee, ed. *Major Documents of the People's Republic of China: Selected Important Documents since the Third Plenary Session of the Eleventh CCP Central Committee*. Beijing: Foreign Languages Press, 1991.

Taiwan Affairs Office and the Information Office, PRC State Council. "The One-China Principle and the Taiwan Issue, February 2000." In *White Papers of the Chinese Government, 2000–2001*. Beijing: Foreign Languages Press, 2003.

U.S. Defense Intelligence Agency. *China Military Power: Modernizing a Force to Fight and Win*. Washington, DC: U.S. Government Printing Office, 2019.

U.S. Department of Defense. *Annual Report to Congress: Military Power of the People's Republic of China, 2008*. http://www.defenselink.mil/pubs/pdfs/China_Military_Report_08.pdf.

U.S. Department of Defense. *Annual Report to Congress: Military Power of the People's Republic of China, 2009*. http://www.defenselink.mil/pubs/pdfs/China_Military_Report_09.pdf.

U.S. Department of Defense. *Military and Security Developments Involving the People's Republic of China, 2013*. http://www.defenselink.mil/pubs/pdfs/China_Military_Report_13.pdf.

U.S. Department of State. *Foreign Relations of the United States: China, Korea, Vietnam, and Indochina, 1945–1972*. 8 vols. Washington, DC: U.S. Government Printing Office, 1982–1997.

Weathersby, Kathryn, trans. and ed. "New Russian Documents on the Korean War." In *Cold War International History Project Bulletin No. 6/7 (Winter 1995): The Cold War in Asia*, edited by James G. Hershberg, 30–125. Washington, DC: Woodrow Wilson International Center for Scholars.

Wu Lengxi. "Inside Story of the Decision Making during the Shelling of Jinmen." In "Mao Zedong's Handling of the Taiwan Straits Crisis of 1958: Chinese Recollections and Documents," translated and annotated by Xiaobing Li, Chen Jian, and David L. Wilson, *Cold War International History Project Bulletin No. 6/7* (Winter 1995/1996).

Zhang, Shuguang, and Jian Chen, eds. *Chinese Communist Foreign Policy and the Cold War in Asia: New Documentary Evidence, 1944–1950*. Chicago: Imprint Publications, 1996.

Zhang Liang, ed. *The Tiananmen Papers: The Chinese Leadership's Decision to Use Force against Their Own People—in Their Own Words*. New York: Public Affairs, 2001.

Zhou Baoshan. "China's Crouching Dragon." In *Voices of the Korean War: Personal Stories of American, Korean, and Chinese Soldiers*, by Richard Peters and Xiaobing Li, 85–96. Lexington: University Press of Kentucky, 2004.

***Books and Articles***

Avalist, Nanda. "The Naval Dimension of the Great Power Contest for Global Hegemony: A Case of the US-China-Russia Rivalry." PhD diss., Curtin University, Australia, 2024.

BBC. "Questions and Answers: China-Japan Islands Row." *BBC News* (UK), September 11, 2012. http://www.bbc.co.uk/news/world-asia-pacific-11341139.

*BBC News*. "Hu Jintao Tells China Navy: Prepare for Warfare." December 7, 2011. www.bbc.com/news/world-asia-china-16063607.

Bernstein, Thomas P., and Hua-yu Li, eds. *What China Learns from the Soviet Union, 1949–Present*. Lanham, MD: Lexington Books, 2010.

Bitzinger, Richard A., Michael Raska, Collin Koh Swee Lean, and Kelvin Wong Ka Weng. "Locating China's Place in the Global Defense Economy." In *Forging China's Military Might: A New Framework for Assessing Innovation*, edited by Tai Ming Cheung, 169–212. Baltimore, MD: Johns Hopkins University Press, 2014.

Brands, Hal, ed. *The New Makers of Modern Strategy: From the Ancient World to the Digital Age*. Princeton, NJ: Princeton University Press, 2023.

Burkitt, Laurie, Andrew Scobell, and Larry M. Wortzel, eds. *The Lessons of History: The Chinese People's Liberation Army at 75*. Carlisle, PA: Army War College Strategic Studies Institute, 2003.

Burr, William, ed. *The Kissinger Transcripts: The Top-Secret Talks with Beijing and Moscow*. New York: New Press, 1999.

Bussert, James C., and Bruce A. Elleman. *People's Liberation Army Navy: Combat Systems Technology, 1949–2010*. Annapolis, MD: Naval Institute Press, 2018.

Chen, Dean. "Sea Power and the Chinese State: China's Maritime Ambitions." *The Heritage Foundation*, July 11, 2011. https://www.heritage.org/asia/report/sea-power-and-the-chinese-state-chinas-maritime-ambitions.

Chen, Dean P. *U.S.-China Rivalry and Taiwan's Mainland Policy: Security, Nationalism, and the 1992 Consensus*. London: Palgrave Macmillan, 2017.

Chen, Jian. *Mao's China and the Cold War*. Chapel Hill: University of North Carolina Press, 2001.

Chen, Jian. *Zhou Enlai: A Life*. Cambridge, MA: Harvard University Press, 2024.

Chen, Jian, and Xiaobing Li. "China and the End of the Cold War." In *The Cold War: From Détente to the Soviet Collapse*, edited by Malcolm Muir Jr., 120–31. Lexington: Virginia Military Institute Press, 2006.

Chen, Qimao. "The Taiwan Strait Crisis: Causes, Scenarios, and Solutions." In *Across the Taiwan Strait: Mainland China, Taiwan, and the 1995–1996 Crisis*, edited by Suisheng Zhao, 127–62. London: Routledge, 1999.

Cheng, Dean. "Assessing Threats to US Vital Interests: China." *The Heritage Foundation*. www.heritage.org/2021-index-us-military-strength/assessing-threats-us-vital-interests/china.

Cheung, Tai Ming, ed. *Forging China's Military Might: A New Framework for Assessing Innovation*. Baltimore, MD: Johns Hopkins University Press, 2014.

Christensen, Thomas J. *Useful Adversaries: Grand Strategy, Domestic Mobilization, and Sino-American Conflict, 1947–1958*. Princeton, NJ: Princeton University Press, 1996.

Christoffersen, Gaye. "Crises as Impetus for Institutionalization: Maritime Crisis Management Mechanisms in China's Near Seas." In *China's Strategic Priorities*, edited by Jonathan H. Ping and Brett McCormick, 62–79. London: Routledge, 2016.

Cohen, Warren I. *America's Response to China: A History of Sino-American Relations*. 6th ed. New York: Columbia University Press, 2019.

Cole, Bernard D. *The Great Wall at Sea: China's Navy in the Twenty-First Century*. 2nd ed. Annapolis, MD: Naval Institute Press, 2010.

Copper, John F. "The Origins of Conflict across the Taiwan Strait: The Problem of Differences in Perceptions." In *Across the Taiwan Strait: Mainland China, Taiwan, and the 1995–1996 Crisis*, edited by Suisheng Zhao, 41–76. London: Routledge, 1999.

Council on Foreign Relations. "Tracking China's Control of Overseas Ports." November 6, 2023. Asia Program and Greenberg Center for Geoeconomic Studies. https://cfr.org/tracker/china-overseas-ports.

Cowley, Robert, ed. *The Cold War: A Military History*. New York: Random House, 2005.

Crowl, Philip A. "Alfred Thayer Mahan: The Naval Historian." In *Makers of Modern Strategy: From Machiavelli to the Nuclear Age*, edited by Peter Paret, 448–67. Princeton, NJ: Princeton University Press, 1986.

Deng Rong. *Deng Xiaoping and the Cultural Revolution: A Daughter Recalls the Critical Years*. Translated by Sidney Shapiro. Beijing: Foreign Languages Press, 2002.

Di Cosmo, Nicola, ed. *Military Culture in Imperial China*. Cambridge, MA: Harvard University Press, 2009.

Dreyer, Edward L. *China at War, 1901–1949*. New York: Longman, 1995.

Dreyer, Edward L. "Continuity and Change." In *A Military History of China*, updated edition, edited by David Graff and Robin Higham, 19–38. Lexington: University Press of Kentucky, 2012.

Elleman, Bruce A. *High Seas Buffer: The Taiwan Patrol Force, 1950–1979*. Newport, RI: Naval War College Press, 2012.

Elleman, Bruce A. *The Making of the Modern Chinese Navy: Special Historical Characteristics*. London: Anthem Press, 2019.

Elleman, Bruce A. *Modern Chinese Warfare, 1795–1989*. London: Routledge, 2001.

Engstrom, Jeffrey. *Systems Confrontation and System Destruction Warfare: How the Chinese People's Liberation Army Seeks to Wage Modern Warfare*. Santa Monica, CA: RAND Corporation, 2018.

Fairbank, John K., and Merle Goldman. *China: A New History*. Enlarged ed. New York: Belknap Press, 1998.

Fairbank, John K., Rosemary Foot, and Frank A. Kierman Jr., eds. *Chinese Ways in Warfare*. Cambridge, MA: Harvard University Press, 1974.

Fairbank, John K., Edwin O. Reischauer, and Albert M. Craig. *East Asian: Transition and Transformation*. Rev. ed. Boston: Houghton Mifflin, 1989.

Fang, Qiang, and Xiaobing Li, eds. *China under Xi Jinping: A New Assessment*. Leiden: Leiden University Press, 2024.

Fang, Qiang, and Xiaobing Li, eds. *Corruption and Anticorruption in Modern China*. Lanham, MD: Lexington Books, 2019.

Finkelstein, David M. "Three Key Issues Affecting Security in the Asia-Pacific Region." In *Asia-Pacific Security: New Issues and New Ideas*, edited by China Association for Military Science, 110–16. Beijing: Military Science Publishing House, 2014.

Finkelstein, David M. *Washington's Taiwan Dilemma, 1949–1950: From Abandonment to Salvation*. Fairfax, VA: George Mason University Press, 1993.

Finkelstein, David M., and Kristen Gunness, eds. *Civil-Military Relations in Today's China: Swimming in a New Sea*. Armonk, NY: M. E. Sharpe, 2007.

Foot, Rosemary. *The Practice of Power: U.S. Relations with China since 1949*. Oxford: Oxford University Press, 1997.

Fravel, M. Taylor. *Active Defense: China's Military Strategy since 1949*. Princeton, NJ: Princeton University Press, 2019.

Fravel, M. Taylor. *Strong Borders, Secure Nation: Cooperation and Conflict in China's Territorial Disputes*. Princeton, NJ: Princeton University Press, 2008.

Freeman, Charles, Jr. "The Process of Rapprochement: Achievements and Problems." In *Sino-American Normalization and Its Policy Implications*, edited by Gene T. Hsiao and Michael Witunsky, 1–22. New York: Praeger, 1983.

Gady, Franz-Stefan. "Russian and China Kick off Naval Exercise in Sea of Japan." *The Diplomat*, August 24, 2015. https://thediplomat.com/2015/08/russia-and-china-kick-off-naval-exercise-in-sea-of-japan/.

Gao Xiaoxing et al. *The PLA Navy*. Beijing: China Intercontinental Press, 2012.

Godwin, Paul H. B., and Alice L. Miller. "China's Forbearance Has Limits: Chinese Threat and Retaliation Signaling and Its Implications for a Sino-American Military Confrontation." In *China Strategic Perspectives* 6. Washington, DC: National Defense University Institute for National Strategic Studies, 2013.

Goldman, Jeffery B. "China's Mahan." U.S. Naval Institute *Proceedings 122*, no. 3 (March 1996). https://www.usni.org/magazines/proceedings/1996/march/chinas-mahan.

Goldman, Merle, and Roderick MacFarquhar, eds. *The Paradox of China's Post-Mao Reforms*. Cambridge, MA: Harvard University Press, 1999.

Gorshkov, Sergey. *The Sea Power of the State*. Annapolis, MD: Naval Institute Press, 1979.

Graff, David A., and Robin Higham, eds. *A Military History of China*. Updated ed. Lexington: University Press of Kentucky, 2012.

Granados, Ulises. "The US Factor in China's Dispute with Japan over the Diaoyu/Senkaku Islands: Balancing Washington's 'Rebalancing' in East Asian Waters." In *China's Strategic Priorities*, edited by Jonathan H. Ping and Brett McCormick, 80–96. London: Routledge, 2016.

Han, Zhongtian. "The PRC's Naval-Air Campaign in the East China Sea, 1954–1955." Conference paper at the Chinese Military History Society annual meeting (virtual), May 10, 2020.

Heck, Timothy, B. A. Friedman, and Walker Mills, eds. *On the Contested Shores: The Evolving Role of Amphibious Operations in the History of Warfare*. Quantico, VA: Marine Corps University Press, 2024.

He Di. "The Last Campaign to Unify China: The CCP's Unrealized Plan to Liberate Taiwan, 1949–1950." In *Chinese Warfighting: The PLA Experience since 1949*, edited by Mark A. Ryan, David M. Finkelstein, and Michael A. McDevitt, 73–90. Armonk, NY: M. E. Sharpe, 2003.

Hensel, Howard M., and Amit Gupta, eds. *Maritime Security in the Indian Ocean and Western Pacific: Heritage and Contemporary Challenges*. London: Routledge, 2018.

Holms, James, and Toshi Yoshihara. "Liu Huaqing, RIP." *The Diplomat*, January 18, 2011. https://thediplomat.com/2011/01/liu-huaqing-rip/.

Hsiao, Gene T., and Michael Witunsky, eds. *Sino-American Normalization and Its Policy Implications*. New York: Praeger, 1983.

Huang, C., and T. Ng. "Xi Jinping Sends Signal to Neighbors with High-Profile Tour of Liaoning Aircraft Carrier." *South Chinese Morning Post*, August 31, 2013.

Jencks, Harlan. "Civil-Military Relations in China: Tiananmen and After." *Problems of Communism* 40 (May–June 1991): 12–27.

Joffe, Ellis. *The Chinese Army after Mao*. Cambridge, MA: Harvard University Press, 1987.

Joffe, Ellis. *Party and Army: Professionalism and Political Control in the Chinese Officer Corps, 1948–1964*. Cambridge, MA: Harvard University Press, 1967.

Johnston, Alastair I. "Prospects for Chinese Nuclear Force Modernization: Limited Deterrence versus Multilateral Arms Control." In *China's Military in Transition*, edited by David Shambaugh and Richard H. Yang, 548–76. New York: Oxford University Press, 1997.

Kamphausen, Roy, David Lai, and Travis Tanner, eds. *Assessing the People's Liberation Army in the Hu Jintao Era*. Carlisle, PA: U.S. Army War College, 2014.

Kau, Michael Y. M., ed. *The Lin Biao Affair: Power Politics and Military Coup*. White Plains, NY: International Arts and Science Press, 1975.

Keegan, John. *A History of Warfare*. New York: Knopf, 1993.

Kenny, Henry J. "Vietnamese Perceptions of the 1979 War with China." In *Chinese Warfighting: The PLA Experience since 1949*, edited by David Finkelstein, Mark A. Ryan, and Michael A. McDevitt, 217–40. Armonk, NY: M. E. Sharpe, 2003.

Khoo, Nicholas. *Collateral Damage: Sino-Soviet Rivalry and the Termination of the Sino-Vietnamese Alliance*. New York: Columbia University Press, 2011.

Koo, Min Gyo. *Island Disputes and Maritime Regime Building in East Asia*. New York: Springer, 2010.

Lai, Benjamin. *The Chinese People's Liberation Army since 1949*. Oxford: Osprey, 2012.

Lai, Sherman Xiaogang. "Ensured Loyalty versus Professionalism at Sea: A Historical Review of the PLA Navy, 1949–1982." Conference paper at the annual meeting of Chinese Military History Society (CMHS), Ottawa, Ontario, Canada, April 16, 2016.

Lewis, John, and Xue Litai. *China Builds the Bomb*. Stanford, CA: Stanford University Press, 1991.

Li, Cheng. *China's Leaders: The New Generation*. Lanham, MD: Rowman & Littlefield, 2001.

Li, Nan. "China's Evolving Naval Strategy and Capabilities in the Hu Jintao Era." In *Assessing the People's Liberation Army in the Hu Jintao Era*, edited by Roy Kamphausen, David Lai, and Travis Tanner, 257–99. Carlisle, PA: U.S. Army War College, 2014.

Li, Nan, ed. *Chinese Civil-Military Relations: The Transformation of the People's Liberation Army*. New York: Routledge, 2006.

Li, Xiaobing. *Attack at Chosin: The Chinese Second Offensive in Korea.* Norman: University of Oklahoma Press, 2020.

Li, Xiaobing. "Beijing's Strategy Shifts and US-China Relations." *American Review of China Studies* 23, no. 2 (Fall 2022): 1–25.

Li, Xiaobing. *China's Battle for Korea: The 1951 Spring Offensive.* Bloomington: Indiana University Press, 2014.

Li, Xiaobing. "China's Intervention and the CPVF Experience in the Korean War." In *The Korean War at Fifty: International Perspectives*, edited by Mark F. Wilkinson, 130–49. Lexington: Virginia Military Institute Press, 2004.

Li, Xiaobing. "China's Intervention and the End of the Communist Alliance in Vietnam." In *Beyond the Quagmire: New Interpretations of the Vietnam War*, edited by Geoffrey W. Jensen and Matthew M. Smith, 209–42. Denton: University of North Texas Press, 2019.

Li, Xiaobing. "China's Military Strategy from Mao Zedong to Xi Jinping." In *The Practice of Strategy: A Global History*, edited by Jeremy Black, 521–42. Rome: Nadir Media, 2024.

Li, Xiaobing. *China's New Navy: The Evolution of PLAN from the People's Revolution to a 21st Century Cold War.* Annapolis, MD: Naval Institute Press, 2023.

Li, Xiaobing. "China's Support to the Vietnamese Communists." In *The Brown Water War at 50: A Retrospective on the Coastal and Riverine Conflict in Vietnam*, edited by Thomas Culter and Edward Marolda, 190–204. Annapolis, MD: Naval Institute Press, 2023.

Li, Xiaobing. *China's War in Korea: Strategic Culture and Geopolitics.* London: Palgrave Macmillan, 2019.

Li, Xiaobing. *The Cold War in East Asia.* London: Routledge, 2018.

Li, Xiaobing. *The Dragon in the Jungle: the Chinese Army in the Vietnam War.* New York: Oxford University Press, 2020.

Li, Xiaobing. "The East and South China Seas in Sino-US Relations." In *Sino-American Relations: A New Cold War*, edited by Xiaobing Li and Qiang Fang, 319–44. Amsterdam: Amsterdam University Press, 2022.

Li, Xiaobing. *A History of the Modern Chinese Army.* Lexington: University Press of Kentucky, 2007.

Li, Xiaobing. *History of Taiwan.* Santa Barbara, CA: ABC-CLIO/Greenwood, 2019.

Li, Xiaobing. "How to Train the Dragon: Soviet Advisors and Assistance to the Chinese Navy, 1949–1960." In *Naval Advising and Assistance: History, Challenges, and Analysis*, edited by Donald Stoker and Michael T. McMaster, 220–42. Warwick, UK: Helion, 2017.

Li, Xiaobing. "The Impact of Social Changes on the PLA: A Chinese Military Perspective." In *Civil-Military Relations in Today's China: Swimming in a New Sea*, edited by David M. Finkelstein and Kristen Gunness, 26–47. Armonk, NY: M. E. Sharpe, 2007.

Li, Xiaobing. "Large-Scale Amphibious Warfare in Chinese Military Strategy." A conference paper presented at the naval symposium organized by China Maritime Studies Institute, U.S. Naval War College, May 4–6, 2021.

Li, Xiaobing. "New War of Nerves." *Journal of Chinese Political Science* 3, no. 1 (Summer 1997): 56–73.

Li, Xiaobing. "PLA Amphibious Campaigns and the Origins of the Joint Island Landing Campaign." In *On Contested Shores: The Evolving Role of Amphibious Operations in the History of Warfare*, edited by Timothy Heck, B. A. Friedman, and Walker D. Mills, 2:228–46. Quantico, VA: Marine Corps University Press, 2024.

Li, Xiaobing. "PLA Attacks and Amphibious Operations during the Taiwan Strait Crises of 1954–55 and 1958." In *Chinese Warfighting: The PLA Experience since 1949*, edited by Mark A. Ryan, David M. Finkelstein, and Michael A. McDevitt, 143–72. New York: M. E. Sharpe, 2003.

Li, Xiaobing. "Reforming the People's Army: Military Modernization in China." *Journal of Southwest Conference on Asian Studies* 5 (2005): 1–19.

Li, Xiaobing. "Security Challenge and Global Strategy: Modernization of Chinese Military." *Journal of American Review of China Studies* 15, no. 1 (Spring 2014): 45–64.

Li, Xiaobing. "Sino-Japanese Maritime Conflicts and Security Concerns in the East China Sea." In *Maritime Security in the Indian Ocean and Western Pacific: Heritage and Contemporary Challenges*, edited by Howard M. Hensel and Amit Gupta, 243–60. London: Routledge, 2018.

Li, Xiaobing. "Sino-Soviet Border Disputes." In *Magill's Guide to Military History*, edited by John Powell, 4:1421–24. Amenia, NY: Salem Press, 2001.

Li, Xiaobing. "The Status of Taiwan and Hong Kong." In *Security Dynamics in the South China Sea: Contemporary Challenges and Opportunities*, edited by Howard M. Hensel, 162–78. London: Routledge, 2024.

Li, Xiaobing. "Truman's Foreign Aid Legacy in East Asia: The Communist Chinese Perspective." In *Foreign Aid and the Legacy of Harry S. Truman*, edited Raymond H. Geselbracht, 101–28. Kirksville, MO: Truman State University Press, 2015.

Li, Xiaobing. "Truman and Taiwan: A U.S. Policy Change from Face to Faith." In *Northeast Asia and the Legacy of Harry S. Truman: Japan, China, and the Two Koreas*, edited by James I. Matray, 119–44. Kirksville, MO: Truman State University Press, 2012.

Li, Xiaobing. *Voices from the Vietnam War: Stories from American, Asian, and Russian Veterans*. Lexington: University Press of Kentucky, 2010.

Li, Xiaobing. "What Did the PLA Learn from the Jinmen, Hainan, and Yijiangshan Landing Campaign?" In *Chinese Amphibious Warfare: Prospects for a Cross-Strait Invasion*, edited by Andrew S. Erickson, Conor M. Kennedy, and Ryan D. Martinson, 29–44. Newport, RI: Naval War College Press, 2024.

Li, Xiaobing, and Qiang Fang, eds. *China under Xi Jinping: A New Assessment*. Leiden: Leiden University Press, 2024.

Li, Xiaobing, and Qiang Fang, eds. *Sino-American Relations: A New Cold War*. Amsterdam: Amsterdam University Press, 2022.

Li, Xiaobing, Allan R. Millett, and Bin Yu, trans. and eds. *Mao's Generals Remember Korea*. Lawrence: University Press of Kansas, 2001.

Li, Zhisui. *The Private Life of Chairman Mao: The Memoirs of Mao's Personal Physician*. New York: Random House, 1994.

Li Danhui, and Yafeng Xia. *Mao and the Sino-Soviet Split, 1959–1973: A New History*. Lanham, MD: Lexington Books, 2018.

Lim, Louisa. *The People's Republic of Amnesia*. New York: Oxford University Press, 2014.

Lo, Jung-Pang. *China as a Sea Power, 1127–368: A Preliminary Survey of the Maritime Expansion and Naval Exploits of the Chinese People during the Southern Song and Yuan Periods*. Singapore: National University of Singapore Press, 2012.

Lorge, Peter A. *The Asian Military Revolution: From Gunpowder to the Bomb*. New York: Cambridge University Press, 2008.

Low De Wei. "Full Text of Xi Jinping's Speech at China's Party Congress." *Bloomberg*, October 18, 2022. https://www.bloomberg.com/news/articles/2022-10-18/full-text-of-xi-jinping-s-speech-at-china-20th-party-congress-2022.

Luthi, Lorenz M. *The Sino-Soviet Split:. Cold War in the Communist World*. Princeton, NJ: Princeton University Press, 2008.

Lu Xiaoping. *The PLA Air Force*. Beijing: China Intercontinental Press, 2012.

Macaes, Bruno. *Belt and Road: A Chinese World Order*. London: Hurst, 2019.

Mann, Jim. *About Face: A History of America's Curious Relationship with China, from Nixon to Clinton*. New York: Knopf, 1999.

Mattis, Peter. *Analyzing the Chinese Military: A Review Essay and Resource Guide on the People's Liberation Army*. Erie, PA: Amazon Kindle Edition, 2015.

Maurer, John H. "Alfred Thayer Mahan and the Strategy of Sea Power." In *The New Makers of Modern Strategy: From the Ancient World to the Digital Age*, edited by Hal Brands, 169–92. Princeton, NJ: Princeton University Press, 2023.

McDevitt, Michael A. *China as a Twenty-First Century Naval Power: Theory, Practice, and Implications*. Annapolis, MD: Naval Institute Press, 2020.

Meisner, Maurice. *The Deng Xiaoping Era: An Inquiry into the Fate of Chinese Socialism, 1978–1994*. New York: Hill & Wang, 1996.

Meisner, Maurice. *Mao's China and After: A History of the People's Republic*. New York: Free Press, 1999.

Muir, Malcolm, Jr., and Mark F. Wilkinson, eds. *The Most Dangerous Years: The Cold War, 1953–1975*. Lexington: Virginia Military Institute, 2005.

Nixon, Richard. *The Memoirs of Richard Nixon*. New York: Grosset & Dunlap, 1978.

O'Dowd, Edward C. *Chinese Military Strategy in the Third Indochina War: The Last Maoist War*. London: Routledge, 2007.

Ogden, Suzanne, Kathleen Hartford, Lawrence Sullivan, and David Zweig. *China's Search for Democracy: The Student and the Mass Movement of 1989*. Armonk, NY: M. E. Sharpe, 1992.

Paret, Peter, ed. *Makers of Modern Strategy: From Machiavelli to the Nuclear Age*. Princeton, NJ: Princeton University Press, 1986.

Perry, William, and Ashton Carter. *Preventive Defense: A New Security for America*. Washington, DC: Brookings Institute, 1999.

Peters, Richard, and Xiaobing Li. *Voices of the Korean War: Personal Stories of American, Korean, and Chinese Soldiers*. Lexington: University Press of Kentucky, 2004.

*PLA Daily*. "China's Establishment of the Air Defense Identification Zone (ADIZ) in the East China Sea, January 22, 2014." http://eng.chinamil.com.cn/view/2014-01.

Polmar, Norman C., Thomas A. Brooks, and George E. Fedoroff. *Admiral Gorshkov: The Man Who Challenged the U.S. Navy*. Annapolis, MD: Naval Institute Press, 2019.

Raine, Sarah, and Christian Miere. *Regional Disorder: The South China Sea Disputes*. London: Routledge, 2013.

Robinson, Thomas. "The Sino-Soviet Border Conflicts of 1969: New Evidence Three Decades Later." In *Chinese Warfighting: The PLA Experience since 1949*, edited by Mark A. Ryan, Daniel M. Finkelstein, and Michael A. McDevitt, 198–216. Armonk, NY: M. E. Sharpe, 2003.

Ross, Robert. *Negotiating Cooperation: The United States and China, 1969–1989*. Stanford, CA: Stanford University Press, 1995.

Ryan, Mark A., David M. Finkelstein, and Michael A. McDevitt, eds. *Chinese Warfighting: The PLA Experience since 1949*. Armonk, NY: M. E. Sharpe, 2003.

Saich, Anthony, ed. *The Rise to Power of the Chinese Communist Party: Documents and Analysis*. Armonk, NY: M. E. Sharpe, 1996.

Saunders, Phillip C., Arthur S. Ding, Andrew Scobell, Andrew N. D. Yang, and Joel Wuthnow, eds. *Chairman Xi Remakes the PLA: Assessing Chinese Military Reforms*. Washington, DC: National Defense University Press, 2019.

Sawyer, Ralph D. *Fire and Water: The Art of Incendiary and Aquatic Warfare in China*. Boulder, CO: Westview, 2004.

Schoppa, R. Keith. *Revolution and Its Past: Identities and Change in Modern Chinese History*. 3rd ed. New York: Prentice Hall, 2011.

Scobell, Andrew. *China's Use of Military Force: Beyond the Great Wall and the Long March*. Cambridge: Cambridge University Press, 2003.

Shambaugh, David. *Modernizing China's Military: Progress, Problems, and Prospects*. Berkeley: University of California Press, 2002.

Shambaugh, David, and Richard H. Yang, eds. *China's Military in Transition*. New York: Oxford University Press, 1997.

Shen Zhihua, and Danhui Li. *After Leaning to One Side: China and Its Allies in the Cold War*. Stanford, CA: Stanford University Press, 2011.

Shen Zhihua, and Yafeng Xia. *Mao and the Sino-Soviet Partnership, 1945–1959: A New History*. Lanham, MD: Lexington Books, 2017.

Smoot, Roland N. "As I Recall: The US Taiwan Defense Command." U.S. Naval Institute *Proceedings* 110/9/979 (September 1984): 46–63.

Spence, Jonathan D. *The Search for Modern China*. 4th ed. New York: W. W. Norton, 2025.

Swope, Kenneth, ed. *Warfare in China since 1600*. New York: Routledge, 2005.

Szonyi, Michael. *Cold War Island: Quemoy on the Front Line*. New York: Cambridge University Press, 2008.

Tian, Xiansheng. "When Chongqing Challenges Beijing: The Bo Xilai Case." In *Evolution of Power: China's Struggle, Survival, and Success*, edited by Xiaobing Li and Xiansheng Tian, 323–50. Lanham, MD: Lexington Books, 2014.

Tsai, Ming-Yen. *From Adversaries to Partners: Chinese and Russian Military Cooperation after the Cold War.* Westport, CT: Praeger, 2003.

Tsao, Nadia. "Hong Kong Crackdown Sparks 'Fundamental Change' in U.S. Taiwan Policy: Trump Adviser." *Radio Free Asia*, November 13, 2020. www.rfa.org/english/news/china/crackdown-11132020095826.html.

Tucker, Nancy Bernkopf. *Strait Talk: United States–Taiwan Relations and the Crisis with China.* Cambridge, MA: Harvard University Press, 2009.

Tucker, Spencer C. *Vietnam.* Lexington: University Press of Kentucky, 1999.

Tyler, Patric. *A Great Wall: Six Presidents and China.* New York: Public Affairs, 1999.

Wakeman, Frederic, Jr. *The Fall of Imperial China.* New York: Free Press, 1977.

Wang Guangqun. "China Rises to Top in Ranks of Ship Makers." Xinhua News Agency, May 9, 2011. http://news.xinhuanet.com/english2010/china/2011-05/09/c_13865547.htm.

Westad, Odd Arne, ed. *Brothers in Arms*; *Brothers in Arms: The Rise and Fall of the Sino-Soviet Alliance, 1945–1963.* Washington, DC, and Stanford, CA: Woodrow Wilson Center Press and Stanford University Press, 1998.

Worthing, Peter. *A Military History of Modern China: From the Manchu Conquest to Tiananmen Square.* Westport, CT: Praeger, 2007.

Wortzel, Larry M. "China's Foreign Conflicts since 1949." In *A Military History of China*, updated ed., edited by David Graff and Robin Higham, 267–84. Lexington: University Press of Kentucky, 2012.

Wortzel, Larry M. *The Dragon Extends Its Reach: Chinese Military Power Goes Global.* Herndon, VA: Potomac Books, 2013.

Xinhua News Agency. *China's Foreign Relations: A Chronology of Events, 1949–1988.* Beijing: Foreign Languages Press, 1989.

Xiong Guangkai. *International Strategy and Revolution in Military Affairs.* Beijing: Tsinghua University Press, 2003.

Xiong Guangkai. "On Revolution in Military Affairs." Conference presentation at the Chinese Scientists' Forum on Humanities on April 16, 2003.

Xu Yan. "Chinese Forces and Their Casualties in the Korean War." Translated by Xiaobing Li. *Chinese Historians* 6, no. 2 (Fall 1991): 45–64.

Yoshihara, Toshi. "China's Vision of Its Seascape: The First Island Chain and Chinese Seapower." *Asian Politics and Policy* 4, no. 3 (July 2012): 239–314.

Yoshihara, Toshi. *Mao's Army Goes to Sea: The Island Campaigns and the Founding of China's Navy.* Washington, DC: Georgetown University Press, 2022.

Yoshihara, Toshi, and James R. Holmes. *Red Star over the Pacific: China's Rise and the Challenge to U.S. Maritime Strategy.* 2nd ed. Annapolis, MD: Naval Institute Press, 2018.

You, Ji. *The Armed Forces of China.* New York: I. B. Tauris, 1999.

You, Ji. "Changing Leadership Consensus: The Domestic Context of War Game." In *Across the Taiwan Strait: Mainland China, Taiwan, and the 1995–1996 Crisis*, edited by Suisheng Zhao, 77–98. London: Routledge, 1999.

You, Ji. *China's Military Transformation: Politics and War Preparation*. Cambridge: Polity, 2016.

You, Ji. "The Soviet Model and the Breakdown of the Military Alliance." In *China Learns from the Soviet Union, 1949–Present*, edited by Thomas P. Bernstein and Hua-yu Li, 131–49. Lanham, MD: Lexington Books, 2010.

Yu, Bin. "China's Gun-Control Problem: Jiang vs. Hu?" *PacNet*, no. 40. Honolulu: Pacific Forum CSIS, September 16, 2004. www.csis.org/pacfor/ccejournal.html.

Yu, Bin. "What China Learned from Its 'Foreign War' in Korea." In *Mao's Generals Remember Korea*, translated and edited by Xiaobing Li, Allen R. Millet, and Bin Yu, 9–29. Lawrence: University Press of Kansas, 2001.

Zhang, Shuguang. "Beijing's Aid to Hanoi and the United States–China Confrontations, 1964–1968." In *Behind the Bamboo Curtain: China, Vietnam, and the World beyond Asia*, edited by Priscilla Roberts, 259–88. Stanford, CA: Stanford University Press, 2006.

Zhang, Shuguang. *Deterrence and Strategic Culture: Chinese American Confrontations, 1949–1958*. Ithaca, NY: Cornell University, 1992.

Zhang, Xiaoming. *Deng Xiaoping's Long War: The Military Conflict between China and Vietnam, 1979–1991*. Chapel Hill: University of North Carolina Press, 2015.

Zhang, Xiaoming. "High-Altitude Duel: The CIA's U-2 Spy Plane Overflights and China's Air Defense Force, 1961–1968." *Journal of Military History* 86, no. 1 (January 2022): 132–59.

Zhao, Suisheng, ed. *Across the Taiwan Strait: Mainland China, Taiwan, and the 1995–1996 Crisis*. London: Routledge, 1999.

Zhu, Fang. *Gun Barrel Politics: Party-Army Relations in Mao's China*. Boulder, CO: Westview Press, 1998.

# INDEX

## ABOUT THE AUTHOR

**XIAOBING LI**, professor of history and Don Betz Endowed Chair in International Studies at the University of Central Oklahoma, is the author of *China's New Navy: The Evolution of PLAN from the People's Revolution to a 21st Century Cold War* and more than a dozen other books on the PLA, in which he served in the 1970s. He is the executive editor of the *Chinese Historical Review*.

**THE NAVAL INSTITUTE PRESS** is the book-publishing arm of the U.S. Naval Institute, a private, nonprofit, membership society for sea service professionals and others who share an interest in naval and maritime affairs. Established in 1873 at the U.S. Naval Academy in Annapolis, Maryland, where its offices remain today, the Naval Institute has members worldwide.

Members of the Naval Institute support the education programs of the society and receive the influential monthly magazine *Proceedings* or the colorful bimonthly magazine *Naval History* and discounts on fine nautical prints and on ship and aircraft photos. They also have access to the transcripts of the Institute's Oral History Program and get discounted admission to any of the Institute-sponsored seminars offered around the country.

The Naval Institute's book-publishing program, begun in 1898 with basic guides to naval practices, has broadened its scope to include books of more general interest. Now the Naval Institute Press publishes about seventy titles each year, ranging from how-to books on boating and navigation to battle histories, biographies, ship and aircraft guides, and novels. Institute members receive significant discounts on the Press' more than eight hundred books in print.

Full-time students are eligible for special half-price membership rates. Life memberships are also available.

For more information about Naval Institute Press books that are currently available, visit www.usni.org/press/books. To learn about joining the U.S. Naval Institute, please write to:

Member Services
**U.S. NAVAL INSTITUTE**
291 Wood Road
Annapolis, MD 21402-5034

Telephone: (800) 233-8764
Fax: (410) 571-1703
Web address: www.usni.org